FOREVER'S TEAM

FOREVER'S TEAM

John Feinstein

Villard Books New York 1990

Library of Congress Cataloging-in-Publication Data
Feinstein, John.
Forever's team/by John Feinstein.
    p. cm.
ISBN 0-394-56892-3
1. Duke University—Basketball—History. 2. Basketball players—
United States—Biography. I. Title.
GV885.43.D85F45 1990
796.323'63'09756563—dc20

Manufactured in the United States of America
9 8 7 6 5 4 3 2
First Edition

This book is dedicated to the players, coaches, managers, and trainer of the 1978 Duke basketball team

and
to Tom Mickle,

who dreamed the dream then and still dreams it now.

Acknowledgments

It has been quite a year for me.

In a little more than twelve months I have gotten married, left the newspaper where I worked for eleven years, arrived at and departed from the magazine where I always wanted to work, and written this book.

The best thing I did was get married. The fact that Mary Clare Gibbons actually walked down the aisle and said, "I do," amazes me even more than it amazes our friends.

The toughest thing I did was leave *The Washington Post*. It was, without question, something that had to be done, but that doesn't mean it wasn't painful. Almost a year later, my memories of the place tend to focus on all I learned while I was there, on the good times and on all the terrific people I worked with.

The most surprising thing I did was leave *Sports Illustrated* less than a year after being thrilled to have the opportunity to work there. But Frank Deford made me an offer I couldn't refuse and I look forward eagerly to working for him at *The National*, America's new daily sports newspaper.

And, finally, the most enjoyable thing I did was research this book. Going into your past is a gamble because you don't know what you'll find. People can disappoint you. Fond memories can turn out to be innacurate. None of that happened to me. The players, coaches, managers and trainer of the 1978 Duke team brought back wonderful memories and were generous with their time and their stories.

They are the first group I have to thank: Bill Foster, Lou Goetz, Bob Wenzel, Ray Jones, Bruce Bell, Jim Spanarkel, Harold Morrison, Scott Goetsch, Steve Gray, Rob Hardy, John Harrell, Mike Gminski, Bob Bender, Gene Banks, Kenny Dennard, Jim Suddath, Kevin Hannon, Mary Kay Bass Haynes, Debbie Ridley, and last—but certainly not least—the Pride of Cherryville, Max Crowder. Thanks also go to Shirley Foster, Neva Wenzel, Jennifer Bell, Elizabeth Hardy, Stacy Anderson, Nadine Dennard, Jennifer Suddath, and Chris Haynes. Special thanks to Tate Armstrong, who, like me, graduated one year too soon.

There are others at Duke who must be thanked for their help: Athletic Director Tom Butters; Sports Information Director John Roth and his assistants, Mike Cragg and Mike Sobb. And a special thank-you to Johnny Moore and the indefatigable Jill Mixon. As for Tom Mickle, anything I say here will be inadequate.

At *Sports Illustrated*, I owe thanks to Mark Mulvoy, Alex Wolff, Armen Keteyian, Sandy Padwe, David Bauer, Steve Robinson, Liz Greco, Peggy Terry and, most of all, Rob Fleder. They could not have been nicer to me.

At *The Washington Post*, I will always appreciate the fact that Ben Bradlee never wanted me to leave and that Bob Woodward was still my friend long after he stopped being my editor. There are many others: David Maraniss, Ken Denlinger, Lexie Verdon and Steve Barr, Doug Feaver, Bill McAllister, Gene Bachinski, Martin Weil, Rich Pearson, Carla Hall, Sandy Boodman, Juan Williams, Larry Meyer, Tom Kenworthy, Fred Hiatt and Margaret (Pooh-Bear) Shapiro, Jackson Diehl, Len Shapiro, Sandy Bailey, O. D. Wilson, Donald Huff, Richard Justice, Sally Jenkins, Tony Kornheiser, Bill Gildea, Mark Asher, Chris Brennan, Byron Rosen, Ben Gieser, Kevin Coughlin, David Levine, Elizabeth Cale, and Joyce Manglass. I will never forget Mike Trilling. It is the dedication to the news and the newspaper of people like him that made the *Post* a special place for me.

I also owe thanks to many friends who put up with me during a turbulent year: Keith and Barbie Drum, Dick (Hoops) Weiss, Linda Mickle, Dave Kindred, Bill Brill, Doug Doughty, Bob and Anne DeStefano, Ray Ratto, John Hewig, Bud and Mary Lou Collins, Pete (Ivan) Alfano, Jennifer (Wailin') Proud(-to-be-a)Mearns, Lesley Visser, Norbert (the international political analyst) Doyle, Tom Hammond, Al McGuire, Rick Brewer, Jeff Neuman, Rick Barnes, Gary Williams, Mike McGee, Analee Thurston, Ted Tinling, Dewey Blanton, Peter Lawler, and Tom Ross.

Last but not at all least is Sandy (Flailin') Genelius, a wonderful friend *and*, in fact, the person who introduced me to my wife.

The people I work for at Villard Books cannot be thanked enough for their patience with me, especially my editor Peter Gethers, who may have been the only person other than me who believed this book could work when I first proposed it. Thanks also go to Janis Donnaud, Heather Lehr, Janet Bolen and Corinne Lewkowicz and, at ICM, Kathy Pohl.

And of course there is Esther Newberg. She is, no doubt, the best literary agent anyone can hope to have but she is a much better friend. The measure of friendship is how you respond in times of trouble. Esther is always there when you need her. Always.

As for my family, there is no way to measure what they mean to me. My mom and dad may disagree with me at times, but they always stand by me. My brother Bobby was a hell of a best man but is a better brother. My sister Margaret is five-two, weighs 105 pounds and, believe me, you wouldn't want to meet her in a dark alley—especially if you have crossed a member of her family or a friend. Her fiancé, David Sattler, is a lucky—and courageous—person. I got amazingly lucky when it came to in-laws, with Arlene and Jim Gibbons becoming my parents-in-law and Kathleen, Annie, Jimmy, and the folk hero of Holy Cross, Brendan, as siblings-in-law.

As for Mary Clare Gibbons Feinstein (I like the way that sounds), well, everyone who knows us insists that after one year of marriage she deserves to be sainted. I disagree. Sainthood isn't quite good enough for her.

Contents

Introduction

Sunday morning, December 12, 1982, was a cold, clear morning in Washington, D.C., the kind that pumps energy into you when you step outside the door. I wanted an early start that day because I was working on a long story about the speaker of the Maryland House of Delegates.

I arrived in the newsroom of *The Washington Post* just before 10 A.M.—early is a relative term—and started to walk downstairs to the cafeteria for a cup of coffee. To do so, I had to walk through the sports department. I had left sports the previous January to pursue my fascination with politics but still wrote occasional pieces for the section.

Len Shapiro, the deputy sports editor, who runs sports on Sundays, stopped me by calling my name. There was an urgency in his voice, especially for a Sunday morning. I walked over to where he was sitting. Pointing to a story on his computer, he said, "Have you heard about this yet?"

I looked at the story. The first sentence was all I had to read: "South Carolina basketball coach Bill Foster was listed in critical but stable condition early this morning after suffering an apparent heart attack last night following the Gamecocks' upset victory over 15th-ranked Purdue."

By the time I finished the sentence my legs felt a little bit wobbly. It had been eight months since my father suffered a heart attack and I was familiar with the trauma that accompanied one. My dad had done everything right: He had started feeling sick at work and had gone straight to George Washington University Hospital, only a few blocks away. He actually had the attack in the hospital, which is one of the top heart treatment centers in the country. It had been a mild attack and he had been home within ten days.

Even so, the experience was frightening for everyone in my family. Now, looking over Shapiro's shoulder, I searched the story for details. How serious was the attack? How much danger was Foster in? I knew from experience that the first twenty-four hours would be critical. I also wondered if he would ever coach again.

The story I was supposed to write that day was quickly forgotten. So was the coffee. Bill Foster had been the basketball coach at Duke when I was a student there. I had been sports editor of the student paper and had watched from close up as he went through the agonizing process of trying to rebuild a fallen program. Duke's record in Atlantic Coast Conference play during my four years as an undergraduate was 11–49. I saw every loss, many of them torturous. But I also saw improvement as Foster brought players like Jim Spanarkel and Mike Gminski into the program. During my senior year came the epic recruitment of Gene Banks.

And then came 1978. From last place in the ACC in 1977, Duke wrote one of the more remarkable Cinderella stories in college basketball history. With Banks and Kenny Dennard, both freshmen, starting at the forward spots, Duke won the ACC Tournament, won the East Regional of the NCAA Tournament, and then shocked Notre Dame in the national semifinals in St. Louis. The dream ended in the final, a 94–88 loss to Kentucky, but that didn't diminish the achievement.

Duke was America's Team before the term had become popular. The players were brash, funny, and articulate. Unlike Kentucky's players, who had to win or be labeled failures, they were kids having fun. They were playing a game. There was none of that "basketball is religion" garbage that has created so much sickness around the Kentucky program. They lost the game but won the country.

To me, less than a year out of Duke, the experience was extraordinary. I had known the players not as a reporter but as fellow students. Foster's three assistant coaches were all young enough to be friends and Foster himself was the kind of person who was impossible not to like. He had a self-deprecating sense of humor though he was driven and intense about rebuilding. He also had time to talk to a student reporter, win or lose, day or night—often *late* at night. That alone made him unusual.

My most vivid memory of St. Louis came after the Kentucky game, when the Duke players and coaches came back onto the court to receive their awards. Their arms were linked, their message apparent: you can beat us but you can't break us. As they walked onto the court, the Duke fans spotted them and immediately began chanting, "We'll be back, we'll be back." It was so loud that it drowned out the celebration of the Kentucky fans. I stood there, tingling, thinking, "Damn right they'll be back."

And why not? The only senior was Bruce Bell, who had come to Duke as a walk-on. Bell was a great guy but a limited player. The fact was, *the first ten players* would be back. This was *clearly* only the beginning.

Only it didn't turn out that way. The pressure of expectations, inability to deal with sudden success, changes in the coaching staff, injuries and immaturity kept them from coming back. Duke had excellent teams the next two years: 22–8 in '79 and 24–9 with another ACC title and a trip to the final eight in '80. But the magic was gone. It was replaced by frustrations that eventually drove Foster to flee in pursuit of happiness at South Carolina.

Foster's departure devastated me. I thought it was a mistake for him and for Duke. I was half right. Mike Krzyzewski succeeded Foster and has done a superb job. Back then, though, to the old student reporter, Foster *was* Duke basketball.

I kept in touch with him after he went to South Carolina and with the assistants—now scattered—as well as a lot of the players. I had talked to Foster a couple of weeks earlier, just before the '82–'83 season began, and he had been optimistic about his third team at South Carolina.

"We're actually not bad," he had said, which from him was rampant praise. "You ought to come down when we play Clemson. Stay at the house if you want, we've got loads of room."

And now, on the night of a major victory, a heart attack. I walked to my desk and dialed Foster's home number. No answer. I called Lou Goetz next. If anyone was likely to have news about Foster it was Goetz, who had spent fourteen years with him as a player and assistant coach.

"I'm about to drive down there," said Goetz, who had quit coaching the previous year and moved back to Durham. "I spoke to the hospital and they said he isn't in any danger. But I want to see him."

That made sense. In a lot of ways Goetz was the son Foster (who has four daughters) had never had. Goetz said he would call me if he had any news.

I then called Tom Mickle, who had been the sports information director when I was at Duke. He was now promotions director and had been as close to Foster as almost anyone. I needed to talk to people who had been there through the bad times and the good. Catharsis in crisis, I suppose.

Mickle and I talked at length about the inevitability of it all; Foster was so driven, so unable to take things easy, so torn up after every defeat. "My God, Fein," Mickle said, "it still seems like St. Louis was last week. How can it be almost five years?"

I thought about that for a minute. It was remarkable how vivid my memories of that season were. In my mind's eye I could still see John Harrell, the quiet point guard, making the two free throws to beat Notre Dame, and Bob Bender's length-of-the-floor pass to Banks in that same game. I saw Dennard's backwards dunk against Villanova and Gminski blocking all those shots against Pennsylvania. I saw Lefty Driesell burying his head as Spanarkel went over, under, and through his team for 33 points. I couldn't see Rhode Island's three missed shots at the buzzer in the first round of the NCAA Tournament because I had had my head down during that sequence, listening for the crowd's reaction. I hadn't been able to look.

Just thinking back gave me chills. "That was a great time," I said to Mickle. "I wonder if any team ever had as much *fun* as those guys did that year."

Mickle, who had been with them every step of the way, laughed. "I doubt it," he said. "How many teams have ever had Dennard *and* Banks *and* Spanarkel *and* Harold Morrison *and* Ray Jones . . ." He stopped but his point was well taken. During that phone call, the idea for this book was born.

Bill Foster recovered. Nine weeks later he was back on the bench, even though Goetz and many of his friends—myself included—tried to convince him to give up coaching. I went down to South Carolina for his return game and talked to him at length about life, about basketball, about coaching, and about 1978.

"When I was in the hospital, almost all the guys called," Foster said. "Except for Lou and Wenz [Assistant Coach Bob Wenzel]. They both came to see me. When Tink [Banks] called and didn't reverse the charges I almost had another heart attack I was so shocked."

Foster's heart attack, as it turned out, started a shocking run of bad luck for people connected with that team: Wenzel needed radical brain surgery; Dennard and Ray Jones both had testicular cancer; Banks snapped an Achilles tendon in a summer league basketball game. A year before Foster got sick, Mike Gminski had almost been killed by a staph infection and Steve Gray had been in a serious automobile accident. In 1986, Foster got fired from South Carolina and was tainted by an NCAA investigation into the program there.

For a group so young, the bad luck and bad health was remarkable. Sixteen men—twelve players, four coaches—only one of them (Foster) older than thirty-one in 1978 and only one of the twelve players (Bell) even twenty-one. And all this had happened.

How had they dealt with the adversity? They had known extraordinary success very young and then, in many cases, extraordinary misfortune. I wanted to know how all of them were doing and what '78 meant to them ten years later. If it had meant so much to me, a spectator, then it must have profoundly affected each of them, the participants. I wanted to write this book for personal reasons, because I thought it would be fun to sit down with people I had known years ago and talk about a special time in our lives. But the reporter in me was convinced there was a story here too: that these men (and two women managers) could mean something not just to Duke people but to anyone who could identify with innocence and the loss of it, success and failure, joy and sadness.

I set out not certain I could find them all and not certain how they would react to the concept. In some cases, it had been ten years since I had seen or talked to them. Maybe their memories wouldn't be as warm or as vivid as mine were. Maybe they wouldn't want to talk—or at least not talk *frankly* about what had gone wrong in 1979 and 1980.

None of my fears proved valid. I found everyone. And, in every case, they were not only willing to talk, they talked at length. Some told me they found the discussions cathartic. My belief that the '78 season and the friendships that were forged that year had been important to all of them proved correct—and then some. Many of them cried at some point in retelling their stories. Often, I cried too.

I can honestly say I enjoyed almost every minute of the research process of this book. Spending time with all the guys again was not only a gratifying experience as a reporter, it was fun, period.

There is one story that best sums up how they all still feel about each other. Sitting in the trailer that Jim Suddath lived in with his wife and three children at the Columbia Bible College, I asked Suddath how he would feel walking into a room with all his ex-teammates.

Suddath was four months short of completing his work in the seminary and becoming a minister, and we had talked during the day about his belief that sin (selfishness, immaturity, lack of discipline) had brought about the team's downfall in 1979. When I asked him about seeing his teammates again, Suddath took a long time before he answered.

"I'd want to give everyone a hug, of course," he said. "But I'm a preacher and there's part of me that would want to preach to them."

"How do you think they would react to that?" I asked.

Suddath laughed. "They would all say, 'Oh come on, Sudds, cut it out with that religious stuff!' "

"And how," I asked, "would you react to that, being a preacher?"

"I'd laugh and I'd stop," he said. "With anyone else, I would feel obligated to try and get my message across. But not with those guys. With them, if you can't laugh at yourself, you won't last very long. That's what I remember most about '78. We laughed all the time. And when it was over, we cried."

He paused. His voice was very soft now. "Everything we did though, as a basketball team, we always did it together. Win, lose, laugh, cry. In a way, even though we're spread out now, we're still together. For me, the bond will always be there. I don't know about anyone else, but that's the way I feel."

I do know about everyone else, Sudds. They all feel the same way.

—JOHN FEINSTEIN
Shelter Island, N.Y.
June 11, 1989

I

THE PUZZLE

From left to right, kneeling: Coach Bill Foster, Team Captain Jim Spanarkel; seated: Kenny Dennard, Bob Bender, John Harrell, Steve Gray, Rob Hardy, Bruce Bell, Jim Suddath; standing: Assistant Coach Lou Goetz, Assistant Coach Ray Jones, Manager Kevin Hannon, Manager Mary Kay Bass, Harold Morrison, Cameron Hall, Mike Gminski, Scott Goetsch, Gene Banks, Trainer Max Crowder, Manager Deborah Ridley, Assistant Coach Bob Wenzel.

THAD SPARKS

1

The Reunion

April 7, 1989 ...

For at least the fourth time since midnight, Bill Foster looked at his watch. "I have to get going," he said—again—thinking about the wake-up call that was now only five hours away.

Bruce Bell, sitting a few feet from Foster, put his beer on the table and shook his head vehemently. His voice, high-pitched under the most serious of circumstances, was half an octave higher after an evening of drinking. "You can't leave yet, Coach," he insisted. "We haven't even called H yet." Foster, who had been sipping white wine while everyone around him was guzzling beer, smiled. Harold Morrison—H—had been recruited by Foster out of West Orange, New Jersey, in 1975. At the time, the coach thought H would help him turn the basketball program at Duke University around.

As it turned out, Morrison *had* been a key man in Duke's rise as a basketball power. But not in the way that either he or Foster had imagined or wanted. Now, however, ten years later, Foster didn't remember the problems and frustrations—his or Morrison's. Like the other men in the room, he thought not about Harold Morrison, the unhappy senior, but about H, the team wit of 1978.

"See if you can get him, Juice," Foster said, calling Bell by his nickname. Bell was on his feet heading for the phone almost before Foster's sentence was finished. It had been almost ten years since he had spoken to Harold Morrison, yet calling him seemed the most natural thing in the world.

When Morrison picked up the phone, Bell, in a voice rapidly ap-

3

proaching soprano, said, "God-dog, Willie hit me in the head with an elbow."

Morrison, three thousand miles away, said, "Excuse me?" Bell repeated himself, squealing, "God-dog, Willie hit me in the head with an elbow."

Morrison got it the second time, remembering the line and the voice. *"No! No way!"* he screamed. *"It can't be! Juice? Is that you, Juice?"* Then he stopped himself. "Of course it's you. No one else in the world can talk like that." Bell was dissolving in laughter. Foster took the phone. "H, guess who?" he said. And then, a little nervously, "It's Coach Foster."

"Coach!" Morrison seemed genuinely happy to hear Foster's voice. The bad memories went into recess, at least for the moment. Foster was laughing by now, his mind off his watch, the wake-up call, and the crucial group of recruits waiting for him back at Northwestern. "We ate dinner at The Kanki in your honor, H," he said, a reference to a restaurant where Morrison had twice become desperately sick while a Duke undergraduate. Shifting gears quickly, as the men around him smiled, he said, "You've got a family now, don't you?"

"Four kids," Morrison replied. "Two are my wife's by her first marriage. I guess you could say I got them in the draft."

Morrison's old teammates were now lining up to take the phone from Foster. "Got to go, H. There's some other guys here who want to talk to you. In fact, I think this next guy wants to try to straighten you out." As he handed the phone to Jim Suddath, who was two months away from being ordained as a minister, Foster turned to Bell. "Are you going to try to get Gray, too?"

Bell was stunned. If there was a player Foster had coached in six years at Duke who he would have reason *not* to want to talk to it was Steve Gray. If Morrison's college basketball career had been one of broken dreams, Gray's had been a nightmare. Every person in the room had two distinct memories of Gray: the pass off the rim and the dribble off the foot. It may have been unfair, but it was true. Even Gray, thinking back to those two heartbreaking disasters in his sophomore season, had once shaken his head and said, "After that, if I had been smart, I would have just gone and sat in the stands with all the other students and *watched* the games."

Apparently, though, the evening had become giddy enough that even Gray, the angry man of the team (his nickname had been Charlie Manson), could now take part. To the delight of everyone, Foster was actually relaxed and enjoying himself. For his former players, this was a side of him they had almost never seen. It had been nine years since any of them had played for him but to all of them he was still, "Coach."

■

They were all adults now, most of them with families, all of them with jobs and pressures and anxieties. Yet, returning to their alma mater for an unofficial reunion eleven years after their most glorious moment, they had quickly reverted to their college roles. Coach was Coach. Bruce Bell, father of three, a successful lawyer in Lexington, Kentucky, was again Juice, his old teammates screechingly imitating his voice. Rob Hardy, also a Kentucky lawyer, was a walk-on, just as he had been eleven years earlier. Suddath, even if he had worn his minister's collar, was Sudds, the naive lefty shooter whose Georgia drawl matched Bell's. Jim Spanarkel, the team captain, was definitely still the team captain, the guy everyone looked up to, the most likely person in the room to nail anyone—even Coach—with a one-liner. Scott Goetsch might weigh more than three hundred pounds but he hadn't stopped being The Fonz. Bob Bender was about to become a head coach himself. He wore wire-rimmed glasses and talked about "the kids" on the *current* Duke team. To his old teammates, though, this was still Benny talking: suave, sophisticated and—no doubt—full-of-it Benny. Gene Banks, even if he showed up looking like the cover of next month's *GQ*, would always be Tink, short for Tinkerbell. And if Tink said he'd meet you outside in fifteen minutes, you knew he might—might—be outside anytime in the next hour. Kenny Dennard—Dog and Dirt—was different only in the sense that the testicle he had lost to cancer gave everyone something new to tease him about.

■

The idea to bring the 1978 team back to Duke had come about after several of the players had contributed to the Max Crowder Endowment, a scholarship fund Duke was setting up in honor of Max Crowder, the school's basketball trainer since 1962, a man who had worked with every Duke basketball player of the past thirty years. Crowder was to be honored at the annual Hall of Fame Banquet on April 8. Why not, reasoned Tom Mickle, the man putting the Crowder Endowment together, invite the whole '78 team to come back that weekend?

After all, Duke had done nothing the year before to mark the tenth anniversary of this team's miraculous run in March of 1978. "Too soon," said Tom Butters, the athletic director. "Maybe you do it after twenty years, but not after ten."

Maybe. They were not the first Duke team to reach the Final Four, or the last, but they were the most unlikely. In 1977, Foster's third Duke team had finished last in the Atlantic Coast Conference, the fourth straight season that Duke had been last or tied for last. Forgotten were the glory years of the 1960s, when in 1963, 1964, and 1966 the school had gotten to the Final Four. Duke had become a laughingstock, a doormat, a school that in four years had an aggregate 11–49 record against ACC teams.

Then, suddenly, without warning, it had all turned around for Duke. A team with only one senior—Bell, a onetime walk-on—and with two freshmen and two sophomores in the starting lineup, went from the bottom to the top, winning the ACC Tournament. From there, they had gone on to become national darlings, going to the Final Four, then actually reaching the national championship game. The 94–88 loss to Kentucky in the final couldn't dampen what they had done. They were America's Team before the term was popularized by the Dallas Cowboys. They were bright, funny, irreverent, and they could play.

Best of all, with only Bell graduating, they would surely get their national title the next year. Or the year after. Or both. But they never came close again. Not this team, anyway. Not this coach.

On the campus where Foster had once been a hero, the man who succeeded him, Mike Krzyzewski, was now an icon, having finally put together a perennial powerhouse. Foster could have walked across the quad on this April afternoon without turning five heads. He had come back to Duke with mixed emotions. But in the glow of this reunion, as with most reunions, the bad times were either forgotten or ignored. They had been a special team once and now those were the times they remembered. For these few hours, they were special once again.

Four of them had not come back. H had wanted to, but to come three thousand miles from San Francisco and leave his wife with four kids for the weekend was impossible. Charlie Manson might have come the three thousand miles from Los Angeles if H had—they had stayed in touch over the years—but when Morrison couldn't make it, neither could Gray. John Hunnell—Johnny Gun to his teammates—had to work, or at least said he had to work.

And then there was Mikey. No one would have enjoyed this weekend more than Mike Gminski. He would have ripped and been ripped more than anyone. But Mikey was still playing. He had just signed a five-year, eight-million-dollar contract with the Philadelphia 76ers. This amazed and delighted his old teammates. But it did not prevent them from abusing him or from waking him up at 1 A.M. to remind him that no matter how much money he made he was still a 6-11 Polack with no neck.

In many ways, this group was no different from any other that was brought back together after several years. There were familiar stories and old jokes and fond memories. But this team *was* different. Perhaps never in college basketball's long history has a group of characters so diverse become so close.

The 1978 team was too young to understand what it was doing. There had been so much failure in the past at Duke that no one cared *how* they won, as long as they won. Players like Bell, Gray, Morrison and Goetsch, who might have objected to younger players like Banks, Dennard, Suddath and Harrell relegating them to the bench, really didn't mind, as long as the team won. A year later that all changed. But that was later.

Banks, black, from the Philadelphia ghetto, and Dennard, white, from a rural North Carolina town, became close friends. Suddath, the born-again Christian from Georgia, looked up to Spanarkel, the wise guy from Jersey City. Harrell and Bender, both transfers, became the point guards. Harrell was the son of a math professor at North Carolina Central, a small black college in Durham. Bender was a coach's son from the Midwest. Harrell transferred to Duke without a scholarship, a move across town in 1976 noticed by no one. Two months later, Bender also transferred to Duke, but he came from Indiana, which had just won the national championship, and his arrival made headlines.

They didn't win a national championship. In some ways, that didn't matter then. It doesn't really matter now. They were a team that represented *innocence*. They had never won, they had never felt jealousy or envy, they had never failed to meet expectations. Dennard and Banks didn't know that the sight of a black teenager and a white teenager hugging unabashedly on national television would make them celebrities. Spanarkel couldn't possibly understand that seeing a knock-kneed, pigeon-toed guard dominate a basketball game would send people into ecstasy.

It came so fast and went even faster. There was no second chance for this team, just the one joyride. Only two people associated with that 1978 team have ever been to another Final Four. Crowder, the trainer, who comes with the franchise, has been a part of all seven Final Four teams at the university. Bender, as an assistant coach at Duke, has been to Krzyzewski's three Final Fours. But the other eleven players, the four coaches, and the three managers got there once.

"The teams I've been part of as a coach that made it to the Final Four all expected to be, or at least *hoped* to be there," Bender said. "In '78, we had no clue. It came out of nowhere. We started the season hoping we would at least be good enough to get to the NIT. Just being in the NCAA Tournament surpassed our wildest dreams. To play for the national championship was something we never gave any thought to. Until we were there. Then we all looked around and kind of said, 'Oh my God, look where we are now.' We never thought about where we were going. All we thought about was how much fun we were having. As long as we kept winning, we got to keep having fun. All we wanted to do was play basketball because we had figured out that we were good, damn good, and beating people was fun. We were having fun, that's all it was."

It was never that way again at Duke after 1978. In fact, it is probably fair to say, in this era when so much money is involved in college basketball, that it has never been quite that way again *anywhere*. College basketball lost its innocence long ago. But that Duke team had it. The morning after the Blue Devils lost the national championship game, one of the headlines in *The Durham Sun* said this: "DUKE FANS EXPECT NATIONAL TITLE NEXT YEAR."

They weren't alone. Almost from the minute that headline appeared, everything changed. But during the 1977–78 season, Duke was a place found in fairy tales. It didn't last—fairy tales never do in real life. The extraordinary success the members of that team found at such a young age was followed, in many cases, by extraordinary adversity. Cancer. Heart attack. Brain tumor. Automobile accident. *Failure.*

Through it all, in a very real sense, all of them hung on to 1978. Gray, Morrison, and Harrell, who all left Duke unhappy, still wear their 1978 rings. No matter what else happens to them, they all still have '78. Even as the years pass, even if they haven't seen one another, the feeling persists.

"I could walk into a room with any of them and it would be as if we hadn't seen each other for ten minutes, not ten years," said Goetsch, who practices law in Baltimore. "That goes for any of them. Gray. H. Sudds. Kenny. Tink. Every one of them. There is a bond between us that will never go away, even if we never see each other again.

"When we walked into that locker room in St. Louis after losing to Kentucky, we all cried. Not because we had lost, but because it was over. We knew then we'd been through something that would never happen again. Never. The feeling in that locker room was a feeling of closeness I've never felt in my life. Nothing close."

Every member of the team says the same thing about that locker room scene. Every one. In the retelling, most begin to cry, or at least choke up, their eyes glistening at the memory. But what makes that moment most remarkable is that this was not an era where basketball teams spent every waking moment together.

"We didn't hang around together all that much away from the locker room," Bender remembered. "We were all different and we all had a lot of friends away from basketball. But when we walked into the locker room or onto the floor, for whatever reason, we were everything a team should be."

A team that won. A team that lost. But always a team. Then. Now.

It was after 2 A.M. when Bill Foster looked at his watch one last time. The beer was gone. The police had come twice to ask for quiet. Foster had enjoyed himself. For his players, seeing him like this made the entire weekend worthwhile. They had never seen him so loose, so relaxed. They all worry about him, the way he once worried about them. As important as the other coaches were, as vital as each player's contribution was, Bill Foster was the architect, the man who built the foundation. He was Duke basketball when each of them arrived; in many ways he is still Duke basketball to each of them today.

"I'm glad I came," Foster yawned as he said good-bye to everyone, his wake-up call less than four hours away. "I wasn't sure I would feel that way. The guys haven't changed at all, they're all still the same."

In truth, all of them had changed; Foster too. But the feelings they shared hadn't changed a bit. They never will.

2

The Beginning

It was a warm, rainy Friday evening in Durham when Bill Foster was introduced to the world as Duke's new basketball coach. In less than a week, Foster had gone from New York—where his Utah team had lost the National Invitation Tournament final to Purdue—to Durham for a tour of the Duke campus; to Greensboro to watch the national championship game between N.C. State and Marquette; to Salt Lake City to talk to his wife Shirley about the Duke job; and then back to Durham.

"I'm really happy to be here," Foster said, "I think."

The "I think" was supposed to be a joke, but there was a lot of truth in those two words. Foster really wasn't sure he was doing the right thing. In fact, on his way to Durham, changing planes in Chicago, he had almost turned back.

"I panicked," he remembered, years later. "I got cold feet. I said, 'Why are you doing this?' I had a good thing going at Utah. We had gotten through the rough times and now I'm going to another place to start over. Shirley was pregnant, she certainly didn't need a move right then. But I had made a commitment so, really, there was no backing out. But if I had understood just how tough things were, I might have turned around and gone home anyway, commitment or no commitment."

There was no way that Foster, as an outsider, could understand how bad the basketball situation at Duke had become. This was a school living on its past. From 1960 to 1969 with Vic Bubas as the coach,

Duke was one of the glamor basketball programs in America. Players like Art Heyman, Jeff Mullins, Jack Marin, Bob Verga, and Mike Lewis were All-Americans for Bubas and, between 1960 and 1966, the Blue Devils won four ACC titles and reached three Final Fours.

But by 1967, Dean Smith had built his own powerhouse eight miles down the road at the University of North Carolina. Bubas still had good teams, but not dominant ones. Nonetheless, when he announced that he was going to retire at the end of the 1968–69 season at the age of forty-eight, everyone at Duke was stunned.

Bucky Waters, a former Duke assistant who had gone on to become the head coach at West Virginia, was hired to replace Bubas. Waters was a stern disciplinarian, a no-nonsense type of coach. He believed in short hair and long practices.

This was during the Vietnam era. Duke had been the scene of a student takeover of the administration building in 1969. Antiwar and anti-Nixon feelings were running high on campus, even among athletes, normally the most conservative members of any student body. Waters recruited well during his first two years, but his style didn't fit the times. Four of his players, from a freshman team that had gone 16–0, transferred before their junior and senior years. The next recruiting class went 13–3 as freshmen—this was before freshmen were eligible to play on the varsity—and three of those players also transferred.

With many of his key recruits deserting (and with others who stayed extremely unhappy) Waters's record slipped steadily: 20–8, 20–10, 14–12, 12–14. The student newspaper, *The Chronicle*, wanted him gone. "Dump Bucky" signs began to crop up in the student section at home games. At the end of that fourth season, with one year left on his contract, Waters asked for an extension. He was told no. Duke didn't fire coaches. Waters's contract would be honored. But there was no indication he would be given a new one. In fact, the implication was that, barring a major turnaround during the 1973–74 season, the coach would be fired.

Waters understood. He knew he was in an impossible position. Without a new contract he was a virtual lame duck. That, combined with all the previous problems, made recruiting virtually impossible. On September 10, a week in to the fall semester, Waters resigned. He had been offered a job at the Duke hospital and decided the opportunity was too good to turn down.

This was everyone's easy way out. Waters didn't have to spend a season as a lame duck. Duke didn't have to face questions about why it had kept Waters around for a fifth year if the decision to dump him had already been made. Fine for Waters. Fine for the administration. But horrible for the basketball program. Coaches just don't resign in September, five weeks before practice is set to begin. Coaches resign— or get fired—at the end of the season so that a successor can be found during the spring. Duke was in an impossible situation, trying to find a coach when school was already underway.

The logical thing to do was name Neill McGeachy, Waters's top assistant, as interim coach for the season. If McGeachy did well, he would be considered as a candidate to replace Waters on a full-time basis. But Athletic Director Carl James, never a man who did anything the simple way, wasn't about to change his ways now. He began calling head coaches, hoping that someone might be enticed—even at this time of year—to jump to Duke.

One of the coaches James called was Bill Foster. "I was shocked," Foster said. "Partly because of the timing, but also because I was not exactly setting the world on fire at Utah. I wasn't quite sure why anyone would want me."

Foster was forty-three at the time and had just completed his second year at Utah with an 8–19 record. "If we don't upset Brigham Young in the last game of the season, we become the first Utah team to lose twenty games," Foster said. "It had not been a great season. Now, all of a sudden a guy calls me and says, 'Would you be interested in coaching Duke?' "

The answer was yes. But *not* one month before practice began and *not* coming off a losing season during which Foster had played several freshmen extensively. Not only did this upcoming season promise much more, Foster was not about to leave Utah without a coach one month before practice started. So James said he understood and told Foster he might hear from him again, which was fine with Foster.

The next person James called was Adolph Rupp. Yes, *that* Adolph Rupp. The Baron of the Bluegrass, the winningest college basketball coach of all time. The year before, at the age of seventy, Rupp had been forced into retirement by the University of Kentucky. James had the notion that if he could bring Rupp out of retirement for a year or two, he would certainly gain some national attention for his moribund program; he might even get some of the glamor back into it.

Rupp was interested. Very interested. He was angry that Kentucky had forced him out and he saw Duke as a way to prove to the world that he was not too old to coach. Duke had tradition, it had a big name, and it needed a winner. The Baron was, after all, a winner. A few days before practice was to begin, Rupp told James he would take the job.

No one at Duke had any idea what was going on. McGeachy, the top assistant, was in charge for the moment, waiting like everyone else, for something to happen. Then, on October 14, the day before practice was to start, Art Chansky, the sports editor of the *Durham Morning Herald*, broke the story: Duke was trying to hire Adolph Rupp.

"After Bucky quit, I kept trying to find out from my Duke sources who Carl was trying to hire," Chansky said. "I was getting nowhere. Even McGeachy didn't know what was going on. Then, I heard they were talking to Adolph Rupp. I ignored it. It was just too preposterous. Then I heard it again. And again.

"The funny thing was, I had Rupp's home phone number because when I had worked at *The Atlanta Constitution* one of the rituals they had for new reporters was to assign them to call Rupp. The idea was, you'd think there was no way you could get Adolph Rupp on the phone and then you'd find out that not only could you get him *on* the phone, you couldn't get him *off*. He'd talk to anyone, any time, because he was so pissed off that Kentucky was running him off.

"So, I called him. And, he said, 'Sure I've talked to Carl James about coming over to Durham to coach.' I called Carl and he gave me a very stiff 'No comment.' I remember thinking to myself, 'My God, the old man isn't hallucinating. They might actually hire him.'"

Chansky's story did not exactly set off dancing in the streets of Durham. Rupp may have been a god in Kentucky but to Duke people he was just an over-the-hill old man who had fought integration throughout the 1960s and had given every indication during his last few years at Kentucky that he was well past it as a coach. How in the world, the players wanted to know, do you rebuild a basketball program with a seventy-one-year-old coach?

By now, James had a fiasco on his hands. Practice had started. He had no coach. He was being laughed at because of his flirtation with Rupp. In *The Chronicle* that day, Bob Fleischer, the starting center, had an angry letter denouncing the athletic department for its handling of the coaching vacancy.

On October 17, Duke announced it would hold a 10 A.M. press conference the next day to name the new coach. Chansky called Rupp again. "I'm so glad you called," Rupp told him. "We've got a terrible storm down here and my phone has been out for hours. I still can't make a call out and I have to reach Carl James. My farm manager died today [Rupp owned a 1,500-acre farm outside Lexington] and I just can't leave here to take the coaching job at Duke. Will you call him for me and ask him to give me a call?"

Chansky called James, who mumbled something about not knowing what Chansky was talking about, hung up and, no doubt, called Rupp. Now, James had a 10 A.M. press conference to name a coach, and no coach. Finally, he called McGeachy and asked him to be in his office at 9 A.M. There, he offered him a one-year contract.

At the press conference an hour later, James denied Chansky's assertion that McGeachy had just been offered the job that morning. "Who is your source on that?" James demanded to know.

Chansky's source was McGeachy, who had told him just before the press conference what had happened. James and Chansky stood yelling at one another while the rest of the media watched both amused and amazed by what had become of Duke basketball. In the back of the room, the members of the team watched the scene with equal bemusement.

The press release handed out that day heralded "A New Era At Duke." Indeed it was.

■

Six months later, Carl James insisted that he had told McGeachy when he was hired that he was only an interim coach and that he was continuing his search for a permanent replacement. McGeachy insists that he refused the job on an interim basis and was given a one-year contract with the promise that he would be given a chance to prove he deserved a longer contract.

The press conference was a harbinger of what was to come. The '73–74 season was a disaster. The players were happy McGeachy had finally been given the job but uncertain about his future—with good reason. The Blue Devils played well some nights, poorly on some others. There were some embarrassing blowouts and some heartbreaking losses. But none of the losses compared to what happened in Chapel Hill on March 2, 1974.

This was the regular season finale. Duke was 10–14. North Carolina, strong as always, was 22–5. One of those victories had come in Durham back in January. With the score tied at 71 and four seconds left, Carolina's Bobby Jones had stolen a crosscourt inbounds pass thrown by Duke guard Paul Fox and hit the winning lay-up at the buzzer.

That had been Duke's big chance for a major upset; the kind, the players thought, that would give McGeachy a chance to retain his job. Their chances of winning in Chapel Hill were extremely slim, especially since Duke had not won in Carmichael Auditorium since 1966.

But the Blue Devils had one of those days. With seventeen seconds left, they led 82–74 and Carmichael was a morgue. Jones made two free throws to make it 82–76, but so what? All Duke had to do was kill seventeen seconds. A couple of inbounds passes and the game would be over.

It didn't quite work out that way.

Carolina stole one inbounds pass and scored. Then another. Amazingly, it was 82–80 with five seconds left. On the third try, Duke finally got the ball inbounds—to junior forward Pete Kramer. He was fouled with three seconds left. All he had to do was make the front end of the one-and-one and the game would finally be over.

Kramer missed.

Mitch Kupchak rebounded for Carolina and immediately called time. Since this was Chapel Hill, the clock stayed right at three seconds. Still, the Tar Heels had to go ninety-four feet and score in three seconds. The ball came in to freshman Walter Davis. From just beyond halfcourt, he heaved a desperation shot. It hit the top of the backboard—*and dropped in.* Overtime. Which was merely a formality. Duke was finished.

Neither school has ever forgotten that game. At Carolina, it is considered one of the great moments in the school's history. In March of 1989, the *Charlotte Observer* ran a huge story commemorating the 15th anniversary of what is known as "the eight-point game." At Duke, students today still whisper about those seventeen seconds. No lead is considered safe, especially against Carolina.

For the players on that team it was the nadir of what had already been a horrendous experience. Five days later, in the opening round of the ACC Tournament, they lost meekly to Maryland, finishing the season with a 10–16 record—the worst in Duke history. By then, it had been announced that a search for a new basketball coach had formally begun and the players were angrily saying that McGeachy deserved more time and a fair chance.

He would get neither. In truth, Carl James had never stopped recruiting Bill Foster, even after giving the job to McGeachy. He had flown to Salt Lake City to see Utah play and to talk to Foster— informally—about moving to Duke. Foster, even though his team was built around sophomores and en route to a 22–8 record, was most definitely interested.

Foster was, after all, an easterner. He had grown up in Norwood, Pennsylvania, just outside of Philadelphia, and gone to college at Elizabethtown. He had coached and taught for six years in Pennsylvania high schools before becoming the coach at Bloomsburg State in 1960 at the age of thirty. Three years later he had moved to Rutgers. After eight very successful seasons there, he had been lured west by Utah, largely because he felt he had taken Rutgers about as far as he could. He was also very aware that he had a chance to be a star in Salt Lake City, away from the glutted New York media market.

"Going to Utah was a gamble but I felt like it was one I sort of had to take," Foster said. "I loved it at Rutgers. We had a house we loved and the school had always been good to me. But this was the kind of experience I just didn't think I was going to get if I stayed at Rutgers. I mean, fifteen thousand, five hundred seats. A television show, a radio show. It wasn't so much the money as the experience. This was a whole different type of job for me."

Not an easy one, though. Utah basketball was down when Foster took over. The Utes were 13–12 his first season but graduated several seniors off that team. Foster had to play with freshmen the next year and that produced the 8–19 mark. But that one poor season did not damage his reputation as a builder. He had turned a horrendous program around at Rutgers and had been popular with the students, his players, and the media while he was doing it. Carl James was intrigued by Foster. And Foster was intrigued, almost fascinated by Duke.

"I remember my first reaction was, 'What a great school,' " he said. "But I also remembered [former Duke All-American] Jack Marin telling me once, 'It's a great school but you can't win there anymore.' I knew there was a risk involved but there were still a lot of reasons for me to be interested."

Location was one reason. Foster's mother lived alone in Tyrone, Pennsylvania, and could not fly. Sometimes during the season, Foster would fly red-eyes back and forth from Utah just to spend a day with his mother when she wasn't feeling well. Durham would be much closer than Salt Lake City. She might even get to see her grandchildren on occasion.

What's more, Foster owned and operated a lucrative basketball camp in the Pocono Mountains each summer. Going back and forth between the camp and his home at Utah was exhausting.

There was more. Foster had always been aware of Duke. As a freshman at tiny Goldey Business College, a small college prep school in Wilmington, Delaware, he had been recruited briefly by Duke as a basketball player. He still carried in his wallet the newspaper clipping that reported Duke's interest in "The Goldey Flash."

Back at Duke, rumors were flying. Bob Boyd, the coach at Southern California, had reportedly been interviewed by James. Some alumni were pushing Lefty Driesell, a Duke alumnus who had built powerhouses at Davidson and Maryland, for the job. James kept saying he wanted "a super-coach," but wouldn't say who it would be. Maybe, the players joked, he was going to hire John Wooden.

Regardless of who became the coach, he would have a massive rebuilding job on his hands. Duke had ended with a 2–10 record in the ACC, finishing in last place for the first time in the school's history. The 10–16 overall record was also the worst in history. Recruiting, especially with a coaching change, was a likely disaster. Lou Goetz, who had played for Foster at Rutgers and then coached under him at Rutgers and Utah, remembers thinking the move to Duke was a fabulous idea when Foster first broached it to him. "It was only after we got there that we began to understand what we had gotten ourselves into," Goetz said. "There were times, a lot of times during those first three years, when we all wondered whether we could get the job done. We came close to failing."

Failure is something Bill Foster can't deal with. He is a driven, single-minded person who is always his own worst critic. After his second year at Utah, he was honestly concerned about the possibility that Utah might fire him. In fact, the officials at the school were delighted with the way he had put things in place for the program to succeed—which it did that year.

But simple success wasn't enough for Bill Foster. If he had a good team, he wondered why it wasn't a great team. And, even though he liked living in Salt Lake City, he felt cut off from the world he had grown up in back east. He wondered if, in ten years, anyone outside of Utah would know who he was if he remained there.

"The thing you must remember about Bill is that he's never been truly happy," said Goetz, who has known him for almost twenty-five years. "That's just not in his nature. Even when he has had success, he has always worried that failure is waiting right around the corner. I think that's one of the reasons why he's always kept moving. Somehow he worries that if he stays in one place too long, failure will catch up to him."

Foster had been a college coach for fourteen years when James approached him about moving to Duke. He had had only one losing season (his first) at Rutgers and one at Utah. Other than that, he had always coached winners. But not *big* winners. He had been to four NIT's, but never to the NCAA's. He was about to become the president of the National Association of Basketball Coaches, but he wondered if he belonged in the same room with the top names in his profession. Duke was down, but it was a place that had been *up*. It was in the most prestigious conference in America. It had a beautiful campus, a student body Foster thought he could relate to, and the money to recruit on a national level, which Foster knew he would have to do if he was going to make Duke competitive again.

Foster told James he would take the job—even though he wasn't certain it had really been offered to him. "I don't actually remember Carl saying, 'We'd like you to be the coach,' " Foster said. "But when I told him I'd take the job, he seemed happy about it. At least I think he was happy about it."

James was a difficult man for anybody to read. He was, to say the least, circumspect. Once, he had told a student reporter that Duke's swimming coach was retiring the following season. When the student called the coach for a comment on his retirement, the coach wasn't quite sure what to say. "I was in Carl's office yesterday talking about next season," he said. "This is the first I've heard of it."

James was actually a hardworking, decent man who, as a Duke graduate, genuinely cared about the school. But he would never be mistaken for The Great Communicator. Apparently, though, he did want Foster to be his coach: as soon as Foster accepted what had not been offered, a press conference was called to introduce him.

Before he met the press, Foster met his new team. Since Duke had not exactly dominated the national limelight, Foster had to take a media guide into the meeting so he would know who the players were.

There were four seniors—and since they had played freshman basketball in 1972, Foster would be their fourth coach. No one in the room bore any resemblance to David Thompson, who had just led N.C. State to the national title. Looking at the players in the room and thinking about those at some of the other ACC schools, Foster came up with a quick assessment of the program for his new boss.

"We've got six problems, Carl," he said. "N.C. State, North Carolina, Maryland, Wake Forest, Clemson and Virginia."

It was intended as a wisecrack but the ring of truth was loud and clear. Duke's talent had fallen way behind the rest of the ACC.

In order to change that, Foster would need a strong staff, an aggressive group of assistants who would comb the country for players with talent *and* good grades, who wanted to be part of a rebuilding process. "We'll sell two things," Foster decided. "The academics and playing time."

Duke *had* to stress academics to recruits. That was the only area in which it might have an advantage over other schools. Many top players simply couldn't be recruited by Duke because of the admissions standards. Even though that narrowed the talent pool, it meant that a lot of the players it *would* want to get involved with would be the kind who might want to go to a school like Duke. Foster had to push that concept hard.

His first task was to hire a staff. He had already decided that Goetz would come with him from Utah. Goetz had been a good, but not great player for Foster at Rutgers, a 6-2 forward who survived because of his smarts. After Goetz graduated, Foster hired him as a graduate assistant and then took him to Utah. Even though Goetz was only twenty-seven, he would be the number one assistant at Duke.

Joining him would be another Rutgers graduate, Bob Wenzel. Three years younger than Goetz, Wenzel had spent two seasons as a graduate assistant at Utah before leaving to get a full-time job at Yale. Foster wanted him on the staff, too. Wenzel was packing his bags almost before he hung up the phone after Goetz called to say, "Coach wants you down here."

The third assistant would be Jim Lewis, a holdover from the Waters/McGeachy staff. Foster thought it was important to have some continuity, both for the sake of the players and because Lewis had been in contact with the players Duke was recruiting that spring.

Picking his staff was relatively easy for Foster. His next job was a lot harder: He had to win the players over.

The team had liked McGeachy; they weren't happy with the way he had been treated, and Foster told them in his first meeting that he was pleased that they felt that loyalty. He said he hoped, in time, he would earn that same feeling from them. He pointed out that he had not been at Duke during the fiasco that had passed for the previous season and asked them to start on square one with him, just as he planned on doing with them. He also told them that if anyone wanted to transfer he would try to help them do so.

No one did. "Part of it was Duke," said Tate Armstrong, a freshman on that McGeachy team. "It isn't exactly a place you want to leave even if basketball is going terribly for you. But a lot of it was Bill. I think he struck all of us as being a very sincere guy who would work very hard to turn it around. We all knew he was going to be the coach no matter what we thought so why not give him a fair shot?"

The next step was winning the student body back.

Duke students have always thought of the basketball team as being *theirs*. Football games at Duke are little more than an excuse to drink beer in the sun and get a head start on that night's party. But basketball is another story.

■

Cameron Indoor Stadium is one of college basketball's special places. It is an old relic with a low ceiling and bleacher seats running around the entire court. More and more, as big money has come into college basketball, arenas have been built with plush, expensive seats close to the court. The big-money contributors sit in these seats; the only thing that can get them on their feet is the national anthem and, perhaps, the need to go to the bathroom at halftime.

This is not the case at Duke. Downstairs is for the students; the bleachers are within a few feet of the court. Given this proximity, the students believe it is their *obligation* to play a role in the outcome of the game. Their participation goes well beyond noise. If an opponent has had the misfortune to get into some kind of trouble before playing at Duke, heaven help him.

When N.C. State's Moe Rivers was arrested for allegedly shoplifting a bottle of aspirin in 1974, he was pelted with aspirin tablets when he appeared before the Duke students. A few years later when two other State players were picked up for trying to steal underwear (yes, underwear), they were bombarded with underwear that had been painted red and white, State's colors. In 1983 when State's Lorenzo Charles was charged with mugging a Domino's Pizza delivery man, twenty Domino's Pizzas were delivered to the State bench just before tip-off.

And it wasn't just State that got picked on. Whenever Lefty Driesell came to town the students showed up en masse wearing bald skullcaps. They always had different chants waiting for North Carolina that were usually *just* obnoxious enough to enrage Coach Dean Smith. "I suppose you think they're funny," Smith once said to a reporter who had graduated from Duke. "Well, I guess you would—since you went to Duke."

Duke students clearly looked upon basketball as a participation—not a spectator—sport. But some of that had been lost during the Waters/ McGeachy era. In '74, the student section had been full for just three games—N.C. State, North Carolina, and Maryland—all ranked teams. With all the chaos that had gone before, Foster knew he had a lot of work to do to get the students involved with "their" basketball team again.

"The notion that the students were really important to the success of the team at home had always been there," Foster said. "I had to get it back to that point and I thought I had to get it back quickly for the sake of the team the next year but also for the sake of recruiting. You didn't want to bring a kid in and tell him this was one of the great home courts in America and then have him look across and see the bleachers half empty."

Foster spent most of his first spring at Duke and a large portion of the next fall going to fraternities and dormitories to speak to student groups. He answered questions for as long as they wanted to ask them. Very quickly, even before he had coached a game, Foster became a popular figure in the student body.

Promotions have always been a passion of Foster's, dating back to the business classes he took at Goldey and the business-education major he pursued at Elizabethtown College. "I always figured that if I ended up not liking teaching or coaching that I would have my business background to fall back on," he said. "As it turned out, I used a lot of my business background in my coaching."

Foster was one of the first business-minded college basketball coaches. As far back as the 1950s when he was coaching high school, he had organized an annual clinic in suburban Philadelphia, bringing in speakers one weekend each spring to talk to the area's high school coaches. When the clinic grew steadily, Foster went another step, putting up $2,500 to promote an exhibition basketball game between the Philadelphia Warriors and the Minneapolis Lakers. This was 1958 and the Warriors had a rookie who had gotten some attention. His name was Wilt Chamberlain.

Foster made his $2,500 back—and more. He also set up one of the first pure basketball camps in the country. Most camps were just general camps in those days; the notion of a one-sport camp was brand new. By the time Foster and his partner, Harry Litwack sold the camp in 1987, it ran eleven weeks a year and was one of the top basketball camps in the country. And by then, *everyone* was running basketball camps.

At Rutgers and at Utah, Foster had been heavily involved in the promotion of his teams. When he arrived in Salt Lake City, the Utah Stars of the American Basketball Association were the hot ticket in town. Foster immediately asked for a meeting with the Stars management so that Utah could make sure it scheduled home games on nights when the Stars wouldn't be playing. He then dubbed his team "The Runnin' Utes," and went about trying to sell out a 15,500-seat arena.

At Duke, Foster had a smaller—8,800 seats—arena but he also had a recent tradition of losing. He also had N.C. State, the new national champions, twenty miles to the east and perennial power North Carolina eight miles to the south. So Foster called his new team "The Runnin' Dukes," and talked about the run-and-gun style the Blue Devils would play.

"Of course, we didn't have any speed at all," Tate Armstrong said. "But he felt if we could push the ball down the court intelligently, we would get better shots, even if we didn't get lay-ups. He was right."

Foster also felt that the push-it-up style of play would be more attractive to potential recruits than a methodical, walk-it-up-and-pass-it-twenty-times approach. As it turned out, he was right about that, too.

The Runnin' Dukes of Bill Foster were not going to run anybody out of the gym, especially not in the ACC. But very quickly, Foster had done a lot to get Duke basketball turned back around from the nosedive it had been in for five years. He had the players on his side, he had the students on the way, he was getting attention by promising to play aggressively, and he had a very young staff on the road looking for the right players for the future.

3

The Recruiting Road

Basketball recruiting is different from any other sport because a basketball team contains so few people. Football coaches go out and look for big bodies that they can make bigger. They don't worry about personality because when you bring in thirty players a year, attrition will take care of personality problems. No one notices when a football player at a major school flunks out or transfers, unless he's a star player at a glamor position. The coaches just go out and get thirty more future weightlifters the next year.

Basketball isn't like that. It demands closeness in order to achieve success because there are only twelve players on a team. Most college programs sign no more than three, maybe four players in a given year. If one leaves or flunks out, it is a big deal. If two leave, it is a catastrophe—they are almost twenty percent of the team. Players are very conscious about who else a school is recruiting. If a school is recruiting two point guards, invariably each will want to know which one is their top priority. Or, just as often they will ask, "If I'm so good, why are you recruiting *him*?"

Basketball recruiting is politics and deal-making and figuring out what thing or which person is the key to a recruit's heart. Beyond that, it is like piecing a puzzle together. If there is a 6-7 player in the senior class who you like but there's another 6-7 player in the junior class you like better, do you risk taking the senior if it means you might not get the junior? And what if you pass up the senior but then lose the junior? Do you take the first player willing to commit to you or wait for someone you think is better and gamble on losing both of them?

Every college coach deals with these questions every year each and every time he signs a recruit. Some just lie to players. "You're my point guard for the next four years," a coach will say, even while he is dictating a letter to another point guard. Another familiar line is, "I won't recruit anyone else at your position for three years." Then, he will recruit another player at that position and claim he really doesn't play it. "I know he's your height, but he's really a forward, not a guard."

When Bill Foster and his staff went out into the recruiting world in the spring of '74, they weren't even on square one—they were behind it. Square one would come the next fall when they could start out with a fresh class of high school seniors, having seen them in the summer camps, following that scouting up with letters to the players they were most interested in. Now, not wanting to have *no* new players the next fall, Foster and company were out beating the bushes for players who, for one reason or another, had not yet signed with another school. The pickings were slim.

One player that McGeachy's staff had recruited was George Moses, a twenty-six-year-old six-foot-five-inch junior-college player from Texas. Duke had never recruited a JUCO but Moses seemed like a reasonable exception. He had been in the service before enrolling in junior college and was a decent student. He had threatened to look elsewhere if McGeachy was fired but when Foster contacted him right after taking the job, Moses said he still wanted to come. Foster was delighted to have him.

He offered two other players scholarships that spring, both guards from the area he was most familiar with, New Jersey. One was Kenny Young, tiny at 5–10, but lightning-quick; the other was Rick Gomez, a 6–2 youngster originally from Puerto Rico who seemed to have potential as a shooter.

Lou Goetz made a home visit to one other high school senior but did not offer him a scholarship. His name was Bruce Bell and his fondest wish was to play basketball at the University of Kentucky.

Bruce Bell had grown up with Kentucky blue in his blood. His father, Tommy Bell, had played football at UK under a young coach named Bear Bryant. Later, after receiving his law degree, Tommy Bell became one of the best-known football and basketball referees of all time. In fact, he is still the only man in history to referee in both the Super Bowl and the Final Four.

While Bruce was growing up, his father was a member of the board of trustees at Kentucky. The family had season tickets to all the UK basketball games and Bruce still has vivid memories of going to the games with his father, first at Memorial Coliseum and then at Rupp Arena after that 23,000-seat palace opened in 1977.

Bruce Bell was a good—though not great—high school basketball player. He was six feet tall, a steady point guard without a great deal of quickness. As a junior and a senior, playing on excellent teams, he averaged about 10 points a game. That was not enough to attract much attention from the big-time schools but it did attract the attention of Lee Rose, then the coach at Division 3 Transylvania College in Lexington. Rose wanted Bell to come to Transylvania and be his point guard. Bell was tempted.

But the Kentucky dream lingered. Bell had gone to UK's basketball camp for as long as he could remember and, with his father's ties to the school, he knew the coaching staff well. Although Joe B. Hall never recruited him, he did tell Bruce that if he enrolled at Kentucky he could come out for the team as a walk-on. Bell was weighing his options—big fish in a small pond or tiny fish in the pond he had always dreamed about—when Lou Goetz called.

Bell was flattered and delighted. To this day he doesn't know who gave Goetz his name, but he suspects it was his father. Tommy Bell had always liked Duke; it had a great mix of academics and athletics and he had been talking the school up to his son. Goetz visited and explained the situation: Duke did not have a scholarship to offer but if Bruce decided to come, he would be given the chance to walk-on. If he made the team there was a chance he would be put on scholarship later. Goetz promised nothing—except a chance for Bruce to show his stuff. That was really all Bell wanted.

"I guess part of it is ego," he said. "We all think we're a little better, or in some cases a lot better, than we are. I knew I wasn't a great player but I thought I was a pretty good player and that I could handle myself against good players if I had the chance. I knew Duke was a great school and I also knew I would have a better chance of making the team with their talent than I would at Kentucky where, as usual, they were loaded. It was still a tough decision. Part of me really wanted to go to Transylvania because I liked Lee Rose so much and part of me would always want to play for Kentucky. But in the end, I think I figured Duke might just be the best of both worlds for me. Plus, if I didn't like it, I could always transfer back home after a year."

And so it was that Bell decided to go to Duke as a walk-on. Little did he know that he had just become the first piece in Bill Foster's puzzle.

The 1974–75 Duke team was an experienced, though emotionally bruised, team. The four seniors had seen about everything there was to see in their college careers.

Bob Fleischer and Kevin Billerman had both started for two years. Fleischer was a solid player with a nice shooting touch for a man six feet eight inches tall but wasn't quite big enough or quick enough to be a star. Billerman was not a great talent but he was smart and hard-nosed, a member of everyone's all-dirty team. Billerman, according to his teammates, even played dirty in practice. Pete Kramer, at 6-4, wasn't quite big enough to play forward or quick enough to play guard. But he could shoot the ball and was not afraid to take an important shot. Bill Suk would never be a scorer but he played very solid defense.

The junior class, in addition to Moses, had one player, 6-10 Willie Hodge, who had the potential to be a star if he could stop getting into foul trouble; it had another player, 6-6 Dave O'Connell, who might have been a star if he had not damaged his knees; it had a workmanlike guard in 6-2 Paul Fox and it had Terry Chili.

Chili was 6-10, but he played 6-5. He was a hardworking, fun-loving sort who was very popular with the student body. Every time he entered a game, a big sign went up in the student section: "Herm the Sperm." Somehow, it fit. Chili loved to talk, on or off the court. Once, after a game, referee Hank Nichols presented him with a whistle, commenting, "You made more calls out there tonight than I did so you might as well have this." Everyone liked Herm. But when it came to basketball, no one wanted to depend on him to shut down Mitch Kupchak, Kenny Carr or, for that matter, anyone else in the ACC.

There were two sophomores left, Armstrong and Mark Crow.

Crow-bar, as everyone called him, was the team flake. If you were looking for a party, Bar would find one for you. If you were looking for a date, Bar would find that for you, too. In fact, if you were looking for almost *anything*, Bar would find it for you. Bar rarely looked as if anything was registering when you talked to him, usually because nothing was. But he was 6-7 and he could shoot and Foster saw potential in him. The question was, what did he have the most potential for? As a sophomore, he was Spuds McKenzie before anyone ever thought of using a party animal to peddle beer.

Armstrong was a different story although he and Bar were, and still are, close friends. Michel (pronounced Michael) Taylor (Tate) Armstrong is the oldest son of Robert Taylor and Shirley Johnson Armstrong. He was a military brat, living in Moultrie, Georgia; Enid, Oklahoma; Waco and San Antonio, Texas; and Wiesbaden, West Germany, by the time he was ten.

One of the tough things about moving all the time for Armstrong was the first day in a new school. "Without fail, the teacher would look up and say, 'Is Michel Armstrong here?' looking for some little girl. I would answer very quickly, 'There's no Michel Armstrong here and I would appreciate it if you call me Tate.' "

When Tate was ten, he and his mother and sister moved to Houston while his father, an Air Force pilot, went to Vietnam. Robert Armstrong spent two years in Vietnam as a forward air controller (FAC). The job of a FAC was to lead fighter pilots or bombers into the combat zone, flying just above the tree level, then peeling off only after the enemy had been spotted. It was incredibly dangerous work. The man Robert Armstrong replaced had been shot down. The man who eventually replaced him was also shot down. In all, he survived more than ninety-five missions north of the demilitarized zone, one of only three men to do so.

Tate Armstrong was old enough to understand that his father was in danger. But it was only later that he fully understood that his father's survival was remarkable. "Even now, he doesn't talk about that experience very much," Armstrong said. "It's one of those things where I don't think he's proud that he did what he did, but he understood that he didn't have much choice in the matter. His biggest triumph, I guess, was coming back."

Robert Armstrong was a major influence on his son. He was a disciplinarian who believed there was no excuse for not fulfilling your potential. When Tate was eight, he came home with a report card that included two C's. "I had never gotten anything lower than A, but I was really bored in class so I was reading all the time.

"My father sat me down and said I had a choice. I could quit the football team for the rest of the season and play basketball, or I could play football the rest of the season and not play basketball until we saw how I did on my next report card. After that, I never read in class and I never got anything lower than a B."

Armstrong's work ethic came from his mother. She was the one who always pushed him to try new things and not to get down on himself when things didn't come easily. "My dad gave me discipline," he said. "My mom gave me self-confidence."

Armstrong played football, basketball, and baseball through junior high school. Then, he believed he was a better football player than basketball player. But in high school in Texas when you are a little over six feet, slender and not that fast, you are not going to be a football star. So Armstrong stuck to basketball.

By his junior season at Spring Woods High, Armstrong was averaging 28 points a game. Texas, however, is not exactly a basketball hotbed and Armstrong, having never gone to a basketball camp, attracted little notice outside of Texas—except from Brigham Young, which recruited him heavily. "I think they thought I was a Mormon because I had blond hair and blue eyes," he said, laughing.

Duke discovered him by accident. Armstrong's high school coach, Roy Kieval, moonlighted as a scorekeeper at the Houston Rockets home games. Through that job, he struck up a friendship with Mike Newlin, then a starting guard for the Rockets. As a result, Newlin used the Spring Woods gym to work out in the summer. "He needed someone to beat up on," Armstrong said. "Roy gave him me."

Newlin did beat up on Armstrong, but he also helped make him a better player. And, he came away from the sessions thinking that the kid wasn't a bad player. He mentioned that fact to Jack Marin, a teammate on the Rockets. Marin, who had graduated from Duke in 1966, called the Duke coaches and said, "There's a kid here in Houston you should see."

Bucky Waters sent Jim Lewis down to take a look. Lewis was impressed enough to invite Armstrong to visit Duke. Not only could he shoot, he was an A student with 1,250 on his college boards.

"The first place they took me was the Chapel," Armstrong remembers. "The second place they took me was to the Duke Gardens. That was it. I said, 'Where do I sign?' The rest really didn't matter to me. I knew it was a great school, I knew it was in a big-time conference and the campus was like nothing I had ever seen. The problems they were having really didn't concern me. I was young and foolish. I thought I could handle anything."

He almost didn't handle his freshman year. Ten days after Armstrong arrived on campus, Waters quit. That didn't bother him much since the only coach he knew well at that point was Jim Lewis. But then the Rupp story broke. "I was in shock," he said. "I went in to see Carl James and told him that I knew it wouldn't break his heart or anything but if Duke went ahead and hired a guy who would practically be coaching out of an iron lung, my instinct would be to transfer. He just sort of looked at me like I was the man in the moon."

Armstrong made another fruitless trip to James's office to plead McGeachy's case at the end of the season. "I just didn't think he had been given a fair chance. I think most of the guys felt that way. But as soon as Coach Foster got the job, it was easy to see he knew what he was doing. And, it was certainly a lot better than Adolph Rupp."

The key for Armstrong was Wenzel. He was just three years older than the seniors and was pretty near his playing shape. He worked out relentlessly with Armstrong in the off-season. "Wenz was the guy who always wanted to run through walls. I was the same way and we hit it off right away."

Armstrong came back for his sophomore season with a new body. He was twenty pounds lighter and in much better shape than he had been the previous year.

In a lot of leagues, Foster's first Duke team would have done quite well. It had experience with three senior starters. Armstrong was emerging as a fine shooter at the off-guard and Willie Hodge showed flashes of brilliance. Moses was an excellent addition inside and Young's quickness added a dimension off the bench.

But it was not a team that could compete in the upper echelon of the ACC and Foster believed he had his job for only one reason: to get Duke back to the top of the ACC.

Early that first summer, going through one of the many lists of high school players that coaches constantly stare at, Wenzel noticed the name Jim Spanarkel. There was nothing extraordinary about Spanarkel except that, according to this report, he was an excellent student. Since he was from Jersey City, an area the coaches were familiar with, Wenzel called Spanarkel's coach at Hudson Catholic High School, Joe (Rocky) Pope.

Almost fifteen years later, Wenzel still remembered the conversation vividly. "I said, tell me about this Spanarkel kid and Rocky says, 'Well, he's about six foot five inches, he's not very fast or quick, he can't jump, and he's not a very good shooter. But when the other team presses, we give him the ball. When we need a basket, we give him the ball. If we're having trouble stopping a big man, we put him on the guy. If we're having trouble with a guard, we put him on that guy. About the only thing he can do for you is win.'

"Four years later, when Jimmy was a senior at Duke, I got a call from a pro scout and he said, 'Tell me about Spanarkel.' I gave him the same speech Rocky had given me four years earlier because it was still true."

That summer, Kevin Billerman found himself working at the Jersey Shore League. Spanarkel was playing on one of the teams. Billerman called the coaches raving about him. Now, they had to go see for themselves. They liked what they saw.

"He had a toughness about him," Wenzel remembered. "He just wasn't intimidated by anything. And he had great instincts. He knew when to shoot, when to pass, when to put it on the floor. By the end of the summer we were all agreed that we really wanted him."

Since Billerman knew Spanarkel—and, under NCAA rules, personal contact with players during the summer was illegal—he was assigned to ask Spanarkel if he would visit Duke. Like Armstrong, Spanarkel didn't know that much about Duke. "But my father always told me, 'Never say no to anything because that makes it final.' So I told Kevin I'd take a look." Once again two factors helped Duke: one was the fact that Spanarkel was not that highly recruited—a lot of schools were scared off by his lack of quickness; the other was The Chapel.

The Chapel is Duke's symbol, and, very possibly, its chief recruiter. Almost without fail, when a coach picks a recruit up at the airport, the first thing he does is drive him to Chapel Circle. For anyone, much less an impressionable seventeen-year-old, the huge, majestic, Gothic building looming in front of you is memorable.

"Remember, I'm from Jersey City," Spanarkel said. "All of a sudden they show me this incredible place, starting of course with The Chapel, and they're saying to me, 'You can live here for four years.' I'm like, wait a minute, are you serious about this?"

Duke was very serious. When Spanarkel came home and told his parents about his visit he said he still hadn't decided where he was going to school. Later, his father told him, "When you came home from visiting Duke, I knew that's where you were going."

The only drawback was the distance. The Spanarkels are a close family and Jim wasn't certain he wanted to be that far from home. If he went to St. Peter's, he would practically be a long walk from his home on Fairview Avenue. If he went to Holy Cross, he would only be four hours away by car. But Spanarkel liked Wenzel. He had also hit it off with Foster and the Duke players. And the vision of The Chapel kept popping into his brain every time he thought he didn't want to go south. Raymond Spanarkel knew his son well.

When Spanarkel called the coaches and told them he was coming, it set off a minor celebration. Foster, Wenzel, and Goetz all had a feeling they had a player who was going to be a lot better than the experts were projecting. "You can say we got a little lucky when Jimmy became an All-American," Wenzel said. "But you also have to give us some credit because we thought all along he was going to be damn good. We might not have known *how* good, but we knew when we got him it was important."

It was especially important to Foster, suffering through a tough first season. Once Spanarkel committed in early March, Foster's spirits picked up. When people asked about the future he would smile and say, "I only know one thing for sure. This Spanarkel kid knows how to play the game."

Although Spanarkel was considered the key recruit in the Class of '75, he was not the only player pursued by Foster and his coaches that year. With four seniors graduating and five more scheduled to leave the following spring, Foster needed bodies.

Four players, in addition to Spanarkel, signed with Duke. The one the coaches had the highest hopes for was Steve Gray, a 6-2 guard from suburban Los Angeles. Gray was a great all-around athlete, a highly recruited football player who seriously considered going to UCLA or USC as a linebacker. He was also a prolific scorer on the basketball court. When Goetz saw him play he thought he was looking at a potential All-American.

"There is no question that when I looked at that class after we recruited it, I honestly thought that Gray was potentially the best player in the group," Goetz said. "He was an *athlete*. He was quick, he was strong, and he could shoot the ball. Spanarkel was a better *player* but Gray looked to me like he was only going to get better and better."

All Duke had to do was convince Gray that he wanted to play basketball *and* that he wanted to play basketball for Duke.

The former was tougher than the latter. "I really wasn't interested when they first approached me," Gray said. "But I thought it would be fun to see the East Coast. That was why I agreed to visit. At that point, I still thought I was going to play football." Two things changed Gray's mind: the visit to Duke—naturally—and a visit to the locker rooms after the UCLA–USC football game. Gray was a linebacker who loved to hit. When he walked into the locker room and was introduced to some of the players, he was struck by one thing: their size. "Reading that a guy is six foot four inches and two hundred fifty pounds is different than standing next to him," he said. "I mean, these guys were behemoths. I could run at some of them from ten yards and give them my best shot and I was just going to bounce off them. That really had an effect on me." Enough of an effect that when Duke offered him a scholarship, he accepted.

Gray was not the only Californian in that freshman class. The other was Scott Goetsch, also from suburban Los Angeles. Goetsch was not the scorer that Gray was but he was 6-9 and shot the ball reasonably well. Goetz thought he had potential. Like Gray, he was an excellent student who probably would have ended up in the Ivy League if he had not been recruited by Duke.

Along with the Californians, Foster signed a Canadian, Cameron Hall, who was also 6-9. He was much more slender than Goetsch and a better shooter, another player whom the coaching staff took based more on potential than on the kind of player he was at the time.

The fifth recruit was Harold Morrison, probably the best-known player of the group. Although he and Spanarkel lived only a few miles apart, Spanarkel in Jersey City and Morrison in West Orange, their paths had never crossed.

Spanarkel was white, a street kid from the city, the fourth of six children, a tough guy who would gladly punch your lights out if you crossed him. Morrison was black; he had moved from Newark to a suburban Jewish neighborhood in fifth grade and had gone to a 99-percent-white junior high school. He was an only child, the son of a prominent union leader, shy at first and as gentle as Spanarkel was hard-nosed. His basketball hero and role model was Pete Maravich.

Morrison had been a Five-Star prodigy, having first attended that famous All-Star camp the summer before ninth grade. He got his first recruiting letter—from Marshall University—that fall and was eventually recruited by schools like Indiana, Villanova, Cincinnati, Southern Methodist, and the entire Ivy League.

"My parents' whole thing was that I go to a good school," Morrison said. "When the University of Hawaii called and offered me a visit they said not to even *think* about it. They probably would have been happiest if I had gone to Harvard. But Duke was fine because it had a good reputation academically."

Morrison knew about Duke because of Kenny Young. They had played together in the Elmore Park League in East Orange and had been friends. When Young went to Duke, Morrison followed his progress. And, when he visited, he felt more comfortable there than anyplace else he had seen.

But what sold Morrison on Duke, as was the case to at least some degree with all of his classmates, was the opportunity to play right away. Goetz and Jim Lewis both pointed out to him that the freshman and sophomore classes at Duke that year consisted of four guards and one forward. That meant there would be plenty of openings up front for young players in the future.

Still, Morrison almost went to Villanova—because of Rollie Massimino. "There is no question that I felt a lot more at ease around Coach Massimino than around Coach Foster," he said. "But I really liked Lou and Jim and I liked the campus. If Villanova had been a little farther away, though, I might have gone there. I just didn't want to be too close to home. I thought it was time to leave the nest."

So that was the first recruiting class: the tough kid from Jersey City who knew how to play, the black kid from the white neighborhood, the two Californians who seemed to have potential, and the Canadian with the soft shooting touch. The coaches had no idea what a cross section of personalities they had on their hands. But that wasn't their concern at the time. They needed people who could play. They would worry about meshing the personalities later.

4

Tough Times

While Foster was piecing together his future team, he was also trying to pick up the pieces of the current team after the disastrous end to the '73–74 season.

The first month was encouraging. With George Moses providing both strength and stability inside and the team playing their new up-tempo offense, the Blue Devils got off to a 6–1 start.

Then came the annual Big Four Tournament in Greensboro.

The Big Four had become an annual disaster for Duke but it was, quite simply, a financial bonanza for them, North Carolina, North Carolina State, and Wake Forest. The four schools got together for a weekend at the neutral Greensboro Coliseum, sold sixteen thousand tickets a night, and played four intense although, if truth be told, meaningless basketball games.

Duke was paired the first night with North Carolina. The last time they had played had been the Chapel Hill debacle in March. This game was similar: Duke playing over its head, the game going back and forth and, finally, overtime. But there was no blown eight-point lead this time and, amazingly, Duke pulled the game out, 99–96. It was a stunning victory although it was overshadowed by the fact that Wake Forest had beaten defending national champion N.C. State in the other game.

That didn't matter to Foster or his players, however. "After what had happened in Chapel Hill," Foster remembered, "to turn around and beat them the next time we played in another close game was very important. It got a big monkey off our back. I really felt then, with the experience we had on the team, that we could build on that win and put together a decent season."

It didn't happen that way, though. The next night, Wake Forest, still walking on air after beating State, beat the Blue Devils for the Big Four title. That was a disappointment. But the really bad news came the next day: Moses had flunked out of school. He could return in the fall if he wanted but he was finished for the season.

This was a blow. Moses had been more than just a good rebounder—he had been a steadying force in the locker room. He was older than the other players and had not lived through the trials and tribulations of the previous year. He played as if he believed Duke was going to win every night because he had not gone through the losing of the recent past.

Even without Moses, the Blue Devils opened ACC play with a respectable six-point loss at Maryland and a solid win at home over a good Clemson team. Armstrong hit the key shot down the stretch and suddenly people were noticing that a team that had won only ten games the previous season was 8–3. Even when it lost, the games were close. A year earlier, Duke had lost by 30 at Maryland. This time, the game wasn't decided until the final minute.

Then came the game at Virginia. The Cavaliers were in the same kind of rebuilding mode that Duke was. They too had a first-year coach in Terry Holland and if there was any team Duke might hope to finish in front of in the ACC it was probably Virginia. The Blue Devils led most of the game. But at the end the shots didn't fall and a freshman named Mark Iavaroni got every key rebound down the stretch. The Cavaliers won the game, 60–56.

This was the first time the players had seen Foster really lose it. He was one step short of hysterical—one *small* step. He couldn't understand how they could let this team beat them and he let them know it in no uncertain terms. "That was probably the first time we realized how much losing tore him up," Armstrong said. "I mean, none of us wanted to lose, in fact we were sort of sick of it. But it got to him worse than it got to any of us."

That loss set a tone for Duke on the road. The Blue Devils could stay close with most teams, but they just couldn't win. Foster's initial analysis of Duke's six problems turned out to be correct. The ACC schedule was just too tough. N.C. State buried them in Cameron; Wake buried them at Wake. Virginia came to Cameron on a Saturday afternoon and, with the gym half empty, beat Duke again. This time Foster was completely out of control. Losing to Virginia on the road was bad enough, but at home?

Ten days later at Carolina, Armstrong, who was playing with a bruised thigh, got kneed hard in the thigh and went down. Foster, who had grown weary of Kenny Young's erratic play, sent Paul Fox in for him, hoping Fox would provide some stability and shooting. Fox played well and Foster announced that—even with Armstrong out—Young would not start in the next game, three nights later at Clemson. Fox would take his place.

This did not sit well with Kenny Young. The little guard had shown flashes of great talent but did not seem to understand his own limitations. The best example of that lack of understanding may have come when he told a reporter, "The only difference between Phil Ford and me is playing time." *Ford was already the best guard in the ACC as a freshman—a future All-American.*

Now, with his playing time about to be reduced further, Young didn't react well. He was late for the team bus to Clemson. Foster went ahead without him and left word that Young was not welcome to join the team even if he could find transportation to the game. The Blue Devils got their doors blown off at Clemson, 100–66, in a game that wasn't even *that* close. The Clemson lead was 25 points after only ten minutes.

Armstrong tried to play in the game but had to come out, holding his thigh in apparent agony. Goetz, frustrated by the way the season was falling apart, questioned whether Armstrong was really hurt. In pain and embarrassed, Armstrong screamed at him and Goetz screamed back. It was not a pretty scene.

The next day Armstrong had two hundred cc's of blood removed from his thigh. The doctors told the coaches that this was a badly hurt young man who had been crazy to go into the game at all. He would not play again that season. Goetz apologized.

The apology was accepted but it didn't help the situation. Duke's next game was at N.C. State. The timing could not have been worse. This would be the last home game for the great David Thompson, after he had brought glory, a national championship, and a 79–7 three-year record to State. The Wolfpack would be wound up and Coach Norman Sloan had a penchant for running up the score anyway.

And Duke didn't have any guards. Armstrong was done. Foster had suspended Young for missing the bus to Clemson. Billerman had a serious case of bronchitis and was doubtful. The only guards Foster had left, facing the quickest team in the ACC, were Paul Fox and freshman Rick Gomez, who had barely played all season. Bruce Bell, whose college basketball playing experience consisted of eight junior varsity games, was brought up to the varsity and given a uniform—just in case.

"I don't think I've ever been so terrified in my life," Bell said. "I had never been in a real college game and I'm sitting on the bench in Reynolds Coliseum and there's David Thompson on the floor right in front of me. I could still remember seeing Thompson block Bill Walton's shot the year before in the Final Four and now I might be playing against him? My God was I scared."

Bell had reason to be scared. Even with Bob Fleischer dropping back to help Fox and Gomez bring the ball up the court, they had a terrible time. The game was out of control early and the only real question was how big the margin would be. Then, with considerable time still left on the clock, Fox fouled out. Foster marched down the bench to where Bell and Billerman sat, both of them shivering—Bell with fear, Billerman with a fever.

"He looked right at me," Bell said. "I thought I was going to faint."

Foster, seeing all the color drain from Bell's face, turned to Billerman. "Think you can go a few minutes, Kev?" Billerman coughed, got off the bench, and shuffled into the game, hacking all the way. He still remembers having a coughing fit right in front of the press table late in the game. Lefty Driesell, scouting the game, was sitting a few feet away. "Kevin, you okay?" Driesell asked. "You sound like you gonna *die*."

The season had become something of a Bataan Death March.

In the ACC Tournament, they played Clemson right to the buzzer, finally losing 78–76. In the final seconds, the Tigers' seven-foot center, Wayne (Tree) Rollins, knocked Fox cold with an elbow as Fox tried desperately to foul him.

It was a fitting epitaph to the season. Duke had never given up, never quit, but had never quite gotten itself off the mat. The final record was 13–13, certainly an improvement but disappointing after the 8–3 beginning. The ACC record was 2–10, the same as McGeachy's 2–10. Still, there were signs of life.

There's no question we were better," Armstrong said. "When we were healthy, we were in every game. And, at the end, even with George gone and me not playing, the guys hung in. I think we all felt like we weren't that far away." Foster didn't feel that way. To him, there was no such thing as a moral victory. Even as the team was being lauded for giving Clemson such a hard time in the ACC Tournament, he was racing for the door to catch a plane out of Greensboro.

"I have to get out there and find some players," he said. "God knows I don't want to live through another season like this one. Not ever. It's too painful."

He had no way of knowing that his pain had just begun.

∎

The coaches were back on the road that summer, hoping to spot another Jim Spanarkel, or for that matter, Harold Morrison or Steve Gray, at the summer camps. They had high hopes for their freshman class but they knew the puzzle was far from complete.

"We had to have a big guy," Wenzel remembered. "That was a big thing with us. We felt good about the guard situation because Tate was back for two more years and Spanarkel and Gray were coming in. But we needed a big man and a pounder inside."

The coaches, especially Foster, loved Mike O'Koren, a teammate of Spanarkel's at Hudson Catholic. He was a 6-7 version of Spanarkel, tough and smart but more inclined to play inside than Spanarkel was. They thought he would make a perfect complement for Spanarkel. Getting him would not be easy, though. North Carolina, among others, coveted O'Koren. But with Spanarkel at Duke, the coaches thought they had a shot.

They also thought they might get Jim Graziano, a 6-9 center from Long Island being pursued by almost everyone. If those two could be wooed, the puzzle would not be that far from completion.

Goetz, Wenzel, and Lewis were on the road constantly that summer. Foster was out a lot, too, although he was running his camps, one at Duke, one in the Poconos. If the coaches found someone they wanted him to see, they called him and he came. But the crucial phone call of the summer came not from any of the assistants but from Terry Chili.

Chili, who would be one of five seniors on the team in the coming season, was working as a counselor at Lefty Driesell's camp at the University of Maryland. There he had befriended a huge young camper named Mike Gminski. Gminski was 6-11 and 250 pounds. He was surprisingly well coordinated for a youngster who was not quite sixteen yet. Most remarkably, he had a soft shooting touch.

One day he mentioned to Chili, almost casually, that because he was so advanced academically and because the league he played in back home in Monroe, Connecticut, was so weak, he had decided to consolidate his junior and senior years of high school to one year. He would graduate from high school in June of 1976, one year early.

The Duke coaches had heard of Gminski but hadn't paid much attention to him since he still had two more years of high school. Wrong, Chili told them when he called. The coaches immediately asked Chili to find out if Gminski would talk to them.

Earlier that summer, after attending a camp at Davidson, Gminski and his parents had stopped for an unofficial visit at North Carolina. "I had no idea that I was eight miles away from Duke," he said. "I had heard of the school, but that was it. I had no idea where it was or what it was."

During his visit with Dean Smith, Gminski mentioned that he hoped to play a lot as a freshman. That notion must not have sat well with Smith. Two weeks after the visit, Gminski got a letter from Assistant Coach Bill Guthridge informing him that North Carolina did not plan to recruit him.

Carolina was out. Duke wanted in. Early in September Goetz and Wenzel visited the Gminski's. Their mission was simple: convince Gminski to visit Duke. "I remember that we all liked Wenz and Lou," Gminski said. "But the thing I remember the most was Wenz saying to me, 'come down for a visit and I guarantee you'll come.' "

So Gminski agreed to visit Duke. The October weekend that he spent there was a big one for the basketball program. It was homecoming for the football team and three recruits were in town. The most important one was O'Koren. Next came Graziano. And then there was Gminski, the big kid from Connecticut whom no one knew much about.

"A lot of my career, I've been the guy people didn't think could make the transition to the next level," Gminski said. "When I won the punt-pass-and-kick competition at eleven, people said I'd never be any good in high school. In high school, they said I'd never be a very good college player. And when I left college a lot of people said I wouldn't adjust to the pros."

The Duke coaches weren't negative on Gminski by any means. They just saw him as a gamble. When someone is 6-11 and can shoot, even if he has played against weak competition, you take a chance on him, especially when you haven't got anyone comparable. But if the coaches had a wish list on that October weekend, Gminski would have been third.

On Gminski's list Duke jumped right to number one that weekend.

He loved everything about the school—the campus, the other players on the team and, of course, The Chapel.

On Saturday night, Spanarkel took him to a party in the SAE fraternity section. Gminski still remembers sitting on the fraternity's bench at about five in the morning giddily drunk and happy and convinced this was the place for him. Duke was the first and last school he officially visited. He returned home and canceled the rest of his visits.

Foster was delighted to get Gminski. He was, obviously, an excellent student. He was huge. And he seemed like a good kid. From the beginning, Foster and Gminski hit it off. Gminski enjoyed Foster's deadpan, sarcastic sense of humor, which a lot of players either missed or were uncomfortable with because it could be so biting. Gminski enjoyed it from day one.

What Foster didn't know—and couldn't know—was that the package he had just acquired did not consist merely of a 6-11 player with a lot of potential.

Mike Gminski is the only child of Joe and Kirsten Gminski. His size comes from his father, who is almost 6-8. Joe Gminski was an athlete in high school and went to the University of Connecticut hoping to play basketball. But as soon as practice started, Joe Gminski began losing weight. He started at 205 and within a few weeks he was down to 165. Whether it was tension or something else, no one ever found out. But his college basketball career ended before it started.

After two years of college, Joe Gminski dropped out. After giving up basketball he had turned his attention to golf and found it a lot more challenging than his class work. His new goal was to become a golf pro and go out on the tour. First, though, came the Army. Joe Gminski was stationed in Germany. While on leave he took a trip to Copenhagen and visited Tivoli Gardens. There, he met Kirsten Morkegaard, one of the park's tour guides. She spotted Gminski listening to a band and wandered over to ask him where he had found the chair he was standing on. Gminski wasn't standing on a chair.

The two obviously found things to talk about anyway because a year later they were married.

After he got out of the Army, Joe Gminski took his new wife—who already spoke fluent English and several other languages—back home to Connecticut. Joe went to work as a salesman to support Kirsten and their son, who was born in August 1959, checking into the world at twenty-four inches and ten pounds. "When I tell people I was always big," Mike says, "I mean I was *always* big."

When not-so-little Mike was five, his father decided to take his shot at the pro golf tour. He had continued to play golf after getting out of the Army and was a scratch player. He moved his family to Palo Alto, California, set up headquarters there, and gave it a whirl. He did not succeed. One year later, unable to qualify for any tournaments, Joe Gminski moved his family back to Connecticut. Two years after that, when Mike was eight, he quit his job to devote all his time to developing Mike as an athlete.

"When his dream died, I became his dream," Mike said. "In fact, I think to him, I became *him*. It's never been something he and I could really talk about because neither one of us is that way. We tend to hold things in. But I think maybe he remembered how my grandfather had to work three jobs when he was a boy during the Depression and never really spent any time at home. Part of him, I think, thought that he might have made it if his dad had been able to give him more time. Whatever it was, it has never been an easy thing for me to deal with."

Kirsten Gminski went to work supporting the family, working in a department store. Joe Gminski drove a school bus, the one that took Mike to and from school. He worked out with Mike alone and he was always at Mike's practices, first in baseball, later in basketball. When Mike chose his college, there was little doubt in his mind that his parents would follow him. "I guess you could say my dad was the ultimate Little League parent," Mike said.

The Duke coaches knew Joe Gminski took a proprietary interest in his son. But they would not know until later just how difficult that interest would make life for them—and for Mike. For now, as the 1976–77 season began, Bill Foster was hopeful that he had signed his center for the next four years.

A critical piece of the puzzle had arrived, but it arrived with a jagged edge.

■

Foster's second season at Duke was a lot like his first. George Moses had come back to school. Willie Hodge was the starting center—still talented, still foul-prone. Once, getting off the bus in Chapel Hill before a game, someone asked Foster if he had seen Willie. Deadpan as always, Foster answered, "I think he fouled out on the way over."

Spanarkel was a starter from the first day of practice. To almost everyone, this made perfect sense. The other players could see that Spanarkel had an instinct for the game that more than made up for his inexperience. He was a superb passer, rarely made mistakes at either end of the floor and, even though he wasn't a great shooter, he was a natural scorer. And he was tough.

The one person who had trouble dealing with the oohing and aahing over Spanarkel was Gray. When the freshmen arrived on campus that fall, Gray noticed a preseason prospectus put out by the sports information department that listed the five freshmen and their credentials. Next to Spanarkel's name was a star, indicating this was a player to be watched. "Why does he rate?" Gray asked Goetsch, his roommate. "We haven't even started practice yet and they've anointed him."

Morrison didn't disagree with Gray. "I remember thinking that Coach Foster hadn't really seen me a lot and he had already decided that Jimmy was ahead of me," he said. "It didn't seem fair. When we were playing pickup games in the gym, he didn't seem all that good. Of course that was always the way it was with Jim. I can remember calling friends back in Jersey and saying, 'Who the hell is Jim Spanarkel?' Steve and I always thought they had made their minds up even before we started practice."

In a sense, that was true. The coaches felt that if any of the freshmen was going to be ready to play extensively it was Spanarkel. The others had potential, and in Gray's case they felt, *great* potential. But none of them was as precocious as Spanarkel.

It probably would have surprised his classmates to learn that Spanarkel was having a tough time adjusting to college life. He was, in a word, homesick. "I remember when my parents and I were leaving to drive down, I started crying," he said. "It just hit me as a very sad thing. All the way down I kept thinking, 'Are you sure you want to do this?' My older brother was at St. Peter's. I could go there and know everyone. I thought about that a lot first semester. A lot of nights I can remember thinking, 'What the hell are you doing here?' "

Spanarkel was aware of the rivalry with Gray. "There were five freshmen and two of us were guards," he said. "It was only natural that we be competitive with one another. I felt like I had something he wanted and I wasn't going to do anything to give him a chance to get it. Steve was a great athlete and he was tough. But I always thought, to be honest, that I was a better player than he was."

That would be borne out in the future. Back then though, Gray honestly believed that when his chance came, he would be a better player than Spanarkel. His chance would come . . . later.

All the freshmen had difficult moments, like college freshmen anywhere. Duke has no athletic dorms and it doesn't believe in baby-sitting athletes. Tutor them, yes. Baby-sit them, no. Goetsch, Gray and Morrison all thought about transferring at one stage or another during that freshman year but their frustrations had more to do with basketball than with homesickness. Even though he thought of himself as shy, Morrison fit in as quickly as anyone with the team, thanks to his sharp wit and easygoing manner. He had little trouble adjusting to Duke's almost all-white environment; it was similar to what he had become accustomed to growing up.

"I had always felt comfortable playing basketball in Newark with city blacks or hanging out in West Orange with suburban whites," he said. "Being an only child, I didn't mind spending time by myself. I either spent time with people I was comfortable with or by myself. Either way was fine. I liked the guys on the team right off, so I didn't have any problems adjusting."

Morrison did get hassled once by another black student. One night, walking out of the on-campus student hangout, the Cambridge Inn, with the other freshmen players, he was stopped by a young woman who informed him that other black students had noticed that he spent a lot of time with his white teammates. "If you expect to be accepted by the black community at Duke," she said, "you better start sitting at the tables."

The tables were three tables in the CI where the blacks congregated. There was nothing official about it, but the blacks sat there and the white students usually stayed away. "I laughed at her," Morrison said. "First of all, most of the blacks were as suburban and wealthy as the white students so I thought it was kind of funny when they tried to act 'black.' I didn't think I had anything to prove to anyone, black or white. I just told her if it bothered people that I didn't sit at the tables, that was their problem, not mine. No one ever said another word to me about it again."

Spanarkel was the only freshman who was going to play a lot—that was apparent soon after practice began. What was also apparent was that this was now Tate Armstrong's team. With Billerman gone, Armstrong was the point guard. He was also the team leader because the seniors were quiet by nature. What's more, he had improved immeasurably over the summer.

After sitting out the last five games of the season with his thigh injury, Armstrong had gotten himself into an almost fanatical workout routine during the off-season. By the end of the summer he was running nineteen miles *a day* in the awful humidity of Houston. Playing forty minutes of basketball without ever letting up must have seemed easy after that.

Armstrong had always been a good shooter. Now, though, he was quick, he was strong, and he was almost unstoppable. He started the season well, as did the Blue Devils. Again they jumped out to a 6–1 start. Then they lost two close games in the Big Four. Armstrong was averaging more than 20 points a game, Spanarkel was the best freshman in the conference, but the team still couldn't get it done against the ACC teams.

Then came the game at N.C. State. The Wolfpack wasn't the same—Thompson and Monty Towe were gone—but it still had Kenny Carr and it was still formidable. Carr had destroyed the Blue Devils in the Big Four Tournament and he was just as overwhelming in this game. Early in the second half, with the game turning into a rout, Armstrong got fed up. "We were trying to get the ball inside and it just wasn't working," he said. "I finally just said, 'Screw it, I'm shooting every time.' I know that sounds selfish but we were getting killed. So, I just starting shooting and it started going in."

And in and in and in. Armstrong hit seven straight shots during one stretch. The Blue Devils didn't win, but they rallied. Armstrong finished with 34 points. The rest of the season was a lot like that game. Armstrong was brilliant, but his team wasn't quite good enough. Except at home against Maryland.

It was the second-to-last Saturday of the season and if a team had ever been desperate for a victory, it was Duke. The close losses were getting to everyone. (Duke was 2–7 in ACC play and the seven losses were by a total of 15 points.) The students had become so frustrated that, for the first time in memory, they had started throwing things on the court. With N.C. State coming to Cameron on Wednesday followed by Maryland on Saturday, William Griffith, the dean of student affairs, called a meeting involving athletic council members, Carl James, Bill Foster, and members of the student government to discuss the problem of fan behavior.

Foster agreed to write an open letter to the student newspaper, *The Chronicle*, asking that the students stop the obscene cheers and not throw things during the two home games. The sports editor of *The Chronicle*, a volatile sort himself, wrote a column pleading with his fellow students not to lower themselves to the level of fans at other schools.

Something worked. During yet another wrenching loss to State, the students behaved impeccably. But everyone worried about the Maryland game. During the game in College Park three weeks earlier, Driesell and Goetz had gotten into an ugly shouting match and, at the finish, the Maryland players had taunted the Duke players.

The second game clearly had the potential to get out of hand.

Early in the game, Spanarkel went down hard, hurting his ankle and never returning. Nonetheless, the Blue Devils led all night. But as had happened all season long, the opponent rallied. Armstrong kept hitting from outside, Maryland kept answering. With four minutes left, Hodge fouled out. Chili had to take his place. The Duke fans waited for the roof to cave in.

With four seconds left and Duke clinging to a one-point lead, Chili went to the foul line. If he missed, Maryland would have a chance to win at the buzzer. If he made the first but not the second, the Terrapins could force overtime with a basket. If Chili made both, Duke would win. Cameron was as quiet as it ever gets. Lefty Driesell called time to let Chili, a 60-percent free throw shooter, think about the shot. In four years at Duke, Chili had never been in a situation like this one.

It had been four seasons since Duke had beaten a ranked team and everyone in the building knew it. Chili took the ball—for once he had nothing to say to the referee—looked at the basket and shot. Swish. The cheer was hearty, but muted. He still needed one more because everyone fully expected Maryland to score at the other end. Chili took the ball again and shot. Swish.

A Maryland basket at the buzzer made the final score 66–65 but it didn't matter. Duke had the upset—finally. Four years of frustration came pouring out of the student body. They stormed the floor, mobbing Chili, Armstrong, and Foster. They cut down the net where Chili had made his free throws and presented it to Foster. By the next morning it was hanging on a picture frame right next to Foster's desk. It stayed there until the day he left Duke.

The celebration went on into the night. Lefty was hanged in effigy. The other net came down too. No one wanted to go. This one had been a long time coming. "I think we all thought the same thing," Armstrong said. "We'd been good enough to win so many times but we just hadn't won. We knew it was killing Coach Foster every single time and I think we wanted to win a game like that as much for the sake of his sanity as anything else."

The victory meant a lot to Foster. Even though he was very popular on campus he was already questioning himself. Why couldn't his team win the close game? Was it coaching? "After a while," he said, "you look around and you wonder, am I the problem?"

At least for one night, Foster didn't have to wonder anymore.

But there wasn't much time to celebrate. Spanarkel's ankle was X-rayed the next morning and the X ray confirmed what Trainer Max Crowder had suspected: torn ligaments. Spanarkel had become Duke's second-best player, taking pressure off Armstrong offensively and giving the team a toughness that Duke teams often lacked. Now, he was gone.

And the team couldn't help but feel the loss.

They closed the regular season by losing their last two games. The ACC record was 3–9. Last place. Again.

In the first game of the ACC Tournament, they lost to Maryland. But it wasn't just a loss. It was a heartbreaking and humiliating end to their year.

With thirty-three seconds left, the Blue Devils led 72–70. Mark Crow was fouled. For the season, he had hit 84 percent of his free throws. Crow stepped up, shot—and missed. But George Moses, always alert, grabbed the rebound and fed it back outside. Duke ran the clock to eighteen seconds before Paul Fox was fouled. He went to the line, shot—and *he* missed. Amazingly, Moses got the rebound again. This time Duke ran the clock to five seconds before Crow was fouled again. Surely, he couldn't miss again. All he had to do was make the first shot and the game would be over. Even if he missed, Maryland was out of time-outs and would have to race the ball downcourt and take a quick shot to try to force overtime. By this time the entire crowd in the Capital Centre was on its feet, thinking it was about to see something that had never happened in the history of the ACC Tournament: the No. 7 seed upsetting the No. 2 seed.

Crow missed. Reaching for the rebound, Moses fouled a Maryland player—Steve Sheppard who, naturally, made both free throws. Tie game. Overtime. Maryland won it, 80–78.

Armstrong, who had scored 38 points, lost control. He threw things around the locker room, pounded his fists against lockers and cried and cried. "All season long, it was the same thing," he said thirteen years later. "That game *still* upsets me. If we had won, we could have gone a long way. I really believe that. But we let it get away."

Foster was inconsolable. "This is like losing a loved one, that's how I feel," he told the press. "It was our game."

Later, Foster regretted what he had said. "To compare losing a basketball game to someone dying is a little bit sick," he said. "But I had such an empty feeling right at that moment. It just seemed as if no matter what we did, we got beat."

For the second straight year, less than an hour after his season had ended, Foster was on his way out the door. "Players," he said, walking out. "We need more players."

■

Foster was beaten in his recruiting effort also. The only new player—other than Gminski—he signed was Marco Bonamico, an Italian who had been recommended by a friend of Foster's who had coached in Italy. Mike O'Koren had opted for North Carolina and Graziano for South Carolina. Foster took the loss of O'Koren especially hard. After seeing just how good Spanarkel was, Foster had dreamed of pairing the two Jersey City kids together for three years. Now, he would see plenty of O'Koren—but in the wrong shade of blue.

It was Christmas Eve when O'Koren phoned Foster to tell him his decision. "It was not a great Christmas at our house," Shirley Foster remembered. "I just wish Mike had waited two more days to tell us."

Foster was not comfortable with the power forward situation that summer. He had Cameron Hall and Harold Morrison. Hall had a tender back and whether he could play thirty-five minutes a game on a regular basis was questionable. Morrison, even though he had built himself up to 230 pounds at the coaches' request, was more comfortable playing outside than inside. And so, Bonamico was signed in the hope that he could add depth at both forward spots, perhaps even become a starter. Foster felt set at three spots: Armstrong at point guard, Spanarkel at big guard and, at small forward, Crow, who in spite of the missed free throws against Maryland had become a dangerous outside shooter. Gminski was penciled in as the starting center. Hall or Morrison would be the other forward.

The coach was now down to ten recruited players. Rick Gomez, the guard recruited out of New Jersey during that first desperate spring, lasted through his sophomore year, but no further. He flunked out.

That meant six players who had started the year in the program—the five seniors and Gomez—were gone. Foster used the extra scholarships to put Bruce Bell and Rob Hardy on scholarship. He did that partly because he needed bodies to fill out the bench and partly to be nice. Either way, the decision proved correct.

Bell, after agreeing to come to Duke in the fall of '74 as a walk-on, had been miserable his first semester. "When I got there in September

I heard the basketball players were working out in the gym every afternoon," he said. "So, I went over there looking to play. But none of the guys had any idea who I was. The older guys just told me the games were for varsity players only. I wasn't too happy with that. I hung around waiting for a chance to get into the games and every once in a while I did. But I really didn't get much chance.

"The coaches told me that I would get the chance to try out for the JV team in October. That didn't thrill me because I was hoping to get a chance to try out for the varsity. Then, it turned out the JV practices were at seven in the morning. I kept stumbling out of bed wondering why in the world I was putting myself through this to play an eight-game JV schedule. It was no fun at all."

Bell stuck with it, though, and Goetz, coaching the JV team, liked what he saw. Bell was smart, and even though he looked to be about fourteen years old with his baby face, blond hair and blue eyes, he never backed down from anything or anyone.

"The first day of the second semester after George Moses flunked out, Coach Foster called me in and said that I was being put on partial scholarship [meals, books, room and board] and that they wanted me to start practicing with the varsity when the JV season was over. I was shocked, but really happy."

Shortly after joining the varsity, Bell caught an accidental Willie Hodge elbow square in the mouth. He went down in a heap. When he sat up, everyone asked him what happened. In the high-pitched Kentucky drawl that his teammates would mimic forever, Bell said, "Gaad-dawg, Willie hit me in the mouth with an elbow!" Maybe it was the way it came out or maybe it was the fact that Bell had been so quiet since joining the team but the high-pitched yelp left everyone laughing hysterically. "The worst thing about it, though," Bell said, "was that all those dang guys"—dang is the strongest word Bell ever uses— "thought I said *hot*-dawg. I tried to tell them I said *gaad*-dawg but they just liked it better the other way. So, every time I got hit in practice from that day on, everyone would start yelling, '*Hot-dawg, Willie hit Bruce with an elbow.*' Heck, they kept yelling it long after Willie had graduated."

With his outgoing, friendly manner and his willingness to take a joke, Bell quickly became very popular with his new teammates. It was so late in the season that he was given a uniform without his name on it. "Except for my buddies, no one had any idea who I was," he said, laughing.

Rob Hardy's story was similar to Bell's. He too was from Kentucky, born in Frankfort, the capital, halfway between Lexington and Louisville. In eighth grade, his family moved to Columbus, Ohio. There, Hardy played football, basketball and golf. His *best* sport might have been golf—he was about a two-handicapper—but his *obsession* was basketball.

"I used to drive my parents crazy playing in the house all the time when I was a kid," he said. "I knew I wasn't going to be a football player because I was too skinny. So, I just focused on basketball. I was never a great player, but I was always pretty good."

When Hardy was ten, his parents sent him to Vic Bubas's basketball camp at Duke. This was in the late 1960s when Bubas was still Duke's coach and one of the big names in coaching. Hardy fell in love with the school. "I knew when I was ten years old that I wanted to go to Duke," he said. "I never applied to school anyplace else or thought about going anyplace else. The only question was whether I would be able to play basketball. If I couldn't play there, I was going to go to school there, no matter what."

Hardy continued to go to Bubas's basketball camp even after Bubas quit coaching. Then, while in high school, he started going to a second camp, one in the Poconos run by a man named Bill Foster. "The second year I went there was the year he moved to Duke," Hardy said. "I was going into my senior year of high school and I wanted him to see me play. But the day of the All-Star game, just as the game was starting, he got called away to a phone call. I played great in the game, but he didn't see me."

Hardy applied for an early decision to the school of his dreams. With a 3.3 grade point average and 1,200 on his college boards, he was not a lock to be accepted as a regular student. But he got in. "Happiest day of my whole life," he said.

The day he was accepted, Hardy sent a tape of himself to Foster with a letter saying he would like to try to walk on the basketball team the next fall. He had become a good enough point guard as a senior—averaging about twenty points a game—that several Ohio Valley schools had wanted to recruit him. Hardy had eyes only for Duke.

Foster had already signed five freshmen. He wrote Hardy back saying he was welcome to try out for the JV team. That was fine with Hardy. "All I knew," he said, "was I was going to Duke."

That fall, he received the same treatment from the varsity players that Bell had gotten a year earlier. But it didn't faze him. He waited his turn, played when he could and worked out on his own. The early morning JV practices didn't thrill him, but he stuck with it. The story of what had happened to Bell the year before—being called up to varsity when Moses flunked out—was familiar to everyone on the JV. "I really looked up to Bruce back then," Hardy said. "He would still play in the JV games, but we looked at him as a varsity player because he never practiced with us. To us, he had it made."

When the school year ended with six players gone and only Gminski signed, Foster called Hardy in and told him he might be called up to the varsity the next fall. Two other JV players, Rick Mainwaring and Geoff Northrup, would also be given tryouts. Hardy spent the summer working strenuously to build up his body. "I went from 148 pounds to 175 pounds over the summer," Hardy said. "Of course, there were probably a few beers thrown in there too."

Hardy came back in the fall still not on scholarship, but working out with the varsity. He remembers that, with the exception of Spanarkel, an established star by that point, the other sophomores were standoffish. "I think they saw me as someone who maybe didn't belong. None of them had really established themselves with a role on the team yet and now I come along. Spanarkel and Bell were the two guys I was close to right off the bat. The other guys came later."

Even with Bell added to the team, Foster had only eleven scholarship players when the team reported back to campus during the last week of August in 1976. One week later, the number was down to ten.

5

Breaks of the (Recruiting) Game

Like all top young players in Italy, Marco Bonamico was the property of one of the teams in the Italian professional league. Initially, the club had liked the idea of Bonamico playing in the U.S. for a couple of years before returning to Italy and joining the team on a full-time basis. But he had progressed as a player faster than anyone anticipated and the team now wanted him home playing right away.

There was nothing Foster could do. If Bonamico had been on campus he might have been able to convince him to fight the edict to return home. But Bonamico was still in Italy. When word came that he wasn't coming, the case was closed.

That reduced the number of scholarship players—including Bell—to ten. It also meant that Gminski was the only freshman and thus didn't have a roommate. Foster put him in a room with sophomore manager Kevin Hannon. Ostensibly, Hannon was supposed to keep an eye on the kid, make sure he went to class and didn't stay out too late at night. After all, Gminski had only just turned seventeen. "I never had to do anything," Hannon said. "The big guy took to college like a duck to water."

Gminski did make the adjustment to college life with astonishing quickness. He was quiet at first but as he began to feel more a part of the team he became an unofficial assistant to Spanarkel in ragging and playing practical jokes. "A lot of times Mike wouldn't want to rip a guy himself," Spanarkel remembered. "But he knew I would do it. So he would egg me on until I would get going. Or, he would get Harold to do it."

The personality of the team was changing. Armstrong and Crow were the only players left from the Waters/McGeachy era, and they had played most of their careers and experienced all their success under Foster. Spanarkel, now an established star, was growing rapidly into a leadership role. Morrison, because of his sharp wit, had taken over as the team funny man. Gminski, even as a freshman, was handing out nicknames. Hardy, dark and slender with a hawk nose, became "Klinger" after a character in *M*A*S*H*. And Ray Jones, the new assistant coach, was "Electric."

Jones had replaced Jim Lewis during the summer when Lewis left to become the head coach at South Lakes High School in Virginia. His hiring was a departure for Foster. He was not one of Foster's former players; in fact, he wasn't a former player for anyone. Ray Jones was 5-3 when standing up very straight.

Nonetheless, he had been a successful recruiter at Jacksonville, Houston, and Cincinnati. Those three names raised eyebrows when people looked at Jones's resumé because all had come under NCAA scrutiny in the recent past for alleged rules violations.

Foster knew this when he hired Jones. But he thought he needed a hard-nosed recruiter who knew where bodies were buried and how to get in a back door. He didn't want Jones breaking any rules, but he did want Jones's experience in recruiting the kind of players that the cheaters often tried to buy.

Although he was never going to do much coaching on the floor, Jones was immediately popular with the players. He was a whirling dervish, instant energy when he walked into a room, a man capable of saying anything. On the bench during games he was constantly yelling at the players, "Take no prisoners!" No one knew exactly what that meant but the implication was clear.

Jones also took over the JV program from Goetz, allowing Goetz to finally get some sleep. In his second game as JV coach, Jones was hit with two technical fouls, and when asked by a reporter after the game what had happened, he answered, "It's simple. Those refs sucked."

That quote hit a couple of newspapers and caused Foster to call Electric into his office to suggest he take the JV games a little less seriously. Even so, Max Crowder had given Jones another nickname after the incident: "Short Fuse."

The player Short Fuse was closest to from day one was Gminski. They were as odd a couple as could be found: the 6-11 teenager and the 5-3 coach. Sports Information Director Tom Mickle, a man with a dry sense of humor, couldn't resist picturing Jones watching Gminski shoot a hook shot for the new coach's media guide photo.

There was one other new face that September, a person as quiet as Jones was gregarious. He was so quiet and unassuming that his presence went virtually unnoticed until practice started. When it did, the other players noticed him very quickly. His name was John Harrell.

John David Harrell III had grown up in Durham. His father, John David Harrell, Jr., was the oldest of seventeen children from a remarkable family. The Harrells lived on a farm in Ahoskie, North Carolina, and, all through school, John Jr. as the oldest was expected to come home and work every day. "I think he saw college as a way to escape the farm," his son says today.

John Harrell, Jr., went to North Carolina Central University in Durham. There he met Fannie Johnson, who had also grown up on a farm, in nearby Roxboro. They were married shortly after college. The example set by John Harrell must have been an inspiration to his younger brothers and sisters because all fourteen of his siblings who survived eventually went to college. Today, three of them are doctors, three are lawyers—one of them a judge—and a half-dozen are teachers.

John Harrell went on to get his master's degree in math and became a professor at North Carolina A&T. He was teaching there when John III was born. Shortly after that, he got the job he had dreamed about: teaching math at his alma mater, North Carolina Central.

Once settled in Durham, John Harrell put up a basketball net on the family carport and started teaching little John and his younger brother (by five years) Ivan how to play the game he loved. "My dad was a frustrated ballplayer," John Harrell said. "He never pushed me to play the game but whenever I wanted to play he was always available to play with me. The message that he wanted me to play was pretty clear. That was fine with me. I always liked the game. The first time I ever took a shot, it went in. After that I was hooked."

In sixth grade, John Harrell attended a basketball camp at Durham High School run by Pete Maravich. He noticed two things: Even though he was small for his age—about five feet tall—he was better than the other kids. And Maravich always seemed to pick him out to use for demonstrations. "That was the first time I thought I might be pretty good," he said.

He eventually grew to be six feet tall and became a star at Hillside High School, yet he was never recruited as a college basketball player. Harrell was heavily recruited as a *student,* though. He was an honor student and scored close to 1,300 on the college boards. Being black from a North Carolina public school, this made him a highly sought-after property. "Growing up I always told people that I was going to go to North Carolina Central and become a math professor just like my dad," he said. "All the other kids were going to be policemen or firemen and I was going to be a math professor. I guess I always liked being different. But now I had people from Harvard and Yale and MIT coming in to talk to me. I was interested but in the end I wanted to stay close to home and go to Central.

Harrell remembers getting one recruiting letter from a basketball coach. "Catawba College," he said. "That was it. Duke didn't recruit me as a ballplayer or as a student. But that didn't surprise me. That was the way Duke was."

Duke was in Durham, but not *of* Durham. "It was like a separate city," Harrell said. "Duke was an island no one from my neighborhood ever gave much thought to. My high school was about a mile from campus but if three kids from there were at Duke at any one time it was a lot. We were all Carolina fans."

It had been *years* since Duke had successfully recruited a player from North Carolina. In-state it was viewed by most people as the Yankee school, one filled with upper class white kids from the Northeast who couldn't get into Ivy League schools. In the early 1970s, with Terry Sanford, the former North Carolina governor, as the school's president, this was changing. But the process was a slow one. The fact that John Harrell, both the student and the athlete, could go unnoticed attending high school a mile from campus in 1975 was evidence of how slow.

Harrell ended up going to N.C. Central on a combined basketball/math scholarship. Having grown up within blocks of the campus he was extremely happy there as a freshman. "The ratio of women to men was seven-to-one," he said, laughing. "How could I not be happy?"

There was one way. Harrell was easily the best player on the basketball team, playing point guard and averaging almost 20 points a game. But Central had a disappointing season, going 9–20. At the end of the season Coach Sterling Holt was fired. That was fine with Harrell—the conference's rookie of the year—who hadn't really gotten along well with Holt.

But Holt fought the firing. He charged that the school had violated his contract and threatened to sue. Rather than face a lawsuit, Central reinstated him. He then began telling people that John Harrell and his father had been responsible for his firing.

"I think he blamed me because I was the best player and I hadn't supported him," Harrell said. "It's true, I didn't support him. I didn't think he was a very good coach. But I wasn't going around trying to get him fired and neither was my dad. But he blamed us. It was like a soap opera. The way I saw it, there was no way I could play for him again."

Harrell's first thought was not to play basketball as a sophomore and hope that Holt would be fired at the end of that season. He and his father were discussing his options one night that summer when Dr. Joseph Battle came by the house to visit. Battle was a long-time family friend who taught statistics in the Duke business school. Why not, he suggested, transfer to Duke? With his grades, getting in shouldn't be hard. He wouldn't have to leave home and, what's more, the basketball program was in tough shape. John might just be able to make the team and earn a scholarship.

"The idea had never really crossed our minds," Harrell said. "No one ever really thought about Duke in our house. But when Dr. Battle brought it up it made sense. I had played some summer pickup games against the Duke and Carolina players and didn't feel like they were all that tough. I didn't want to go to Carolina because most of my high school was going there. I still wanted to be a little different. So, I figured I'd just give Duke a shot and see."

Harrell drove over to Duke the next day, transcript in hand, and presented himself at the admissions office. This was in June. He was told it was too late to apply to school for the fall semester. "But I play basketball," he said. Fine, said the admissions people, go over to the basketball office and talk to them. Harrell did exactly that. The first person he ran into was Lou Goetz.

Goetz was familiar with Harrell, more from the newspaper than anyplace else, but knew he had a reputation as a talented player with the kind of quickness Duke didn't have except in the person of the troubled Kenny Young. "It was an amazing thing if you look back at it," Goetz said. "We hadn't recruited a basketball player from North Carolina in a hundred years and this kid just walks into the office and says he'd like to *pay* to come to Duke. To say no to that would have been foolish. We had nothing to lose and everything to gain, especially when we found out what kind of student he was. Even if he couldn't play he would be good to have around."

The fact that Harrell was black didn't hurt either. At that moment, the only black players on the roster for the '76–77 season were Harold

Morrison and Kenny Young. The era when all-white teams could be successful in college basketball had long since passed. Duke had to start recruiting more blacks. The coaches were painfully aware of this but also in the Catch-22 position of needing blacks to come to Duke and succeed in order to convince others to follow. Goetz called admissions immediately: "We want Harrell" was the message. Harrell was accepted a week later.

■

The players noticed Harrell's shot even before they noticed his quickness. Because his right wrist lacks normal flexibility, Harrell had always been more comfortable pushing the ball out of his hand rather than flicking his wrist to give it power. As a result, his shots had no rotation at all. They went up to the basket with no spin at all. They also went in. Morrison quickly dubbed the new guy "Johnny Gun."

Whenever Harrell, who always practiced with the second team since he had to sit out the season as a transfer student, began to light up the starters, Morrison would always point at him and say, "Okay, Johnny Gun. That's fine now. Let's see what happens next year when you get to play."

Harrell would almost always break out laughing at Morrison, a sound that surprised his teammates. Quiet as he was, Harrell had a loud, piercing laugh. Morrison, more than anyone else, put him at ease. Whenever Morrison would draw Harrell out, his new teammates would smile. They liked seeing Johnny Gun that way.

"Most of the time he was a blur," Spanarkel said. "On and off the court. He was just very quiet. But, he was also very damn good and we noticed it right away."

The person who noticed it most was Kenny Young.

Starting from the day he missed the bus to Clemson, Kenny Young had struggled. He had gone from a freshman with all sorts of potential to a struggling sophomore who gave the coaches all sorts of headaches. His second season he shot an anemic 33 percent from the field and his playing time continued to dwindle.

To make matters worse, that summer Young was arrested in Chapel Hill for allegedly breaking into a Coke machine. The charges were eventually dropped after the Duke coaches intervened but the incident was an embarrassing one. Given the way the Duke students liked to treat players from other schools who got into trouble, this was a real black eye. "The only good thing about it," Foster joked, "is that I don't think even *our* students would throw Coke bottles at a guy."

Young was on thin ice academically, too. Shortly after practice started, having gotten a look at Harrell, Young went to Foster and demanded a spot in the starting lineup. This startled Foster, who had Armstrong and Spanarkel as starters and felt that, to that point, Steve Gray had outplayed Young for the third guard spot. He told Young that. Young announced that if he didn't start, he was leaving school. Foster advised Young to think about that for a while. He did—and was gone within a week. He landed at Bucknell and would later write to Foster, signing his letters "Kenny Duke Young." But Kenny Young was no longer at Duke. Happily for the coaches, John Harrell was.

■

As good as Harrell looked in practice, the coaches couldn't be sure how he would do in competition when he became eligible the next season. Already they had seen some evidence that Gray, as good a player as he was in practice, could not maintain that level in games. There was no way to tell how Harrell would react to competing in the ACC until he got the chance. With Armstrong graduating, someone would have to step in at point guard the next season. Harrell might be the answer. Gray might be the answer. Or, perhaps, neither one.

That was why everyone on campus went a little ga-ga when Bob Bender showed up, coming almost as out of the blue as Harrell had. Bender and Harrell had two things in common: They were both point guards and they were both named after their fathers. The similarities ended there.

Bender was a midwestern Catholic, his parents both coming from Illinois. They had met at Quincy College, a small Catholic school, and had gotten married just before Bob Sr. went into the Marines. While he was in the service, three children were born: Bob, Kathy, and Margaret, all one year apart. Once out of the Marines, Bob Bender, Sr., became a coach and a teacher. In 1971 when Bob Jr. was about to enter the ninth grade, his father got a break, being named head basketball coach at a Catholic high school in Quincy. His starting point guard after the first three games was his son.

"That wasn't easy," Bob Jr. remembered. "When you start as a freshman, a lot of people are going to be jealous. And when you start as a freshman *and* your dad is the coach, it's really tough."

Bob Jr. played well and the team did so well that Bob Sr. was offered the job as coach at Bloomington (Illinois) High School. This was a step up. Naturally, his son went with him. By the end of his junior year, Bender was tabbed as one of three top guard prospects in the Midwest.

Knowing that his son's recruitment was going to be intense, Bob Bender, Sr., resigned as Bloomington's coach before Bob's senior year. "He was concerned that if he was still coaching it might create awkward situations," Bob Jr. said. "He didn't want anyone to think he was trying to use me to get a college job like a lot of high school coaches do. And he wasn't very comfortable being in a dual role. So he decided to let his assistant coach the team and he just focused on my recruitment."

In 1975 the many restrictive rules that exist today in recruiting did not exist. A player could visit as many schools as he wanted and have as many contacts with coaches as he desired. Bender took full advantage.

"There were three schools I was really interested in," he said. "Indiana, Kansas, and N.C. State. I was smart enough to know that I was not going to go somewhere and be a major impact player. I needed to be in a program where I would be with other good players. State had just won the national championship; Kansas had been in the Final Four and had a player [Norm Cook] who had played in my high school league. Indiana had Bob Knight."

Then, Bob Knight was the enfant terrible of college basketball. He had just finished his third season at Indiana and had already been to one Final Four, even though he was only thirty-four years old. He was building a monster at Indiana and Bender knew it. What's more, his father was a big fan of Knight's, using the book Knight had written on how to play defense as a model for his own man-to-man defense.

Once Bender had visited Indiana it was a virtual certainty he would go there. Knight, straight up as always, told him that he was the guard Indiana wanted but if he did not make a decision soon, Indiana would recruit someone else.

When Knight came to the Bender home for his visit with the family, he brought three assistants with him: Dave Bliss, Bob Weltlich, and a young graduate assistant named Mike Krzyzewski. "It's funny, but there were two assistant coaches my mom really liked during my recruitment," Bender said. "One was Mike Krzyzewski and the other was Bob Wenzel."

Although Duke never officially visited the Benders, Wenzel was in the house after games on several occasions. Rather than have the coaches wait around after games to try to bump Bob—still legal in those days—the Benders would go home and put out sandwiches for any of the coaches who wanted to drop by. Wenzel was one of those coaches.

The other coach who made an impression on Bob Bender was an assistant coach from Cincinnati named Ray Jones. "If I had changed my mind about Indiana, I might have ended up at Cincinnati just because of Ray," Bender said. "He just seemed like a great guy. Boy, did he work hard trying to recruit me."

It was Indiana all the way, though, and Bender arrived on campus the next fall along with two other recruited freshman, Richard Valevicious and Scott Eeals. There was also a walk-on who would later become a scholarship player, Jim Roberson. On the first day of practice the three scholarship freshmen made a bet on which of them would get yelled at the most by Knight. "By the end of the first day I had the bet won hands down," Bender said, laughing now at the memory. "The older guys had all warned us before the first day to make sure when we started doing drills to get paired with an upperclassman. That way you were with someone who knew what they were doing. Well, somehow I got paired with Roberson. We had no clue. Knight just stood there screaming at us the whole time."

That didn't really bother Bender because he had been told by the other players that was part of the deal. What did bother him was feeling so overmatched every day in practice against players like Quinn Buckner and Bob Wilkerson. "I was six foot two inches and I weighed 150 pounds," Bender said. "These guys were men. I had no chance. I was so overmatched that in preseason scrimmages I didn't score a single point. That's almost impossible to do, but I managed. Not one point."

Bender did achieve his goal of making the ten-man traveling squad that would go to the season opener in St. Louis against defending national champion UCLA. Indiana, with most of the key players back from a team that had gone 29–1 the year before, was favored to win the national title. This was the season that the NCAA, as a budget-cutting measure, limited traveling squads in basketball to ten players. Knight was furious with the rule and vowed to fight it in court. The rule was repealed after one semester but when Bender made the trip to St. Louis he was thrilled.

He even got in the game, an 86–66 Indiana rout. "I went in during the last minute and somehow I got the ball on the baseline with about five seconds left," he said. "I shot and amazingly it goes in. I was just so excited to have scored that I ran back down the court waving my arms and screaming and pointing up at where my parents were sitting. After the game, Coach Knight came into the locker room and said, 'I'm sure glad you made that basket, Bender, it really saved the day.' Everyone cracked up."

Bender was part of an undefeated national championship team that season. The Hoosiers went 32–0 and Bender even got into the national championship game against Michigan, an 86–68 rout reminiscent of the opener. That was the good news. The bad news was that Bender was genuinely struggling to succeed in Knight's system. "I just had trouble getting a lot better at it," he said. "I still remember Knight saying, 'Bender, you are without question the worst defensive player I have ever recruited.' I know he says stuff like that to everybody but in my case he was exactly right."

Bender worked hard during the off-season to prepare for increased playing time as a sophomore. He returned to Indiana in September of 1976 to find a highly touted recruiting class on campus and began to realize that Knight's constant scrutiny and harping wasn't getting easier to live with. In fact, it was getting more difficult.

"I was incredibly uptight," he said. "I was afraid to make a mistake because I was afraid of the way Coach Knight would react. It wasn't his problem, it was mine. This was the way he coached, the way he's always coached. I just couldn't adjust to it."

With the first day of practice rapidly approaching, Bender found himself dreading the coming season. He called his dad, who suggested he go talk to Knight. "Just going in there to his office was the hardest thing I've ever done," Bender said. "I started trying to explain what was bothering me and after about three minutes I started crying.

"He was really great about it. He got me settled down and looked at me and said, 'Bob, what's wrong?' I kept blathering away because I couldn't bring myself to say, 'I want to leave.' Finally, he said it. He just asked me if I wanted to leave. I said, 'Yes, I do.' He wanted me to think about it overnight, talk to my folks and then come back and tell him where I stood. That's what I did. I knew I wanted to leave though because as soon as it was out in the open I felt better. I stopped crying and calmed down. The next morning I went back in and said I wanted to leave. Coach Knight looked at me and said, 'Bob, I wouldn't try to talk Jesus Christ into staying if he didn't want to.'

"After that, we started talking about places I could go. I really can't imagine anyone handling a situation like that better than he did. The one thing he told me was that I shouldn't think of myself as being recruited again. I should just figure out where I might want to go and then check it out. But I shouldn't put myself back out on the market.

"Naturally, the places I mentioned first were the ones I had considered before—Kansas, Cincinnati. I even thought about Providence because of Ernie DiGregorio having gone there. Then I thought of Duke. I remembered two things. One was how much my mom had liked Wenz. The other was that it seemed like every school that came into our house tried to compare itself academically to Duke. I also had just read in *Street and Smith's Basketball Yearbook* about Spanarkel and Gminski, so it seemed like they were getting some good players. When I mentioned Duke, Coach Knight liked that idea a lot."

Things moved swiftly after that. Bender left Indiana on October 14, the day before practice began. "The tough thing about leaving was walking into the locker room that day to say good-bye to the guys," he said. "You play at Indiana, even if it's only for a year, and the guys become family to you because you go through so much together. None of them knew I was leaving so when I said it, it was a shock. I just shook hands with everyone, picked up my stuff and left."

He went home for a few days while his father called both Bill Foster and Carl Tacy at Wake Forest. Wake was one of the few schools where Bender would not have to wait until January to enroll in school, so he had decided to visit there also. But he went to Duke first.

Bill Foster knew that getting Bender would be a coup. He had just been part of a team that had won the national championship. Duke had not even had a winning season since 1972 and had not been in the NCAA Tournament since 1966. Having a player with that connection in the program could only be a boon. Also, even though his playing time at Indiana had been limited, Bender was a known quantity; the Duke coaches had seen him play in high school. At worst, he would create competition for the point guard spot in 1978. At best, he would *be* the point guard. Finally, it certainly would not hurt Foster's image as a recruiter to have it come out that Bob Knight had recommended Duke to Bender.

Foster picked Bender up at the airport himself. The first thing he said impressed Bender because it echoed what Knight had said: "Bob, we'd love to have you at Duke. But we aren't going to recruit you. We're going to show you the campus, introduce you to our players, and then when you decide what you want to do, let us know."

That was fine with Bender. He met the players—and liked them. He was delighted to see that Ray Jones was on the staff. And, of course, there was The Chapel. Bender arrived at Duke at ten in the morning. That afternoon, after practice, he went back in to see Foster. "Coach," he said, "this is where I want to go."

Needless to say, Foster didn't argue. Bender couldn't enroll in school—or practice with the team—until January. But he and Foster agreed it would be a good idea for him to come to Durham, get a job—he ended up delivering lighting fixtures for a Duke booster named K. D. Kennedy—and get used to his new environment.

Bender's decision made major headlines in North Carolina. This was the first high-profile player Foster had recruited. Neither Spanarkel nor Gminski had been as well known when they made the decision to come to Duke. As Foster prepared for his third season, the puzzle was suddenly coming together. Spanarkel was set at one guard spot for three years. Gminski would be the center for four. Harrell and Bender would both have eligibility for three seasons after they sat out their transfer years, meaning that Gminski would have two classmates. There was depth, most of it in the current sophomore class. They still needed a forward with some quickness. And, most of all, they needed a strong-man, a power player to dominate the inside. Thirty months after taking over a program in shambles, Foster could see some hope.

"It still wasn't there though," he said. "There were signs of progress but that wasn't what we were looking for. We were looking for results."

6

More Heartbreak

One of the signs of progress that fall was the media guide. On the cover was an Olympic gold medal with a Duke basketball player bursting through it, looking like the prototypical golden American hero.

The golden boy was Tate Armstrong, who had earned his invitation to the Olympic Trials with his sensational '75–76 season and then had surprised most everyone by making the team. Dean Smith had given him minimal playing time in Montreal, which frustrated Armstrong a great deal, but nonetheless he had come home with the gold medal. For the first time in a long time Duke had a genuine star in its program.

Foster's third team had the potential to be much improved in spite of the lack of depth—*if* Gminski was ready to play center in the ACC. That was the big question in everybody's mind.

The season opened against Wake Forest in Greensboro; the opening round of the Big Four Tournament. When the team walked onto the floor for their noontime shoot-around at the Greensboro Coliseum, one of the grand old arenas in college basketball, Gminski looked at the sixteen thousand empty seats and said, "Do they fill this place?" No Duke player had ever played a game in the Coliseum when it wasn't filled, so Gminski's innocent comment not only set off gales of laughter, it became a team cliché. Every time the Blue Devils walked into an arena someone would inevitably say, "Do they fill this place?"

"My entire hometown could fit into that arena and you would have had about six thousand seats left over," Gminski said. "I had played in a high school gym that seated about twelve hundred people. I had no idea what I was getting into."

He looked that way that night. Gminski was completely outplayed by Wake Forest's Larry Harrison and the Blue Devils lost, 81–80. It was a beginning discouragingly similar to the ending the previous year. And, it looked like Gminski might be in for a very tough rookie season.

"I remember watching Gminski that night and thinking he had potential," TV analyst Billy Packer said. "I told someone, 'Two or three years from now, that kid will be a very good center.' I came back twenty-four hours later and he was there."

It was true. The timid, frightened freshman of Friday, after a pep talk from the coaches, was a calm veteran on Saturday against N.C. State. He only scored 8 points but he got 14 rebounds and blocked two key shots down the stretch in another gut-wrenching game. Only this time, Duke didn't let the game get away. The Blue Devils won 84–82, then put on what may have been the most fervent postgame celebration ever seen after a November game.

The team then went on the first real roll of Bill Foster's tenure. They beat Johns Hopkins with ease, then Armstrong beat a good Washington team with a buzzer-beating jump shot—his 35th point—in an 83–81 victory. Three nights after that, playing in Knoxville in the game that marked the return of superstar Bernard King from a suspension, Armstrong (29 points), Spanarkel (19 points, 9 rebounds, 9 assists), and Gminski (15 points, 11 boards) took over. The final was 81–78 but it wasn't that close. Duke took the lead with ten minutes left in the first half and Tennessee never caught up.

The whooping in the Duke locker room was genuine and no one whooped louder than Foster. He knew that winning at Tennessee would draw some attention across the country. And he knew that he had a team with three big-time scoring threats, only one of them a senior. The suffering looked to be over.

The rest of the month was a joyride. Armstrong beat Richmond at the buzzer, then proved he was human by missing the last shot against Connecticut in Madison Square Garden. Didn't matter. The Blue Devils won in overtime, Gminski scoring 20 in front of several hundred people who had driven down from Monroe for the game. By the time ACC play began, the Blue Devils were 10–1 and their name was starting to appear in some top twenty's around the country.

Cameron was packed for the ACC opener against Clemson. The pregame atmosphere reminded old-timers of the Bubas days. Unfortunately, the game still bore the stamp of the recent past. Armstrong had the last shot of regulation to win the game but the ball spun out and it went into overtime. Surprised by the reprieve, Clemson played textbook basketball for five minutes and won going away, 90–83.

It was discouraging, as was a loss three days later at Carolina. The record dropped to 10–3, 0–2 in the ACC. Some people shrugged and said, "same old Duke." Not the team. "We knew we were good," Armstrong said. "Tennessee was proof of that. We shouldn't have lost that game to Clemson but they weren't exactly a slouch team with Tree Rollins at center. We knew we had to win a tough game to really make a move and we had to do it on the road. Virginia was certainly a golden opportunity."

Forty-eight hours after the Carolina loss, Duke played at Virginia. Foster's mood was a cross between funereal and furious. He practiced the team for two hours in Charlottesville on Sunday. The message was clear: The almosts had to stop, if only for the sake of the coach's sanity.

The close losses were eating at Foster day and night. He had developed the habit at Utah of staying up until dawn after losses, often dragging the assistants with him to an all-night restaurant to sit up and figure out ways to turn the team around. "I don't think Lou [Goetz] ever had a girlfriend in Salt Lake," Foster joked. "He was always with me."

Now, after losses, Foster was pulling back even from Goetz and Wenzel. He would get in his car, pop in a country music tape, and drive around, trying to push the game images from his mind. Everyone worried about him but no one knew what to say to him. "For me to say, 'Bill, this is craziness,' wouldn't do a lot of good," his wife Shirley said. "Intellectually, he understood that. But emotionally he was no more capable of stopping than he is capable of stopping coaching."

The players had long ago nicknamed him "Wild Bill," for obvious reasons. They felt helpless when he would go bananas after a loss but knew the only thing they could do to help was not lose. In the ACC that was easier said than done.

"One of the first things that struck me after I started being able to travel with the team was just how much Bill *hurt*," Bender said. "It was almost physical pain. You could see it on his face. The rest of us hurt too, but it wasn't the same. We wanted to win a game. To him, this was life itself."

Foster really can't pinpoint where this drive comes from. All successful people in any competitive profession have a will to win that goes beyond the norm, but in Foster it was different. On the surface he seemed low-key, almost easygoing. His wit was sarcastic and self-deprecating, usually disarming. Something ate at his insides, though.

"Maybe it's my background," he said, trying to explain it. "I didn't grow up poor or anything but I was never a varsity basketball player until my senior year of high school. Then, I went to Goldey College for one year and Elizabethtown. Good schools but not exactly giants in basketball. I always wondered just how good I was.

"The same thing in coaching. I started in high school figuring I would end up being a teacher. Then I get the job at Bloomsburg. Tiny school. Then Rutgers, two-thousand-seat gym until the day I left eight years later. We did well but we were never an NCAA team. Utah had a big gym but we were on square one. Same thing at Duke. Always, in the back of my mind I wondered how good I was. Other people would tell me I was good and people kept wanting to hire me. That was very nice and I was making a good living. But still the questions were there: 'How good are you? Will you ever make the NCAA Tournament? When you think you're unlucky all the time is it maybe that you aren't that good?' You think about those things. You can't help it. At least *I* couldn't help it."

All the players saw was a forty-six-year-old coach who had steadily climbed the ladder in his profession to the top league in the country and was quietly piecing together a team that would be a power in the future. They couldn't understand the insecurities that raged inside him.

That Sunday afternoon in Charlottesville, the rage was on display for all to see. As the players headed for their rooms that night with the snow falling hard, they knew the next night's game was as important as any they had played at Duke.

Terry Holland, in three years at Virginia, had been rebuilding the same way Foster had. But the previous March, in the same ACC Tournament where Duke might have made the big breakthrough, Virginia *had* made it. On consecutive nights, the Cavaliers had beaten third-seeded N.C. State, second-seeded Maryland (ripe to be picked as Duke had proven the first day), and then, stunningly, top-seeded North Carolina.

It was the school's first ACC championship ever and put it into the NCAA Tournament. Even a first-round loss to DePaul could not dampen what Virginia and Holland had accomplished. Basketball was very much on the rise at Virginia and, unlike at Duke, there was tangible evidence: the banner in University Hall that proudly proclaimed, "University of Virginia, ACC Champions 1976."

This was not the same Virginia team, though, not with Wally

Walker, the tournament MVP, in the NBA. Nonetheless, Duke had not won an ACC road game in five years, a 27-game losing streak that stretched back to 1972. To say the least, no ACC road game was going to be easy.

Armstrong started the game by hitting a jump shot. Seconds later, with the ball loose on the boards, Armstrong tried to box out Virginia's Billy Langloh. Their legs got tangled and Armstrong tripped and fell, landing on his right arm. He came up rubbing his wrist but waved Crowder off when he started to come on the court to take a look.

The game went back and forth. Midway through the first half, Morrison had an allergy attack. Crowder had to take him into the locker room, call a doctor and get him taken care of. In the meantime, Armstrong's wrist had started to throb. "I thought about calling time out a couple of times because it hurt so much," Armstrong said. "But I was afraid if Max took a look at it he might make me come out. I couldn't come out. We *had* to win that game."

Even in pain, Armstrong kept shooting. At halftime he had 16 points and Duke led by 4. During the break, Crowder was preoccupied with Morrison, who was quite sick. He gave Armstrong some ice for his wrist, which dulled the pain. The second half was like the first. Duke led. Virginia led. The Cavaliers had the last shot of regulation—it went in and out. Armstrong dominated the overtime, hitting two jump shots at the start and four free throws at the end. "By that time I was almost screaming in pain on the foul shots," he said.

The Blue Devils won the game, 82–74. Armstrong had scored 33 points. And the road losing streak was finally over. But when Crowder finally got a look at Armstrong's wrist in the locker room he was shocked. He took Foster aside and said quietly, "I'm pretty sure he's got a broken wrist."

The glow of the biggest victory of his Duke career drained out of Foster in an instant. A broken wrist in January meant that Armstrong's college career was over. The dream of converting what was now an 11–3 record into a postseason tournament bid of some kind was probably out the window, too. "If Max had kicked me in the stomach I think it would have hurt less," Foster said.

He was ashen by the time he walked into the interview room to meet the press. "There isn't a lot of celebrating going on right now," Foster said. "We just have to wait until tomorrow to see how bad Tate is."

Armstrong got the official word the next morning. The break was in the navicular bone. Not only was his college career over but, the doctor said, "I have to be honest with you, Tate. Sometimes injuries like this never heal."

The words "never heal" sent Armstrong reeling. He was being projected at that moment as a certain first-round draft pick. That meant a great shot at a pro career and long-term financial stability. The doctor put the cast on and Armstrong walked out into the cool January sunshine. It was a gorgeous day at Duke. Armstrong was a senior. He was in love with a beautiful cheerleader and she was in love with him. He would graduate in May with his whole life ahead of him. He started to cry.

Twelve years later, recreating that morning he smiled and said, "It was the best of times, it was the worst of times. . . ."

For Foster and the team, it was only the worst of times. They had to play at Wake Forest two nights later, a tough task *with* Armstrong. Steve Gray would be the starting point guard. Gray had started at Virginia because of a minor injury to Mark Crow and he was playing respectable basketball as the third guard. Now a giant responsibility had been dropped in his lap.

"I wasn't sure how to feel," he said. "I was excited about the chance to really get to play but sorry that it happened that way. I definitely thought I could do the job though."

The offense would have to be changed. Instead of trying to set screens and create shots for Armstrong, the team would now look to get the ball to Spanarkel and Gminski. Crow would have to shoot more often. And Morrison, who had taken over the starting power forward spot, would have to take some shots too.

The loss at Wake Forest was not unexpected. This was a Top Twenty team playing at home. But three nights later, N.C. State came to town. The Blue Devils had beaten the Wolfpack in November on a neutral court. They were certainly capable of doing it in Cameron. As usual, the game came down to the final seconds. With twenty-five seconds left, Morrison hit a follow shot to put Duke up, 78–77. State came down and missed. Gminski rebounded. Now, Duke just had to run the clock out or wait to get fouled. The ball went to Gray, an 82 percent foul shooter. The clock was under ten seconds by now. But as Gray spun away from the defense, the ball, somehow hit his foot. It slid onto the floor, rolled away and went out of bounds as Gray stood frozen, watching in horror.

With eight seconds left, State came down, set up for the last shot. The ball went to Hawkeye Whitney. He went up, shot and—*swish*. It was over. State–79, Duke–78.

Gray was mortified. His teammates were horrified. His coaches were speechless. "I kid him about it now," Morrison said. "I tell him because of his stupid foot I missed my chance to be a hero. But that's now. Back then, it wasn't funny."

Nothing was funny at this stage. The team went on a nightmarish trip the following week, having to bus fourteen hours to Morgantown, West Virginia, because a snowstorm had shut down all the airports and interstates in the East. There was an energy crisis and the heat in the West Virginia Coliseum was set at 58 degrees. In the half-empty building, it felt a lot colder than that. The game fit the mood. If the Blue Devils had tried, it was unlikely they could have played worse. They lost, 70–65.

Foster was wilder than ever. He threw a garbage can across the locker room in disgust and stormed off into the snow. Two nights later, in another frigid near-empty arena in Pittsburgh, the Blue Devils finally got their first win A.T. (After Tate), routing a Duquesne team that included Norm Nixon, 76–49.

Even the victory had an eerie side to it. In the final seconds, Foster cleared the bench, giving Rob Hardy a rare chance to play. With time winding down, Gminski threw Hardy a long lead pass and Hardy went to the basket against a Duquesne player named B. B. Flennory. Flennory tried to take a charge. Hardy ran over him and hit the lay-up. There was no whistle, the officials undoubtedly just wanting the game over with. But Flennory had fallen straight back when Hardy collided with him and had hit his head on the hard Civic Arena floor. He lay there not moving, out cold.

He was taken to the hospital where X rays showed a concussion. Foster and the assistants went to see him late that night and were assured he was going to be just fine. They reported back to the shaken Hardy that his first varsity field goal—his only one of the season as it turned out—had not been fatal to anyone.

The victory didn't cheer anybody up much, although the trip was not without moments that would be remembered years later. On the endless bus trip up, the bus had stopped at a light right next to a house where a family was just sitting down to dinner. Seeing this was too much for Gminski. "Maybe we could stop and see if they have something to eat," he said, not really kidding. "I'll eat anything right now."

Gminski finally had a nickname that would stick: Mikey, as in the character in the Life cereal commercial who would eat anything.

Bell also immortalized himself that evening. When the bus finally arrived in Morgantown, the players had a long walk in the cold to their hotel. By the time Bell made it to his room he was screaming: "My hands are frozen, my hands are frozen! I can't feel my hands, I can't feel my hands!"

He was genuinely scared but his high-pitched yelps sent Hardy, Spanarkel, and Hall into hysterics. Hardy was alert enough, however, to stop Bell when he raced toward the bathroom to run his hands under hot water. The next day as the team walked to the bus, cries of, "Hot dawg, I can't feel my hands!" were everywhere.

Most of it was gallows humor. The season was rapidly slipping away. Wake came to town and beat Duke for the third time, and then, on February 5, Maryland came in for a Saturday afternoon game. Duke was 12–7 and 1–5 in the ACC, the ill-fated Virginia game the only victory. It needed an ACC win. Spanarkel was brilliant that day, scoring a career-high 30 points. His three-point play made it 54–49 with forty-seven seconds left and it looked like Maryland would lose in Cameron for a second straight year. Maryland scored to make it 54–51 but the clock was under twenty seconds. Desperate, the Terrapins pressed. Gray picked up his dribble on the right side of the Duke basket and looked for someone to pass to.

He was double-teamed. Afraid of getting trapped, he committed a cardinal sin, throwing a crosscourt pass. That was bad enough. What was worse was that the pass was so far off line that *it hit the rim*. It bounced high in the air and Maryland's James "Turkey" Tillman grabbed it and went up to dunk. Even if he made the shot Duke would still have the lead and the ball. But Gray, reacting instinctively, tried to stop him. He succeeded only in fouling him as Tillman rammed the shot home.

It was as if Cameron was a balloon and someone had stuck a pin into it. After Tillman tied the game with his free throw, the air went out of everyone. Maryland won in overtime, 65–64.

This one was the worst. The days of blowing unblowable leads were supposedly in the past. But they weren't. Spanarkel could barely talk. Foster *couldn't* talk. He had the flu, a bad case of laryngitis and a sore throat. It was probably a good thing. No one was more devastated than Gray.

"To this day I can't believe that happened," he said. "It was as if someone plotted it. My career, realistically, ended right there. The coaches never had confidence in me again and I don't think anyone else at Duke did either. I might as well have quit right then because I would probably have been a lot less frustrated when I left Duke if I had."

That night, Foster was scheduled to fly to Louisville on a private plane to see Jeff Lamp play. The plane got halfway there and then ran into awful head winds. The pilot was forced to turn around and go back to Durham. The plane bounced all over the sky on the way back. As soon as it landed, Foster got off, ran into a bathroom and got sick. "I'm not sure up to that moment in my life I had ever felt worse," he said. "I was really starting to be convinced that it just wasn't going to turn around. All I could think was, 'What next?' One more disaster and I might have been done. I mean really. Done."

Bill Foster had never felt lower in his coaching career than he felt in the first hours of February 6, 1977.

7

The Final Piece

When the phone rang the next day, it was Shirley Foster who answered it. Bill was lying next to her, literally waiting for the next disaster to happen. Shirley talked for a couple of minutes and then handed the phone to her husband. "It's Gene Banks," she told him.

Foster cannot remember any particular thoughts registering as he took the phone. Normally, the name Gene Banks would have sent his mind racing: Why was he calling? Was it good news? Bad news? A question he couldn't answer? When was the last time he had talked to him? Gene Banks was, quite simply, the best basketball player Foster had ever recruited. And, certainly on this morning, the most important.

But Foster was too sick and too tired to think any of those thoughts. All he could see in his mind's eye was Gray's pass hitting the rim. Banks knew none of this, of course. He knew Duke had had a tough loss the day before but he couldn't understand what Foster had been going through.

Cheerfully, he said to Foster: "Coach, can you make it up to Philadelphia tomorrow?"

Foster thought he could, but why? What was up? "Well Coach," Banks said, not without a dramatic pause, "I've called a press conference for tomorrow. I'm coming to Duke."

When Foster heard Banks say, "I'm coming to Duke," his first thought was that he was still asleep, having a dream, and would wake up any minute to the reality of Gray's pass. But a minute later, Foster was still sitting there wide awake and Banks was still talking and he was still telling him he was going to come to Duke.

"I'll be there in the morning," Foster said, even though he knew, under NCAA rules, he wasn't allowed to actually attend the announcement. He hung up the phone and called his assistants. Goetz, low-key as always, was very happy but pointed out it would be two months before Banks could formally sign an NCAA letter of intent. Wenzel was ecstatic. He had spent almost a year chasing Banks.

"Coach," Wenzel said, "this is it. The worm has turned." For the next week, Wenzel kept saying those words over and over again: "The worm has turned."

Gene Banks was exactly the kind of player it seemed impossible for Duke to recruit. He was from the West Philadelphia projects and he had low college board scores. He was a schoolboy legend, a player anointed as a sophomore after leading West Philadelphia High School to a 25–0 record and the city championship. He was listed as 6-7—although he was really barely 6-6—and he had a body that looked like it had been sculpted from stone.

By the spring of 1976, Banks and Albert King, both high school juniors, were larger-than-life figures, Banks from the Philly schoolyards, King from Fort Hamilton High School in Brooklyn. There was a third junior getting a lot of attention but he was from the Midwest—Lansing, Michigan—and didn't get quite as much attention as a result. His name was Earvin Johnson. Went by the nickname "Magic."

Banks had a nickname, too: "Tinkerbell."

"It started my sophomore year," he said. "A couple of days before the city championship game, my cousin Theo and I ducked out of school during a fire drill and went downtown to go to the movies. The only movie open at that hour was *Peter Pan*. We went in. I was trying to come up with a nickname for myself at the time. I liked 'Magnum Force.' But during the movie Tinkerbell was flying all around and my cousin said, 'That's it, that's it, we'll call you Tinkerbell!'

"I said, 'Don't you dare call me that. Call me Magnum Force.' But he liked it. He said that Tinkerbell flew through the air with the greatest of ease, just like me. He started calling all my friends before we played for the city championship and telling them my new nickname was Tinkerbell. When the game started, I scored the first basket and this whole section of people stood up and yelled, 'Tinkerbell!'

"I didn't like it a bit. But after we won, all the papers the next day were writing stuff like, 'There's a new Bell in Philadelphia,' things like that. So, I decided I liked it."

He liked it so much that he began signing his autographs that way. Today, at the age of thirty, he still signs Tinkerbell on autographs.

Realistically, Duke had little chance to sign Gene "Tinkerbell" Banks. Everyone in the country was recruiting him. He was a superstar with suspect board scores, not exactly the perfect Duke profile.

But Banks was not your stereotypical black superstar. In some ways yes: his parents had separated when he was very young and both had remarried. His mother, Barbara, had a total of eight children. Derrick, Gene's oldest brother, had been born before Barbara had met Eugene Banks, Sr., in a Pentecostal church. Gene, Venesse, and Darryl were the products of their marriage and Gene's four youngest sisters were the children of his stepfather, Walter Williams.

During junior high, Gene had lived with his father and bussed to a predominantly white school. He had moved back in with his mother in the tenth grade and enrolled at West Philadelphia. He had become such a big star as a ninth grader that his high school coach, Joey Goldenberg, was accused of convincing Gene to move from one parent to the other in order to get him into West Philadelphia's district.

One thing set Gene Banks apart, though. He was very image-conscious. He enjoyed the attention showered on him and the adoration he felt whenever he played; he wanted very much to live up to the image that had been created for him. He had an English teacher at West Philadelphia named William H. Deadwyler, Jr., who couldn't have cared less about basketball. But Deadwyler didn't allow any street talk or lingo in his class. When he heard Gene Banks say "ain't" during a radio interview, he berated him in front of the class. Banks hated that. He worked hard on his public speaking and by the time he was a senior he was as smooth as most professional athletes who have been getting paid to talk for years.

What's more, he had the gift of the bull. Few people in history, whether they be Winston Churchill, Abraham Lincoln or Franklin D. Roosevelt, have been gifted with the ability to convince people that up is down and left is right the way Gene Banks is. "Remember this about con men," said Kenny Dennard, Banks's best basketball-playing friend in college. "The best ones are the ones who you *know* are conning you but you want to believe them anyway. They look right at you, tell you something you know can't be so and you believe it anyway. That was Gene. He is without doubt the most charming person I have ever met. I've never met anyone Gene couldn't charm."

With his bodybuilder's physique, his superstardom on the basketball court *and* his charm, Banks was the consummate ladies' man. He had a beautiful girlfriend named Princess and, during his senior year at

West Philadelphia, he fathered a son named Benjamin. "This girl and I fell in love and it just happened," he said, years later.

"Was that Princess?"

"Oh no. Princess was my girlfriend. This was another girl."

Of course.

Bill Foster and his assistants didn't really care how many women Banks charmed or how many stories he told about his heroics. All they knew was he was a great player who, in spite of his low board scores (610), was clearly bright enough to do the necessary schoolwork if he wanted to. And, most important, he was interested in Duke. It might be years before another player of his caliber might come along and be interested in Duke.

At the end of his junior year, Banks and Goldenberg made a list of six schools he wanted to visit: UCLA, N.C. State, North Carolina, Notre Dame, Michigan, and Duke. Banks would also visit Villanova and Pennsylvania unofficially, the two schools being several miles and several blocks respectively from where Banks lived.

The only school in the group that didn't make sense was Duke. UCLA had more tradition than anyone. N.C. State had won the national title two years earlier and North Carolina was a perennial power. So was Notre Dame—and Banks was a big fan of Notre Dame star Adrian Dantley. That March, Michigan had played in the national championship game. Villanova and Penn were both at home and Penn, a power at the time, was in the Ivy League, something that would appeal to Banks.

But Duke? "I didn't know a thing about the school," Banks said. "In fact, I always thought Duke was Duquesne because they wore Dukes on their uniform. But during my junior year, Bill left brochures and stuff with Goldenberg. It was when I read the brochure that I first realized Duke was in the ACC and North Carolina. After that, something just told me to put Duke on the list. I don't really know why. I knew they had tradition and my coach told me that Bill Foster was a good coach so I thought I should give them a look."

Foster, being from the Philadelphia area, knew Goldenberg well. So did Rollie Massimino at Villanova and Chuck Daly at Penn, but if Banks looked outside of Philadelphia, Foster's connections there would help. Wenzel began the recruiting process and to this day Foster gives him a lot of credit for the success with Banks. But Wenzel will tell you that Banks ultimately chose Duke for one reason: Foster.

"The first time they met there were sparks," Wenzel said. "Don't ask me why but I could tell they just hit it off. It was as if Gene enjoyed the fact that Bill didn't come in as if he was in the presence of God."

In fact, one of Banks's first questions to Foster was to ask him why he had not stopped to introduce himself the first time Foster had come to see him play. "Bumps"—coaches talking to players at their games—were still legal, and paying postgame homage to superstars like Banks was considered a requisite for any coach going to see a player.

"So how come you didn't stop to say hello?" Banks asked Foster.

Deadpan, Foster said, "Well, Gene, to tell you the truth I wasn't sure you could play for us."

Banks's mouth dropped open. Wenzel's heart stopped beating for a second. Then, Banks got it. He cracked up. "I've never forgotten that," Banks said. "I was so used to coaches coming in and telling me I was the greatest this and the greatest that and Bill came in and started giving me a hard time. I really liked that."

After that initial meeting, Wenzel was convinced that unless someone stole (read: "bought") him, Duke was going to get Banks. Two days after that meeting, sitting in his office, he told a student reporter, "Mark it down. We're going to get him."

Part of this was pure optimism. Part of this was Wenzel. He was the guy on the staff who never seemed to get down. When the staff would sit around and talk about an upcoming game, Foster would inevitably shake his head and say to Goetz, "Have we got any shot?" Goetz would answer, "Well, if we play very well, we can stay with them." Foster, still convinced defeat was inevitable, would turn to Wenzel and ask: "What do you think, Wenz?" Wenzel would jump out of his chair and say, "We're gonna kick their ass!"

And he believed it. Banks remembers liking Wenzel when he first met him, "because he was always geeked up." That was Wenzel. Now he was geeked up about getting Gene Banks. "If we get him," Wenzel said, "people better watch out."

The coaches were also excited about Kenny Dennard, who had committed in late November, although they knew he was not the typical high school senior. Since his official visit in October, Dennard had spent almost every weekend on the Duke campus, sleeping on the floor of Crow's room.

"Kenny was the only one of us who spent five years at Duke, not four," Bender said. "He was also probably the brightest of any of us. And, of course, he was the only one not to graduate on time."

That was Dennard. He never did anything that was easy—and

school was always easy. Basketball came harder. He was a late bloomer, a player who had averaged only nine points a game as a *junior varsity* player his sophomore year at South Stokes High School, and then became a star as a junior. Wenzel had discovered him the previous summer at the Five-Star camp quite by accident.

"I walked in the first day I was there, another coach came by and said to me, 'Hey Wenz, you must be looking at that big white kid from North Carolina.' I had no idea who he was talking about. But I bluffed. I said, 'Yeah, yeah, where's he playing right now?' He told me. I got over there and quickly figured out that this wild man who was taking charges on the concrete outdoor courts was the guy he was talking about. I can't even remember who it was who said that to me, but I owe him."

Dennard had gone from 6-3 and 210 pounds as a chubby sophomore to 6-7 and 190 as a rock-hard junior. Wenzel was so geeked up by what he saw that week that rather than write the Dennard family the customary form letter introducing Duke, he called them directly.

What was most ironic about Wenzel's discovery of Dennard was that the only reason he was at Five-Star was Neill McGeachy. McGeachy had become an assistant at Wake Forest after being forced out at Duke. Dennard was from King, North Carolina, a small town about twenty-five miles north of Winston-Salem. McGeachy had seen Dennard play at South Stokes High that year and had talked him into going to Five-Star. He thought it would help Dennard to play against top competition.

"No one had really heard of me before Five-Star," Dennard said. "I was worried that being from a rural school in North Carolina, no one would *ever* discover me. If Neill hadn't convinced me to go to Five-Star, Wake might have been the only school that ever recruited me. After Five-Star, the letters started coming in from everywhere."

Dennard visited Duke in October. His escort for the weekend was Mark Crow. Dennard had met Crow the previous summer when Crow had worked as a counselor at Wake Forest's summer camp. Clearly, having his players work at other ACC schools' summer camps was a boon to Foster's recruiting. Crow-bar was Dennard's hero and role model. "Bar was the greatest," Dennard said. "He never locked the door to his room unless he was, you know, occupied—which he often was. He just knew how to have a good time."

Crow-bar showed Dennard and Pete Budko, another recruit, a very good time that weekend. Late Saturday night—or early Sunday morning—the three of them were crossing the quad when Crow-bar suddenly pulled off the fatigue jacket he was wearing and said to the two recruits, "Are you coming to Duke or not?"

Dennard's mind was made up. Budko said his was too. Crow-bar sat down and, on the back of his fatigue jacket, wrote out a letter of intent. Dennard and Budko both signed it. To Dennard, that was like a blood oath, his signature on his hero's fatigues. Budko, who ended up at North Carolina, didn't take it quite as seriously.

Several weeks later, Dennard announced he was coming to Duke. Back then, preseason commitments were almost unheard of but Dennard's mind was made up. "I liked the idea that I'd have a chance to play," he said. "I liked Bill and I liked the team's sense of humor. There were a lot of funny guys. I thought I would enjoy that."

The same weekend that Crow-bar was showing Dennard and Budko around, Harold Morrison was doing the same thing with Banks. It was only natural that the coaches would put Banks in Morrison's hands. Kenny Young was gone. John Harrell was still a walk-on. Morrison was the only black scholarship player on the team. He would introduce Banks to the black community at Duke—most notably the black women—and he would give Banks an honest idea of what it was like to be black in Duke's almost lily-white society.

"What I liked about Harold first was that he was one of the funniest people I had ever met," Banks said. "But when we started talking seriously, he was honest. He told me there was definitely a social life for blacks at Duke but most of the time you were around whites, some of whom would talk to you only because you were a basketball player. I understood that. I think going to a white junior high school helped.

"I had visited State and Chapel Hill [North Carolina] already and it just seemed to me like the whites at Duke were more comfortable talking to blacks than the whites had been at the other two schools. Maybe it was because there are more northerners at Duke. Or, maybe I was just more comfortable with them because I knew they were from the North."

This was an important weekend for Morrison. To him, Banks was his escape from playing the power forward position he dreaded. He knew Banks was reputed to be as good as anyone in the country. "All I could think was that if we got this guy, I could be the starting small forward the next year," Morrison said. "Crow-bar was graduating and the spot was going to be open. I had no idea who Kenny Dennard was. All I knew was *we* needed Gene Banks and *I* needed Gene Banks."

It became apparent to Morrison very quickly that Banks was not your typical visiting recruit. "We went to a party on Friday night and when we got there I was figuring I would start introducing Gene to some of the girls and hope he would feel okay talking to them. But as soon as we walked in the door he just said to me, 'Check you later,' and he was gone. He didn't need any help at all."

Banks tells a story about that party that may or may not be apocryphal. "I started talking to this girl and she said to me that she was really excited because Gene Banks was visiting Duke that weekend and she was just dying to meet him and she wanted to know if I knew who he was. I told her that I had met him earlier that day and he was really a great guy. She was just really excited about meeting Gene Banks. I liked that."

Who wouldn't. Banks liked Duke and liked the campus. But as he freely admits today he liked UCLA and he liked State and he liked Carolina and he liked Penn and he liked Villanova. "Every place I visited, I liked," he said. "That's why I decided not to visit Notre Dame and Michigan. It was just all getting to me. Everyone being so nice and me feeling like every time I visited a campus that was where I wanted to go."

Like all the other coaches recruiting him, Foster kept close tabs on Banks after his visit. He or Wenzel went to see him play whenever possible. There were the usual phone calls, letters, post cards and calls from Morrison too. Princess, who was a straight-A student, was admitted to Duke, a kind and generous thing for the admissions department to do.

Admissions was not so certain, though, about admitting Banks. Generally speaking, admissions frowned on admitting any athlete with less than 1,000 on his boards, and it had never taken anyone below 800. That was the cutoff point. But Foster pointed out that Banks had always had good grades and that coming from an inner city school had certainly played a role in his low SAT score. "At least talk to him and see what you think," Foster said. Admissions agreed.

Banks, during his visit, met the admissions people, turned on the charm and won them over. They didn't say they would absolutely take Banks if he decided he wanted to go there, but Foster felt very confident that they would. He was right. Now, on February 7, with every TV and radio station in the city and every newspaper for miles around represented, Banks stepped to a microphone and told the world, "I've decided to go to Duke."

The announcement stunned the city of Philadelphia, shocked UCLA and angered Notre Dame. Banks had chosen Duke because he liked Foster but also for one other very important reason. "I can make them a national power," he said. "The other schools were already there. Duke wasn't. I wanted to go there and be the guy who took them to the top. I thought I could do it."

With Spanarkel, Gminski, Bender, Harrell, and to a lesser extent Dennard already in place, Foster agreed with Banks. "In a lot of ways, Gene was the last piece of the puzzle," he said, years later. "We could not have gotten him if we hadn't had the other guys already there. If we had recruited him the year we recruited Spanarkel, I don't think he would have come. The other side of it is that if we hadn't recruited Gene, even with the other guys there, we wouldn't have been as good as we became."

Irony is a constant in recruiting. This is another one: If O'Koren had chosen Duke a year earlier, Banks would never have followed him. The fact that he would be *the* star at forward appealed to him.

Banks's announcement transformed the Duke campus. The pall that had fallen after the Maryland game, the feeling that the good guys were destined always to lose, turned around 180 degrees almost overnight. This season was probably gone. A shame. But Gene was coming. Some of Gminski's fraternity brothers had a shirt made up that said just that: "Gene is coming." For the first time in years the light at the end of the tunnel wasn't another train.

To understand the significance of Banks's decision to the students at Duke, one must know a little more about Duke. People are always shocked to learn that it has a total student population of less than nine thousand, less than six thousand of them undergraduates. It isn't a tiny school—Wake Forest is half its size—but in the world of big-time college athletics it is quite small.

Football, for all intents and purposes, ceased to exist at Duke in the early 1960s. Duke played in the 1961 Cotton Bowl and even with the proliferation of bowls to the point where simply fielding a team makes you a contender for a spot, it has not been back to a bowl game since. It hasn't won an ACC title in football for almost twenty-five years— and winning the ACC in football is not exactly a big deal.

In the 1970s, when Carl James was the athletic director, the football team regularly played road games against Southern California, Michigan, Tennessee, and Florida. That was the way James balanced his budget. He fed his team to the wolves (or the Wolverines, if you will) a couple of times a year, took home a big guarantee and then couldn't understand why the team was so beat up by ACC time that it couldn't compete.

In the 1980s, James's successor, Tom Butters, went in the opposite direction. Now Duke regularly jumps to a 3–0 start (5–0 in 1988) by beating up on the Citadel, Northwestern, and Ohio University. Then the team limps through the ACC schedule at 4–3 or 3–4 and finishes with five to seven victories. Steve Spurrier was chosen ACC coach of the year for going 7–3–1 in 1988. He is, no doubt, a good coach. But no one at Duke is fooled. If the Blue Devils went back to playing the nonconference schedules they played back in the '70s, they would get killed all over again. At best, Duke can be a nice regional team, maybe even get a bid to the Peach Bowl or some other nonentity bowl.

Basketball is *different.*

Basketball has always been the sport where the Duke team can compete with anybody. The Final Four banners in Cameron Indoor Stadium attest to that. More than anything, basketball has given Duke its name nationally. That is no knock on what Terry Sanford did in the 1970s to upgrade the school academically. Duke's medical school is one of the very best in the country and the law school is not that far behind. Its Institute of Public Policy has gained national attention. But Sanford would be the first one to tell you that the basketball team gives the school more visibility than anything else can.

That's why the early and mid-'70s were so painful to Duke people, specifically to the students. They knew of the tradition, they knew that games in Cameron were special, and they knew Duke was capable of competing on that highest level. But as each year passed and the losses mounted, they became more and more painful.

Foster had brought hope. But the breakthrough hadn't come. Everyone sensed it was near, but no one was sure it was a certainty. Banks's saying he was coming to Duke made it a certainty. Now, it wasn't *if,* it was *when.*

That was the mood when Virginia came to Cameron four days after the Gray off-the-rim pass and two days after the Banks announcement. There was a feeling of joy in the building, a "Happy Days Are Here Again" atmosphere.

With Spanarkel playing point guard for much of the contest, the Blue Devils beat Virginia 65–49 in a truly ugly game. It didn't matter. It was an ACC victory and Banks was coming. Three nights later, Duke beat St. Joseph's to up its record to 14–8. This was a watershed victory—it clinched the first winning season for the Blue Devils since 1972. No small thing.

That was the good news. The bad news was that Foster knew he could not play Spanarkel at point guard against N.C. State, Maryland, Clemson, and North Carolina, the last four opponents of the regular season. They were too strong for him to play out of position. He also felt that to put Gray back out there would be suicidal for the team and cruel to Gray. So, he decided to start Bruce Bell.

This decision was a melding, in a sense, of the old—Foster's first days at Duke—and the new—the future that included Gene Banks.

Bell was, by now, very much established as a member of the team. He had worked hard at his game and had played well in practice. But the fact remained that with big things supposedly just ahead, Duke was starting a one-time walk-on at point guard—in the middle of the ACC season. "In a way I was very proud of myself for getting to that point," Bell said. "I realize that it took a lot of different circumstances to make me a starter but I was the first walk-on that anyone could remember to start an ACC game.

"And I didn't think my being a starter meant we were surrendering. I went into every one of those games thinking there was no reason we couldn't win. If I could get the ball to Jimmy or Mike or Crow-bar, they could score on anyone."

Bell did nothing to embarrass himself. He played respectably and so did the team. But the Blue Devils lost the last four games of the regular season, then dropped their first-round game in the ACC Tournament to Clemson. That left them with a 14–13 record—their best in five years but still disappointing. Once again, they were last in the ACC.

—

While the team was crawling to the finish line, Banks was making the coaching staff nervous—to use an understated word.

His announcement that he was coming to Duke did not end his recruitment, not by any means. Notre Dame and UCLA were still hot on his trail.

Both coaching staffs insisted later that Banks told them he was having second thoughts about Duke. In fact, two weeks after his big announcement, Banks told a Philadelphia newspaper that he might change his mind. Hearing this, Foster called Banks immediately. Banks told him it was true, he *was* reconsidering his decision.

Foster and Wenzel were on the next plane. This was a strange situation. Duke had used up all of its legal visits to Banks, so even though they were in Philadelphia, they could not go see him face-to-face. They checked into a downtown hotel, and Foster called Banks from one phone while Wenzel called room service on the other.

Foster and Banks were on the phone for four hours. Foster's dinner had gotten quite cold by the time he hung up the phone, but he felt better. At the end of the conversation, Banks had said, "Coach, I'm still coming to Duke, don't you worry about it."

Foster would worry until Banks could sign a letter of intent. That was not until April 9. Banks had been hearing a lot of things: He had heard Duke was a bad place for blacks, that Spanarkel and Gminski were overrated, that the team could never be a true national contender. He had heard that Jim Lewis had been replaced on the staff by Ray Jones because Foster was more comfortable with white assistant coaches.

In short, he had heard a lot of things from a lot of people trying to undermine Duke. For all of his physical maturity, Banks was still a seventeen-year-old kid being pulled in a hundred different directions at once. He remembers today how the different schools tried to get to him through different people. "UCLA was going to put my stepfather in business in Los Angeles," he said. "I think Villanova was going to give my coach a job the next year. I had another buddy who was trying to get me to go to Michigan because they were talking to him. And my mother thought Norm Sloan was the greatest. She loved him."

Everyone tugged at Tinkerbell. Part of him loved every second of the attention. But part of him was confused. All Duke and Foster could do was hope he would be true to his word.

On March 18, West Philadelphia traveled to Washington, D.C., to play in the Knights of Columbus Tournament. This was an annual eight-team postseason tournament, once a top showcase for talent. But with the advent of high school all-star games, the K. of C. had fallen on hard times. As it turned out, this would be the last year the tournament was held.

The D.C. Armory is an ancient building that sits in the shadow of Robert F. Kennedy Stadium and the old D.C. jail. It is almost never used now and it was cold and dank on that rainy March night when West Philadelphia easily beat Georgetown Prep. Banks didn't play much because he was in foul trouble. Wenzel, on baby-sitting duty, was there to watch. Sitting across from him in the stands was Notre Dame Coach Digger Phelps. With him sat Bob Whitmore, Sid Catlett, and Gary Brokaw, three of Phelps's biggest stars of the 1970s.

When the game ended, Banks went downstairs to change. Five minutes later, he appeared at the top of the steps. Wenzel was standing to the left, Phelps and company a few steps away on the right. "Gene," Phelps said, getting the jump on Wenzel, "I've got some people here I'd like you to say hello to."

Banks recognized the stars right away. They crowded around while Wenzel stood rooted to the spot, steam coming out of his ears. "It's amazing that I didn't do something stupid," he said. "I was so pissed off I would gladly have killed Digger."

Although it may not seem that way, there are certain ethics that go with recruiting: honor among thieves. One of the unwritten rules is: Don't mess with a kid who has made a verbal commitment. Constant violation of that rule created the early signing date, which now allows players to sign a letter of intent during an eight-day period in November if they wish. Most players do sign then to take the pressure off. But in 1977, there was no early signing date and Digger Phelps was putting the club rush on Banks.

Wenzel felt helpless. But he knew if he panicked and let the situation become ugly, it could only hurt Duke. So he bided his time, waiting for Phelps to finish his pitch. The whole thing took five minutes. To Wenzel it seemed like hours. Phelps and company finally moved off. If Wenzel had heard Phelps's final words to Banks, he almost certainly would have blown his cool.

"The last thing he said to me," Banks remembered, "was, 'Sure Duke's a good school, Gene. But so are we. Choosing their basketball program over ours is like choosing a Volkswagen over a Cadillac.' The whole thing blew my mind. If he had pulled out a letter of intent right there, I was so intimidated by all those guys I might have signed it. I couldn't believe the whole thing." Neither could Wenzel. When Banks finally came over to him, he looked at him and said, "Gene, are you okay?"

Banks nodded. "I'm fine, Coach. But what about you? You look white as a sheet."

"I'll be okay on April 9th," Wenzel said.

On the morning of April 9th, Banks walked outside his house at 8 A.M. and put a letter of intent in his mailbox. Once he had gone back inside the house, Foster, sitting in his car down the street, drove up to the mailbox and pulled the envelope out. This had actually been planned, since all visits had been used up (Wenzel's contact in Washington had been legal because it had been at a game site) and Foster wanted the letter of intent in hand the moment it was legal. Foster ripped open the envelope and looked at the letter. At the bottom, Banks had signed his name. It was official. "Our roster looks a little bit better than yesterday," he said aloud.

Foster had been Duke's coach for three years. His record was 40–40. But the puzzle now had pieces. The worm had finally turned.

II

AMERICA'S TEAM

8

The Worm Turns

Banks was in Durham that summer, taking classes as part of a prepara-
tory program set up for marginal students. Dennard, who had practically lived at Duke the previous semester, was there too. So was Bender
and so was Harrell and some other former players. At night, they would
get together in the intramural building and play.

"I remember one thing about those games," Bender said. "Kenny
knocking Gene on his ass. It was his way of saying, 'Hey big shot, I can
play too.' Gene liked that. He respected Kenny for it."

He respected Dennard enough to get up, go to the other end of the
floor and knock Dennard flying. Neither one said a word. No one
squared off. It was just basketball. Right there, a bond started to build.

"I came in with something to prove, there's no doubt about it,"
Dennard said. "Everyone knew who Gene was. He was like a movie star
or something. He had been a superstar in the tenth grade when I was
still playing for a JV team. I wanted him to know right off that I wasn't
intimidated and that I could play."

That was apparent to Banks. And, it was just fine with him. "I knew
all about Jimmy [Spanarkel] and Mike [Gminski] when I decided to go
to Duke," he said. "But I had never heard of Kenny Dennard. The fact
that here was another freshman who could play and wanted to play,
that was fine with me. I lost two games in three years in high school.
I didn't want to come to college and play on a loser."

Night after night Banks and Dennard would play on opposing teams
in the I.M. building and go after one another. Watching this, the other
players could see a relationship developing.

"They both had an enthusiasm for the game that Duke teams just didn't have before," Bender said. "Jimmy was always the quiet leader, the guy who got it done by playing tough and hard. Mikey was quiet. I was a verbal player but not a physical one the way Gene and Kenny were. They just seemed to enjoy playing together right from the start."

Their backgrounds could not have been more different: Dennard, the white kid from rural North Carolina, and Banks, the black kid from Philadelphia. Their feeling for the game, however, was similar.

"Our differences were what made us click," Dennard said. "If we had been the same, then we would have been a threat to one another. But that was never the case. Gene was going to be the power forward. There wasn't any question about that and I had no desire to compete with him for that. He was going to be the star freshman and I understood that too. My competition was going to be Harold Morrison. I had a lot to prove to everyone. Gene had a lot to prove but it was different. He had to prove he was as good as he had been built up to be. I had to prove that I was good, period."

Dennard was a little taller, Banks a little heavier. Neither one was a great shooter, but both were excellent athletes who loved to run the floor, pound the boards and scream and yell when they did something good. They were freshmen coming into a program that needed not only their ability but their enthusiasm.

"They gave us a kind of leadership that year that was completely different than anything we had ever had," Lou Goetz said. "They could do things that might seem silly or childish and get away with it because they were freshmen. Spanarkel couldn't do what they did any more than they could do what he did."

By the time the other players came back to campus at the end of August, Banks and Dennard were already friends and partners in crime. Each learned quickly that in spite of the difference in their backgrounds, they shared two common interests: basketball and women. At eighteen, those two things are more than enough to build a friendship around.

The September pickup games that year were in Card Gym, the ancient edifice that was Duke's main gym until Cameron Indoor Stadium opened in 1938. Card is used now for physical education classes and for pickup basketball. But in September of 1977, a new floor was being put down in Cameron—a symbolic act if there ever was one—and that meant the varsity basketball players had to use Card for their afternoon games.

Preseason pickup games are as much a part of college basketball as the NCAA Tournament. Technically, coaches cannot require their players to do anything until practice begins on October 15. But preseason conditioning drills and the daily pickup games are as required as showing up for the first day of practice. If you can't play on a September afternoon, you better have a reason.

None of the Duke players had any desire to miss the games in Card. This was now Foster's team from top to bottom. Armstrong and Crow, the last players recruited during the Waters/McGeachy era, had graduated in May. Both would be difficult to replace. Armstrong had been an All-American before his injury and Crow had averaged 14 points and six rebounds a game as a senior.

—

Bell was the only senior on the team. Remarkably, he was the only senior associated with the team in any way. Kevin Hannon and Mary Kay Bass, both juniors, were the managers with the most seniority. Two years earlier, as a freshman, Bass had been the first female manager in the history of the ACC. Her success—or survival—had started a trend. The following year, ten women had tried out as managers—"some for reasons that had nothing to do with basketball," Bass said, smiling—and now Bass and sophomore Debbie Ridley were both very much a part of the team.

Bell began that September thinking he had a chance to hang on to his starting spot, at least at the start of the season. His thinking was simple: Bender would not be eligible until January, Harrell still hadn't proven himself in game situations, and he had moved past Gray at the end of the previous season.

As it turned out, Bell's playing time in his senior season would be limited. But it never affected his attitude. "I would have liked to have played forty minutes in every game," Bell said. "Heck, there isn't a player alive who doesn't feel that way. But I think all of us went into that season with only one concern and that was winning."

Bell's attitude and that of the non-Spanarkel juniors—Morrison, Goetsch, Gray, and Hardy—would be critical as the season evolved. Cameron Hall was still with the team when the season began but by the end of the first semester his bad back and limited playing time moved him to decide to leave and focus on academics. It was clear to him that his future did not lie in basketball, so he wanted to devote his time to things that were going to matter to him after college.

The other juniors, like Bell, were all looking to prove something. Morrison thought of the small forward spot as his. But when he saw Dennard in the September pickup games, he knew he would have to fight for that spot. Their rivalry throughout the six-week prepractice period was heated.

To his credit, Gray had not let his disastrous sophomore season destroy him. He had worked out all summer and was in the best shape of his life. With Armstrong gone he thought he had a chance to beat Harrell and Bender out for the starting point guard spot and he played that way throughout preseason.

Scott Goetsch had been perhaps the most improved player on the team. He had gone from a player incapable of dealing with ACC competition as a freshman to a credible backup center as a sophomore. He had been productive coming off the bench and wanted to build on that by earning more playing time in his junior year.

Hardy was thrilled to be part of the team, regardless of his role. Of the three walk-ons added to the team the previous year, he had emerged as the one who fit into the team the best. He had boundless energy, loved to play anywhere, anytime, and was always around for a game of one-on-one, two-on-two, or any other type of competition. He was the team's unofficial cheerleader, the guy always up, always yelling. His teammates imitated him by cupping their hands together and yelling, *"Block-out!"* since Hardy was perpetually yelling those two words whenever the other team was on the free throw line.

The only person guaranteed to start in the junior and senior classes was, of course, Spanarkel. He had become a genuine star during the post-Armstrong period of the '77 season and there was no question that he would be the captain of this team. That was no knock on Bell. Bell was very much a *part* of the team, but Spanarkel was the leader. He was not one of those leaders who screams and yells at people, but he was someone whose message came across loud and clear every day.

Jim Suddath, the 6-6 Georgia freshman who, of the three freshmen, would receive the least attention as the season wore on, remembers failing to dive for a loose ball during one of the early pickup games. "Jimmy just grabbed me a couple seconds later and, without raising his voice at all, said, 'Don't ever let Coach Foster catch you not going after a loose ball in practice. Not ever.' He said Coach Foster because I don't think he wanted me to think he was acting like a big shot but I think he meant himself. He just couldn't stand not seeing anyone work hard."

Spanarkel's work ethic would be important to this team. He had been brought up to believe that hustle was something that anyone could do, regardless of talent level. Then, during his first two years at Duke, he had seen how much individual work could pay off by watching Armstrong.

"I learned a lot from watching Tate," he said. "When I was in high school, I was always looking for a game. All I wanted to do was get some guys and play. Compete. All the time. But Tate taught me that if you shoot one hundred free throws every day, you'll become a better free throw shooter. If you work on going left for thirty minutes a day, you'll be better going left. You didn't need coaches or other players around to work on those things. You could do it yourself.

"I saw the way he would schedule his classes so that he always had a break in the morning to get over to the gym to work out on his own. I started doing that too. By the time I was a junior, Rob [Hardy] used to come over almost every day too and we would play full-court, working on our conditioning but also on our one-on-one moves."

Spanarkel was also the player with the best relationship with Foster. To some, Foster was hard to fathom. They all appreciated his sense of humor and understood how badly he wanted to win. He was loyal and he cared about all his players. But some of them, especially the junior nonstarters, had trouble really opening up with him. They were more inclined to go to Goetz with a problem than to Foster.

Spanarkel never had this problem—he and Foster had hit it off from day one. Now, after two years, Spanarkel probably understood what Foster wanted from the team on a day-to-day basis better than anyone. And that understanding was important because, in his quiet way, Spanarkel could always let his teammates know what *he* wanted from them.

There were three sophomores, but only Gminski had played in a Duke uniform. He had ended up averaging 15 points and almost 11 rebounds a game as a freshman and had answered all of those who had doubted whether he could make the early transition to college. Now, he was an established star. In fact, he and Spanarkel were the only returning starters. Morrison had started the entire second half of the season but that had been at power forward, a spot that now clearly belonged to Banks.

The other sophomores were the two transfer point guards, Harrell and Bender. Harrell was very much a contender to start. He would give the team a dimension of quickness it had never had before. Everyone knew about his quickness. What would be a revelation would be his steadiness. Johnny Gun simply did not turn the ball over.

Bender did turn it over because he was more of a risk-taker. He would go for the spectacular pass, Harrell wouldn't. "The interesting thing about Harrell and Bender was that they belied the black-white guard stereotypes," Goetz said. "Harrell was the 'white' guard. He took care of the ball, didn't take chances, and only shot the ball when he was open. Bender was the 'black' guard. He was always looking for the fast break and would force things sometimes."

They would end up being an excellent combination at the point guard spot once Bender became eligible. But during those September games the feeling was that Harrell and Gray would be first semester caretakers at the point until Bender was ready to step in and claim the position that had been his since the day he made the decision to transfer to Duke.

Of course, there were also the freshmen: Banks, Dennard, and Suddath. Perhaps never in history has a freshman class contained three people so wildly different than these three. Each was—and is—a major personality in his own way.

Banks was a living legend from the first day he set foot on campus. "The first time I met him, it was like meeting a movie star," Gminski remembered. "We all wanted to see what he was going to be like. But we were also all a little bit in awe of him."

Of all the memories the players have of that season, one that is most vivid is Banks during the preseason pickup games. "It was like being in the presence of a god," Bender said. "First of all, he had this body that was chiseled from stone. I mean the guy had never lifted a weight in his life and he was Adonis. Then when we started playing, he was just amazing. He never said anything, because he still wasn't comfortable with the rest of us yet. But he was as gifted a basketball player as I've ever been around."

Banks didn't stay quiet for long. He became a major personality on the team, often in tandem with Dennard, but also on his own. His teammates marveled at his ability to charm the socks off almost anyone: the coaches, the media and, most definitely, women. Eventually Foster would go out and buy a can labeled "bullshit repellant" that he would keep in his drawer, always ready for Banks.

There was one other trait Banks had that would become very much a part of his character. That was his ability to pass gas. Anywhere, anytime, Banks could clear out a room. His teammates took great pleasure in this—and quickly changed Banks's nickname from Tink to Stink.

When Spanarkel and Morrison discovered that milk often played a role in Banks's unusual talent, they sat him down for a serious talk. By this time, Banks had worked his way through a large percentage of the female population of North Carolina and showed no sign of slowing down. Spanarkel and Morrison decided it was time for a talk with the freshman.

"You know, Gene," Spanarkel said one day, "we all only have a certain amount of semen in our bodies. If you have sex *all* the time, eventually you may run out of semen."

Banks went a little bit wide-eyed at this. Morrison was right behind Spanarkel. "But there is one thing, isn't there, Jimmy? If you drink a lot of milk, that will replenish your semen supply and you won't have a problem."

Spanarkel nodded his head vigorously. "Yeah, I think they've done studies on that, H. That's true. Lots of milk."

For all his worldliness, Banks was, after all, just eighteen and he *was* in the hands of two of the great deadpan artists of the twentieth century. For weeks after that, Banks would load his tray up at lunch and dinner with three and four glasses of milk. And, inevitably, he would send his teammates scurrying for cover in the locker room.

Dennard was the wild man of the group. He would say anything, do anything, try anything. To Dennard, college was a great adventure and he didn't plan to miss a minute of it. He had untamed curly hair and an equally untamed sense of humor. Dennard was as obvious as Spanarkel and Morrison were subtle.

But he loved to play basketball and he loved to play hard and that earned him the respect of the other players. "Kenny could screw around and screw around but when it was time to go on the court and do his work, he did it," Spanarkel said. "That was all we cared about. What he did the rest of the time was okay with the rest of us as long as he worked hard. And no one ever worked harder than Kenny. We knew he was crazy but we were *all* a little bit crazy. Kenny was just more up front about it than the rest of us."

Dennard's roommate was Suddath, one of the most extraordinary matchups in sports history. "Those two being roommates was God proving that he has a sense of humor," Gminski said, years later.

Suddath was a born-again Christian, someone whose faith was the most important thing in his life. This was not, by any means, a passing phase—in June of 1989, after three years in the seminary, he was ordained as a minister.

"The first day I got to campus, Coach Foster called me in and told me I was going to be rooming with Dennard," Suddath said. "He said he was putting us together because both our fathers had gone to Georgia Tech. I'm not sure whether he was joking or not."

Foster was joking . . . sort of. There were a couple of reasons he wanted to put Dennard and Suddath together. One was simple: Banks had a single and Dennard and Suddath were the other two freshmen. Beyond that, though, Foster hoped that some of Suddath would rub off on Dennard.

It didn't. But their time together as roommates was the stuff legends are made of. Each still has warm memories of the other; as different as they were, they would often stay up well into the night talking—and arguing—about life.

"To this day Kenny's one of the brightest people I've ever come in contact with," Suddath said. "He was someone you *had* to listen to and he was *worth* listening to. It was just that we didn't agree on very much."

Dennard says the same thing. But this is twelve years later. Then, the room they shared often seemed quite small. Dennard would come in at all hours of the night, often loud, sometimes drunk, but always happy. Suddath had never met anyone like Dennard and didn't quite know what to make of him. Dennard had never met anyone like Suddath and had no idea what to make of him.

One story, the one that is told every time their teammates get together, sums up the Dennard-Suddath relationship. Dennard tells it this way:

"I was out one night with a bunch of people and we all started drinking gin and tonics. I'm not sure why, but we did. I'd never had them in my life. I'd always been a beer drinker. Anyway, I end up in deep conversation with this girl who was sort of, you know, the welcome wagon for athletes at Duke.

"After a while we're pretty drunk and we decide to go back to the room. We walk in and Sudds is asleep with the pillow over his head— that was the way he always slept. So we get into bed and we're going at it the way you do when you're in college and after a while she looks up at me and says, 'You ought to bottle it and sell it.'

"Well, you know, I'm just kind of having a good time. I think I may have yelled something like, 'God, college is the greatest!' at some point but through it all Sudds never moves. At least I didn't notice if he did. Finally, we're finished and we kind of roll over and go to sleep. A few minutes later, Sudds pulls the pillow off his head and starts yelling, 'Get her out! Get her out! Right now, get her out!'

"I'm very groggy at this point but I say, 'Okay, okay, calm down.' I get her up, walk her back to her dorm and come back. Jimmy's still up. So I say to him, 'Sudds, how much of that were you awake for?'

And he looks at me and says, 'Let's put it this way, I don't think you'd have much luck selling it.' "

The Dennard-Suddath relationship was, in some ways, a microcosm of this basketball team. They were about as diverse a group as could be found in a room with only twelve people. It was a team full of nicknames: Mikey and Johnny Gun; H and Charlie Manson; Fonz (Goetsch) and Juice. Dennard and Banks each had two nicknames. Dennard was Dirt for his playing style and Dog for his social style. Banks, of course, was Tink and Stink.

They came from New Jersey, North Carolina, California, and Kentucky. And from Pennsylvania, Georgia, and Connecticut. They came from the inner city and from farms. They were the sons of lawyers and coaches and clerks. Three were only children; one was the youngest of four brothers who all grew to be at least 6-5.

Even the coaching staff represented a cross-section of characters: Foster, the only child from outside Philadelphia; Goetz, the Jewish kid from Jersey; Wenzel, the second of six kids from a middle class Long Island Catholic family; and Jones, the little fighter whose parents had been told he probably wouldn't live to be twelve because he was born with two holes in his heart.

The case can certainly be made that any locker room is full of diverse personalities and backgrounds, but this one had both character and characters. Bob Bender, one of the five new players in the mix that year, may have explained it best:

"We were not a team that hung out together all the time. It wasn't as if every night when practice was over we all went and ate together. In those days we didn't have training meals except on game days. We didn't have an athletic dorm. We lived all over the place and we all had friends away from basketball. I hung out with Juice and Rob a lot, Gene and Kenny spent time together, and Steve and Harold, but most of us would probably have named a non-basketball player as his best friend. That was one of the things about Duke. The team was important but it wasn't *all* that was important.

"And yet, when we walked into the locker room, we were everything a team should be. There was, without question, a closeness and a camaraderie. A lot of it had to do with humor. We always enjoyed getting on each other. Our game-day meals were nonstop rip sessions and everyone was included and everyone got ripped. If you had put us into a computer, the thing probably would have tilted. It just wouldn't have worked. But it did. That year there was a feeling we all had that still exists today. It's never gone away."

It began, according to everyone involved, with those pickup games in old Card Gym. Banks and Dennard began to develop a feel for each other's game. Everyone recognized that Spanarkel was now the leader and Gminski was a force to be reckoned with. Harrell, Bender, Gray, and Bell dueled one another each afternoon, looking for an edge.

"We became a team during those games," Bender said. "Remember, we had five new guys. But each day we went out there and learned something about each other. We began trying things: lob passes, different ways of running the break. A lot of it was stuff you'd never use in a game but it was still fun to try. And it was fun to see how good we were. I think it was obvious to all of us that we were pretty good."

Goetsch, who was fighting for playing time even then, remembers thinking, "This is not a team that will be easy for anyone to beat. It's easy to look good in practice, everyone knows that," he said. "But it didn't take a genius to know that this team had talent on another level from where we had been before."

It was anticipation of that new level that packed Cameron Indoor Stadium on October 15. The first day of practice fell on a Saturday; Foster scheduled a scrimmage to follow the football game. But by the end of the third quarter, with Duke taking yet another shellacking on a rainy afternoon, Cameron was almost packed, everyone wanting to see the new Blue Devils. When they walked onto the court the ovation was such that it was easy to forget that this was the same school that just four years earlier had started practice without a head coach.

Now, the head coach stood in the packed gym, looked at the team he would put on the floor and almost smiled. "We've worked a long time to put this group together," Foster told his coaches. "Let's make sure we keep them working to reach their potential."

Two hundred and seventy-three college basketball teams began practice that day, each of them aware to some degree that March 27 and

St. Louis were the date and the city they were all pointing for. At Duke, even with all the excitement surrounding the arrival of Banks, St. Louis was nothing more than fantasy. Reality was 20 victories and a trip to the NIT. That would be a successful season. No one in Cameron that day—*no one*—had any idea where the journey that was about to begin would take this team.

9

Slow Progress

On that first day of practice, the most disappointed person in Cameron was probably Harold Morrison. Because when Foster divided the team into white (first) and blue (second) teams, Dennard was with the white team.

It is against NCAA rules for coaches to watch their players work out before October 15, but this is a universally ignored rule. The coaches were aware of Dennard's athletic ability, his meshing with Banks and his enthusiasm; they had decided to give him the first shot at starting opposite his new friend. Morrison was, to say the least, unhappy.

"I felt as if their minds were already made up," he said. "I didn't mind competing for the job. That was okay with me. But I felt like I was the junior and if you had to start one of us with the white team just to get things going, it should be me. When they put Kenny with the white team right away it told me they had already made a decision."

In truth, they probably had. Dennard could have played his way out of the lineup or Morrison might have played his way in but if the status remained quo, Dennard would start. Early on that first day, Dennard took a couple of quick shots and Foster called him over for a chat.

"Kenny, look out on that court, what do you see?" he asked rhetorically. "You see Jim Spanarkel, Mike Gminski, and Gene Banks, right? They're going to score sixty points a game. I don't need you to score another twenty. I need you on the floor, taking charges, diving for loose balls. Understand?"

Dennard understood. He took more dives the rest of that afternoon than a boxer on the take. He gave Foster exactly what he was looking for and the chemistry between himself and Banks was apparent. To anyone watching that day it was apparent that Foster was going to start two freshman forwards, something almost unheard of in the ACC.

"I think one of the strengths of that team, especially in the preseason, was that everyone felt he had something to prove," Foster said. "Jimmy and Mike were the stars but they had been stars on a lousy team. They wanted to change that. Everyone else was trying to prove he could play in the ACC, including Gene. We got very lucky with him. A lot of guys with his reputation would not have taken the approach he took."

The approach Banks took was to let his play do the talking for him. He didn't want to show up Spanarkel or Gminski and he wanted very much to be liked and accepted by his teammates. The ego was there and everyone recognized and accepted it. But it was overshadowed by a burning desire to be part of a winner.

Wanting to win, to shed the losing image that had become as much a part of Duke as The Chapel, was the driving force for this team. Every day in practice was a war, everyone trying to prove himself. The first game was an exhibition against a Canadian team, St. Francis. The game meant nothing and the competition would be minimal but Cameron was packed and the team was more than ready to play after five weeks of practicing against only each other.

"I still remember Gene and Kenny grabbing each other in the locker room just before we went out and saying, 'Let's go, this is it,' " Goetsch said. "I remember thinking that was nice that we hadn't played a game yet and these two guys had a real feeling for one another. We just hadn't had that kind of feeling before."

Everyone has a memory of that night it seems. The game was a rout—122-79—but that didn't matter. Sitting upstairs in the Cameron end zone, Shirley Foster can still see Banks, Dennard and Harrell running the fast break, Harrell in the middle, the two freshman on the wings, and feeling as if she was seeing the game played on a different level than before. "I looked down and saw this and it was like something out of a dream," she said. "It was just so perfect. We could do things we had never done before."

The first two games of the regular season were almost as one-sided, not surprising since they were against Division 3 teams. Then came a cold dose of reality, a 79-66 loss to North Carolina in the opening round of the Big Four. The Tar Heels had played in the national championship game the previous season and with Phil Ford, Mike O'Koren, and Tom Zaligiaris they were a mature, tested basketball team.

The loss brought everyone back to earth a little bit. But the next night, trailing a good Wake Forest team by 15 points in the second half, the Blue Devils suddenly caught fire and wound up romping to a 97–84 victory. This was worth noting not only because it was a victory but because it was a decisive, come-from-behind victory against a very good team. It takes talent to do that.

In the ACC, the word went out: This was a new Duke team. Banks was averaging 17 points a game in the early going and that was no surprise. But Dennard was averaging 12. That was a surprise. Robert Noell, a sportswriter in Winston-Salem who had seen Dennard play in high school, had bet a friend one hundred dollars that Dennard would not score one hundred points during his college *career.* In four games, he had 47. Noell would lose his bet within ten games.

Dennard and Banks were already becoming folk heroes in North Carolina. Before the St. Francis game, Dennard was introduced first; when Banks came out after him the two of them bear-hugged so hard the building vibrated. The crowd went wild and, from that day forth, that became the Dennard-Banks signature, the pregame hug, complete with shared primal screams. They did it every game they played together for four years.

"It was never a planned thing," Dennard said. "If it had been it probably wouldn't have worked. What happened was that in practice when we would get psyched Gene and I would slap each other five. He would slap my hand so damn hard my hand would get sore. So, that first game when I saw him coming out I thought, 'He's going to slap my hand so hard I'm not going to be able to play.' So, I threw my arms open and he ran into them and we hugged and everybody thought it was great. So we just kept doing it. We never once talked about it. We just did it."

This was before the era of the choreographed high-five, low-five, elbow-five. This was pure spontaneity, two freshmen having a good time, and people understood that. They loved it. Only later would people talk about the fact that one player was black and the other one white.

But even though the ACC was quickly becoming aware of Duke's new prowess, the rest of the country knew little about what was going on. A victory over Wake Forest, while an upset at the time, did not exactly set off screaming headlines. Again, timing was important here.

This was a year before ESPN began to make college basketball a nightly event in homes across the country. Nationally televised games were few and far between. It was also a year before the epic Larry Bird–Magic Johnson national championship confrontation that once and for all catapulted college basketball into the national consciousness.

Today, Duke would be on ESPN four times before the end of December and Dick Vitale would be screeching about Dennard and Banks, Gminski and Spanarkel. *USA Today* would do a cover story on Foster and *Sports Illustrated* would not be far behind. But this was a gentler time in college basketball and the Blue Devils were allowed to evolve.

"I don't think we could have become what we became then if we had been playing today," Dennard said. "This is the satellite, fast-food generation. Immediacy is everything. Half the media in the world would have covered Gene Banks' first college game if it had been in 1987 instead of 1977. We had a chance to develop, to grow up in peace and not start to think we were good before we *were* good. We were talented from the start but we didn't really become good until February. By then, we were ready to handle it. In December or even January, we weren't ready."

That they weren't ready was evident when they went to Southern California and fell behind a good, but certainly not great, USC team by 18 points. A furious comeback tied the game and on the final play of regulation Gminski drove to the basket and got hammered. There was no call, the game went into overtime, and the Trojans won, 87–81. Later that week, the commissioner of the Pacific 8 (now the Pac-10) would write Foster apologizing for the officiating. But that wasn't going to change the result and Foster did his first Wild Bill routine of the season in the locker room.

Tom Mickle, the sports information director, was standing outside the locker room with his new assistant, Johnny Moore, when a USC official came up and told him it was time for Foster to come to the interview room. Mickle knew damn well that Foster was several thrown chairs away from being ready to go to the interview room. "I think he needs a few more minutes," he said.

"We need him now," the USC man said.

Moore, eager to please his new boss, chimed in at this point. "Tom, I'll go in and get him."

Mickle, knowing a baptism of fire when he saw one, smiled. "Fine, Johnny, go on and get him," he said.

Moore got one step inside the door and had to duck a flying stool. He walked out the door, looked at the USC man and said, "Like Tom said, it'll be a few more minutes."

■

Three days after the Southern Cal game, the team was back home to play another walkover game against the University of Chicago. The players had gathered in the student union for pregame meal. This was the seventh game of the season and the pregame meals had become major rip sessions by now, with Morrison and Spanarkel in charge.

At home, the meals were prepared by a very sweet, elderly woman named Margot who looked upon the players as her children. She always checked to make sure everyone liked the food. One night she had prepared tacos for everyone. Midway through the meal, Bell had to excuse himself to go to the bathroom. While he was away, Spanarkel and Morrison did their work, loading up the inside of Bell's taco with hot sauce. They then told Margot that Bruce had commented on how much he liked the tacos. When Bell returned, he took one bite and broke into a cold sweat. Just then Margot came by and said, "How's your taco, Bruce?" Near death, Bell managed to croak, "It's great, Margot, thanks."

As soon as Margot exited, the entire team, which had been holding back its laughter collectively, broke up. "God-dang, guys," Bell said. "They almost killed me."

It had now become a tradition at the pregame meal that when a player thought he had a good joke to tell, he would clank his spoon against a glass to get everyone's attention, yelling, "joke, joke, joke," as he did. Everyone would get quiet and the joke would be told. If it wasn't funny, the joker had better be ready to duck. The coaches never came to these sessions at home so there was no telling what would happen during the course of a simple meal.

On this particular evening, before the Chicago game, the jokes were flying in all directions. When it was Banks's turn, he grabbed his spoon, banged it against his glass and yelled, "joke, joke, joke." But as he finished, Banks looked up and saw his teammates looking stunningly somber. He turned around and standing behind him was Foster, who had walked in unannounced to say a few words to his team, which he assumed was as distraught as he was about the loss to Southern Cal.

All eyes were on Foster, who was not smiling in anticipation of the joke Banks was about to tell. "Joke?" Foster said. "You want a joke?

I'll tell you a joke. Goddamn Southern California! That was a joke, alright!"

With that he turned on his heel and walked out. There was a moment of shocked silence, then uncontrollable laughter. Banks never did tell his joke but from that day forward the first time someone dinged a glass to tell a joke in pregame meal, the rest of the team would yell, "Joke? I'll tell you a joke. Goddamn Southern California!"

They easily beat Chicago on the night of Banks's "joke," and rolled to an 8–2 record in their pre-ACC games. There was nothing surprising in any of this. The competition wasn't overwhelming and, after all, Foster's December records in the past had been 7–2, 6–3 and 9–1.

The first real test would come at Maryland, a place where Duke hadn't won since 1970—Lefty Driesell and Bucky Waters's first seasons at Maryland and Duke. Driesell had gone on from there to build Maryland into a formidable power; not "The UCLA of the East," as he had promised upon taking the job, but certainly one of the top dozen programs in the country.

In 1977 he had a team a lot like Duke's: young but still looking to find out how good it was. Albert King, Banks's New York counterpart, had landed at Maryland after a recruiting circus that made what Banks had been through look tame. Like Banks, King had two talented classmates, Greg Manning and Ernest Graham. And, as always, Driesell had several strong, hard-nosed players up front and a couple of lightning-quick guards in Billy Bryant and Jo Jo Hunter, the latter having dominated the Blue Devils in both games between the teams in 1977.

It was Hunter's play the season before that led Foster to make his first critical decision of the season. For the first ten games, Gray had been the starting point guard. The coaches had gone with Gray for several reasons: he had played well in preseason practice, they were hoping he would regain his shattered confidence by playing and they wanted Harrell to work his way into the lineup gradually.

Bender would be eligible when second semester started but that would come after the first two ACC games—at Maryland and at N.C. State. Foster didn't want to throw him into the starting lineup from day one because he knew Bender's every move would be chronicled almost as closely as Banks's had been.

Going to Maryland, though, the coaches felt they needed Harrell to play a major role if they were to win the game. Harrell had been waiting for this chance since he first arrived at Duke. He had been amazed during the early days of his transfer year at how easily he could handle defensive pressure from his new teammates. "To tell you the truth, it was a piece of cake," he said. "I expected it to be tougher. I knew I could help them if they just let me."

Harrell found the preseason baffling. He thought he should be the starter ahead of Gray and he wasn't. "And yet, when they finally made the change, there really wasn't any reason for it. They [Foster] just came to me the afternoon of the game and said, 'John, you're starting against Maryland tonight.' "

It wasn't quite that simple. Two nights earlier against Virginia Tech, Gray had gotten in foul trouble and Harrell had played a lot of minutes. Ironically, Virginia Tech's point guard was Marshall Ashford, whom Harrell had played against since the seventh grade. "I knew I could handle him, so I felt very free and easy all night," Harrell said.

Whether the move made sense to Harrell or not, he really didn't care. He called home and told his parents to be sure and watch on TV that night because he was going to start. "It surprised me because I thought they were going to go with Steve until Bob was eligible and then give the job to him," Harrell said. "I was surprised when Bill came to the room and said I was starting."

One factor that Harrell was unaware of at the time was Spanarkel. Almost from the day Harrell arrived, Spanarkel had felt he could give Duke an element of speed it had always lacked and whenever he had a chance, he would mention this to Foster. The decision to make the change was a consensus among the coaches but Spanarkel's input was undoubtedly a factor.

Cole Field House on the night of January 4, 1978, was packed to the rafters. Maryland was 9–1 and this was the ACC debut for both King and Banks. Maryland was favored but everyone knew this was a different Duke team from the one that the Terrapins had brushed aside in this grand old building for seven straight seasons.

The beginning of the game hardly seemed different from the recent past. Maryland blew to an 8–0 lead, the last two of those points coming when Billy Bryant, running the right wing on the fast break, took a pass from Hunter and *slammed* the ball right in Banks's face. The place went crazy, Foster had to call a quick time-out, and it looked like business as usual in Cole.

It wasn't, though. Calmly, the Blue Devils came back. Spanarkel ran so many backdoor cuts on the overplaying Maryland defense, it began to look like a broken television tape that kept running the same play over and over again. Gminski took over the inside and Duke's defense began to force Maryland into bad shots. Duke took the lead for good with ten minutes left on—what else—a Spanarkel backdoor cut. The lead built to 10 and Maryland went to pressure defense, waiting for Duke to self-destruct the way it had in Cameron a year earlier.

Not this time. From that point on it was the Johnny Gun and Spanky show, the two Duke guards playing keepaway from the Terrapins. Sitting on the bench, manager Kevin Hannon, who had charted every game in his three seasons at Duke, knew he was seeing something new. "The last five minutes of that game made me realize we had something special going here," he said. "In the old days, we would have been panicked, just trying to hang on, hoping not to turn it over too quickly. Now, there was no doubt about what was going to happen. We just got the ball to Johnny and he did the rest. He wasn't going to turn it over. That was obvious. Not only could he handle the ball, he *wanted* the ball."

The final was 88–78 Duke, and the shocked crowd was heading for the exits before it was over. Spanarkel finished with 33 points and 9 assists. Gminski had 19 points and 13 rebounds. Harrell only had four points but he had eight assists and just one turnover. They had beaten Maryland *at* Maryland and they had done it easily. This was a watershed victory.

"One win does not a season make," Foster told the press. But he couldn't resist a grin. "Shakespeare said that, right?"

Shakespeare might have had some things to say about this victory— it was so sweet that poetry was appropriate. Maryland had inflicted the two most painful defeats of the Foster regime—the ACC Tournament game in 1976 and the pass-off-the-rim game of 1977. At last, some of that pain had been alleviated.

Not surprisingly, the young team overreacted to this victory. Instead of heeding Foster's—or was it Shakespeare's?—words, they spent the next couple of days thinking they were God's new gift to college basketball. When they went into N.C. State and quickly led 19–12 they were convinced of it. State quickly divested them of that notion. In the last thirty minutes of the game the Wolfpack outscored the Blue Devils by a 62–31 margin. The final was 74–50, the kind of loss that hadn't happened even in the darkest days of Foster's first couple of years.

Glen Sudhop, a gawky 7-2 center who wasn't fit to carry Gminski's schoolbooks, completely outplayed him. Spanarkel and Gminski, who had combined for 52 points against Maryland, had 6 apiece. Only

Harrell, with 12 points and 6 assists, played anything approaching decent basketball.

Wild Bill was back after this one. Bender, standing outside the locker room, remembers hearing the shouting and the crashing chairs. When Spanarkel came out he looked at Bender and said, "We can never let that happen again." Bender, who would play his first game two nights later against Lehigh, knew Spanarkel was right. He also knew it would be almost impossible to play that poorly again.

Looking back, the coaches agree that that loss and the thoroughness of it helped in the long run. "After Maryland, I think we all felt a little invincible," Wenzel said. "Which was, of course, ridiculous. We were still a team going into ACC play with two freshman forwards, a sophomore center and two point guards with almost zero ACC experience. We had one good win and got cocky." After State, it would be a while before anyone got cocky again.

In fact, over the next seven days, Duke played the best basketball seen at the school since Bubas had retired. It started with, as was expected, a rout of Lehigh. Bender made his long-awaited debut almost fifteen months after transferring, coming off the bench to spell Harrell. He scored seven points and heard wild shrieks every time he did something positive.

The only person not caught up in Bender-mania was Gray, who, in keeping with the kind of luck that dogged him throughout his career, had broken a bone in his foot against N.C. State. "That made it easy for them," Gray said, looking back. "I wasn't playing badly, but I wasn't playing so well that I would be missed. I went down, Bob came in, and by the time I was ready to play again [five games later] I had been phased out."

Gray might have been phased out even if he had not been injured. He never once got a break (except in his foot) at Duke. He was talented enough and worked hard enough that one big game or even one big play might have turned him around and made him into an effective player. But it never happened for him. During the rest of his junior year and throughout his senior year he was, without question, the unhappiest player on the team.

"In a lot of ways, I wish I had had the guts to just walk away from it, the way Cameron Hall did," Gray said. "He knew he wasn't going to play and he didn't want to deal with the frustration of just watching, so he just said, 'enough,' and left. I've often wondered if I should have done that. But I had too much pride to give up. I kept thinking I could somehow turn it back around. But I never did."

Goetz, who recruited Gray and saw greatness in him, still shakes his head when he thinks about him. "Every coach has players who don't make it for reasons you can't explain," Goetz said. "That doesn't make it any easier to deal with. No one ever worked harder on his basketball than Steve Gray. Guys hated to play against him in practice because he was tough and talented. He made the other guys better because he was such a worker in practice. But in the games. . . ."

The games now belonged to Harrell and Bender and they quickly became an effective combination. Harrell provided steadiness, Bender pizzazz. They were full of confidence and eagerness and glad to share time. Harrell, thinking the job would be turned over to Bender, was delighted to see the starting job was still his. Bender had no problem coming off the bench because he had never been a starter in college and he knew that Harrell's play had earned him the starting spot.

After the Lehigh victory, Duke traveled to Clemson, another place that had been full of misery in recent years. Here, they put on a forty-minute clinic, blowing the Tigers out 107–85, breaking the record for points scored by a visiting team in Littlejohn Coliseum. Even with the N.C. State debacle in between, the fact remained that Duke had won two ACC road games in eight days—after winning only one ACC road game in the six previous seasons.

And then, three days later, on January 14, Carolina came to Cameron.

It is not easy to explain the unique nature of the Duke-North Carolina rivalry. The two schools are located eight miles apart. One is a large public school, the other a small private school. Both pride themselves on academics. Their students often share the same bars—most of them in Chapel Hill, a quintessential college town—and their alumni share the same offices and neighborhoods, although there are more Carolina alumni in the state of North Carolina than there are Duke alumni in the world.

Because a majority of Carolina's students come from in-state and a majority of Duke's students from out-of-state, their backgrounds are very different. Carolina people tend to see Duke as a Yankee school while Duke people often look at Carolina as a grit school. Neither assessment is entirely accurate or inaccurate. Duke certainly has a lot of southerners; Carolina a lot of northerners.

The rivalry is different from many of the heated college rivalries in sports because of two things: geography and respect. Even though it has boomed in recent years, the Durham-Chapel Hill corridor is still, essentially, a small town where, in daily life, it is almost impossible not to run into people with ties to one of the two schools. It is not like Los Angeles, a huge city where graduates of UCLA and USC might never cross paths except at a game. It is not like Michigan and Ohio State, which are several hundred miles apart, or even South Carolina and Clemson, whose alumni are spread out over an entire state.

Duke and Carolina alumni live together on a daily basis year-round. There is no hatred in this rivalry. Intensity, yes; hatred, no. Duke people can't stand losing to Carolina—and vice versa—for the simple reason that they know they must face the victors the next morning.

Being from Duke during the 1970s was not an easy thing. Duke won the annual football game exactly once (1973), and from 1974 through 1977 it won one of ten basketball games. Even in Cameron, where the Blue Devils had once been so dominant, Carolina won five straight times beginning in 1973. While Duke was becoming a marshmallow in basketball, Carolina, under Dean Smith, had become a juggernaut.

To go through a losing cycle, especially at a place as proud of its tradition as Duke, is difficult. To go through it at a time when your most heated rival is near its zenith is worse, much worse. The most painful thing about that period in the mid-'70s for Duke people was that the rivalry with Carolina was so one-sided it ceased being that big a deal to the Tar Heels. N.C. State, going through the David Thompson era, became UNC's number one rival. Duke was just a team the Tar Heels flicked away a couple of times a year, like a gnat. Duke could be annoying at times but it wasn't really a threat.

To Duke people this was galling. Losing to the Tar Heels was bad enough. Knowing that, at Carolina, winning those games wasn't even considered worthy of celebration, was awful.

Miraculously, Foster had won his first encounter with Smith, the Big Four overtime game in 1974. But since then the Tar Heels had won eight straight, including the victory in the Big Four in November. Some of those losses had been agonizing; some of them quite thorough. Now, the Tar Heels came into Cameron on a snowy Saturday afternoon ranked No. 2 in the nation.

Even in the days when the program was at its nadir, Cameron was packed when Carolina made the drive up Rte. 15–501 to play Duke. This time, the students camped out for two days before the game to make sure they got the best seats; by the time game day rolled around the campus was hopping. "I still remember the feeling," Bender said. "It was like this was our time. But we knew we still had to go out and do it."

They did. Gminski was fabulous, with 29 points and 10 rebounds. Spanarkel was himself with 23 and Banks had 15. Bender added 11 off the bench and Dennard, even though he only scored 7 points, was everywhere, diving and scratching at anything and everything that moved. Duke blew open a close game in the last five minutes and cruised to a 92–84 victory. For everyone in the program, from the alumni upstairs, to the students downstairs, to the coaches on the bench and the players on the court, this was a cathartic moment.

"I remember standing on the foul line with a few seconds to go and it was over, we were going to win," Gminski said. "The noise was like nothing I've ever heard in my life. I really thought the whole building was shaking. It was unbelievable. I don't think I'll ever forget that."

No one in the building will forget that afternoon. On the cover of the postseason media guide that Tom Mickle put together that March, there is a picture that says everything that need be said about that game. The buzzer has just sounded. Foster, usually so low-key in victory, is off the bench, his arms over his head, leaping for joy. To his right, Bender is lying on the floor, feet up in the air, shaking his fists. Just behind Bender, head down, is Smith, walking down to try to shake hands with Foster, refusing to look up into the crowd. Behind them, the entire crowd is standing, arms raised in the air just like Foster, everyone screaming for joy.

You aren't supposed to go bananas over a victory in January, but when it is one over an archrival that has not been beaten at home since the school's current senior class were high school sophomores, you celebrate. "Bill, I tried to shake your hand after the game but you were jumping up and down so much I didn't get the chance," Smith said in the postgame press conference.

This was a classic Smith swipe. What he meant was, "You see what a big deal it is for you to beat me, even once?" He was absolutely right, though. At this juncture, it was about as big a deal as you could find.

"That game established in our minds the idea that we were good enough to play with anyone," Dennard said. "I don't think we had thought in those terms before. Carolina was ranked second. Maybe they were overrated, but we didn't know that. Sure, we were playing at home but it isn't like playing at home had helped us against them before. After that, our feeling was that if someone was going to beat us, they were going to have to be damn good."

The next two games were victories over Wake Forest at home and LaSalle in Philadelphia, a homecoming for Banks in which he had 24 points and 13 rebounds. The Blue Devils were 14–3 and, for the first time since 1971, they were in the Top Twenty, ranked 11th.

Roles were now clearly established. The leaders were Spanarkel and Banks, each in a completely different way. Spanarkel had blossomed into one of the best all-around players in the country, someone who went out every night and scored, rebounded, passed, and played defense. Foster had even invented a new verb in his honor: Spanarkeling. When you were Spanarkeling on a basketball court you were doing everything. A Duke player could not be paid a higher compliment than to have Foster say he had been Spanarkeling.

While Spanarkel was the rock, Banks was the glitz, the guy whose every act needed an exclamation point. The other players had been in awe of his image when he arrived. By midseason, they were in awe of his play. "Gene had something special that year," Steve Gray remembered. "After a while, we all knew that when a big play had to be made, Gene would make it. It was different than Jim and Mike [Gminski]. They played at a consistently high level every game, all game. But Gene, when we needed it most, would just explode into a game. He would take hold of the game for a couple of minutes and then turn it back to Mike and Jimmy. We all came to count on that after a while."

What was perhaps most remarkable about Banks was his consistency. Most freshmen go up and down from brilliant to brutal during a season. Banks was in double figures in thirty-one of thirty-four games and he shot 53 percent from the field, meaning he rarely took bad shots. He was fire and Spanarkel was ice.

Gminski was as much a star as Spanarkel and Banks, but he did things quietly. The coaches often got on him about not being aggressive enough as a rebounder, but he averaged 10 a game and only had one game all season where he got less than seven. At LaSalle, he had one rebound at halftime. Looking at the stat sheet just before the second half started, Foster said, "Nice half Mike, you got a rebound." Gminski said nothing. He then got 15 in the second half.

If all three of the stars had been in the same class, there might have been problems dividing up the glory. If they had been seniors—or if one or two had been seniors—there might have been jealousies over who was going to get the best pro contract. But with Spanarkel a junior, Gminski a sophomore and Banks a freshman, there was none of that. Each got recognition in his own way and each was, for the most part, happy that way.

The rest of the team gladly fell in behind the Big Three. Dennard was Banks's alter ego. Harrell and Bender understood their role was to get the ball to the scorers. Goetsch and Suddath, the seventh and eighth men, each understood his role and reveled in being able to contribute. Bell and Hardy, as former walk-ons, knew that on a team this talented their playing time would be limited. And Morrison and Gray, the two players most likely to be upset about their diminishing roles, were caught up in the joyride like everyone else, thrilled at last to be winning.

"If Spanarkel, Gminski and Banks had been egomaniacs or bad guys, it might have been different," Morrison said. "But they weren't. Just the opposite in fact. Even if I had taken off the uniform and just been a student I would have rooted for them because they were my friends. That year, I still felt like I was part of it, that I was a contributor. Plus, I wasn't a senior. I didn't see the end coming. I could still say to myself, 'next year.' Steve was the same way. We were all having too much fun to start letting petty things mess it up."

Very few college basketball teams go through an entire season without the benchwarmers becoming bitter, or at least frustrated. Very few teams can have more than one star without sniping. That would all become very evident in a year, but that winter, through both luck and skill, Foster had put together a team that truly was a team from player one to player twelve.

The same was true of the coaching staff. All four coaches knew exactly what their role was. Foster was the worrier, the mother hen who looked at 14–3 and moaned about how tough the next three games would be. He was the organizer, the person responsible for two-man drills beginning at precisely 3:37 and ending at 3:44. He believed in management by objective on both a daily basis and a long-term basis. The other coaches took their cue from him.

More than anyone, Foster understood that assuming next year would be better than this year was dangerous. He had been in coaching long enough to know that one takes *nothing* for granted. At forty-seven, he was sixteen years older than Ray Jones, the second-oldest member of the staff, and almost thirty years older than the players.

"It wasn't that I didn't think we could get better or I didn't think we weren't going to keep recruiting good players," Foster said. "It was just that I didn't want to use the 'next time' theme as a copout. If we had a shot to do something, we needed to try like hell to do it right then. Beat Carolina, win the ACC, get into the NCAA, make the Final Four, win the whole thing. Whatever it was, my thinking was there was no guarantee we'd be back next year. If we were, hey, we could try to do it twice and that would be twice as good. But I had reached the point that year where I had been in coaching for twenty years and had never been in the NCAA. After that long, you begin to wonder."

The assistants knew that Foster would wonder and worry and there was nothing they could do about it. Goetz had been around him long enough that he could read his moods and usually calm him down when he became anxious about something. Goetz was the one who was always pushing everyone, demanding more from them, wanting to know why something couldn't be done.

"A lot of times my first two years at school I would leave practice hating Lou Goetz," Gminski said. "Nothing ever seemed good enough for him. If you got fifteen boards in a game, he'd show you film where you could have gotten five more. If you made a move well once, he wanted you to do it twice. I never understood until later how important he was to me. I've been in the NBA for nine years and one of the main reasons for that is the work he did with me."

Goetz knew exactly what his role had to be. Wenzel was the players' pal, their contemporary in many ways, the guy they went to and talked to about women. He and Jones shared an office; often the players would congregate in there for BS and rip sessions. Goetz's office was much quieter, much more businesslike.

"I never minded that," Goetz said of his bad-cop role. "I came from a family where my mother always wanted us to do better. If you made a B, she couldn't understand why it wasn't an A. If you came back next term with an A, she wanted to know why not A-plus. Then if you came back with the A-plus she would shake her head and wonder why it took you so long to live up to your potential. I always saw potential in the kids to do more because we all have the potential to do more."

When Goetz was told that Gminski had described him in terms almost exactly the same as the ones he had used to describe his mother, he smiled. "You have a Jewish mother, I guess you become one," he said.

Those traits went beyond being demanding. Goetz was also the one who made sure the guys on the end of the bench were reminded how important they were. He had coached Bell and Hardy on the JV team and he had recruited Morrison, Gray, and Goetsch. He felt one of his jobs was to make certain they felt as much a part of the team's success as they had felt a part of its failures.

"Those guys *were* important," Goetz said. "One of the reasons we were good that year was that we had such competitive practices. People can't understand the significance of that. Those guys had become pretty good players and they made it tough on the starters every day. If they had given up or stopped caring, they wouldn't have done that. I wanted to be sure they knew it was appreciated."

This was a critical time for Goetz. He had just turned thirty and he had been married in December. As the team began to get attention, so did he, and the thought that this might be his last year at Duke crossed his mind as the postseason approached. He had been with Foster for fourteen seasons and the notion of leaving him was not easy to deal with. But Goetz knew this might be his best chance. If he wanted to stay in coaching he would have to make the move up someday.

"I felt a little like Peter Pan that season," he said. "I knew it was time to grow up, but I wasn't all that sure I wanted to."

The Blue Devils were now rapidly growing up and, ever so slowly, the national media was starting to notice. The story was a natural: a school with great tradition that has been down coming back, led by a wise-cracking coach and a bunch of funny, articulate kids. Banks talked very sincerely about wanting someday to be governor of Pennsylvania. While the media listened with rapt attention, his teammates would snicker quietly, knowing that Banks meant he wanted to *own* Pennsylvania. Or at least Philadelphia. Spanarkel and Gminski were the stereotype All-American types, white and attractive, excellent students, good interviews. Bender was asked nine million times about playing for Bob Knight and about leaving him. Harrell was the Cinderella story. Dennard was the flake. The only thing the media missed was Morrison, whose sharp wit was never publicized because he wasn't playing enough to be interviewed very often.

Foster was delighted with the attention the team was getting, although he worried at times that the players might start to think they were better than they were.

But just when it seemed as if the team might sail through to the regular season finale in Chapel Hill without another loss, disaster struck in the exact place where it had struck a year ago—Virginia.

Like Duke, the Cavaliers were a vastly improved team with their own pair of freshman forwards, Jeff Lamp and Lee Raker; they came into the game also in the Top Twenty at No. 18. They had savvy guards and the experience up front of senior Marc Iavaroni.

Going into the game, Banks, fighting a winter cold, was not quite himself. Early on, Gminski went down with a sprained ankle. He limped off, replaced by Goetsch, who promptly twisted a knee. One could almost hear Tate Armstrong's wrist hitting the floor all over again. Virginia led 41–34 at halftime as Foster moved Spanarkel to forward and played Harrell and Bender together in the backcourt.

Gminski came back to play in the second half even though he couldn't jump—he finished the game with one rebound—and he, Spanarkel, and Banks led Duke back. The Blue Devils took the lead on a Banks steal and jarring dunk and led 73–72 with Gminski on the foul line and eleven seconds to go.

The Blue Devils would finish the season shooting a remarkable 79 percent from the foul line and Gminski would end up hitting 84 percent. But in University Hall, none of that mattered. Gminski's free throw rattled out, Dave Koesters hit a jumper with time running down, and Virginia had a 74–73 victory.

That Virginia celebrated on the court at the buzzer was a tribute to how far Duke had come. It had been a long time since a victory over Duke—especially at home—had been cause for anyone to celebrate. That didn't lessen the disappointment in the Duke locker room.

"We were angry," Rob Hardy said, looking back. "We knew damn well that Virginia wasn't as good as we were and that we had handed them the game. Sure, we had some bad luck with Mike and Fonz getting hurt, but that shouldn't have mattered. We just looked at each other and said, 'This is bullshit.' "

Whatever it was, Gminski's ankle was hurt badly enough that he had to sit out the next two games. His absence didn't matter against East Carolina but it mattered greatly at Wake Forest, where the Demon Deacons played superbly and pounded the Blue Devils, 79–60.

Gminski was back when Virginia came to Cameron. It had been just two weeks since the game in Charlottesville and all the anger the players had felt in the locker room came out, fueled by the Cameron crowd. It was 25–6 after seven minutes and it was 100–75 when the clock mercifully hit zero. Spanarkel had 30, Gminski hit seven of eight from the field, and Banks had 17 points and 14 rebounds. Those who had lumped Duke and Virginia together as rising young teams in the ACC needed to rethink that analysis. Virginia was good. Duke was becoming a monster.

That game was the first of five straight at home, and it was a delirious time at Duke. After all the years of embarrassment and horrific losses, the basketball team was not only competing in the ACC again, it was dominating. Cameron, half empty for so many home games from 1973 to 1977, was now the toughest ticket around. The announced attendance at each home game—for the benefit of the fire marshals—was 8,333, but if they had ever gone into the student section and taken a count they might have found 8,333 squeezed into four thousand seats.

N.C. State came to town, the same N.C. State that had humiliated Duke in January. It was never close. Maryland came in and was down 20 in the first half on a Saturday night when the noise was so loud it seemed the roof might come off. Duke was 19–5 when Clemson came to Cameron for the home finale.

This would be Bruce Bell's last home game. The farewell for a player who would finish his career with a total of 58 points is not, in most places, a very big deal. Introduce him to the crowd, give him a round of applause, and get on with the game. But Bell was not your average former walk-on and Duke not your average place.

He had come a long way since those first days as a freshman when he couldn't get into pickup games and wanted to go home to Lexington. Everyone enjoyed Juice. He had a self-deprecating sense of humor and he enjoyed a joke played on himself as much as a joke played on someone else. He had taken Suddath, who was at times overwhelmed by the bawdiness of the locker room, under his wing and helped get him through the year. He was someone everyone felt they could talk to and he was also someone respected for his toughness and his knowledge of the game. "Juice was one of those guys you had to respect," Bender said. "On the one hand, he was as nice a guy as you'll ever meet, naive but really *not* naive because he *knew* he was naive. Also a guy who you'd want in your corner in a fight even if he looked like everybody's little brother."

Juice was both big brother and little brother to this team. He was the one guy who had been around since Foster's first days on campus, who remembered *all* the bad times and who fully understood how important it was to savor what was now happening. He was bright and mature and there was no question in anyone's mind that he would follow in his father's footsteps and become a lawyer.

But he was also Juice, so nicknamed not because it rhymed with Bruce but because he had made the mistake of letting people see him putting lemon juice in his hair at the beach as a freshman. For Juice, the Cameron finale would be special. His teammates would see to that.

Because the students were always in their seats at least two hours before tip-off, the team would generally make two entrances. The second one was the formal one thirty minutes before tip-off when the band would play the fight song and Spanarkel would lead them out for the traditional lay-up line. The first was usually at least an hour before the game, much less formal, the players walking out just to informally shoot around and get loose.

On this night, as the players were getting ready to go out for the informal shoot-around, a couple of the players came up to Bell and suggested he walk out first—"just for the heck of it"—and they would all follow right behind him. Bell thought that was a nice gesture. He walked to the door, turned left toward the court, picked up a basketball, and looked over his shoulder for his teammates.

They were nowhere in sight. The students had started to applaud when Bell first came into sight, expecting to see several players right behind him. But no one else was coming. The students understood— this was a setup. As Bell stood there, stunned, they all stood and began chanting his nickname, "Juice, Juice, Juice." Then the two sides of the arena started throwing his name back and forth: "Bruce!"—"Bell!"— "Bruce!"—"Bell!" Through it all, Bell tried to nonchalantly shoot as if the other guys would show up any second. Finally, he knew they wouldn't. He stopped and waved his thanks to all four sides of the arena. It was as warm a moment as one could imagine.

Then, just before tip-off, Bell had one more moment to remember. Foster started him and he was the first player introduced. The lights were all out and Bell stood at center court in the darkness, the spotlight shining on him as the entire building, led by the Duke bench, stood and clapped for him. *The Chronicle* ran a front-page picture of that scene the next morning. In it, Bell is biting his lip, clearly fighting back tears.

The memory of that night still stirs Bell's emotions. "The feeling I had for all those people that night is something I still love to think about," he said. "Part of it was the guys, but even beyond that, it was all the students. There's always such feeling between the team at Duke and the students, it's difficult to describe. But to stand out there all by myself, first while they chanted my name and then when they intro-duced me, that was a kind of warmth and love I've only felt a couple of times in my life. I still get choked up thinking about it."

The game, almost inevitably, was an anticlimax. Duke was in control from the start and the 78–62 final was not really a full measure of the ease of the victory. Duke was now 20–5—its first twenty-victory season since 1971—and, even more important, was 8–3 in the ACC. That meant that the team that had been dead the last four years in a row would travel to Chapel Hill in three days to play North Carolina for the regular season championship.

10

Contenders

They had come a long way since Steve Gray's pass and Foster's aborted plane trip to Louisville. They had no way of knowing, though, that they had only just begun.

At this stage, Foster really wasn't sure how to feel. One year earlier, when the season had crashed after Armstrong's injury, the thought that he could not get the job done at Duke had crossed his mind more than once.

"If we had not signed Banks at the end of that season, I think I might have left," he said. "They bring you in to do a job. I didn't think in those first three years I had done the job they were paying me for. I'm not a big believer in hanging on because someone has to pay you or anything like that. I would have sat down with Lou and Wenz and tried to make an honest assessment of where we were. If I didn't think we were going to be considerably better, I would have been gone."

The Banks signing changed that but it didn't change Foster. Where he saw failure during those first three seasons, virtually everyone else at Duke saw progress. No one liked losing close games but everyone—students, faculty, administration—appreciated the way the team competed and the way Foster integrated himself and his team into campus life. Never once during those first three seasons was anything resembling a boo heard in Cameron Indoor Stadium. The students, especially, understood—perhaps even better than Foster did—that this was a building process. As long as Spanarkel got better and Gminski improved and they knew the coaches were out looking under every rock for the missing ingredients, they were willing to wait out the bumps in the ride.

Now the waiting was over. That was why the joy was so palpable during the last home game against Clemson. It was for Bruce Bell, but it was also for Spanarkel, Gminski, Banks, and the rest. And for the coaches. And, for that matter, it was for Tate Armstrong and his contemporaries, because even though they weren't there everyone knew they had been part of the process too. The Clemson game was almost like a graduation. Four years after 10–16, they were 20–5 and the world was waiting to see just how much they had learned. If ever a team was eager to show off, it was this one.

"We were on a roll by then," Dennard said. "It was one of those things where if you asked us what we were doing we really couldn't tell you. We might mouth some clichés about playing hard and playing together but every team that's winning does those things. A lot of teams that *don't* win do those things. But something was *right* with us at that stage. Gene and I were matched perfectly and Mike gave us that balance in the middle. The guards were doing what they wanted to do and everyone was happy.

"It's funny, because a lot of what happened to us in February and March is a blur for me. It just went by so fast."

Dennard isn't alone in this feeling. Just as the next season seemed to pass in slow motion, this one seemed speeded up because everything was so easy. It was all brand new and so much fun.

Chapel Hill, though, was not fun. No one expected it to be. Duke had not won in Carmichael Auditorium since the year the building opened, 1966, and this would be Phil Ford's last home game. Ford may well be the greatest guard ever to play in the ACC, a blur with the basketball, an extraordinary competitor who found ways to win when everyone else had given up.

This Carolina team did not have the talent of the one that had played Marquette for the national title a year earlier. Walter Davis was gone and so were Tommy LaGarde and John Kuester. The cupboard was far from bare, though, with Ford and O'Koren and Tom Zaligiaris and a group of interchangeable big men who would take turns pounding on Gminski the whole game.

Even so, Duke was probably the better team at this point. If Foster had been able to hypnotize his team into believing it was playing anywhere but at Carolina that afternoon, Duke might very well have won the game.

"I don't think we ever went into Carolina thinking we were going to win," said Rob Hardy, the unofficial team psychiatrist. "It was something you could feel in the locker room. Duke *never* won at Carolina back then and even though we thought we were real good, we still were thinking, 'Well, we *are* playing in Chapel Hill.' "

It was a superb basketball game. Ford again did the impossible, taking his game to a higher plane than he ever had before, pouring in 34 points, refusing to miss, refusing to lose.

"I remember one play in that game where Phil was coming right at me on the break," Dennard said. "I thought, 'If he drives at me, I'll have to pound him,' at least put him on the line and not give him the lay-up. All of a sudden he stops at the top of the key on a dime and *whooosh* puts in a jumper. Then I look at him and he's wiping tears out of his eyes. The guy was so emotionally wound up it was unreal."

Every time Ford would seemingly bury Duke with another jumper, the Blue Devils would come back. Carolina led the entire afternoon, but Duke wouldn't die. The team may not have believed yet that it could win here, but it knew it could compete. Finally, with fifteen seconds left and the Tar Heels up 85–83, Spanarkel made a steal and was fouled. He would go to the line for a one-and-one. If he made both shots the game would be tied—no doubt setting the stage for a Ford jumper at the buzzer to win it.

Maybe, deep down, Spanarkel knew this was Ford's day. He missed the free throw, something he almost never did in the clutch. Ford made two more foul shots to wrap it up and Carolina escaped, 87–83. It was a brilliant basketball game between two very good teams. In the past, when Duke played a close game with Carolina it was because the Tar Heels came down a little bit or because the Blue Devils moved up. That was not the case here.

"When it was over and we had a chance to think about it I think we all knew we should have won the game," Spanarkel said. "I missed the free throw so I take the blame but it was more than that. Great as Phil was, we were the better team. But we hadn't figured that out yet. We were still reacting in our minds to who they were and what we had been. We learned a lesson that day."

Doctor Hardy/Freud agrees. "I think that game fueled the fire," he said. "I can remember all of us looking at each other in the locker room and saying, 'Wait a minute, we're better than they are.' Phil plays the game of his life, maybe of anyone's life, they've got ten thousand people going crazy for them and Jimmy's on the line with a chance to tie it at the end. No one ever said it but I think we all walked out of there thinking that if we got to play them in the ACC Tournament the next week we were going to pound their ass. Because we knew we were good enough to do it."

Carolina's victory gave it the first seed for the ACC Tournament with a 9–3 league record. Duke was second at 8–4 and State third at 7–5, followed by Wake Forest and Virginia at 6–6. Everyone in the league expected a Duke–Carolina final. Jim Thacker, the long-time play-by-play man on the ACC Saturday afternoon telecasts, had summed it up best at the end of the game in Chapel Hill when he said, "There is no doubt that these are the two class teams in this league right now, a clear notch above everyone else."

And yet, Duke was not in a position to take anything for granted. The Blue Devils had not won a *game* in the tournament since 1972 and had not even sniffed at playing in the final since Bubas's retirement in 1969. Foster was 0–3 in the tournament and he often joked, "I've never had to pack anything but a handkerchief for the tournament." This year, he took a full suitcase.

▬

Today, every conference has a tournament. Not in 1978. From 1954 to 1974, the ACC Tournament had determined who would be the league's one representative in the NCAA Tournament. A team could go undefeated in the regular season and if it lost in the tournament, *sayonara*. That fact had created an aura around the tournament, one that had not faded even in 1975 when the NCAA expanded to thirty-two teams, meaning that *two* ACC teams would be invited.

Under the new setup, the regular season champion was already in the tournament even though officially the tournament champion still got the only automatic bid. That meant Carolina was in. If Carolina and Duke played in the final and the Tar Heels won, Duke would get the second bid because it was clearly the No. 2 team in the conference. But if someone other than Duke or Carolina won the tournament, the Blue Devils would be out of the NCAA's. In October, if someone had told Foster that his team would win 20 games in the regular season and enter the ACC Tournament with at least an NIT bid wrapped up, he would have been delighted. But now everyone connected with the team wanted more. Everyone knew they were capable of more.

On Monday afternoon, after practice, Goetz explained the situation to the team. "If State, Virginia, Wake Forest, Maryland, or Clemson win the tournament they will go to the NCAA with Carolina," he said. "We will get a bid to play in the NIT. Next week is spring break. If you would rather not play in the NIT because of that, you can vote that way as a team."

Goetz and Foster knew their players would accept any postseason bid, even if it was to the second-level NIT, but they wanted their players to make the trip to Greensboro thinking that anything less than an NCAA bid would be a disappointment. The NCAA was something to be sought; the NIT something to be accepted.

In keeping with the notion that this was a new era, Foster had booked the team at the Hyatt Winston-Salem as opposed to the Holiday Inn where they had stayed in the past. The thinking here was simple: get the players thinking that this was not an overnight—read Holiday Inn—experience. In the Greensboro/Winston-Salem area, the Hyatt was as high class as it got. The Blue Devils bussed down there on Tuesday to get settled in for the tournament opener at three P.M. Wednesday against Clemson.

This was a new schedule for the tournament, one brought on by ABC–TV. The network, as an experiment, had bought the rights to televise the final on its Saturday afternoon *Wide World of Sports* show. With the final pushed up from the traditional eight-thirty P.M. start to four P.M. the league didn't think it fair to ask the semifinal winners to play Friday night and then Saturday afternoon. So, the opening day had moved from Thursday to Wednesday; the semifinals to Thursday and there was now a rest day on Friday.

Clemson had finished last in the league and Duke had easily beaten the Tigers twice during the regular season. Still, Foster remembered how close his teams had come as a prohibitive underdog to pulling first-round upsets in the past (remember Maryland?), and he had a team that knew nothing about winning in the ACC Tournament. He was—of course—nervous when he walked onto the floor wearing a blue blazer and blue-and-white-checked pants. The pants were new, given to him by his wife for good luck in postseason play.

Clemson's strategy for this game was simple: make Kenny Dennard shoot the ball. Every time the ball went inside to Gminski, the Tigers would double-team, ignoring Dennard, who had gained a reputation as someone who was dangerous only on the drive or going to the boards.

What Clemson didn't know was that Dennard had spent the last month in remedial shooting sessions with Bob Wenzel, who had changed his shot, shortening his release. Dennard had always shot the ball from behind his head. Now, Wenzel had him keeping the ball in front and shooting from there. It was almost like taking the loop out of a golf swing—more compact, more efficient, less chance to make a mechanical error.

And so, each time Gminski was double-teamed, Dennard was wide open in the corner. His teammates got him the ball and Dennard stood on the same spot and kept firing away. He hit four in a row to start the game and Duke was up 14–4 before you could say "blowout." The Tigers never got within 10 and the second half was strictly a coast job, the bench getting some playing time. The final was a not-as-close-as-it-looked 83–72, and Dennard finished with a career-high 22 points.

Foster felt as if the combined weight of Bucky Waters, Adolph Rupp, and Neill McGeachy had been removed from his shoulders. His team had won an ACC Tournament game and it had done so in a laugher. To most, Duke beating Clemson was no big deal—the second seed was supposed to beat the seventh seed—but to the Duke contingent, this was one more stigma finally shed.

That evening, sixth-seeded Maryland upset N.C. State in triple overtime and Wake Forest easily beat Virginia. The Cavaliers, rated on the same plane with the Blue Devils six weeks ago, would go to the NIT. The Duke players honestly felt they had left that level behind long ago.

The semifinals matched Duke and Maryland and Carolina (which had a first-round bye as the top seed) and Wake Forest. As was the case with Clemson, Duke had beaten Maryland twice during the regular season. Banks had easily beaten Albert King out for the rookie of the year award (Duke's third straight, Spanarkel and Gminski having won before) and was the clear winner of their personal battle at that stage. Of course, the Johnson kid at Michigan State was turning some heads but that was not a concern to anyone in the ACC.

Duke was a loose and confident team. But disaster almost struck before tip-off. When the players went out for their pregame shoot-around an hour before the game started, a small group of Maryland's most vociferous fans were already in their seats. As soon as Gminski appeared they began yelling at him. "Hey, Gminski, where's your neck? What's it like having no neck?"

Gminski was shaken. Cool as he seemed at the time, he was still only eighteen, the youngest player on the team. Back in the locker room he stood in front of the mirror examining himself. "I've got a neck, don't I?" he asked everyone. Unanimously, his teammates told him he had a neck. Only later, in less stressful moments, did they start calling him "No-neck."

For thirty minutes, the Terrapins hung with the Blue Devils. But with a little over ten minutes left, Lefty Driesell made a mistake. As Bender stepped to the foul line to shoot a one-and-one, the wound-up lefthander grabbed his throat, giving Bender the choke sign. This was a Lefty staple, something he did more out of pure emotion than to psyche anyone. Bender stared at Driesell for a moment as if he was crazy, then made both free throws. The Blue Devils picked up the pace from that moment on and never looked back. The margin at the end was 81–69.

They were in the final. For some, this might have been cause for ecstasy. But having won two games easily, the players and coaches now felt that they were the team to beat. There was no reason—or excuse—for losing. They wanted to play Carolina in the final. From a pragmatic standpoint, if they lost to Carolina they'd still be the second-best team in the league and would clinch an NCAA bid. More important, though, was Hardy's post-Chapel Hill notion: They wanted to pound the Tar Heels.

They never got the chance. Wake Forest whipped Carolina in the second semifinal. UNC, after having played in three straight finals, was gone. It would be Duke and Wake Forest for the championship. The winner would not only be the ACC champion but would go to the NCAA's. The loser would get a pat on the back and a trip to the NIT.

"Wake winning changed everything, put a lot more pressure on us," Foster said. "Now, we *had* to win. If it had been Carolina, if we lose, we're disappointed but still in the NCAA and everyone says, 'Well, they lost to Carolina.' Now, if we lose, we aren't in the tournament and everyone is going to say, 'How in the world did you lose to Wake?'"

It snowed in Greensboro on Friday. Two days earlier, the temperature had been in the 70s, but on March 3, a half-foot of snow paralyzed the central part of North Carolina. Both teams were brought in for a press conference that morning and Foster, noting the snow, announced, "They said it would be a snowy March day in Greensboro before Foster made the ACC final and I guess they were right," he said. Everyone laughed. Except Foster. He was too tight.

"I was afraid with all the people around telling the guys they had already had a great year that they would relax and maybe even use the idea that there was always the future as a copout," he said. "My attitude was you deal with the immediate. There were no guarantees for the future. There never are. I was afraid we might not come to play really hungry and then we would spend the whole summer regretting it."

Foster's fears were understandable. Duke had beaten Wake Forest in their first two meetings of the season but had lost to the Deacons in their third game—without Gminski. Both teams were hot and both had plenty of motivation: Duke had not won an ACC Tournament since 1966; Wake hadn't won one since 1962.

And, the game being on national TV was a big deal to everyone.

In terms of television exposure for college basketball, 1978 was eons ago. That season, NBC televised a dozen regular season games—most of them, it seemed, involving Notre Dame—and another dozen NCAA Tournament games. CBS and ABC combined to televise one game— this one. There was no ESPN, no USA, no FNN (Financial News Network).

None of the Duke players had ever been on national television. In fact, no Duke team had ever appeared on national network television. Not ever. "The *Wide World of Sports* thing was something we all talked about," Gminski remembered. "In fact, after we beat Maryland in the semis that was one of the things that came up right away: Now we would be on national TV. It was something the coaches didn't want us to pay any attention to, but we couldn't help it."

It was a big thing for Wake too, but perhaps not *as* big since the Deacons had been on NBC the previous year during the NCAA's. Even so, the mood in the Greensboro Coliseum was tense on Saturday afternoon as the two teams warmed up. In a sense, this was a throwback to the old days of the ACC Tournament—only the winner was going on to the NCAA's.

Foster was dressed, for the third straight day, in the blue blazer and the checked pants. Coaches are a superstitious lot and Foster was no exception. The outfit was 2–0 and Foster wasn't about to change.

Everyone remembers pregame meal being a little quieter than normal that day. They told their jokes and got on each other a little but not as much as usual. This was bigger than any game they had ever played. So much was at stake and no one was trying to pretend that wasn't the case.

"Except for the freshmen, we all still remembered the days when we would head for Florida on spring break the day after our first-round game," Bender said. "We would get down there and put it out of our minds but we all wondered at some point what it would feel like to stay the whole weekend, to play in the final, to actually *win* the final. Now, we were going through it and it felt great. But we were nervous too."

There was also a feeling of wanting to win for Foster, to get him into the NCAA Tournament, to make him the coach who ended Duke's twelve years without an ACC championship.

"I think it was something every one of us thought about," Bell said. "We all knew what Bill put himself through and how much he suffered. We wanted to win for ourselves, there was no doubt about that, but we also knew how happy it would make him. A lot of coaches spend years in the ACC and never win the thing once. We wanted to make sure that didn't happen to him."

The first half did not go well.

At the buzzer, the Deacons led, 43–37. When Gminski was a freshman, the coaches had been gentle with him when Larry Harrison, Wake's gawky center, used his experience to take advantage of him. Not now. Foster and Goetz were both on Gminski at halftime, demanding to know how he could be outplayed by Harrison. This was not an All-American! Gminski had just six points and three rebounds! "I wasn't nervous in the first half, I just didn't feel quite right," Gminski said. "I don't know exactly what it was. I think we were all that way a little bit. Part of it was Wake. They were shooting the ball well and they had a lot of confidence. None of us had expected an easy game and we weren't getting it."

Twenty minutes is a long time in college basketball and even though the coaches were stern at halftime, there was no reason to panic. They just wanted to be sure the players understood that, unlike a week ago in Chapel Hill, there was no second chance this time. Being part of a wonderful game that was a loss would not be satisfying to anyone.

The players understood. From the start of the second half, Gminski was a different player. He was on the boards aggressively. His shot began to fall and that opened things up for everyone else. Every time Wake missed it seemed as if Gminski was on the boards and pitching a quick pass out to Harrell, Bender, or Spanarkel.

It took the Blue Devils five minutes to get the lead. From there, they never looked back. Wake hung in, but it never got even again. With seventeen seconds to go, it was 83–75 Duke, the same eight-point lead that a Duke team had been unable to protect almost exactly four years earlier. But this team wasn't going to blow any such lead. When the buzzer went off, it was 85–77 and the floor of the Coliseum resembled Times Square at midnight on New Year's Eve.

The Duke students lucky enough to have tickets, having postponed their spring trips to see this, stormed the floor. Banks had grabbed the Blue Devil mascot's pitchfork and was parading around the court waving it at everyone, even as the nets were cut down. There was a feeling of overwhelming joy. Foster, who almost never used profanity, pushed a couple of tears out of his eyes as he hugged Lou Goetz and said, "About fucking time."

This was an extremely big moment in Bill Foster's life. "I have to be honest," he told the press. "There have been nights where I've lain awake in bed worrying that I would never get to coach in the NCAA Tournament. There were times in the first half today where I wondered again. But in the second half, well, the guys were just great." His voice caught on the word "guys."

Everyone got a cut of the net. All the players, all the coaches, all the managers. Spanarkel, with 20 points in the final and 53 in the tournament, was a more than deserving MVP. But the second half had belonged to Gminski. Pushed and prodded to raise his game when it mattered most, Gminski had scored 19 points and pulled down 13 rebounds in the second *half*. His totals for the game were 25 and 16. Even beyond that, when the fire had been lit in Gminski, it had caught in everyone else.

"Jimmy, you always knew would be in there doing everything he possibly could," Banks said. "But the big guy sometimes was a little tentative maybe. It just wasn't his way to be screaming and yelling and going crazy like Kenny and me. But when we saw him come out there in the second half breathing fire like that, we were all caught up in it. Once I saw that I knew there was no way we were losing."

Banks had played a major role himself with 22 points and 10 rebounds in the final. That gave him 51 points and 27 rebounds for the tournament, excellent numbers for anyone, amazing ones for a freshman.

Banks was so good, he was almost taken for granted. As good as they were, neither Gminski nor Spanarkel would have been able to produce those kinds of numbers in their freshman years. Banks was *expected* to be great and he *was* great. Often, people forget how difficult that is to do. His buildup had been as a Superman. That he had somehow lived up to that buildup was remarkable.

"You had the feeling that year that as long as Gene was on your side, you were going to win," Wenzel said. "I remember having that feeling watching him in high school, where he lost two games in three years, and then feeling as if he brought that with him when he came to play with us. Part of it was just his sheer physical ability. But part of it was emotional. Some players just have the ability to make their teams win. It isn't always points or rebounds. A lot of the time it's getting other guys to play better because they know if they hang in, you'll find a way. Whatever the hell it was, Gene had it and we all felt it that year."

Later, Banks would come to feel some resentment for not getting the recognition he felt he deserved. He would begin to worry about individual honors and glory. But not now, not in the month of March, 1978. Not only were Spanarkel, Gminski, and Banks a single unit, the whole team was. No one could know the pain they had felt in the past and no one could know the joy they felt that evening on the floor of the Greensboro Coliseum celebrating a victory that five months earlier had been nothing more than a fantasy.

"The best time for all of us was out there on the floor, just letting loose," Hardy said. "It was something we all wanted to savor, not let go of, and make sure we always remembered. Later, we would get all the congratulations from the fans and everyone else and that was great. But this was *us*, no one else, and we didn't want to let the feeling go for a long, long time."

■

That night, while the players threw themselves a well-deserved party, Bill and Shirley Foster and some friends celebrated in the very expensive restaurant of the Hyatt Winston-Salem. If the roads had been clear, Foster might have considered going home to prepare for the next day when Duke would find out who it would play in the NCAA Tournament. But the roads were icy and this was a night for savoring what had been done, not for worrying about what was left to do. By the time dessert was served, the group, led by Shirley Foster, had started singing "Meet Me in St. Louis," that being the site of the Final Four. More fantasies. A few of the other diners in the restaurant—which was half empty by this late hour—were casting glances toward the table. That was all the incentive Tom Mickle needed. Under normal circumstances the Duke SID was so quiet and laid-back that Foster had nicknamed him "Eddie Sominex." But in the right setting with a few drinks in him, Mickle was transformed.

As the last strains of "Meet Me in St. Louis" were being butchered, Mickle leaped onto his end of the table, turned toward the rest of the restaurant and shouted, "All right, everybody sing!" He then launched into a raucous, way-off-key version of the Duke fight song, holding his glass up to give a toast as he warbled on. By halfway through the song the entire table—even Foster—was standing, glasses in hand. So was a good portion of the restaurant. No doubt the black-tied waiters had never seen anything quite like this.

"Of all the memories I have of that year, one of the most vivid is Tom Mickle standing on that table singing," Foster said. "The damn guy had me laughing so hard I had tears in my eyes."

That was exactly what Mickle was trying to do. He was a 1972 Duke graduate who had come to Duke just as the program was starting to slide. He had been a football manager as a student even while he worked toward his engineering degree. Even with Duke spiraling downward in every possible way, he had been bitten by the bug and had accepted Sports Information Director Richard Giannini's offer to stay on as assistant sports information director after he graduated.

When Giannini left in 1976, Mickle, who is so quiet many people underestimate him, took over. Foster had figured out early that Mickle was bright, had good ideas, and was intensely loyal. Mickle had suffered through every twist and turn in the road at Duke in the '70s. After Foster's agonizing first three years, he wanted to be certain that Foster enjoyed what he had worked so hard to accomplish.

"I did enjoy it, but not as much as I should have," Foster said. "I enjoyed coaching that team because it was so easy to work with and because the guys had such a good time. But when it was over, I didn't really enjoy what we had accomplished as much as I should have. We really did come an awful long way that year, when you realize we had been last in the ACC the year before."

By the next afternoon, Foster would be worrying about how his team would bounce back to play in the NCAA's. But on this night, with some help from his wife and from Tom Mickle, he paused briefly to appreciate what he and his coaches and his players had done.

"Mick, you're the best," Foster said when Mickle was finished.

"No, Coach," Mickle said, still standing on the table, *"you* are the best." He raised his glass in a toast. So did everyone else. Even Foster. For one brief moment at least, he actually felt that way.

11

Joyride

The NCAA Tournament draw was announced on Sunday afternoon. Duke was sent to the East Regional to play a first-round game against Rhode Island in Charlotte. There was no formal seeding back then but few considered Duke a serious threat to win the regional and advance to the Final Four. More experienced teams like Indiana, Pennsylvania and Villanova were more highly regarded by most people.

Kent Hannon of *Sports Illustrated,* writing the magazine's ACC Tournament story, summed up the general feeling about Duke when he wrote, "Duke is a team of the future, too young to make a serious run this year." This didn't bother the players a bit. They were far more interested in giving Banks a hard time about being on the magazine's cover. That issue, heralding Duke's victory, sold out in Durham in two hours.

For the players, it was a relatively quiet week. Campus was almost deserted because of spring break. Some of them felt a little bit empty because there was no one around to share their grand triumph with.

"I really got upset when I got back to campus and there was no one around," Dennard said. "I wanted to go crazy, just go out and savor what we had done. We had two days off to rest and party. How many chances do you get to do that in life? But there was nobody there. I had all this pent-up energy and no place to get it out."

Foster was justifiably concerned about a letdown. The only player on the team who knew anything about Rhode Island was Gminski, who was familiar with the Rams' best player, Sly Williams, because both were from Connecticut. No one else had any clue or notion about Rhode Island. The coaches could talk twenty-four hours a day about the fact that any team that made the tournament was a good team and the players weren't likely to hear a word.

In a sense, it was difficult for them to get uptight for this game. Even if they lost, they would finish the season with twenty-three victories, an ACC championship, and the school's first trip to the NCAA's in twelve years. No one, not even Foster, would label that record a disappointment. It was difficult for the players to understand what the NCAA's were about because they had never been there.

The exception to this was Bender, who had not only been there two years earlier with Indiana but wore a belt that said "NCAA Champions" on it.

"I tried to explain to the guys that walking out on the court to play in the tournament would be an entirely different feeling than anything else they had ever gone through," Bender said. "It's tough to explain it, though. You have to go through it. The ACC Tournament is a huge thing—to people in the ACC. But when you get into the NCAA's, now the *whole country* is watching every single game. It's an amazing thing to be a part of but you really don't know how amazing until you've been there."

In short, the Blue Devils were flying blind. They were only playing 150 miles away from home but the Charlotte Coliseum certainly didn't have the comfortable familiarity of the Greensboro Coliseum. They knew the game was big, but they really didn't know why. They knew Rhode Island must be good, but they didn't know specifics the way they did playing Wake Forest or North Carolina or Maryland.

For five minutes, none of that seemed to matter. Duke blew to a quick lead. Then, naturally, the team relaxed. "I think we felt like all the talk that this was going to be so difficult was a lot of pregame hype," Dennard said. "We took a deep breath, relaxed, and the next thing we knew, we were behind."

Never far behind, but consistently behind. The shooting, so good throughout the ACC Tournament, was horrendous—41 percent for the game. Williams was as good an offensive player going to the basket as they had faced all season. With a minute to go, it was Rhode Island's game to win. The Rams led 62–59 and had the ball. There was no shot clock. Duke didn't have the quickness to steal the ball so it had to foul and hope Rhode Island would miss.

The Rams did just that. Duke got the ball back with a chance to cut the lead to one. Gminski, with thirty-three seconds left, hit a short jumper, making it 62–61. Rhode Island spread out again and put the ball in the hands of Williams. He was fouled with seventeen seconds left and went to the line to shoot one-and-one. Amazingly, he missed. Gminski rebounded and, even more amazingly, he was fouled by Williams, his fifth. The last thing in the world Rhode Island Coach Jack Kraft wanted was to give Duke a chance to go ahead at the foul line.

Two months earlier, at Virginia, in a situation that had seemed huge at the time, Gminski had missed the front end of a one-and-one. Now, with fifteen seconds left and the season on the line, he coolly made both free throws. Duke led 63–62. Still, Rhode Island would get the last shot. Forward Stan Wright put up a long jump shot, with six seconds left. It rolled off the rim. But the Ram's John Nelson had perfect rebounding position on the weak side of the basket (away from the ball). He grabbed the ball. With three seconds left, he went up for a wide-open lay-up.

"I can still see it sitting here right now," Bender said eleven years later. "I mean, it's a wide-open lay-up. We had no one even close enough to foul him. All I remember thinking is, 'It's over. We're done.' "

Spanarkel, who had been jostled on the play, was on his hands and knees. When he saw Nelson with the ball, he couldn't look. "I just looked at the floor and listened to the crowd reaction. But I knew we were dead."

On the bench, Foster hadn't given up. "I was hoping the guys would be alert enough to call time-out real quick," he said. "Then we might at least have a chance to get a long inbounds pass and a shot at the basket."

Banks, a couple of steps away from Nelson, was lunging toward him. "All I wanted to do was grab him and foul him," he said. "I wanted to make him beat us at the foul line, not with a wide-open lay-up. But by the time I got to him, the ball was out of his hand."

It was a shot that a college basketball player will make ninety-nine times out of one hundred. But this was the one hundredth time. The enormity of the moment, the adrenaline pumping through him were too much for Nelson. The shot was too strong, going right over the rim.

There was one last scramble for the loose ball. Finally, light years after Gminski had made the two free throws to put Duke ahead, the buzzer sounded. Rhode Island had had three chances to win—one of them a gimme—and had somehow not converted. The scoreboard said it all: Duke–63, Rhode Island–62, and in between those numbers, the :00 that meant it was over.

There was none of the ecstasy of the week before. The hugs this time were the product of exhaustion and relief, the kind one sees when a plane has landed safely after the pilot has told the passengers that the landing gear may be locked.

They knew they had been lucky. Years later, when asked to speak to children's groups, Dennard would bring up the Rhode Island game. "A lot of you know who I am because I played in the Final Four," he would tell them. "But if a guy makes a wide-open lay-up, I never get there. You have to remember there are a lot of things in life you *can't* control. Knowing that, you should understand how important it is that you handle what you *can* control."

They had not played well, but they had survived. They had won on a day when only four players in Duke uniforms had scored: Gminski, the hero, had scored 25; Spanarkel had 18; Banks had 14; and Suddath had come off the bench with Dennard in foul trouble and played a vital role with six points and four rebounds. Dennard, Harrell, and Bender had gone scoreless.

Suddath's contribution was a perfect example of why this team was successful. Shunted into the background all season by the flash and dash of his two freshman partners, he had worked hard anyway and when Foster and the team had needed him most, he had produced. Without Suddath, Duke never gets past the first round and Rhode Island. The fact that his play went largely unnoticed in the aftermath of the dramatic finish didn't bother him. Like everyone else, he was just happy to still be playing.

Even before the players filed into the locker room, Wenzel had written the number 16 on the blackboard. That was the number of teams still left competing for the national championship. Now, feeling as drained as they had ever felt after a game, they understood what Bender had been talking about. And, when the press came stampeding into the locker room, they began to understand just how big this event was. The press wanted to review every play, every shot and, in great detail, the last sequence.

To some teams, the ones that have received a lot of attention, this kind of "tell me your life story" scrutiny might be oppressive. To the Blue Devils, a group used to living in the shadow of North Carolina and N.C. State, the media attention was fun. They were all articulate, honest, and totally unprogrammed. They told the press they had been lucky as hell to win the game and that they hadn't done a good job of listening to the coaches' pleas to take Rhode Island seriously. This was a team that didn't see any reason to make excuses after a poor performance.

At this time of year the performance didn't matter, the result did. And, as Wenzel had so pithily reminded them, there were now just sixteen teams left. Four would go to Providence to play for the East Regional title: Duke, Pennsylvania, Indiana, and Villanova. The Blue Devils would play Penn in the regional semifinal on Friday night.

The Duke campus was now jumping with anticipation—everyone was back from spring break. The players couldn't turn around without being clapped on the back or being interviewed. Distractions were everywhere. Foster knew this. So, on Monday, to get everyone's attention, he put the team through the kind of grueling workout usually associated with preseason.

"He wanted to remind us that everyone else could have the fun now, we would have our fun later," Bender said. "He wanted us to understand that we still had a lot of work to do, that there was no point in stopping now. We all felt the same way."

For Bender this would not be an easy week. People were already speculating on the very real possibility of a Duke–Indiana regional final, which meant Bender, since he would be facing his old teammates, would be the center of attention.

"I was *just* getting to the point where every reference to me in the paper wasn't 'Indiana-transfer Bob Bender,' " he said. "For a while I thought that was my full name. Now it was back to that stuff. Everyone wanted me to condemn Knight and talk about how much better Foster's way was than Knight's way. Even if I had felt that way I wasn't about to do that. And I didn't feel that way anyway. I was never disgruntled. When I said that to people that week they looked at me like, 'Yeah sure.' It just happened to be true."

They flew to Providence Thursday. By now it was becoming ritual for the players. Practice a couple of days at home, go on the road to a hotel filled with excited Iron Dukes—the Duke booster club—and answer all the questions all over again.

"We were the team from nowhere," Hardy said. "Everyone wanted to know where the hell we had come from. After all, it wasn't as if Duke had made a lot of noise in basketball in the recent past. People wanted to build us up. We were the good guys."

"It was as if the whole world woke up one morning and said, 'Who are these guys?'" Spanarkel observed. "We were perfectly happy to tell people exactly who we were."

Having lucked out against Rhode Island, they came to Providence expecting a difficult game against Penn. Bender had played against starting guard Tom Crowley in high school. The Duke coaches had tried very hard to recruit the other guard, Bobby Willis. Banks knew all the Penn players because he had been recruited by Coach Bob Weinhauer the previous year. For Foster, playing against Penn in the NCAA Tournament was special because he had grown up watching the Quakers play in the Palestra.

Indiana and Villanova played the opener and the Wildcats pulled the game out, 61–60. Although Bender harbored no ill will against his old team, he was relieved by the outcome. Now he knew that if Duke won he would not face two days of questions about Knight. "All I had to do was play," he said.

Easier said than done. Penn was an experienced, savvy team. It was patient with the ball and played excellent defense. The Quakers led from the start and only a flurry in the final minute of the half kept the margin at two points at intermission. The second half was more of the same: Willis, Crowley, and Tony Price controlling the tempo, the Blue Devils unable to get anything going. With the clock under eight minutes, Penn led by eight. It looked as if the Rhode Island miracle had only extended the season by one game. When Weinhauer went to his spread offense, the Duke bench had the look of a desperate group. Even Hardy and Bell, the consummate cheerleaders, looked discouraged. Then fate intervened again.

Instead of milking the clock, taking advantage of their quickness to force Duke to foul, the Penn guards decided to go right at Gminski. Maybe they believed the reports that Gminski wasn't aggressive enough to go after them and block their shots. Maybe they were so confident they didn't even think about Gminski. In any event, on three consecutive possessions, Crowley, Crowley again, and then Willis went right up the middle and right at Mikey.

Gminski responded to the challenge. He blocked Crowley's first shot, then his second one. Then he blocked Willis's shot. In all three

cases, showing his maturity, he blocked the ball inbounds. Some young centers would have swatted the ball as hard as possible and knocked it out of bounds. This was the macho thing to do. The smart thing to do was to keep the ball in play and get it turned the other way. Each block led to a quick Duke basket and, to the surprise of everyone in the building, the lead was suddenly down to two. The momentum had turned 180 degrees.

Now, the Blue Devils were convinced they were meant to win this game. Spanarkel and Banks barged inside and, before the run was over, Duke had outscored Penn 16–4. In the last three minutes it was Duke spreading the floor and Penn having to foul. As always, the guards made their free throws and, in a remarkable reversal, Duke had the victory, 84–80.

In its own way, this win was as stunning as the one over Rhode Island. "We were dead—again," Bender said. "The whole game was decided by those three plays. The funny thing is, Tom Crowley was always a very smart player and he made two stupid plays in a row. And then Willis made a play that was just as stupid."

Gminski was as surprised as anyone when he saw the plays coming right at him. "I know I didn't have a reputation as a great shot blocker but they didn't need to make those plays. I didn't even have to move all that much to get the shots. They just came to me."

Wenzel, beating the players to the locker room just as he had done in Charlotte, had the last word—or number—again. On the blackboard, waiting for them, the players saw the number 8. In the East, there were just two: Duke and Villanova.

Weinhauer did not take the defeat well. He felt, with some justification, that his team had let Duke get away and he said so. That was fine. What wasn't fine, as far as the Blue Devil players were concerned, was what he said afterward. "They don't have any quickness," he said. "I don't see any fast break. They fast-break like a pack of thundering elephants. I don't think they'll be able to keep up with Villanova on Sunday."

Foster should have sent Weinhauer a thank-you note. By the next afternoon, his comments were plastered on the walls of every Duke player's hotel room and all over the locker room. "We were hot," Dennard said. "Hey, whatever you want to say about the game, we beat them. Maybe we weren't the fastest team in the world, but we weren't the slowest either. We'd had enough with this Big Five [Philadelphia's five basketball-playing schools are known as the Big Five] crap. Our attitude after that was bring on Villanova and we'll show you what a stampede of thundering elephants looks like."

They should have been nervous about being one step away from the Final Four. Villanova had beaten a very good Indiana team and it was loaded with experience. But the emphasis from the coaching staff was never about what was at stake. Wenzel's blackboard numbers set the tone because they were a reminder of what had already been accomplished: you are one of sixteen, one of eight, and so on. That done, Foster would quickly establish in practice the next day that this was no time to rest on those laurels.

"The whole time I think the only thing we were aware of was how much fun we were having," Spanarkel said. "None of us ever sat down and said, 'Hey, we're playing for this or for that.' Hell, if we had thought about it or about all the people watching us on television, we probably would have all choked on our food. But we never thought that way. It was always, 'Let's go out and show people just how good we are.'"

On Sunday they did exactly that. Villanova couldn't hit over the Duke zone and Gminski and Banks were getting the ball out on the fast break so quickly that the Wildcats never knew what hit them. It was 21–6 after seven minutes and Villanova never made a run. They were stampeded by a bunch of fired-up elephants.

The afternoon, perhaps the season, was summed up in one play. To this day, everyone on the team simply refers to it it as "Dennard's dunk." It started with Villanova pressing with ten minutes left. Dennard went long, Banks spotted him, open, ahead of the field.

"No one has ever believed me, but I dreamed that play the night before the game," Dennard said. "I called my brother Tommy in the morning and told him I had dreamed that I opened the game with a reverse dunk. He thought I was freaking out. 'Calm down, just calm down,' he told me."

Now Dennard wasn't calm, but he wasn't dreaming either. He went up, twisted his body and dunked behind his head.

This was 1978. The dunk had only been legalized again two years earlier. *No one* dunked like that.

The whole bench went wild—especially Foster, who was furious at Dennard for showboating with so much time left. "I've never felt like that in my life, before or since," Dennard said. "It was like I was moving in slow motion. I didn't think about it, I just did it. The feeling was just incredible. It was completely different than sex, but just as intoxicating. I felt like I was floating above the entire world."

Floating above the entire world was a perfect description of the way they all felt. Shirley Foster's singing in Greensboro had been a harbinger. The final was 90–72. The elephants were stampeding to St. Louis.

This celebration was different from the one in Greensboro. Then, the pressure of years of ACC failures had been lifted. Now, they were going where no one had thought they could go, to the Final Four. They had never even thought in those terms. They had just been having fun and showing people that they could play. First, they had shown themselves. Then they had shown the ACC. Now, they had shown the nation.

This meant so much to Foster. He had been president of the coaches' association. He was friends with all the big-name coaches in his profession. But he had never been *there*, in the arena with Knight and Smith and McGuire and Crum. Now he was. All the work, all the days and nights in dingy high school gyms, the all-night sessions in the coffee shops with Goetz and Wenzel, all the misery, had finally paid off.

"I think for him it was a moment of vindication," said Goetz. "No one ever questioned Bill Foster more than Bill Foster and he needed to prove to himself that he was a good enough coach to take a team to the Final Four. My hope was that doing that would somehow relieve some of that pressure he put on himself. I think it did—at least for a little while."

For the players, there was nothing but jubilation. The exceptions were Morrison and Gray. Both were thrilled for their teammates but neither felt as if he was part of this. Each had scored two points in the three NCAA games and had not played a minute in the ACC final. While their teammates cut the Providence Civic Center nets, Gray and Morrison went back to the locker room.

"It was just my way of saying, 'I'm a spectator, not a participant,'" Morrison said. "I never made a big deal of it. In fact, I don't think any of the coaches ever even knew. But I would have felt funny up there cutting a net." Gray felt the same way. "I had such mixed emotions. For me to say 'we,' talking about the team, seemed wrong at that point. And yet, I had lived through it, I had been right there and I was really,

really excited. But cut the net? That just wasn't something I wanted to do."

In the long run, these feelings of bitterness would come back to haunt the Blue Devils. But for now, with one week left in the basketball season, there was no trouble. Morrison and Gray may not have felt like participants but they were still happy to be along for the ride. And on that snowy night in Providence, it was a joyride for everyone.

Spanarkel's support group, the boys from the Peacock Pub in Jersey City, who made regular road trips to Duke led by Spanarkel's brother Kevin, were in Providence and very much in a partying mood. Banks went out and won a dance contest, which surprised none of his teammates. "By then we were completely convinced that Gene was Superman," Bender said. "There wasn't anything he couldn't do."

But the star of this night was Bruce Bell. In a group overflowing with happiness, Bell was the happiest Blue Devil of them all. Never in his wildest dreams had he thought he would finish his basketball career on a team that was going to the Final Four.

That his boyhood idols from Kentucky would also be there—along with Notre Dame and Arkansas—sharing the same floor, building and spotlight, just added to Bruce Bell's belief that he had somehow landed on Fantasy Island.

Bell had never been a big drinker. In fact, the first time he had gotten drunk at Duke, his fraternity brothers had embarrassed him mightily by coaxing one of his best friends' girlfriends into greeting him at the door of his room in a flimsy nightgown.

"Bruce," she said, "I've been waiting for you all night."

Even drunk, Bell was too much of a gentleman to betray a friend. He became totally flustered trying to explain to the girl that while he certainly found her attractive, he simply couldn't even *think* about kissing her. He awoke the next morning convinced he had dreamed the whole thing.

Bell was almost as convinced that he was dreaming on this snowy night in Providence. The players went out to dinner and toasted themselves into near oblivion. Bell didn't drink a lot, but he drank enough to be feeling extremely happy by the time everyone decided to head for the hotel where the cheerleaders were staying and a major party was reportedly in progress.

The thought of seeing the cheerleaders would have terrorized Bell under normal circumstances, since he had a terminal crush on a blond senior named Kathy Butler. Bell looks and acts like the boy next door, the kind of guy every girl wants to cuddle. But he thought of himself as nothing more than a country boy from Kentucky who would have no shot at a goddess like Kathy Butler. "The thought that she would ever go out with me never once crossed my mind," he said.

The players arrived to find a horde of people at the party. Somehow, Bell ended up sitting on a bed amidst a swarm of people with Kathy Butler sitting right next to him. His teammates, knowing how Bell felt about the beauteous Ms. Butler, were watching closely.

"All of a sudden, in the middle of all this noise, Kathy turns to me and says, 'Will you go to my sorority formal with me?' " Bell's memory of the moment is exact, even eleven years later. "I said, 'Golly yes, will you go to my fraternity formal with me?' She said she would and the next thing I know, we're locked in each other's arms on the bed with fifty people standing there watching."

No doubt many of the fifty weren't paying much attention. But Bell's teammates were. They began chanting, "Juice, Juice, Juice!" as the liplock continued. "They were," Hardy recalled, laughing at the memory, "mashing face."

Eventually it was time for the players to go. They had a very early flight in the morning and it was already late. Several of them piled into a car. Gminski, Bender and Hardy were in the backseat with Bell stretched out across the three of them.

All of them remember the ride back to the hotel vividly, especially Bender. "The whole way back, Juice was lying there screaming over and over again, 'I can't believe it, I can't believe it, we're goin' to the Final Four and I just kissed the girl of my dreams!' He must have said it a hundred times. If there's one single thing I'll never forget about that whole month of March, it's Juice in the back of that car."

Hardy agrees. "You just had to know Juice to understand. The thought that he would play in the Final Four never crossed his mind. The thought that he would date Kathy Butler *never* crossed his mind. Now, in one day, they both happened. He was like a little kid. But then, to some extent that night we were all like little kids."

They had come so far together to reach this point, yet they really didn't understand what they had done. "It was one of those things," Spanarkel said, "where when it was over we all looked at each other and said, 'My God, what did we just do?' But then, we were just doing things we saw no reason not to do."

Even Morrison, on the fringes of the whole thing, admits he still gets chills when he thinks about it. "I look at the Final Four each year now and sometimes it's hard for me to believe that I was part of that once," he said. "We never once thought, 'Boy this is really a big deal,' that whole year. We were too young and innocent to understand."

And no one was a better symbol of that innocence than the oldest player on the team—the only one who had reached the legal drinking age in all fifty states—Bruce Bell.

"I can't believe it, I can't believe it. . . ."

12

Meet Me in St. Louis

By the time the team got home on Monday, Final Four Fever was rampant on campus. Trainer Max Crowder, the only person who had also been associated with the '63, '64, and '66 Final Four Duke teams, remembers the campus as accepting those trips with little fanfare.

"Those teams expected to go," he said. "They were very good and in those days you only had to win two games in the tournament to be in the Final Four. People were *happy* to be going but it wasn't like it was in '78 when the whole thing came from out of nowhere."

This was the Impossible Dream come true. "I think the fact that everyone knew that Duke *had* been good but had lost that luster added to the whole thing," said Ray Jones, the only member of the coaching staff who had ever been to the NCAA's before. "It was as if something that had been lost had been miraculously found. There was a feeling of vindication, a feeling of relief and a feeling of joy all at once."

The players felt all of this. Spring had arrived at Duke and the campus was at its most beautiful. It was the new birth of spring and the new birth of Duke basketball. It was a great place to be and a great time to be there. "If you ever in your life thought you had died and gone to heaven it was that week," Bender said. "It would have been very easy for us to kind of get carried away with the wonder of it all but the fact that we were playing Notre Dame gave us focus. Other than Carolina, they were the team we would want most to beat. For a lot of reasons."

Carolina was long gone from the tournament, losing to San Francisco in the first round of the West Regional. But Notre Dame was still very much alive and most people were already ballyhooing a Notre Dame-Kentucky matchup for the national title.

Like Foster, Digger Phelps was coaching in the Final Four for the first time. But his nationwide persona was much different from Foster's. Seven years earlier, at the age of twenty-nine, he had coached a Fordham team that had captured New York City in much the same way that Duke was now winning over the nation. The Rams went 26–3 that year, reached the NCAA round of sixteen, and made Phelps into a celebrity. He was hired to coach Notre Dame at age thirty and went about building the Irish into a national power, simultaneously building himself into one of the big names in coaching.

In 1974, Notre Dame ended UCLA's eighty-eight-game winning streak on national television. Phelps was the next anointed coach, a man who would start winning national championships shortly and keep on winning them. Notre Dame won a lot of games but kept coming up short in the NCAA Tournament.

Then came the recruiting battle for Banks. When Banks opted to keep his word to Duke, Phelps shrugged and said, "They won the battle, but we won the war," a reference to the fact that Notre Dame had signed Kelly Tripucka and Tracy Jackson, two players almost as highly regarded as Banks. Both had been recruited by Duke. Banks remembered that comment. The coaches did too, and they all remembered the Knights of Columbus scene, Wenzel most of all.

That wasn't all. During the regular season, Notre Dame had beaten Maryland, hardly a major achievement considering the fact that the Terrapins ended up sixth in the ACC. Nonetheless, Digger couldn't resist a jibe. "What's the big deal about the ACC?" he said. "I don't see what's so tough about the ACC."

Add all of that to the fact that NBC seemed to have turned its national game of the week into the Notre Dame game of the week and Duke had every incentive one could need going into the game. There were even individual grudges. Goetsch had played against Notre Dame center Bill Laimbeer in high school and thought he was an obnoxious lout.

"It was all there for us," Wenzel said. "As a staff, we really wanted Digger. We all thought he was an arrogant asshole. The players had heard over and over again how great Notre Dame was and how they were going to bury us. Notre Dame was the national team back then, on TV all the time. They had all the glamor. Our attitude was that we were going to go out there and show people that we were not only just as good as they were, but *better* than they were. It was like a mission. In a lot of ways, it was very easy to coach that week—which was a good thing because we were all nervous as cats."

Except for Foster. He seemed to sense that if he came across to the players as nervous, they would begin to believe that it was all too big for them to handle. Practices that week were very businesslike. If the rest of the campus was going crazy, that was fine. When it was time to go to the gym, Foster wanted everyone thinking about the next game.

"He never talked to us about *where* we were," Dennard said. "He talked about Notre Dame and what we had to do to beat them. There were never any speeches about this being a once-in-a-lifetime opportunity or anything like that. It was just a game we had to play and we would win if we did what we were supposed to."

On Thursday, the students came out to send the team off—the first pep rally in memory at Duke. The team arrived in St. Louis to find the weather cold and their hotel a long way from downtown. "We spent a lot of time in our rooms that weekend," Gminski said. "The coaches didn't want us getting caught up in everything. When it was time to play, we were ready."

What they weren't ready for was walking on the court to practice on Friday afternoon. The St. Louis Arena, which had been bought by Ralston-Purina and renamed the Checkerdome, seats twenty thousand people for basketball. "It made the Greensboro Coliseum look small," Gminski said. And, the place was, if not filled, damn crowded—especially for a practice.

"We were all freaking out," Gminski said. "All these people were there just to watch us practice. You could look into the crowd and see all sorts of famous coaches and you realized they were all there to watch *you*. That was when it hit us that this was really the big time now."

Only Bender had been through this before. But two years earlier, with Indiana, he had been a benchwarmer, more a privileged tourist than a participant. Now, he was a key player and his dad, as an ex-coach, was sitting in the stands with all the other coaches watching his son.

"I have one memory of that practice," Bender said. "We had just run a drill and Bill called us into a huddle. Just as he did, Gene let go with one of his farts. A big one. Bill stepped into the huddle, realized what had happened and said, 'Other end.' I had this vision of all the coaches sitting up there taking notes on how this Final Four team ran practice: 'Run drill, huddle up, go to other end.' Little did they know why we had done that."

For Foster, after years of sitting in the stands watching Final Four practices, this was a special time.

"One of the nice things about that year was that I really did enjoy, at least then, what we were accomplishing," he said. "I was still wound up, still getting tight for every game like I always did, but I was able to look around a little and know that something very good was happening."

The national media certainly understood that. By now, Duke was becoming America's Team. Notre Dame was almost passé; a lot of reporters had tired of Phelps's act. Duke was a genuine Cinderella, last in its own conference only one year ago, now playing in the Final Four—with two freshman forwards and a sophomore center who was younger than the two freshmen. Foster was witty and low-key, not caught up in the notion that he was the biggest story around the way Phelps seemed to be.

That night, Foster learned that he and his long-time friend, Texas Coach Abe Lemons, had been named the national co-coaches of the year by the Coaches' Association. "It was one of the few times in our marriage I can remember him waking me up to tell me something," Shirley Foster said. "He just said very quietly, 'Guess who got coach of the year?' It was about as excited as I've ever seen him. It meant so much coming from the other coaches."

Saturday was an ugly day, cold and rainy. The Duke players had been hoping for snow but they decided the lousy weather was enough of an omen. They were happy to be playing the first game, a 12:30 P.M. Central Time tip-off. Waiting any longer than that would have been unbearable. "I can never remember being so wound up to play a game," said Scott Goetsch. "I was ready to fight somebody or something."

More than anything, Goetsch was ready to fight Laimbeer. His teammates remember him sitting on the bench during the early minutes of the game saying, "Laimbeer sucks," over and over again. When his turn came to spell Gminski midway through the half, Goetsch took a pass on his first possession and hit a jump shot right in Laimbeer's face. For emphasis, he pointed at him as if to say, "In your face." When the two of them began jostling for position at the other end, Goetsch, after a quick check to make sure the referees weren't looking, crashed an elbow into Laimbeer's head. The Duke bench went wild.

"We were all screaming," Gminski said. "None of us had ever seen the Fonz like this. We were never nervous that day after that, we were all just so fired up."

They certainly didn't play nervous. That morning, no less a person than Howard Cosell had done his national radio commentary on the ascension of Digger Phelps to coaching greatness, noting that once Notre Dame had pushed Duke aside, Phelps would meet his greatest challenge in the final against Kentucky.

Duke had other ideas. From the start, the Blue Devils were playing Villanova again, racing the ball up the floor, taking quick shots that Notre Dame couldn't defense, controlling the boards. Gminski was making the Irish big men look silly—aided and abetted by Goetsch; Banks was completely outplaying Tripucka; Harrell and Bender were driving Notre Dame point guard Rich Branning nuts.

Late in the half, with the Blue Devils up by eight, Bender took an outlet pass from Gminski and spotted Banks flying up the right side of the floor. Bender was barely beyond the top of the key at the Duke end of the floor when he whipped a rising line drive pass toward Banks. It was an impossible pass, thrown too hard and too soon. "When I threw it," Bender said, "I thought it was in the fourth row."

So did everyone else in the building. Except Banks. He raced toward the basket, leaped in the air, caught it with one hand and in the same motion scooped it into the basket. The Checkerdome exploded. This was a brand of cerebral basketball you just didn't see at the Final Four. There was too much pressure to even *attempt* a play like that, much less convert it.

A few seconds later, Dennard, scrambling after a loose ball, went flying into press row. He pulled himself up into a sitting position, looked down at the reporters staring at him and said, "Ain't this fun?"

Oh, was it fun. They were running and jumping and playing like they had never played before. With the entire nation watching! And they were doing it to Notre Dame! "We were two feet off the floor the whole first half," Bender said. "We were flying."

They flew to halftime leading 43–29. This was stunning. Didn't they know they were too young? Didn't they know this was Digger's time to shine? They knew none of this. All they knew was this was *fun*.

But Notre Dame was not going to die easily. It was too good and too experienced a team to do that. In the second half, the Irish began to find the range with their jump shots, especially guard Donald (Duck) Williams. Then Tracy Jackson came off the bench and hit five of six shots, all of them with someone in his face. Notre Dame's size began to wear Duke down. The lead whittled. Ten. Eight. Six. Four. The clock was moving in slow motion, or so it seemed.

"We got tired," Spanarkel said. "We were so wound up in that first half that we were bound to run out of gas a little. Notre Dame got hot, we got tired, and then we got a little nervous. We were thinking we couldn't blow the lead but every time we looked at the clock it seemed like there was an eternity to play."

One more Williams jump shot sliced the lead to 88–86 with twenty seconds left. Notre Dame trapped off the inbounds pass. The ball came loose and suddenly it was in Williams's hands again. He was more open than he had been the entire half. Spanarkel's heart sank. "If he ties it there," he said, "we're in trouble."

Williams shot spun around the rim and off. None of Duke's big men were under the basket because they had been deployed down-court to try to break the press. Spanarkel looked up and saw Laimbeer, looking like a lion about to pounce on a piece of meat, reaching for the ball. If he got it, it was an easy dunk. "I knew I couldn't get both hands on the ball," he said. "I just wanted to try to tip it away from him, get it out in the open court and give the other guys a chance to get back."

This was the kind of Spanarkel play that always went unnoticed. Just before Laimbeer could snatch the ball, he lunged and tipped it over his head. Everyone raced for it. The quickest player on the court got to it—John Harrell.

"As soon as I got to it, my first thought was to get it over midcourt and out of danger," he said. "I thought after that, one pass, maybe two and we would run out the clock." Harrell never got a chance to move, though. Branning, understanding time was running out, fouled him as soon as he picked up the ball. Nine seconds were left.

Phelps called time-out to give Harrell a chance to think about the situation. Harrell expected this. He had scored just four points in the game, though he and Bender had been nearly flawless running the offense, getting the ball to the Big Three. He was an excellent free throw shooter—83 percent for the season—but he had never been asked to go to the line with a spot in the national championship game at stake.

In the huddle, Foster talked as if Harrell had already made the two foul shots. He wanted everyone to know where their man was as the players lined up. Without saying it, that was Foster's way of being prepared for a miss. He didn't want Notre Dame to be able to push the ball downcourt for an easy shot because his players didn't know who they were guarding. But he never said that. He knew, in all likelihood, Phelps would call time again if Harrell missed, to set up a play. So, he talked only about playing defense with a four-point lead.

Harrell wasn't really listening. "I knew I had one thing to do and that was make the shots, especially the first one," he said. "Ever since I started shooting foul shots when I was nine years old I always tried to do everything the same way every time. The same number of dribbles, the same time holding the ball, even the same breathing. It's almost like meditation for me. I just wanted to be sure I had my mind focused on the things I did every time up there. I didn't want to think about anything else."

The teams came back on the floor with the Checkerdome tingling with tension. There was no three-point shot then, so if Harrell made the first shot, Notre Dame would be virtually dead. If he missed, overtime seemed more than possible, given the way the Irish had been scoring during the last five minutes of the game.

"It was one of those times when you can feel your heart pounding," Spanarkel said. "It's so damn close, but it can get away real quick too."

Foster, whose blazer and checked pants had become the subject of national newspaper stories with each passing victory, crouched in front of the bench. He, too, could feel his heart pounding. The assistants sat behind him, all eyes on Harrell. Even Jones, for once, was quiet. At the end of the bench Rob Hardy, remembering a foul shooting lesson he had learned years ago in camp, kept murmuring, "school's out, school's out," over and over. It had become his good luck charm.

Harrell walked to the line, watched by twenty million people. He was a long way from his father's carport now. He took the ball, dribbled it twice, picked it up and stared briefly at the basket. The ball came off his right hand, fluttering as it always did like a knuckleball because it had no backspin.

Swish.

Spanarkel wanted to hug Harrell on the spot but he knew that wouldn't do. Instead, he clapped him on the rear end and, in very un-Spanarkel-like fashion, shook his fist gleefully. Foster never moved. He was frozen, knowing in his mind that it was over and yet afraid that if he allowed himself to think that, it wouldn't be. The Duke people, who were seated at the end of the arena where Harrell was shooting, were hugging one another in the stands.

"The minute the ball was out of my hand I knew it was good," Harrell said. "By the time it dropped through I wanted to jump straight up into the air. All the basketball I've played in my life, the best moment for me was when that shot dropped through."

The second one was easy. The Irish raced the ball downcourt hoping to score quickly and call one last time-out. Williams fired. The ball hit the back of the rim and went high into the air. Gminski couldn't grab it so he tapped it back, away from the basket. It landed right in Bender's hands with two seconds left. He was dribbling right toward the Duke bench when he heard the buzzer and began jumping in the air for joy.

Now they didn't have to hold back. While Foster went to shake hands with Phelps, Bender leaped into Wenzel's arms. Spanarkel grabbed Harrell, while Goetz, at last satisfied with Gminski, charged his protégé, who had been extraordinary with 29 points.

And in the middle of it all were Banks and Dennard, arms wrapped around each other, Dennard with his head buried on Banks's shoulder while Banks hugged him so tightly Dennard thought he might break. Each of them was thinking back to the hot nights in the I.M. building, the September days in Card Gym and all the promises they had made to one another. Their hug was long and lingering and the NBC cameras caught it. Right then and there, Duke became America's Team.

This was what sports was supposed to be all about: kids working together toward a goal and then reveling in achieving it. The fact that Dennard was white and Banks was black made the picture, both on television that day and in newspapers around the country the next morning, that much more riveting. The genuine feeling between them moved NBC's Dick Enberg to say simply, "There's a moment that gives you chills."

For Duke, winning the national championship could not have been more emotional than this. The game had been brutally physical; the ending wrenching and draining. Almost no one had expected them to beat Notre Dame and they had done it. *They* had won the war; not

Phelps. Banks, with 22 points and 12 rebounds, had made it clear that Tripucka and Jackson were nice players, but there was only one Tinker Bell, only one Superman. They were so thrilled that if the NCAA officials hadn't stepped in, they might have gone ahead and cut the nets down right there.

Wenzel sprinted to the locker room ahead of everyone else, not wanting to change the ritual now. When the players came through the door it was staring at them on the blackboard: "2." Even Morrison and Gray were caught up in this celebration. Standing at his locker right by the door Gray couldn't help but shout, *"What do you think about the ACC now, Digger?"*

Just as he finished his sentence, the door opened and there stood Phelps. Always a gracious loser, he had stopped to congratulate the players. Gray was embarrassed. "Coach, I'm sorry," he said.

"Perfectly all right," Phelps said. "You won. You can say anything you want to say."

Even then, they really didn't understand what they had done. Harrell, sitting in front of his locker, looked up and saw dozens of reporters heading for him. "My first thought was to look to see if Mike, Gene, or Jimmy was standing next to me," he said. "I figured they wanted to use my space to get close enough to talk to them."

Not this time. They all wanted to know the Johnny Gun story. Harrell didn't understand that making two free throws on this stage was different from making them anywhere else. "I know it now," he said. "My mother still has scrapbooks at home filled with stories about that one game. It was incredible." Perhaps the most emotional person in the locker room that afternoon was Ray Jones. "Because of my height, I always wondered if I would get a chance to coach in the big time," he said. "I thought it was possible I would be buried all my life. Now, I was with a team that was going to play for the national championship. I walked out of the locker room and just burst into tears. It was about as proud a moment as I've ever had in my life."

Foster felt proud, but also relieved. As he walked back onto the floor to watch the Kentucky–Arkansas game, his friend Abe Lemons grabbed him. "It's a damn good thing you won that game, Foster," he said. "Because if you'da lost, there were two hundred coaches ready to come out of the stands and kick your ass for letting that son of a bitch [Phelps] into the final."

Lemons was joking . . . sort of.

The players stayed to watch the first half of the second game. Dennard had gotten his hands on an Arkansas hog hat—the one with the pig snout that you stick on top of your head—and was walking around yelling, *"Whoo-pig-sooey,"* the Arkansas battle cry.

Arkansas had a remarkable team, led by their six-four "triplets," Sidney Moncrief, Ron Brewer, and Marvin Delph. They were coached, ironically, by Eddie Sutton, who would become Kentucky's coach seven years later and eventually resign after getting caught up in the swirling scandal that was bound to catch up with Kentucky's program sooner or later. Unfortunately for Sutton, it would be later. This was sooner and Kentucky won an excellent basketball game, 65–61.

Now, there really were two left: Duke and Kentucky.

Perhaps never in the history of the NCAA basketball tournament have two teams that were so radically different met in the final. Kentucky was the ultimate basketball factory. There was no business bigger or more important in the state of Kentucky than Kentucky basketball. People there honestly thought their program incomparable, even though Adolph Rupp had won the last of his four national titles in 1958 and UCLA had won ten of them in the ensuing twenty years.

Joe B. Hall, Rupp's successor, was a bland, humorless man who could keep the Kentucky fans happy only by winning the national championship. He had come close in 1975, finishing second to John Wooden's last UCLA team, but he had not yet won. Now, the four freshmen who had been key players on that '75 team—Jack Givens, Rick Robey, Mike Phillips, and James Lee—were seniors. Kyle Macy, who had gone to Purdue after Bender decided to go to Indiana, had transferred to Kentucky and was the starting point guard. Truman Claytor and Jay Shidler shared the shooting guard spot. Givens, Robey, and Phillips—the latter two both 6–10—started up front, with Lee the first man off the bench.

It was a deep, experienced team that had started the season as the favorite for the national title. The Wildcats had remained No. 1 almost the entire season and would enter the championship game with a 29–2 record. They were very honest about the fact that only a national title would make their season a success. They said that the season hadn't been any fun because they had a job to do, period. Their theme was "Season Without Joy." It fit.

Their opponents in the championship game didn't know about any of this. They had started the season hoping to get out of last place in the ACC. Kentucky's senior class averaged 56 points and 22 rebounds *per game.* Duke's senior class—Bell—had a total of 25 points and 12 rebounds *for the season.*

The Blue Devils were Cinderella; the Wildcats were the ugly sisters. Hall was the wicked witch; Foster was Prince Charming. The press conferences the next day reinforced the stereotypes. The Duke kids— the five starters and Bender—kept making faces at each other, saying funny things and making fun of one another. "It was one of those deals where years later you look back at pictures and say, 'No, we didn't act like that,'" Dennard said. "But we did. To us, the whole thing was a hoot."

The laughs stopped when Kentucky entered the room. The Wildcat players were as grim-faced as the Duke players had been loose. "We know if we lose," Robey said, speaking for everyone, "we go home labeled as failures."

Looking back, the Duke players are unanimous in saying this was the difference in the game: "We *wanted* to win," Hardy said, "they *had* to win. We went in with the attitude that this was only the beginning for us. They knew that this was the end."

The Duke kids were already heroes; Kentucky still faced the possibility of ending up as goats. "I think we went out to play them thinking we couldn't lose," Gminski said. "We had already won our national championship just by being there. It wasn't that we weren't intense or didn't play hard. We did. But they were on a mission. We weren't."

At the time though, that feeling seemed to make sense. The coaches had watched their team win seven straight pressure-packed games without getting tight. They saw no reason to make them tight now. There was no reason to mess with success: Foster would wear the blazer and the checked pants again and the players would go through their "joke, joke, joke," routine at pregame meal.

"If it ain't broke," Bender said, "why fix it?"

But even though the routine was exactly the same, the players were smart enough to figure out—at last—where they were. Notre Dame had been a vendetta and that had kept them from thinking about everything else that was at stake. But now, as Sunday became Monday, all of them were beginning to understand just how small a number "2" was when 273 had started.

As Bill Foster got ready to attempt to sleep that night, Shirley Foster sat up in bed reading an NCAA program. "You know, Bill," she said, "a lot of the national championship games the last few years have been routs."

Foster groaned. He wasn't going to sleep much anyway and now his wife had given him one more thing to worry about. His mind filled with visions of Robey, Phillips, Givens, and Macy. They had come so far, he thought. "Well," he finally told himself, "everything you could possibly ask for has happened so far. If it can just happen right for one more day. . . ."

13

"We'll Be Back"

It started to go wrong long before the Blue Devils left the hotel for the arena. Early in the afternoon, the front desk called manager Kevin Hannon's room. There were policemen in the lobby and they needed to see Bill Foster. Hannon wasn't about to bother Foster without knowing what was going on so he called Goetz, who went down to meet with the policemen.

There was a problem. A St. Louis television station had received two phone calls with the same message: If Gene Banks stepped on the floor to play in the national championship game tonight, he wouldn't live to see the end of the game.

Goetz felt a chill go straight through his body. He had been thinking that morning about what a wonderful night this was going to be and now all the excitement drained out of him in a second. "It has to be a crank, right?" he said to the policemen.

Almost certainly it was. But a call like this couldn't be ignored, especially when Banks would be in an arena filled with twenty thousand people. Precautions should be taken and Banks, the police said, should be told. After all, it was *his* life. He should be given the option not to play.

Goetz took the police to see Foster, who was just as shocked as Goetz. "My first reaction was it had to be a joke," he said. "I mean, my God, this was still supposed to be a basketball game."

Of course, it *wasn't* a basketball game to Kentucky, it was a crusade. Two days later, writing in *The New York Times*, columnist Dave

Anderson would make reference to the "sick Kentucky fan" who had called in the threat. In response, Anderson would be deluged with mail from Kentucky people infuriated that he would assume the call had been made by a Kentucky fan. Certainly, it could have been someone else. But Anderson's logic wasn't flawed, especially given that Kentucky people were proud of calling UK basketball "a religion." After all, how many people have been killed in the last two thousand years in the name of religion?

Foster called Banks to his room and told him what had happened. Banks had grown up in West Philadelphia hearing gunfire as he played schoolyard basketball. He wasn't going to be scared off by a crank phone call. Foster knew that. But he wanted Banks to know that if he didn't want to play, he understood.

"Coach," Banks said, "be serious."

Foster told the other coaches and he told Tom Mickle and Johnny Moore. Since the threat had been made to a television station, keeping it a secret from the media would be impossible. Mickle and Moore would have to deal with any questions that came up before the game. They would also have to inform NBC and let the network decide how to deal with the threat. If the other players asked about the extra security around the bench, they were to be told it was just in case things got crazy at the end of the game.

Foster couldn't help but be distracted by all this. "I wondered if I had the right to let Gene make the decision," he said. "There was no way he was going to pull himself from the game. Should I call his mother and let her decide? No. That would frighten her, maybe for no reason. Maybe I should just pull him from the game. But the police were very much against entertaining that idea because if you do that you just encourage other nuts to try the same thing."

All these thoughts were swirling through Foster's head when the team arrived at the arena during the consolation game. He forced himself to think about Kentucky.

With the team and the other coaches, he began to review the scouting report. His biggest concern was Gminski, who faced the biggest challenge of his career in this game. In Robey and Phillips he would be taking on two players as big and strong as he was, with much more experience. Robey was the finesse player, the scorer who could hurt you from a lot of places on the floor. Phillips was the banger, the moose who would just knock you around for forty minutes. "The thing we were all most worried about," Goetz said later, "was whether Mike could deal with their two big guys and not get in foul trouble."

Gminski almost never got into foul trouble. He wasn't that kind of player. He would give up a shot rather than commit a foul. But if he did that tonight, Robey and Phillips might spend the game dunking. Duke's two-three zone would have to be very active and force Kentucky to shoot from outside, although Harrell or Bender would have to be sure to spot up on Macy, a deadly outside shooter. The same would be true if Shidler was in the game, although he wasn't nearly as consistent as Macy.

Then there was Givens, known to one and all as Goose. He was Kentucky's leading scorer at 17 points a game, a streak shooter who could be dangerous if he got hot. Bell remembered him from high school, having lost the last game of his high school career to a Givens-led team in the state play-offs. The man assigned to guard Givens for Bell's team that night was James Lee, now Givens's Kentucky teammate.

As Goetz and Wenzel went through the scouting report, they mentioned that Givens could shoot the ball well out to about eighteen or nineteen feet. When they finished, Goetz looked at Bell, knowing how familiar he was with Kentucky and said, "You want to add anything, Bruce?"

Bell nodded. "Coach, I just don't think Givens has the kind of range you're talking about. I think it's more like sixteen or seventeen feet at the most."

That, as it turned out, was a comment Bell would be reminded about for years to come.

Foster took over at that point. His talk wasn't much different from what it had been throughout the tournament. He reemphasized the points Wenzel and Goetz had made and talked about being sure to take good shots because Kentucky was not the kind of team that was going to give up a lot of offensive rebounds. "If he had decided to say something inspirational, I'm not sure any of us would have really heard it," Bender said. "Somehow, when we got in the locker room that night you could tell that it had sort of hit us where we were. It was the first time I felt as if we were at all nervous. All of a sudden, there was no place to go after this game. This was it, one way or the other. I think we all kind of looked around and went, 'Wow.'"

It was easy to do that. There was an electricity in the building that was almost tangible. As the two teams took the court to warm up, public address announcer Frank Fallon put the evening into perspective.

"Ladies and gentleman," he said. "On October 15th, two hundred seventy-three college basketball teams began practicing, each of them pointing for this night. Now, two are left. They are the University of Kentucky and Duke University."

Goetz still remembers those words. "If that didn't give you chills," he said, "then nothing will. It was one of those things you work for and work for knowing there's a good chance you'll never get there. Now, we were there."

The script written for this game was clear and neat: the big bad boys from Kentucky versus the nice boys from Duke. The question was who would bow to the pressure, the team with all the experience that felt a defeat would be humiliating or the team going through all this for the first time? The NBC pregame show harped on this theme. Al McGuire repeatedly said that it didn't really matter if Duke won or lost. "They'll celebrate tonight no matter what," he said. "Everyone back home will love them anyway."

McGuire, like most people, thought it was Kentucky's game to win or lose. If Duke stayed close, that would be a moral victory. Duke's players didn't see it that way. They saw no reason to lose, even to Kentucky. During warm-ups, they kidded Bell about going down to the other end to warm up with his Kentucky teammates.

"I thought we were really ready to go," Bell said. "We knew how good Kentucky was, but by that point, we were pretty good too."

Very good.

Both teams were tight early. It was 2–2 after almost four minutes. Dennard missed two lay-ups. Gminski missed an easy shot. Spanarkel even missed a twisting lay-up. Kentucky jumped ahead 5–2 but couldn't pull away. Duke was shooting poorly, but it was getting to the foul line. Phillips picked up three quick fouls and Lee had to come in for him.

Kentucky maintained its lead throughout the first half, but couldn't build on it. After a slow start, Givens began to warm up. He kept sliding into the hole in the Duke zone just behind the two guards in the foul line area. Gminski, in the middle of the back line of the zone, needed to move up to stop that shot but his mind was on Robey and Phillips. By the time he stepped out towards Givens, it was too late. A couple of times when he did get there, Givens got the shot off over him.

"Step up, Mikey," Foster kept yelling. "Step up."

"My mind was on the two big guys," Gminski said. "When you play zone, there are going to be spots where a guy like Givens is going to get his shot. I didn't adjust fast enough to what he was doing and he got on a roll. After a while, when a guy is hot like that, it doesn't matter what you do, he's going to make his shot."

Even with Givens heated up, Duke hung close. With thirty seconds to go in the half, Banks made a pair of free throws that cut the margin to 39–38. Kentucky came down and fed Givens at his spot. This time, Gminski did move out. Givens faked and appeared to travel. No call. He ducked under Gminski and hit a short jumper to make it 41–38. The Duke bench was up, led by Bell and Hardy, calling for a travel. Referees Jim Bain and Roy Clymer, both from the Midwest, ignored their pleas.

Now, the Blue Devils showed their youth. Instead of waiting for the last shot, Gminski forced a bad one and Robey got the ball to Givens, who was now so hot he didn't even think of waiting for the last shot. With ten seconds left he hit his 19th point—and his 16th in the last ten minutes—to make it 43–38.

Dennard grabbed the ball as it came through the basket and found Banks streaking down the left side. Givens was flying back to cut him off. Banks went in as Givens got between him and the basket. His shot rolled off the rim and the two hit the floor hard. Block or charge? If it was a block, it would be Givens's third foul and Banks could cut the halftime margin to three. But Bain called it on Banks. Instead of Banks at the line, Givens went to the line. He made both shots and Kentucky had its biggest lead of the game, 45–38 at halftime.

The last thirty seconds had been disastrous for Duke. Two calls that could have gone either way—the apparent travel on Givens and the block/charge between Givens and Banks—had gone Kentucky's way. Even a split of the two calls and the lead would have only been three. What's more, a third foul on Givens would have given Hall some serious questions to deal with during the intermission. But none of it had happened.

The coaches, in general, were dismayed by the officiating. But they said nothing. The game was too close for them to get distracted by the officials. "I wasn't thrilled with what was going on but I didn't think we were in bad shape," Foster said. "We had shot the ball poorly [nine for 23], Givens had gone off [21 points], and we hadn't gotten anything from the officials. But we were still only down seven. It wasn't like we hadn't been behind at halftime before. I thought we could handle it, especially if we got a good start."

They got just that, quickly slicing the lead to 45–42. McGuire, who had talked through much of the break about how Kentucky was now at level one with a seven-point lead and would look next to go to level two—a 13 point lead—and then on to level three—a 20-point lead—

was impressed. "These Duke guys don't know they aren't supposed to win," he announced.

The lead went back and forth between three and five for a couple of minutes. Then, with the score 51–46, Banks missed a free throw—his first miss from the line all night. Robey rebounded and flipped a quick pass to Truman Claytor on the left side of the floor, right in front of press row. Claytor turned back toward Robey to catch the pass and as he did, Spanarkel, always alert, jumped up quickly and denied Claytor room to move forward.

The surprise element was vital here. If Claytor saw Spanarkel, he could easily maneuver around him left or right. But because he had his head turned, he didn't have time to think that way. Instead, as often happens, he panicked for a split second. In that moment, having caught the pass with his front foot anchored, he instinctively made a fake using that front foot. He had changed pivot feet, a common mistake made by players when a defender jumps in front of them when they aren't looking. At the end of the Duke bench, Bell and Hardy leaped into the air screaming, "*Yeah!*" when they saw Claytor travel. The Kentucky fans let out an audible gasp, the kind you hear when a player has made an obvious error. Spanarkel screamed "*Walk!*" Claytor actually stopped moving waiting for the whistle.

And Jim Bain, right on the play, never blew his whistle. He just stood there. "I think they had a travel there," McGuire's co-analyst, Billy Packer said, clearly surprised there had been no call.

Foster was stunned. He got off the bench, put his hands out for a moment with his palms turned upward, then gave the traveling signal, as if to say, "Where is the traveling call?" He never said a word and, even if he had, Bain was on the opposite side of the floor from him and could not possibly have heard him.

Bain had blown the call and he knew it. If he had been a good official, he would have blown his whistle, made the call and then apologized to Claytor for making the call late. Instead, he compounded his error. In the national championship game, from across the court, Bain called a technical foul on Foster.

Enberg: "Oh no, I think they've called a technical on Foster."

McGuire: "You see, that happens when a guy misses a call because he's defensive. He missed the travel and then he was quick to call the technical. I don't think Foster even said anything."

Enberg: "Even if Foster said anything, there's no way he could hear him from across the court."

Calls do not come much worse than that one. If Bain had called the travel, Duke would have had the ball with a chance to cut the lead to three. Instead, Macy went to the line, made two free throws to make it 53–46, and then Givens quickly hit a jumper to push the lead to 55–46. Courtesy of Jim Bain, Kentucky had its biggest lead of the night. And, courtesy of Bain, Duke was flustered for the first time all night. Dennard had to come out a moment later after catching an accidental knee in his thigh. Kentucky sensed the kill.

Beginning with the technical, it went on a 15–4 run, widening the lead to 66–50. The highlight of that spree was a Givens jumper from the corner that somehow *banked* in. "When he hit that," Bender said, "it was like lights out time. They just had everything going for them and we had nothing."

Foster called time. He stood staring up at the scoreboard hearing his wife's words: "You know Bill, a lot of finals the last few years have been routs."

"I thought that's what we might be looking at," Foster said. "But our guys were not the type to roll over, even when no one would have criticized them if they did."

Sure enough, the Blue Devils crawled back into the game. They were fighting Kentucky, the clock and, in their opinion, the referees. But they kept fighting them all. Spanarkel and Banks kept going to the basket, Gminski kept taking soft jumpers. Dennard, after a poor first half, came back from his minor injury so angry that his case of nerves disappeared. Bender hit a couple of bombs.

They chipped the lead down to 8 with five minutes left. Kentucky got it back up to 12. They got it back to 8 again. But they couldn't get closer and time was running out quickly. The clock that had seemed so slow on Saturday now seemed to be moving in doubletime. With a minute left and Kentucky leading 90–80, their fans began the "We're number one" chant. Banks hit to make it 90–82, but they had to foul Givens with forty-eight seconds left. Remarkably, he missed. Bender hit a bomb and it was 90–84. Givens then took a foolish shot—any shot was foolish at this stage—and Dennard came down the right side with Lee to beat. He faked, shot, and hit. There were still thirty-two seconds left and the lead was now 90–86. Except it wasn't because there was a whistle. Enter that man Bain again. He called Dennard for a charge. No basket.

"No way was that a charge," Dennard said. "The contact we had was after I shot the ball. The foul should have been on him. But if the guy wants to make the call on me, he's got to count the basket."

Kentucky spread out again and this time Macy was fouled. He hit both free throws with twenty-eight seconds to go. That made it 92–84 and Hall began emptying his bench, wanting to give his starters a chance to come out, get their standing ovation and their hugs.

The Blue Devils had little interest in any of this. Banks quickly got inside with twenty-one seconds left, scored to make it 92–86, and Foster called time. The Kentucky reserves weren't ready to deal with Duke, not in the emotional state the team was now in. Bender quickly stole the ball from Dwayne Casey, who ten years later as an assistant coach would be at the center of the scandal that would bring Kentucky down. Now, Casey was a scared benchwarmer. Bender stripped him and fed Gminski. His basket made it 92–88 with eleven seconds left. A murmur went through the Kentucky crowd. The damn game wasn't over yet.

Hall understood. If he left his reserves out there, Duke might score three times before you could say, "blown national championship," and Hall would be looking for work. He put the starters back in.

"Even now," said Enberg, "Joe Hall can't savor victory."

"He hasn't got the victory yet," McGuire said. "These Duke guys don't know when to quit."

The Blue Devils had to overplay the inbounds pass and try for a quick steal. If that failed, they had to foul right away. For a brief moment, it looked like Macy might not get the ball inbounds in the required five seconds. But then Lee flashed toward midcourt. He was open. Macy threw him the ball as Bender lunged, first for the ball and then for Lee. He got neither. Lee was now behind everyone. He went in and emphatically slammed the ball with four seconds left. Now, at last, it was over. The Kentucky players were mobbing one another, filled with as much relief as joy, as soon as the clock hit zero.

At the time, the rules said that the runner-up team must endure the victor's celebration and wait for the awards ceremony. The coaches from both teams had been briefed about this before the game. But Foster wasn't thinking about any of that. This was Kentucky's moment and he saw no reason for his players to linger. "Locker room," he told them, and off they went, still a little stunned, still not quite realizing that their remarkable journey was over.

Once the door was shut, Foster called them all together to say the brief prayer that had become part of their postgame ritual. As he started to speak, Foster's voice caught and he paused. Bell jumped in immediately. "Coach," he said, "let me do it. Please."

Foster nodded quickly. Next to Suddath, Bell was the most religious person on the team. But that wasn't why it seemed so right to Foster and to everyone else in the room that Bell say the prayer. This was his way of saying good-bye.

Bell was fighting his emotions too as he started to speak. "I had a feeling walking off the floor like I was losing something and I couldn't do anything about it," he said. "It had nothing to do with losing the game, it had to do with the guys. I felt a closeness to them right then like I had never felt in my life and I wanted to hold on to it for as long as I could."

Bell spoke softly and briefly but by the time he was finished, there wasn't a dry eye in the room. "Lord, thank you," he said. "Thank you for letting us be a part of this game and for this season. Thank you for letting me be part of this team and for the people in this room. I know they'll come back and win this tournament next year and no one will cheer harder for them than me. Thank you for making them part of my life. Amen."

They were all crying when Bell finished, hugging each other, hanging on to one another. "It's a feeling I've never had before or since," Goetsch said. "I felt unbelievably close to my wife when our children were born, but it was different. There was a bond in that room that can never be broken. If we never saw each other again that bond would still be there."

Each of them remembers that moment in the locker room with great emotion and each of them says almost the same thing about it. "We cried because we had been through something incredible and now it was over," Bender said. "I don't think any of us felt sadness about losing until later. Right then all our feelings were about the experience and the fact that it was over, not about losing the game."

Reality was on the other side of the door, though, in the form of NCAA officials telling them they had to come back to accept their runner-up awards. As they started out the door, without anyone saying anything, they all linked arms—players and coaches—forming a human chain. They walked back onto the floor like that, their arms around one another.

"The message was, 'Hey, we're together now and we're going to stay together,' " Dennard said. "We were proud of what we had done and we wanted the world to know we were proud of each other and proud to be the team that we were. Losing that game didn't change any of that feeling."

As they walked out onto the court together, the Duke fans spotted them and came to their feet. Somewhere up in the stands the chant started. It grew and grew until it actually began to drown out the gurgling of the happy Kentucky fans: "We'll be back, we'll be back!"

Standing on the floor together, the players heard the chant and looked at one another. "Damn right," said Banks. "Damn right. We'll be back."

And then they accepted their watches and left the floor as they had entered, together. The chant was still there as they exited and all of them knew it was true. They would be back. "We walked off that floor together, as close as a group of people could possibly be," Dennard said. "What we didn't know was that it was the last act of pure innocence we would ever perform together.

"We went to St. Louis as innocent kids. We came back as stars. Our lives were never the same again."

14

Loss of Innocence

The aftermath of the championship game was predictable. During the telecast, NBC had reported the threat on Banks's life. That subject and the officiating dominated Foster's postgame press conference. He wasn't eager to talk about either subject. The threat on Banks had obviously been a crank. It was a sickening, sad thing and Foster had no desire to feel sick or sad on this night. Those feelings would come later. For the moment, he, like his players, felt pride in what had been accomplished.

He was angry, very angry, at Jim Bain, but he wasn't going to say that to the media. He didn't want to sound like a sour grapes loser. "The officiating didn't decide the game," he said. "Jack Givens had forty-one points and Rick Robey had twenty. Givens was unbelievable. That decided the game."

Later, though, looking back at the technical, Foster could not help but feel some bitterness toward Bain. "I hadn't been called for a technical all year," he said. "You would think in a national championship game that the guy would be looking to *not* call a technical unless someone really got out of line." No one connected with the team blames Bain for the loss. But they still resent the role he played in the game. "Looking back, Kentucky was a team that just wasn't going to be beaten," Goetz said. "If Givens had had to score fifty-one instead of forty-one he probably would have. But how can a guy call a technical in that situation? It's just a shame."

What irks some of the players is that time has blurred memories and

167

people have forgotten about some of the critical calls that went against them. Hardy and Bell, both of whom live in Kentucky, come up against this all the time. "I was with a bunch of people who are Kentucky fans at dinner one night and we started talking about that game," Hardy said. "I said that I thought the technical had really hurt us and it was a horrible call. They said, 'What technical?' I couldn't believe it. I had to go back to the tape and show it to them. They thought I was making it up."

In the eleven championship games played since then, no coach has been called for a technical foul, even though there have been outbursts that went far beyond Foster's giving the sign for traveling.

What would have happened had Bain called Claytor for traveling? It is impossible to say but it is, to this day, a question all the Duke people ponder.

"It isn't something I think about every day or anything," Spanarkel said. "But when I think of that game I do wish we could have played it without that happening. Then if we had gone ahead and still lost, okay, we lost and they were better. I can live with that. This way, there's always going to be that question mark in the back of my mind because before that play, we were right on their heels."

■

They left the Checkerdome that night still high on competing, on having been at the highest level of their game and on having played supposedly omnipotent Kentucky to the buzzer. The next day, there was the natural letdown, some of it caused by hangovers, some of it caused by the adrenaline high having passed. "When we went to get on the plane to fly home on Tuesday, there was a feeling that we had let the school down," Morrison said. "We had come close, but we hadn't won. I think we all wondered a little how we would be greeted back home. It wasn't any feeling like we had failed, just that we hadn't succeeded when so many people had been counting on us."

The charter landed at Raleigh-Durham Airport in midafternoon and the players piled onto their bus for the ride back to Duke. The coaches told them that a welcome-home rally had been planned on the quad and they would be going straight there. Exhausted and, in some cases, still hung over, the players weren't thrilled about the notion of waving happily to the few people who would show up to greet them.

As the bus turned up Chapel Drive and headed for the main quad, Morrison shook his head and said, "If there are fifty people here I'll be surprised."

There weren't fifty people there. The number was closer to five thousand. As the bus pulled up to the quad and the players saw that every inch of available space was taken, their mouths dropped.

They walked onto the platform that had been set up and the cheers sent chills through their bodies. They had gotten so caught up in the win-win-win mentality of the Final Four that they had forgotten for a moment that these were the people who had backed them long before anyone else had even heard of them. One by one the players and coaches took the microphone to say thank you, to promise they would be back, and to tell them how much it meant for them to come home to this kind of a welcome.

"I think of all the things I'll never forget about that experience, turning onto the quad and seeing all those people may be what I remember most," Bender said. "I mean those people really did love us. And we loved them. We were part of each other. Duke is just that way. It isn't that people put you on pedestals or anything but the basketball team and the games in Cameron are part of the Duke experience for everyone."

All of them say the same thing about the March 28th love-in on the quad. "The best thing about Duke is that the basketball players really are part of the student body," Goetsch said. "There's no athletic dorm, we all have friends away from the team and people really relate to what we're doing. My greatest joy that year was how excited my fraternity brothers got about the whole thing because they really felt like they were part of it, too."

On that day though, things began to change for Duke. One headline in the *Durham Sun* said, "DUKE FANS EXPECT NATIONAL TITLE NEXT YEAR." The season hadn't been over for twenty-four hours and expectations for next season had begun.

There was more. Once the quad party was over and the bus had taken the players back to Cameron, it was time to split up. Bruce Bell was, suddenly, no longer a member of the Duke basketball team. And neither was Lou Goetz. That day, he had accepted the job as head coach at Richmond.

"I knew it was time to move on and this was a great opportunity for me," Goetz said. "But in the locker room right after the Kentucky game when we were all crying and hugging each other I remember thinking, 'How can I leave these guys?' But I knew I had to do it, even though it was very difficult."

It would be most difficult for Foster. Goetz had been with him for fourteen years, the last eight as his closest advisor. Wenzel would move up to Goetz's job, but he would not be Goetz. Wenzel was not a Jewish mother and he hadn't played the role of number one assistant. He would need time to grow into it.

Beyond that was the question of replacing Wenzel in the second assistant's spot. Jones, naturally, wanted the job and felt he deserved it. But Foster was concerned that because of his height Jones might not receive enough respect from the players on the practice floor. Jones, who was very popular with the players, was crushed when Foster hired twenty-five-year-old Steve Steinwedel (who was six-feet-seven) as the second assistant.

"It killed me," he said. "I don't think Bill understood how important it was to keep continuity as much as possible with Lou gone. I think I had the respect of the players and I would have done the job. But he wanted a guy who could coach the big men and he felt Steve would be better equipped to do it. Leaving Duke was the hardest thing I've ever done. But I felt I had no choice."

When Foster hired Steinwedel, Jones told him he wanted to look for a second assistant's job elsewhere. Foster understood. A few weeks later, Jones was hired as an assistant at Furman. To the players, the departures of Goetz and Jones were disheartening if not shocking. They had all known that their success might lead to Goetz's getting a job, but his actual departure still threw them.

"I think we all were thinking, 'Wait a minute, you can't leave, we aren't finished here yet,' " Gminski said. "To us, the coaches were *our* coaches and we couldn't imagine that changing. Then when Ray left too, all of a sudden we had an entirely different kind of staff."

Whether Foster's fears about Jones's work on the practice floor were justified or not, there was no question that he added a unique element of intensity to the staff. He was replaced by Terry Chili, who was nineteen inches taller but totally lacking in coaching experience. In fact, the seniors and juniors had played with him as a teammate and found it difficult to look up to him—except literally. To them, he was still Herm the Sperm a lot more than he was Coach Chili.

Foster joked about the changes at first, noting that the 6-7 Steinwedel had replaced the 6-2 Goetz and that Chili had replaced Jones by saying, "We've increased the size of our staff more than any school in the country." But the fact was that the smooth-running machine had been broken up: Wenzel could not handle Foster's mood swings the way Goetz had; the players didn't feel nearly as comfortable with

Steinwedel as they had with Wenzel, and Chili was a novice where Jones had seen almost everything.

To the outside world, the changes were hardly worth noting. Spanarkel, Gminski, and Banks were coming back. The rest didn't matter.

—

There would be only one new player, Vince Taylor. Ironically, Taylor was a 6–5 guard from Lexington, Kentucky, who had been one of three high school guards in the East pegged for greatness that year. The others were Dwight Anderson, who was going to Kentucky, and Reggie Jackson, who was going to Maryland.

Taylor would have the luxury of fitting in gradually, something Spanarkel, Gminski, Banks, and Dennard had not had. There were experienced stars ahead of him and Taylor would get to work his way into the lineup. Even though they were from the same hometown, Taylor was completely different from Bell. He was black and highly sought after, a great basketball talent blessed with remarkable quickness. Bell was none of those things. One thing they did have in common, though, was a gentle nature that made them popular with their teammates. While the new coaches would have their problems, Taylor quickly fit into the locker room.

That locker room would be an entirely different place than it had been before. In it now was the No. 1 team in the country, the team picked by all the experts to succeed Kentucky as the national champion. They were celebrities. The Big Three were on preseason All-American teams all around the country. Foster was the hottest commodity in coaching, written about not only in sports magazines but in publications like *The Atlantic* and *Playboy.* The hunger to prove themselves that had pervaded those pickup games in Card Gym the previous September was gone.

No one was more affected by this newfound stardom than Banks and Dennard. Their play, the team's success, and their relationship had made them darlings everywhere they went. Dennard remembers going to a golf tournament in Greensboro the week after the Final Four and being recognized by everybody.

"People fawned on me," he said. "That's when it hit me that we were really big time. I had one guy tell me that his wife wanted to go to bed with me. He was serious, too. And it was *okay* with him. He wanted to go around and tell people that his wife had been with Kenny Dennard. I was nineteen years old and I loved every second of it."

They all loved every second of it but Banks and Dennard most of all. The two of them partied their way through the summer, pausing only occasionally to work out or play basketball. It wasn't a priority, though. They knew they were good and when the time came, they would get back to it.

"Success always changes you," Dennard said. "It has to. It changes the way people look at you and the way they treat you and the way you look at yourself. Especially when you are as young as we were. Maybe if we had gone to the Final Four as juniors, it would have been different. We would have known what failure was. We would have understood better how much work it took to get there. But we went out and did it as freshmen. We just assumed we would do it again. We completely forgot the work and the desire that had gone into getting there in the first place."

It was a summer of great joy and great anticipation for everyone. There was one tragedy, though.

During the Final Four, in addition to the players, one of Duke's managers had become a celebrity: Debbie Ridley, was the classic blond bombshell with the kind of figure that was impossible to miss. NBC didn't miss it or her.

Early in the final game, the cameras caught a close-up shot of her and Dick Enberg introduced her to the nation. "There she is," he said, "Debbie Ridley, the first female manager ever at a Final Four. Looking at her, Al, might help explain why Duke is doing so well."

"Dick," McGuire answered, "I don't think we're going to get into that subject."

Ridley's parents were watching the game at home with a group of friends. As soon as he spotted his daughter, John Ridley jumped out of his chair screaming, "There she is, there's my girl." There was no bigger Duke fan than John Ridley. When she came home that spring, Debbie Ridley gave her NCAA watch to her father. "It was much too big for me anyway because it was a man's watch," she said. "It thrilled him. He wore it all the time."

He was wearing it driving home from work in July when his car collided with a tractor-trailer. John Ridley was killed instantly. When the police asked Debbie Ridley's mother to identify her husband, she looked at his wrist and saw the watch. She knew then that it was her husband. Debbie Ridley still has the watch. "I'm saving it," she said, "to give to my husband when I get married."

She is still single. And still gorgeous.

■

While Banks and Dennard were partying their way through the summer, Rob Hardy was deciding to keep a diary of his senior season. He had watched Bell and knew how much the year had meant to him, even though he had only played sparingly. That, and a conversation with Dick DiVenzio, a former Duke guard, led him to decide to keep a diary of what he hoped would be a championship season. When the players returned to campus the first week in September and began their preseason drills and pickup games, Hardy began to write. Looking back at the diary, one can see warning signs immediately. He makes reference to Banks and Dennard—especially Dennard—not being in good shape. He notes that Dennard wasn't playing hard, sometimes not playing *at all* in the pickup games. Gminski had a bad ankle that was slowing him down but that would come around. So too, wrote Hardy, would Dennard and Banks.

There were five seniors on this team. Only one of them, Spanarkel, would be a starter. Hardy didn't mind not playing; as an ex-walk-on he had long ago accepted his role as cheerleader. But for Morrison, Gray, and Goetsch, playing time was very important. This was their last chance. All had worked hard during the summer and all of them were hoping to push the starters for playing time. Hardy makes reference in the early part of his diary to how well and how hard all three of them were playing and comments that he hopes they get a chance to play. Suddath, though only a sophomore, had worked during the summer to bulk himself up and he too wanted to compete for minutes.

This was now a team with a pecking order. The Big Three came first. They had been selected as co-MVP's at the end of '78, a wise move by Foster. All could make a case for MVP. Spanarkel, the leader by example, had been amazingly consistent, averaging 20.8 points, 4 assists, and 3.4 rebounds a game. Gminski had averaged 20 points and 10 rebounds a game and Banks, getting stronger and stronger as the season progressed, finished at 17.1 points and 8.6 rebounds. They were the nucleus and everyone knew that. With the up-tempo offense the year before, everyone had gotten plenty of shots—the team averaged 85.6 points a game.

One step down from the stars were Dennard, Harrell, and Bender. Dennard's numbers had been solid the previous year—9.7 points and 6.4 rebounds—but his most important contribution had been his willingness to do anything to win, sacrificing his body anytime it was needed. He was the screamer on the team, the wild man, the guy who got everyone pumped up. It was a role he was quite content with.

Harrell and Bender had been a perfect point guard combination. They had each averaged 5.1 points a game and each gave the team a different look. Bender had been happy to come in off the bench. To Harrell, starting was important. He felt he had worked to earn the job; he also felt it was a sign that you didn't have to be highly touted to get the chance to start at Duke.

But Foster felt that Bender had more range than Harrell as a shooter and that he was a little more aggressive, a notion backed up by the stats. Bender had finished the season with 82 assists in 22 games; Harrell had 54 in 34—the last 24 as the starter. When practice began on October 15, Foster said the point guard job was wide open. This stunned—and angered—Harrell.

"It just made no sense to me. Why not say the other positions were open too? I had been the starting point guard on a team that played for the national championship," he said. "I did everything they asked me to and I made the big plays in the clutch all season. No knock on Bobby, but what had I done to deserve to lose my job?"

Nothing. But Foster was concerned that standing still might be the same as taking a step back. He believed that Bender would add versatility to the offense and that his more verbal nature made him the kind of leader one looks to in a point guard.

What Foster did not know was that while Bender might have some qualities that Harrell lacked, the Harrell/Bender combination was stronger than the Bender/Harrell combination would be.

"Hindsight is easy," Bender said. "But looking back, if I had been more mature I think I would have told Bill not to change things. Everyone wants to start and so did I. But I didn't mind coming off the bench the year before and if I had come off the bench that year, it wouldn't have bothered me. I knew I was still contributing that way. But coming off the bench *did* bother Johnny—and we ended up losing a good player."

Harrell was not the only one it bothered. Morrison, Gray, and Goetsch were also upset by the switch. Harrell's best friend on the team was Morrison, so he always spent a lot of time with the blue team group away from the court. He had been their connection to the white team. Now that was taken away.

"We had always looked at Johnny as kind of the blue team's representative on the starting five," Morrison said. "It wasn't anything we

talked about but we felt it. We lived vicariously through his success in
'78. Then he got benched and we all thought it was unfair. It was as
if the plan had been to give the job to Bender all along because he was
the glamor guy."

If Goetz had still been around, things might have been different.
Harrell says to this day that he thinks Goetz would have talked Foster
out of the move. Even if he hadn't, his presence might have prevented
the blue teamers from feeling so alienated and angry.

"Lou was always the guy who kept us feeling as if we were important
to the team," Gray said. "All through '78 he was our connection. He
would explain things to us, not Bill. Wenz had never done that. He
hadn't coached the JV's the way Lou had and he hadn't been the guy
who recruited us. We never felt the kind of closeness with him that
we felt with Lou. We started to feel as if we were a team apart from
the team. It became a them-and-us type of deal."

On the outside of that preseason, the Blue Devils looked like the
same close-knit, eager group that had won over the nation the previous
spring. But inside, the fabric of the team was slowly being torn apart.
The coaching changes started the trouble. The Harrell-Bender switch
made things worse. And, day by day, Banks and Dennard were becoming more and more of a problem.

To the rest of the team it was clear their attitudes had changed
considerably since the end of the season. Neither was in great shape
and neither worked as hard in practice. Banks even got himself arrested
on a charge of trying to sell marijuana to a policeman. It turned out
the cop was out to get Banks because his girlfriend had dumped him
for the player. The charges were dropped and the story somehow didn't
make the papers. But within the team it just added to the sense that
the innocent days of last season were very much in the past.

It wasn't that all the laughter had stopped. Shortly after the Banks
arrest, a Philadelphia tabloid newspaper got wind of the problem. It
couldn't confirm that Banks had been arrested—because the charge
never made the books—but it did write a story in which it reported that
"the Duke team is apparently rife with racial tensions, drug problems
and sexual promiscuity."

That set Foster off. He called a team meeting to clear the air. When
it was over, Gray, whose humor was as sharp as anyone's when he was
in the right mood, stood up and said, "If that's all, I'm going home to
have an orgy and do some drugs. And when I'm done, I want Banks
to come over and clean the place up for me."

Everyone cracked up. But moments like that were rare. This was a team crackling with tension even while everyone was writing about them as if they were still the joyboys of St. Louis. Foster was concerned by the distractions of the national media attention and by Banks and Dennard. He didn't even know the kinds of problems that he was going to face dealing with Harrell and the nonstarting seniors. This was all new for him. He was used to being the builder, the hunter. Now, for the first time in his coaching career, he was the hunted. He wasn't comfortable with the role.

"It was all new for me," he said. "I wish now that I had enjoyed that off-season more than I did. Instead of looking at where we had been and how far we had come, I brooded about the Kentucky game. I really let it bother me that whole summer. Then I started to worry about doing it again, about being labeled a failure if we didn't win it all. I should have let other people worry about that, not me. But I worried about it anyway."

In truth, Duke was in an untenable situation. Like Kentucky the year before, they had been put into a position where anything less than a national championship would be viewed as a failed season. "After that next year, I think we all respected Kentucky a little more than we had before," Dennard said. "They took that situation and handled it. We didn't."

By the time the season started, the team was filled with simmering tension. Goetsch, Morrison, and Gray had surmised from practice that they weren't going to play much and they were angry. Harrell had been told by Foster before the preseason exhibition game that Bender would start and he was disconsolate. He called his parents in tears asking, "Why are they doing this to me?" His parents had no answer.

Foster wasn't thrilled with the opener—at Western Kentucky; a road game where the school had both tradition and a tough building to play in. What's more, they had been selling "Beat Duke" T-shirts for a month. Fortunately, Gminski and Spanarkel both came out hot. The Blue Devils broke open a close game early in the second half to win going away, 78–53.

But there were signs of trouble ahead. Banks and Dennard were sluggish, scoring only six points each. Harrell, in his new role coming off the bench, didn't score. And Goetsch, Morrison, and Gray were upset that Foster waited until the very end of the game to get them in, even with a huge lead. Goetsch, who might have been the most improved player on the team, was especially upset.

"I was really hot," he said. "I had worked hard to create a role for myself the year before. Now, here I was a better player and I was looking at a diminished role. Mikey was going to play more minutes because he was stronger and he was a star and they were going to have to find minutes for Vince because he could play. That took away from the rest of us. When I went in the game that night I was steaming. I remember Dennard kind of grabbing me and saying, 'Fonz, be cool, it'll be okay.' "

But it wasn't okay. The next day in practice during a scramble for position inside, Goetsch and Gminski traded punches. It was a manifestation of all Goetsch's frustrations and Gminski happened to be the person standing there. Gminski, easily the most gentle person on the team, wasn't quick enough or angry enough to really square off, so a real brawl was averted. But Gray and Morrison had jumped to Goetsch's side, fists clenched, so quickly that Goetsch realized on the spot how deep the divisions within the team had become.

"It was as if there were two teams," he said. "The coaches were coaching the starters and we were the opposition. It wasn't as if Steve, Harold, Johnny, and I were being groomed for anything. The players ahead of us were younger than we were. So they didn't really care. And that pissed all of us off. Sudds even became part of it, but he was too nice a person to get really angry the way we did. It was definitely an explosive situation."

Things cooled down for a while after the Goetsch-Gminski square-off. The home opener against SMU was almost a repeat of the quad love-in. The Final Four and ACC Championship banners were unfurled and all the happy memories came flooding back for everyone. The team played sloppily, but still won.

Then came Big Four weekend. Duke had never won the tournament and to do it, it would have to beat N.C. State, which was ranked No. 6 nationally, and North Carolina, which was ranked No. 8. Once again proving that appearances can be deceiving, the Blue Devils did exactly that. Banks hit the winning basket to beat State 65–63 and, after a horrendous start, they blew Carolina away in the last ten minutes to win the championship game, 78–68. Bender played the best game of his Duke career that night, scoring 14 points and handing off for 8 assists. For the third time in four games, Harrell didn't score.

The Big Four victory confirmed their status as the best team in the nation. The next week produced easy victories over LaSalle and a joyful revenge victory over "goddamn Southern California." Dennard still wasn't playing well, but Banks was. He was a man against boys against LaSalle, scoring 32 points. He followed that with a 17-point, 8-rebound game against Southern Cal. Gminski had 25 that night and Spanarkel had 20. The Big Three were right back where they had been.

Now they were 6–0. Bender was playing well and people were writing about the new dimension of leadership he had given the team. They were still the media darlings. *Sports Illustrated's* Kent Hannon had been in and out of Durham for a month putting together a piece on Spanarkel-Gminski-Banks. The premise was that Foster had wrought a miracle, recruiting in successive years players who had become the best in the country at their position.

The preseason tension seemed to be fading. Winning, as always, was a tonic. Even the blue teamers were temporarily mollified. "The thing you have to understand," Morrison said, "is that our feelings towards the coaches never really carried over to the guys. When I sat on the bench during a game, I didn't think about the fact that I was mad at Bill for not playing me more. I looked out there and I saw *the guys.* It was still Jimmy and Mike and Gene and Kenny and Bobby. I liked every one of them. When we won I was happy for them. And when we started the way we did, I think we all thought we were going to roll right to the national championship.

"But then New York changed all of that."

New York would become to Bill Foster and Duke basketball what Normandy had been to Nazi Germany; what Bunker Hill was to the British; what the arrest of seven burglars at Watergate was to Richard Nixon. It was a point that changed their lives forever.

15

The Fall

The trip to New York started out as a triumphant return for Foster. He had left the area eight years earlier. Now, he was coming back with the No. 1 team in the nation, America's Team, the glamor boys of their sport.

Duke was playing in the annual ECAC Holiday Festival, once the country's premier Christmas tournament. Now, due to the demise of college basketball in the New York area, it was a four-team tournament usually filled with floundering teams. Having the No. 1 team in the nation was a fluke—Duke had signed up for it three years earlier when the program was still struggling.

Duke was clearly the star and the favorite but Ohio State had a good, though young team, and St. John's and Rutgers, the two local teams, had both been in the NCAA's the year before. It was a very competitive field. The only question was: Could *anyone* compete with Duke? Reading the New York papers that week one might have thought that Bill Russell, Wilt Chamberlain, Jerry West, and Oscar Robertson had been reincarnated in their prime and put into Duke uniforms.

The first twenty-five minutes of the Duke–Ohio State tournament opener seemed to back up all the paeans of praise. The Blue Devils were brilliant, running the Buckeyes into the ground. Sparnarkel and Gminski were unstoppable and the lead steadily built to 17 points as the Madison Square Garden crowd went bonkers over the artistry of what it was witnessing.

And then, suddenly, it all changed. Ohio State's two best players, point guard Kelvin Ransey and center Herb Williams, began to find the range. They began chipping away at the lead.

Instead of just playing their game and not worrying about Ohio State's run, the Blue Devils became cautious. They stopped running their fast break. They stopped looking to shoot. On one play, Banks broke across center court with the ball and had Spanarkel and Dennard wide open in front of him. All he had to do was decide which one of them he wanted to feed for a lay-up. Instead, he circled back toward center court, looking to make a fancy move and kill some clock. Ransey ducked in behind him, poked the ball loose, and OSU ended up with the lay-up instead of Duke.

Ohio State crept closer and closer. Down the stretch, the ball kept going into Williams and time after time, he was turning and shooting over Gminski. He tied it with fifteen seconds left. Duke still had the last shot of regulation: Gminski missed badly. By now, the Garden crowd was screaming for the upset. All the cool and savvy had gone out of the Blue Devils. The Buckeyes dominated the overtime and won, 90–84.

The upset was, in itself, stunning. The way it had occurred, the nation's No. 1 team folding completely down the stretch against a team that had lost games to Butler, Toledo, and Washington State, was appalling. There was no finger pointing . . . yet. It was a horrendous loss but that was all it was, one loss. They hadn't expected to go undefeated and perhaps some of the pressure would now be off. Foster was angry at the way they had failed to handle Ohio State's rally, but not hysterical.

Actually, the most upset person in the building might have been Kent Hannon. His piece on Spanarkel-Gminski-Banks was complete. The pictures had been shot and this weekend was supposed to be the coronation that would get the piece onto the *SI* cover. Now, it was off the cover. "With my luck," Hannon said, "they'll probably lose tomorrow and the piece will be killed entirely."

He laughed when he said it. After all, the notion was preposterous. Clearly, Duke would come back with a vengeance in the consolation game. St. John's was in for a long night.

That was apparent from the start. Once again, Spanarkel and Gminski were on target. Gminski, in spite of his problems with Williams, had scored 27 points the night before and Spanarkel had scored 30. The Blue Devils again blasted to an early lead. There was only one bad moment in the first half. During a scramble for a loose ball, Dennard hit the floor. As he was lying there, St. John's center Wayne McKoy kicked him in the head. Dennard lay there, stunned for a moment as play went to the other end. When he got up, there was no question about what he was going to do. He ran straight at McKoy, flailing his arms. "I wanted to knock his head off," Dennard said. "That's what he tried to do to me."

McKoy claimed later the kick had been accidental, but on tape it doesn't look that way. Regardless, the referees hadn't seen McKoy's kick. But fifteen thousand people saw Dennard's length-of-the-floor bull charge and he was immediately ejected. Suddath took his place and Dennard's teammates, inspired by what had happened to him, built a 15-point halftime lead. It only got worse for the Redmen after the intermission. Three minutes into the second half it was 55–36. "I was just hoping to make the final score respectable," Coach Lou Carnesecca said later.

With the game in hand, the Blue Devils seemed to relax a little. Suddenly, before you could say "déjà vu," the Ohio State nightmare started all over again. No one wanted to shoot. The turnovers were coming rapid-fire. St. John's was hot. And, for the second straight night, Duke couldn't make free throws. St. John's caught up even faster than Ohio State had. This time, overtime wasn't necessary. The final was 69–66—St. John's.

Twice in twenty-four hours, in college basketball's mecca, they had been humiliated. They had not only lost, they had died right there for all of New York City—and the whole world—to see. Banks had been awful against St. John's, finishing with just seven points. Suddath had not handled the pressure of stepping in for Dennard and Spanarkel and Gminski couldn't hit down the stretch either.

Worse than any of that was the way they had played in the clutch: *not to lose.* They had played scared. All the enthusiasm and joy of playing which had been so much a part of their game the year before—was gone. There were no passes from three-quarter court; no backwards dunks. They had gone from swashbuckling to scared stiff. Instead of thinking, "Let's show them," they had thought, "Let's not get shown up."

"It was everything that happens to teams that have had success," Dennard said. "Teams came at us with the look in their eyes that *we* had had the year before. We recognized it, but we didn't handle it. Instead of getting together and looking at how we had won the year before by staying together, we started pointing fingers. It was never anyone standing up in the locker room and saying, 'You messed up.' It was quieter. In fact, it probably would have been better if we *had* fought.

"After New York, the feeling was never the same again. We felt defensive. We couldn't believe people would criticize us. It freaked us out. And, most of all, it freaked Bill out. There's no doubt that New York was the begining of the end for him at Duke. He was never the same after that trip."

Nothing was the same. The next day, Kent Hannon's editors put his Duke piece on hold. It would never appear in the magazine. The joyride was over. The rollercoaster ride was just beginning.

▬

The day after the St. John's loss—New Year's Eve—the Blue Devils flew to Charlotte for a game on January 2 against Davidson. Everyone was baffled about the two collapses but it was much too early in the season to panic. The emphasis of the day was positive: *Tomorrow is New Year's Day, let's make a fresh start.*

The fresh start lasted until the afternoon paper, the *Durham Sun*, hit the street. In it was a letter to the editor written by Joe Gminski, Mike's father. The headline on the letter said, "OIL AND WATER." The essence of the letter was that Gminski felt the problem with the team was Foster's insistence on continuing to play John Harrell, even in his diminished role. Harrell, according to Gminski, was oil and the rest of the team was water. The two didn't mix. In conclusion, Joe Gminski said, the blame for the New York debacle rested with Foster because, "when the train arrives on time, the engineer gets credit. When it goes off the track, the engineer has to take the blame."

This was a shot below the belt to a team already reeling from a series of body blows. Foster had always been uneasy about Joe Gminski's constant presence around the team but the two had coexisted without problems—as long as the team continued to improve and play well. Now, the simmering rivalry that Mike's father always seemed to feel with Mike's coaches had exploded.

Mike Gminski was already feeling sick that afternoon, exhausted from the travel and disgusted with his and the team's play. He felt worse when Foster and Wenzel came to his room to talk about the letter. "They asked me first if I knew about the letter," he said. "Then they told me what was in it. I was as shocked as they were.

"As soon as they left I called my dad and asked him what in the world was going on. He just said this was the way he felt and he wasn't alone, that the letter really expressed the opinion of a lot of people. I really didn't know what to say to him."

Once again, Gminski was caught squarely in the middle between his father and his coach. "It's something I've been fighting all my life," he said. "I mean, there's never been any question about the fact that my father loves me and cares about me. But I was playing for Bill Foster and with my teammates. Their success was my success and their failure was my failure. You couldn't separate the two. We lost in New York because we all screwed up. I don't remember the games all that well, but I do remember that I stunk.

"Still, it was very hard for me to talk to my father about any of that. It always has been. Instead of having it out with him and maybe clearing the air, I suppressed it, buried it. I know it upset Bill and I'm sure it upset the other guys but they never said anything to me about it."

They didn't say anything because they all liked Gminski too much; they understood that he didn't share his father's opinions any more than he could control them. Even years later, none of them want to say anything critical because it might hurt Mike. One of the players put it this way: "It definitely had an effect on what happened to us that season, but Mike wasn't to blame. All we knew was that all the other parents cared about what was going on with the team, too. Only one of them was causing problems, though."

Joe Gminski was not—and is not—an evil man. He was simply the classic Little League father who wanted his son to become the star he himself had not become.

But now, because of his suppressed frustrations, *everyone* was carrying suppressed frustrations around inside: Foster, who had never before dealt with anyone seriously questioning his coaching; Gminski, caught in the middle between his father and his coach; Harrell, benched first, publicly criticized by a teammate's father second; the other blue-teamers, still not getting to play; Banks and Dennard, who were finding that the sophomore jinx was very real; even Spanarkel, who was baffled and upset by the turmoil around him.

"We never played in '79 the way we played in '78," he said. "Part of it was the other teams. They didn't want to let us run the way we had and they slowed things down on us. But part of it was us. We didn't play with the abandon we had played with the year before. After New York there were times when we were all looking not to be the one that screwed up. It was an entirely different kind of feeling than we had the year before when our basic attitude going into a game was, 'We're going to kick your ass.' "

Gminski, even apart from the problems with his father, felt it too. "I can remember when *Sports Illustrated* came down and a big part of the story was supposed to be how much fun we had playing together and how we were this group of kids who enjoyed ourselves all the time," he said. "I can remember trying to manufacture that kind of feeling because it wasn't really there anymore. It's something you can have when you have nothing to lose and you're on your way up. But when you get there and you're number one, there's a lot more pressure. We felt it before New York. After New York, it almost crushed us totally."

They beat Davidson easily, but didn't play very well in doing so. Dennard scored just two points and looked completely out of the offense. In nine games, he had averaged four points and five rebounds a game and the only reason his rebound average was that high was a 12-rebound night in the home opener against SMU. He had not yet scored in double figures. Before the game against Long Beach State, Foster called him in for a talk.

"He was very straightforward," Dennard said. "He felt we were playing four-on-five on offense and he was right. He never said he was going to bench me but I got the message. He wanted me to get my head straight and produce."

For all of his fooling around, no one wanted the team to succeed more than Dennard. His teammates never minded his escapades; they always knew when it was time to work and time to play a game, Dennard would be ready. But now he wasn't producing and Foster felt the time had come to make some demands. Dennard responded—for one game. He scored a career-high 28 points against Long Beach State and was the reason the Blue Devils escaped with a 79–78 victory.

They opened ACC play with an easy win at home over Clemson. Then came the annual trip to Carolina. The Tar Heels were waiting for them, like a wounded animal. Joe Gminski sat behind the bench and screamed at Foster to take Harrell out every time he went into the game. The Blue Devils lost 74–68.

Even outsiders were now beginning to notice that, even though these were the same Duke players as a year ago, this was not the same Duke team. The fast break was nonexistent. They were playing the way Penn's Weinhauer had claimed they played during the NCAA's—like a herd of elephants. Their game was no longer the controlled fast break but walk-it-up and push-it-inside to Gminski. Fortunately, Gminski was beginning to play very well again. But the thrill was gone—even when they won their next seven in a row to move back into first place in the ACC. The tension was still there, day in and day out.

"You could really see it in Bill," Gminski said. "He seemed to become more and more reclusive all the time. He looked terrible. It seemed as if the only time he ate was when he sent Terry Chili out to get him a Chic-fil-a sandwich or something. He just wasn't the same guy."

Foster was genuinely unhappy. Once as accommodating to the media as any coach in the country, he was available less and less. His open practices were now closed. He even started having the managers tape over the windows so no one could look inside.

The relationship between the players and the rest of the coaching staff was strained at this point. Wenzel was not only different from Goetz, he wasn't as experienced as Goetz. Goetz might have been able to talk Foster out of his bleak moods—or perhaps not. Either way, Wenzel felt helpless watching his coach suffer.

What's more, his relationship with the players had changed. Now he had to play the bad cop sometimes, a role he wasn't comfortable with. Some of the players understood, others didn't The bench warmers resented him because they didn't think he cared about them the way Goetz had. He was struggling.

"I was still learning," he said. "I was twenty-nine and that was a tough year under any circumstances, even if Looey had been there. I'm sure I made mistakes that I wouldn't make now. It just seemed we never got headed in the right direction that entire season."

It was even worse for Steve Steinwedel. He wasn't Wenzel any more than Wenzel was Goetz. In fact, it was worse. Wenzel had recruited most of the key players in the program. Steinwedel had just met them. He was twenty-five and all of a sudden he was an assistant coach for the No. 1 team in the nation. It was overwhelming. Because he was so young and so new, Steinwedel felt he had to assert his authority with the players early. This did not sit well with the group. From Foster, they would accept discipline. From Goetz, too, and to some extent from Wenzel. But not from some newcomer.

The problems started early. One day during preseason, Banks was loafing through a drill in the weight room. Steinwedel jumped on him, screaming in his face, demanding he put more into the drill. Banks raced through the rest of the drill as if to show Steinwedel that he could do it with one hand—he probably could have—then tossed the weight aside and walked away laughing. He had shown Steinwedel up.

Like Wenzel, Steinwedel was being asked to do something he would eventually do well. He is now a highly successful head coach at the University of Delaware. But he wasn't ready for this group. By midseason, he was virtually ignored. Even Jim Suddath, the mildest-mannered player on the team, couldn't stand Steinwedel.

"I really came to believe that Coach Steinwedel was God's way of testing my Christianity," he said. "There was a time when I truly hated him. I had to work very hard to overcome that."

The others didn't work at all to overcome it and the frigid feelings hardened as the season wore on. The team was now ridden by cliques. The coaches had little interaction with the team outside of practice; the white team and the blue team stayed clear of each other more often than not. Even within the cliques there were cliques.

It kept getting worse. Harrell, after losing his starting spot and finding himself in the middle of the Joe Gminski controversy, never adjusted to his role coming off the bench. As he struggled, freshman Vince Taylor kept improving. In mid-January, with Dennard sick on the trip to Virginia, Foster played Taylor for most of the game and he responded by hitting 5-for-5 from the field, scoring 11 points and getting 4 rebounds and 4 assists. After that, Taylor was moved to the white team—the first seven players generally wore white in practice— and Harrell was assigned blue.

"After that happened, I lost interest," Harrell said. "I knew they weren't going to play me and I didn't care. I thought I had lost my job unfairly and then it became obvious that Vince was going to play and not me. I gave up."

He joined Gray and Morrison in that category. The latter two had become so discouraged that they had stopped wearing their shorts under their sweats on occasion because they were convinced—correctly—that they weren't going to get into the games. "I remember one game we had a big lead and I turned to Steve and said, 'Hey, we might get in,' " Morrison said. "Before Steve could answer, Max shook his head and said, 'I'll get into this game before you two guys.' Of course he was right."

Harrell never went to the extreme of not wearing his uniform pants. But he did get into the habit of stopping on the way to the locker room before home games to buy a hot dog—with everything—as a pregame snack. Between January and March he put on eight pounds, even though he was practicing every day.

The winning streak soothed things for a while. When they were good, the Blue Devils were still very good. Gminski played the game of his life in a nationally televised victory at N.C. State, scoring 31 points. Banks had 23 in another national TV game—they were now old hat—against Marquette. Publicly, they were telling people that things were falling into place just as they had in '78, that the chinks had been worked out. But those who were watching the team closely knew better.

The winning streak ended abruptly when Pittsburgh came into Cameron and stunned them 71–69, the first loss at home since the '77 finale. Foster did not take it well. He destroyed a mirror in the locker room.

They were back on the roller coaster after that. An impressive victory over State was followed by an agonizing loss at Maryland, Greg Manning hitting a jumper at the buzzer to win a game that Duke appeared to have under control for most of the last five minutes. That was on a Friday night. For the second time that season, they had to fly direct to Charlotte after a stupefying loss. This time it was for another national TV game, against Louisville on Sunday afternoon.

The night before the game, Foster got a phone call from Durham. His mother had died. She had been living in a nursing home in Durham and she had been ill. That didn't matter. Foster had lost his mother and, like anyone, he was crushed. The players wondered if he would stay for the game.

In the end, Foster had no choice. During the night, Charlotte was hit with a huge snowstorm, a foot of snow being dumped on the city. If the teams had not been staying right across the street from the Charlotte Coliseum, they might not have gotten to the game. As it was, less than three thousand people—the 11,666-seat building was sold out—made it to the game.

Knowing that Foster was hurting, taking note of their old good luck charm—the snow—and still smarting from the loss to Maryland, the Blue Devils became their old selves for one afternoon. The old enthusiasm was back, the verve and panache. The final was 88–72 but it would have been worse if Foster hadn't cleared the bench. The national TV audience, which had now seen Duke beat N.C. State, Marquette, and Louisville with ease, was no doubt baffled by the fact that this juggernaut had lost five games.

But the pent-up emotions that had come streaming out in Charlotte couldn't last. Three nights later at Clemson, they fell apart completely. They were as bad as they had been good against Louisville. The final was a stunning 70–49. It put them one game behind Carolina with one game left to play in the ACC regular season. The Tar Heels would come to Durham for the finale and by now, a lot of people thought they were the best team in the league. Certainly, they were the most consistent.

But Dean Smith wasn't convinced. He knew this would be the last home game for Hardy, Goetsch, Gray, Morrison and, most important, Spanarkel. It was sure to be an emotional night, the crowd would be wound up, and the 9 P.M. start on Sautrday night would mean the students would be in a rowdy mood.

He was right about all of that. The ovations for the seniors were loud. The one for Spanarkel went right off the Richter scale. Even with the frustrations of this season, the Duke supporters understood that everything was relative. This was their last chance to thank Spanarkel for leading them to a high none of them would ever forget. For a couple of minutes, everyone forgot about the troubles and basked in the warmth of the moment.

Then came the game.

Smith wanted to take the crowd out of it and he wanted to frustrate the Blue Devils. So he decided to hold the ball on his team's first possession, trailing 2–0. He held the ball for one minute. Then two. Then three. Then four. The crowd booed. It hissed. It yelled, "borr-ing, borr-ing," at Smith. No matter. Eight minutes. Ten minutes. Foster wasn't going to come out and chase because he knew Smith wanted that. Finally, center Rich Yonaker tried a short baseline jumper. But he was so pumped up after waiting so long to shoot, the shot was two feet long. An air ball. The Blue Devils came down and Taylor hit one free throw to make it 3–0.

Again Carolina held. The clock went under three minutes. Finally, Yonaker shot again. Another air ball. This time, Spanarkel scored to make it 5–0. The stall wasn't working very well. The Tar Heels turned the ball over and Spanarkel scored just before the half ended. A Dave Colescott heave from halfcourt was short. Not only had Carolina been shut out 7–0 in the first half, it had failed to hit the rim. Cameron was completely manic. El Deano had been shot with his own gun.

"That one night it seemed like all the old feeling came back," Goetsch said. "It was as if we were able to put everything aside because it was our last game in Cameron and it was Carolina and then Dean came in and pulled that crap holding the ball. We all forgot about everything except wanting like hell to beat them."

Beyond that, the underclassmen were angry that Smith would conspire to turn Spanarkel's last home game into a circus. Smith had no reason to care about Spanarkel. His job was to win the game. Still, it upset the Duke players. "It was like, 'He's doing this to Jimmy,'" Gminski said. "We all felt it and we were all pissed about it."

Spanarkel found the best way possible to handle it: He took over the game. When Smith came out and actually had his team play the second half—he had no choice down 7–0—Spanarkel was the one Duke player the Tar Heels couldn't stop. The senior guard finished with 17 points. The final was 47–40; the seven first-half points had been the difference.

For Duke it was a strange but gratifying end to the regular season. The victory left them tied with Carolina for first place in the ACC at 9–3 and with an overall record of 20–6—identical to a year ago. They would lose the flip of the coin with the Tar Heels for the top seed and would be the second seed in the ACC Tournament—again, just like a year ago.

The question was whether they could raise their game the way they had a year ago.

The tournament opener was against Wake Forest, a team they had twice beaten easily during the regular season. Once again, the playing-not-to-lose-syndrome hit them. The game became an every-possession-is-life-and-death struggle and only Wake's inexperience saved Duke at the finish. They won, 58–56. The next night was more of the same. This time, Bender made all the big plays and all the big free throws down the stretch and they beat N.C. State, 62–59. Bender had a career-high 16 points. "It was the best game I had ever played," he said. "Afterwards I felt for the first time in a while like maybe we were getting back on track. We hadn't played great the first two nights, but we had still won. And now we were getting Carolina again which was exactly what we wanted."

The Tar Heels had beaten Maryland in their semifinal. Both teams were now in the NCAA Tournament regardless of the outcome of the final. The Blue Devils were starting to pick up some momentum, starting to feel as if all the regular season troubles were going to prove to be minor setbacks when they looked back at it all. If they beat Carolina for a second straight ACC title and got a high seed in the East Regional they would be on their way again.

Bender left the Greensboro Coliseum that night in a buoyant mood. He felt he had finally silenced the doubters who had questioned his replacing Harrell. "I went back to the room after we ate and went to sleep," he said. "But I woke up at about two o'clock. My stomach really hurt. I figured I had eaten something so I got up to go to the bathroom even though I didn't feel like I needed to go."

Hardy, Bender's roommate, was in the bathroom reading. Often, Hardy had trouble sleeping, and rather than turn on a light to read and bother Bender, he would go into the bathroom. When he saw Bender, he wondered what was wrong.

"He looked terrible," Hardy said. "He said it was his stomach so I figured it was the meal we'd had after the game. I figured it was just something to give Max [Crowder always planned the team meals] a hard time about."

It wasn't that simple. Bender was in pain throughout the night. "Finally I figured that I just must be very hungry," he said. "I went downstairs to the breakfast buffet and loaded my plate up with food. I sat down, took one look at it and knew I couldn't eat a bite. I went back up to the room and told Rob he better call Max."

Crowder came in, pressed his fingers in a couple of key places and was pretty certain what the problem was. He decided to take Bender to nearby Wake Forest Hospital for tests. They confirmed what Crowder already thought: appendicitis. When Crowder told Bender, he nodded and asked, "What do I have to do so I can play tonight?"

Crowder shook his head. "Bob," he said softly, "you can't play tonight. You need surgery. We can have you driven to Duke [University] Hospital if you want, but it has to be done today."

Bender was stunned. "It just couldn't be that way," he said. "We were just getting it back to where it should be. We were getting ready to play Carolina for the ACC championship. This couldn't be happening. Not now."

It was, though. Crowder took Bender back to the hotel. They arrived just as the team was walking through the lobby to pregame meal. When Bender saw his teammates, he burst into tears. Needless to say there were no "joke, joke, jokes" during pregame meal.

Foster and Wenzel took Harrell aside to talk to him about starting in Bender's place.

"No way was I ready for this," Harrell said. "I wasn't in shape physically, mentally, or emotionally. If I'd had a couple of days to practice, really work hard and get used to playing with the starters again, it might have been different. But this was four hours before the game. I had to go in cold. There was just no way."

Bender's illness was disastrous. Whether he should have been the starter at the beginning of the season or not, he had established himself as the team's floor leader during the season, as someone not afraid to take a big shot or go to the foul line when it mattered. He had been chosen as the player of the game the night before. Now, as the lineups were introduced for the final, he was on the operating table at Duke Hospital.

Dean Smith wasn't going to mess around with any delays in this game. Carolina came out hot and confident, building a quick lead. Duke came back, got even midway through the second half, but never could take the lead. Considering the circumstances, Harrell didn't play poorly—he had four points and three assists—but Duke clearly missed Bender. Carolina won, 71–63.

■

Disappointing as the loss to Carolina was, it was not a disaster. The NCAA Tournament Committee, knowing Duke had played the final without Bender and noting that Duke and Carolina had split four games during the season, treated the two teams almost equally, sending both to the East Regional in opposite brackets. Both would open the tournament in Raleigh and, if form held, they would decide the season series in a fifth meeting in the regional final.

"We were happy with the draw," Spanarkel said. "We didn't have to travel at all [the regional was in Greensboro] and we had gotten a good seed. And, if we got to the regional final, we'd get Carolina again, which was fine with us."

Harrell would now have a week to prepare for his reprise as a starter; there was even some hope that Bender could play a limited role in the opening round. At worst, he would almost certainly be available the following week, assuming Duke got past the Sunday game in Raleigh.

On Wednesday, Bender was released from the hospital and went directly to Cameron to shoot some free throws while the rest of the team practiced. It was the last week before spring break, the weather was beautiful, and there was a feeling on the team that redemption was still very possible. There was no reason for them not to make another run. If Bender hadn't gotten sick they would have won a second straight ACC Tournament. Everyone, from Foster on down, believed that.

"With all the problems we had been through, we had still played well enough at times that we thought we were good enough to beat anybody," Wenzel said. "There's also something to be said for adversity bringing you together. When Bobby got hurt, we didn't have time to react against Carolina. But during that next week you could feel the team coming together, putting all the rivalries behind. This was the time."

Then, on Wednesday night, Kenny Dennard went over to the Cambridge Inn, the campus hangout, with some friends, none of them basketball players.

"We were having a few beers," Dennard said. "No big deal, nothing wild. There are a lot of stories about how wild I was, but only some of them are true and most of them were during the off-season. During the season, even that season, I didn't drink very much. A friend of mine came up and said, 'Hey, let's get up a group of guys and go play five-on-five.' I figured why not? It sounded like fun."

Dennard's friends all knew he had the keys to Cameron. They had played there at night in the past. Now, while Dennard sat and "had a few more beers," his friends went off to round up a group to play. "We weren't sloppy drunk when we went over to Cameron," Dennard said. "But it was late and we had been drinking and four different guys did get hurt that night."

If Dennard had *not* been one of those guys, that late night game would have been quickly forgotten. "It would have just been another night in college," Dennard said. "A group of guys having fun, male bonding type of stuff."

In the midst of the male bonding, Dennard found himself being guarded by Joel Patton, a six-foot-seven-inch, 250-pound tight end on the football team. They were playing fullcourt and they were playing hard since a keg of beer had been bet on the outcome. "I caught a pass and Joel bumped me," Dennard said. "He was very strong and I lost my balance. I came down wrong on the ankle and felt it blow out."

Dennard limped home to his apartment and immediately iced the ankle. By the next morning, it was still swollen and painful. He called Crowder, who arrived almost simultaneously with Wenzel.

Wenzel's visit had nothing to do with Dennard's ankle. He had received a call that morning about the fact that Dennard had run up $450 in parking tickets. The school was threatening to take action if he didn't pay immediately. Wenzel intended to take Dennard by the hand that morning to go and pay the tickets. He didn't want Foster to know—he had enough on his mind already.

As soon as Wenzel walked into the apartment and saw Dennard's ankle iced and elevated, he knew that the parking tickets were the least of his worries. Crowder, always left to deliver bad news, had just examined the ankle.

"It was a bad sprain, you could tell that," Crowder said. "I didn't think it was broken but at the very least he had stretched ligaments. There was no way he was going to be walking in three days, much less playing basketball."

Crowder filled Wenzel in quickly. Wenzel didn't even want to know how Dennard had gotten hurt. It didn't matter anyway. What were they going to do, suspend Dennard for being irresponsible? About the only way he would play again that season was if Duke made the Final Four. It was at least a two-week type of injury. Wenzel left the apartment angry, sad, and frustrated to go tell Foster. Parking tickets he could handle. This was different.

"There's no question I was foolish," Dennard said, looking back. "If I don't get hurt, it's no big thing. But I did get hurt. Playing seemed like a romantic thing to do. But the time for that sort of thing wasn't then, not with the NCAA Tournament three days away."

It is a measure of the way his teammates felt about Dennard that none of them—then or now—condemned him for his foolishness. "That was just Kenny," Banks said. "His personality was an important part of our success. And part of that personality was doing things like that. If you took that part of him away, then Kenny wouldn't be Kenny."

Spanarkel agrees. "Would I have done it? No. But I wasn't Kenny. All I ever asked of a guy as a teammate was he give everything he had in practice and in the games. Kenny always did that."

Gminski: "The first thing you think is that it was a stupid thing to do. The next thing you think is, well, it was Kenny. That was Kenny. Period."

If the coaches had known at the time how Dennard had gotten hurt, they might not have been as charitable. But they *didn't* know—and they didn't ask. "Right then, our concern was how do we win this game without two starters?" Foster remembered. "In effect, we had three days to get ready with a team that was entirely different from the team that had been playing all season."

The NCAA had expanded to a forty-team field that year. That meant the bottom four seeds in each regional had to play first-round games. On Friday night, Pennsylvania and St. John's won those games in Raleigh, the Quakers earning the chance to play Carolina, the Redmen winning a spot opposite Duke.

The Blue Devils went to Raleigh on Saturday to practice. They knew exactly what they would be dealing with, having been beaten by St. John's during the lost weekend in New York. Bender practiced that day but afterward the doctor told him he wasn't ready to play full-speed. "Next week" was the mandate. Disappointed, Bender went out to dinner with Gminski at a pizza place across the street from the N.C. State campus.

"By the time we got back to the room, I felt sick," Gminski said. "I started throwing up and spent most of the night feeling lousy."

The next day, he was still feeling sick when it was time to go to the arena. Foster now had two starters out and his leading scorer throwing up periodically. Still, everyone's spirits picked up when Penn stunned North Carolina in the first game of the doubleheader. Suddenly, the route to the Final Four was wide open—if they could just get by the first roadblock.

When the game began, it looked easy. Banks, knowing he had to be a dominant force, was just that. Spanarkel was Spanarkeling and Harrell looked much more comfortable. Gminski was sluggish, but even sluggish he was outplaying Wayne McKoy. Quickly, they built a 16–6 lead. Then, just as quickly, St. John's came back. They were even at halftime.

Early in the second half, as McKoy took a pass, Harrell came up behind him looking for a quick steal. McKoy swung his elbow backward to clear room and caught Harrell flush in the eye. Harrell had been playing very well until that moment. Now, he went down hard. He came out, woozy, his eye partially shut. Taylor came in to replace him.

Duke hung in, thanks mostly to Banks—who had 24 points and 10 rebounds—and Spanarkel. Suddath played well in Dennard's place but didn't have the size or quickness that Dennard did. Gminski played respectably on offense, but couldn't stop McKoy on defense. Each time there was a time-out, he would go to the end of the bench and get sick again.

St. John's led most of the second half. But Banks tied it at 78–78 with thirty seconds left. St. John's called time with fourteen seconds left to set up a last shot. Foster, looking for quickness, asked Harrell if he felt up to going back in. Harrell said he did. St. John's swung the ball in the right corner to Reggie Carter, the team's best shooter. Harrell jumped out at him—a second too late. The shot swished through with five seconds left. It was 80–78. Duke called time-out.

They had worked on this sort of situation all year. The evening before, they had practiced a play where Gminski comes to halfcourt to catch the inbounds pass and—with luck—draws the defense toward him. In the meantime, Harrell, having faked toward the ball, runs to one corner while Spanarkel runs to the other. The play worked exactly as Foster had drawn it up. But Gminski was afraid that there wasn't time for a pass and a shot. Instead of finding Harrell or Spanarkel, he turned and, from thirty feet, fired a desperation shot. It hit the backboard, the front of the rim . . . and rolled off, just as the buzzer sounded.

The season was over. There would be no return to the Final Four. The dream of '78 had become the nightmare of '79. "It's almost as if that season balanced the universe," Gminski said. "The year before, everything went right for us. In '79, absolutely everything went wrong. The team we put on the floor against St. John's was not that good a team. And yet, we almost won. But we didn't. We just weren't meant to win."

For the five seniors, the loss was devastating. Even Goetsch, Morrison, and Gray felt the hurt. Hardy, who had abandoned his diary in mid-February when he had sensed the season going sour, was crushed. And Spanarkel was stunned.

"It was all so sudden," he said. "One minute we're out there playing and it's a dogfight just like it should be in the NCAA Tournament. In a lot of ways the game wasn't all that different than Rhode Island the year before. We were struggling, but we were right there in the last minute with a shot to win.

"And then, boom, it's over. It was just hard to believe. Wenz came over and sat down next to me and said, 'You know, you work so hard to get to the top, then you go through a year like this and it makes you wonder if it's all worth it.' He was totally discouraged by the whole experience. The whole thing was just so shocking."

They were all in shock, to one degree or another. The coaches were now in for a long summer of second-guessing. The seniors had never envisioned an ending like this. The underclassmen, who had been able to rationalize the Kentucky loss with the notion that everyone was coming back, saw Spanarkel peeling off his uniform for the last time and knew that was no longer the case. Banks and Dennard had been brought down to earth rudely after their dream freshman season.

More than anyone, Dennard flipped out. "I just couldn't deal with it," he said. "I had to get away. I went down to Key West and just escaped. I felt guilty, then I felt angry. I thought it was all my fault, then I thought it was everyone else's fault. At one point, I said, 'That's it, I'm not going back to Duke.' I just couldn't face everything that had happened to us in the last year. But then I began to calm down. I realized I hadn't dealt with our success well. I looked at how far I had come from no one even knowing who I was as a junior in high school to where we had been the year before in St. Louis. I finally decided I was ready to go back and start all over. I went back, got my hair cut short and went to see Bill."

Dennard was not exactly greeted with open arms by Foster. He had been off contemplating his future for three weeks, meaning he had missed two weeks of school. Foster's first instinct was to throw Dennard off the team. To him, Dennard's irresponsibility had become symbolic of the team's failure that season. Their failure wasn't nearly that simple, but Dennard had done little to endear himself to the coach. All the partying, the traffic tickets—Foster didn't even know about the foolish midnight pickup game—and now, to top it all off, disappearing for three weeks.

The rest of the team had come back to school after the St. John's loss. Why the hell was Dennard different? The answer was easy, of course: Dennard *was* different.

"If he had walked in with more excuses, or looking for me to just forgive him because he was so disappointed about losing, I think I would have told him to look for another school," Foster said. "But he came in, looked me in the eye, and basically said, 'I know I've screwed up. I know I can't go on like this. Work with me and I'll make it up to you.' Bottom line, Kenny never stopped being a good kid. He was immature, no doubt. But you don't give up on a kid because he's immature."

Dennard got a reprieve. He would be back. But Foster did lose one player he thought would be returning—John Harrell. The loss to St. John's hurt Harrell, partly because he felt if he hadn't been knocked silly it never would have happened, and partly because he had been playing well and thought he was about to be redeemed after a disappointing season.

That chance for redemption was now gone. Because of his transfer from N.C. Central, Harrell had been in college for four years but had one more year of basketball eligibility. He would graduate in the spring with a degree in math and could opt to come back as a graduate student. Everyone assumed he would do that.

But when the season ended so abruptly, Harrell began wondering if he wanted to return. Bender would be back and so would Vince Taylor, who had improved steadily all season. "I knew I didn't want to go through another year like this one," he said. "And I knew it was possible that if I came back, I wouldn't play. I had seen what it had been like for Harold and Steve to not play at all their senior seasons and I didn't want to go through that."

Harrell met with Foster and Wenzel. They wanted him to come back but couldn't guarantee him more playing time. The coaches liked Harrell but did not think he had handled losing his job well, sulking rather than fighting to earn more playing time. Harrell thought he was entitled to sulk since he had lost the job unfairly. There was no meeting of the minds, no compromise, no kiss and make up. When the meeting was over, Harrell told the coaches, "I'm not coming back." They weren't surprised.

"If I had it to do over again I would have come back, if only to get a free year of graduate school," Harrell said. "But as it stood, I just didn't want to play for them anymore. I couldn't even look Coach Foster in the eye by the end. It was one of those things. I thought I was right, they thought they were right. Nothing was going to change that."

■

Statistics tell an interesting story when one analyzes what happened to the team that season. In '78, the Blue Devils averaged 85.4 points per game. A year later, the average was 71.9. This is a huge drop, a reflection of the cautious nature of their play.

Each of the top four scorers on the team scored less in '79 than '78. The most drastic drop was Spanarkel, from 20.8 points per game to 15.9. Again, this reflects the change in the way the team was playing. A lot of Spanarkel's points in '78 came in transition. He was allowed to free-lance, push the ball up the court, and look for the quick shot or pass. A year later, that wasn't part of Duke's game. Banks (17.1 to 14.3) and Dennard (9.7 to 6.4) also dropped off. In their cases, inconsistency was the big reason. That was undoubtedly caused by a change in attitude.

The most telling statistic was at the foul line. In '78, Duke was the best free throw shooting team in the country, making 79.1 percent of its foul shots for the season. A year later, the same players dropped to 69.8, an enormous dropoff. Spanarkel fell from 84 percent to 73 percent, Gminski from 86 to 72, Banks from 72 to 63, and Dennard from 67 to 54. Those numbers tell a lot of the story. More than anything else in basketball, free throw shooting is mental. If you are loose and confident, you shoot well. If you are tight, you shoot poorly. If you wanted to write an epitaph that explained what happened in '79 it would be this: "They couldn't make their free throws."

Foster summed the year up best: "All through '78 I kept thinking I was having a dream. In '79, I woke up."

And yet, the dream of '78 wasn't dead. Gminski, Banks, Dennard, and Bender were all coming back for 1980. There was still one more chance.

16

Last Chance

If the '79 disaster did nothing else, it took the Blue Devils out of the national spotlight during the off-season. Teams like DePaul, Kentucky, and Indiana were being looked to as national powers. North Carolina and Virginia—which had signed seven-foot-four-inch Ralph Sampson—were getting most of the attention in the ACC.

This suited Foster and the players fine. Six players—half the team—had graduated. Spanarkel's departure was the one that would really matter. He had been taken in the first round of the NBA draft by the Philadelphia 76ers after leaving Duke as the school's all-time leader in points, assists, and steals. He was the first player in Duke history to score more than two thousand points. Not bad for a slow, pigeon-toed kid from Jersey City.

But as much as Spanarkel would be missed, the same could not be said for the other five graduates. Hardy, accepted at Louisville law school, had certainly established a role for himself as a hard worker and as the leading bench jockey in the ACC, but he had never been a key player. The other four graduates—Goetsch, Harrell, Morrison, and Gray—had all been miserable during their senior year; their college dreams having gradually and bitterly turned to dust.

Their places were taken by four eager freshmen: a pair of guards, Tom Emma and Chip Engelland, and two 6-8 forwards, Allen Williams and Mike Tissaw. None was a superstar but all had potential. More important perhaps was that all were starting fresh. There was no emotional baggage, no anger about not starting. Their presence changed the tone of the locker room from divided to united. They looked to Gminski, Bender, Banks, and Dennard as respected elders.

"It was a much more normal situation than what we had had the two previous years," Bender said. "Before that, we had the young guys playing and the older guys sitting. That was bound to catch up with us sooner or later and it did—in '79. Now, we had the kind of setup you look for in a successful program, the older guys playing, the younger guys working their way in and learning as they went."

Foster seemed more relaxed that fall. Not loose—that would never be the case—but not so loaded down by expectations. As practice began, he liked what he saw of the new players. Banks and Dennard also seemed to have their freshman eagerness back again. The new coaching staff had now been together a year and was more comfortable as a unit. Goetz was still missed, but not as much. After all, one third of the team (the four freshmen) didn't even know who he was.

And, while a lot of people were writing the Blue Devils off—they were picked third in the ACC in preseason—the fact was that four starters were back, led by Gminski, who had been the ACC player of the year in '79. Vince Taylor, now a sophomore, would take Spanarkel's spot, and while he would never be the scorer or all-around threat Spanarkel was, he added an element of quickness that the team had often lacked in the past.

Preseason passed quickly and uneventfully. The season began a week earlier than usual because Duke had been invited to play in the inaugural Tip-Off Classic in Springfield, Massachusetts. Springfield is the home of the Basketball Hall of Fame and the birthplace of basketball. It was at what is now Springfield College that Dr. James Naismith nailed a peach basket up one day in 1891 and thus invented the game. It made perfect sense for the basketball season to start each year in Springfield.

To get the new event started right, the game's sponsors wanted two name teams that were likely to be highly ranked. Ideally, they would have liked to have matched the previous season's NCAA finalists. But Michigan State without Magic Johnson and Indiana State without Larry Bird—they had both turned pro—would not be much of a matchup. The sponsors looked back one year farther to '78. Duke and Kentucky. Perfect.

For Duke, this was an opportunity, not to get even—nothing was going to change the outcome of the '78 final—but to gain a measure of revenge and to find out where *this* team might be going. While most of the '78 Kentucky players were gone, they had a slew of outstanding young players. Most preseason polls had them ranked in the top five.

It was a classic basketball game. Duke's starters all played well but the unsung hero was Suddath, who came off the bench with Dennard in foul trouble and scored 11 points, made 5 steals, and grabbed 4 rebounds. Kentucky was as good as advertised and it took a Bender drive down the middle with two seconds left in regulation to put the game into overtime. On the play, Bender surprised Macy, who was looking for him to pull up and shoot or pass inside to Gminski or Banks. Instead, Bender blew past him, beat the Kentucky big men to the basket, and tied the game. In overtime, the Blue Devils dominated, winning 82–76.

It had been a gut-check game and they had responded. If the innocence of '78 was long gone, they had proved they were now a smart, experienced team that had seen just about everything there was to see in basketball.

After Kentucky came the Big Four. They just got by Wake Forest in the opener—Gminski making a pair of free throws in the last five seconds to clinch the victory—then destroyed North Carolina, 86–74 in the final. Carolina was the team with the expectations this season; everyone was back from the ACC championship team. But all five Duke starters scored in double figures and they beat the Tar Heels with ease. It was the three hundredth victory of Foster's college coaching career.

As Foster walked off the floor, Joe Gminski came up to him, put out his hand and said, "Congratulations Coach, great job." Foster said thank you. But when he got a few steps past Gminski, he exploded.

"Can you believe that guy?" he said. "Tonight it's 'Great job, Coach.' What will it be when we lose a couple of games? If there's one thing I've learned in coaching it's that you have to keep moving. If you don't, your friends come and go and your enemies accumulate."

That was the first time Foster hinted that he might leave Duke. His team had just beaten its archrival convincingly and Foster had just passed a milestone in his coaching career, yet all he could see in his mind's eye was Joe Gminski and others who were constantly second-guessing him.

"Bill is not a person who can handle criticism," Lou Goetz said. "To begin with, he hasn't run into it very often during his life. Beyond that, he wants very badly to have people approve of what he is doing. In the end, if you stay in one place, people are bound to criticize you. It comes with the territory. I think his moving on was, in some ways, inevitable. It fit his character."

After the Big Four, the Blue Devils jumped back up to No. 1 in the polls. They had beaten Carolina while Kentucky, Indiana, and DePaul had all lost. Presto! Welcome back to No. 1. This time it was different, though. It wasn't a life-long dream coming true. And they knew exactly how much being ranked No. 1 in December meant if you lost early in March: nothing.

They did keep winning throughout December. When the month was over, they were 7–0 and still No. 1.

The only down note during this period were the rumors that had started to swirl around Foster. Frank McGuire had announced at the start of the season that he was stepping down as South Carolina's coach at the end of the season. Almost as soon as McGuire's announcement came, Foster's name was linked to the job. South Carolina needed rebuilding and Foster was a builder. The word was out that he wasn't happy at Duke and that South Carolina was putting together a lucrative package to lure him down there.

"We all heard it," Bender said. "But it was one of those things where you didn't just march into Bill's office and demand to know what was going on. To begin with, it was his life. Beyond that, at least at first, I don't think any of us really believed it. Rumors are rumors."

But often as not, there is a reason for a rumor.

Foster had never truly been comfortable at Duke. At first, he had been intimidated by the school's academic reputation. "I always joked when I first got there that I coached there but I never could have gone there," he said. "I always felt a little bit overwhelmed by the people in the Duke community."

Shirley Foster felt it even more. "I always had the sense that people at Duke thought that Bill was very lucky to be able to work at Duke. I think he *was* lucky. But they were also lucky to have *him*. I don't think they saw it that way and we always felt that, as if they looked down on us because we had gone to a place like Elizabethtown."

Real or imagined, these feelings became more important when Foster began to feel heat during the '79 season. To him, most Duke people were frontrunners, there to cheer you on in good times, second-guessing in bad times. Perhaps if Foster had felt that the people who mattered most at Duke were solidly behind him, he might not have let the fans—or the Joe Gminskis—bother him. But he didn't think Athletic Director Tom Butters appreciated him and that bothered him most of all. Eleven years later, Butters says he still cannot understand why Foster felt that way.

"I didn't know I had a problem with Bill Foster until people told me secondhand I had a problem with him," Butters said. "I always thought he was a great coach and, more important, a great coach for Duke. I *thought* I always supported him and gave him what he needed. But *he* didn't feel that way."

Foster's problems with Butters were symptomatic of a larger problem. His insecurity had nothing to do with his job but with a feeling of not being appreciated—or loved.

"Bill is not the kind of guy who would ever go in and ask for a raise," Wenzel said. "What he wants is for you to come in and give him the raise because you feel he deserves it. I think that was the problem with Butters. It wasn't that Butters ever came in and demanded more wins or anything like that. It was that he *didn't* come in and say, 'Hey Bill, we know what a fantastic job you're doing. What can I do to help?' "

The paving of the coaches' parking lot became symbolic of the Butters-Foster relationship. For years, Duke's coaches had parked in a small lot right behind Cameron, only a few steps from the basketball office. The only problem was that the lot was unpaved; when it rained it quickly became soaked and muddy. Foster asked Butters if the lot could be paved. Butters said it could. But then it didn't happen.

"I had given approval for the paving of the lot," Butters said. "The money was there and it was going to be done early in the spring. But for some reason Bill thought I was holding things up. I wasn't."

Whatever the holdup, Foster took it personally. Several players still remember watching him get out of the car one rainy day that season and pull a newly laundered jacket out of the car to take into Cameron. As he did, his foot slipped a little and he dropped the jacket in the mud. "How many fucking games do we have to win here before we get a decent parking lot!" Foster screamed.

During Foster's early years at Duke, he almost never used profanity. Now, while he didn't use it as often, say, as Bob Knight, he used it regularly. The parking lot situation often was the cause.

But that wasn't all. There was also Dean Smith. This is a problem all coaches in the ACC have to deal with in varying degrees, none more so than the Duke coach. Eight miles from Cameron, at Carolina, sat Dean Smith. He had been there since 1961 and had been the dominant force in the league since 1967, when Carolina made the first of seven Smith-led trips to the Final Four.

Dean Smith was—and is—God in North Carolina. The newly built 21,000-seat basketball palace at Carolina is named for him. As the state school, Carolina is always going to have far more fans than Duke, and with a legend as Carolina's coach, Duke is always going to be up against Dean-mania no matter how often it wins.

When he arrived at Duke, Foster seemed able to handle that. He made light of it, often saying, "Before I came down here I thought it was Naismith who invented basketball, not Dean Smith." He delighted in listening to imitations of Smith's nasal midwestern twang, and talked often about using what Smith had achieved at Carolina as a role model for his program at Duke.

But gradually that changed. After Duke's success in '78, Foster thought Duke might be at least competitive with Carolina in terms of public attention, if not public affection. It didn't happen. "Everywhere he went," Wenzel said, "it was Dean, Dean, Dean."

The players were certainly aware of this feeling. As far back as the preseason of 1978, they could sense that Foster was getting tired of Smith-mania. All of them remember walking into a high school gym in Roxboro for a preseason scrimmage that year. A fan walked up to Foster and said, "Which one of these guys is Phil Ford?"

"He went off," Bender said. "We got into the locker room and he started yelling, 'I don't know about you guys but I'm sick and tired of people thinking there's only one team in this goddamn state!' He had a piece of chalk in his hand and when he was finished he threw the chalk down on the floor. It bounced off the floor, flew up into the air and landed perfectly in the chalkholder at the bottom of the black-board. Everybody just stared for a second. Then Bill looked at us and said, 'I'll just bet you don't think I can do that again.'"

Foster could laugh at himself then. By 1980, he wasn't laughing—and the notion of getting away from Dean and the murderous ACC schedule was very tempting. Everyone sensed it. But with the Blue Devils at 11–0 and holding the No. 1 ranking, it hardly seemed conceivable that Foster would be going anywhere.

They won the league opener against ACC newcomer Georgia Tech, a team that had last place locked up before a game was played. That sent them into Clemson with a 12–0 record. The Tigers had perhaps their best team ever, led by Larry Nance and Billy Williams. Littlejohn Coliseum was filled beyond overflowing. The listed attendance that night was 13,500 in a building that seats 11,000. "I've never seen a place so full in my life," Gminski said. "The aisles were packed. You had to wonder if the fire marshals took the night off." It was a superb basketball game. The Blue Devils had a chance to win in regulation. With the score tied, Foster called time and set up a play for Engelland. This surprised the veterans. "We were all a little baffled," Gminski said. "Chip was a good shooter, but he was a freshman. Gene and I were both hot. Why not run something for one of us with Chip as the alternative?"

Foster had confidence in Engelland, but he missed the shot. Clemson won in overtime, 87–82, even though Banks finished with 31 and Gminski with 30. The spell had been broken. There was no time to sulk, however: Carolina was coming to Cameron on Saturday.

This was a game both teams wanted desperately to win. Duke never likes to lose at home and the Tar Heels had been embarrassed by Duke's easy Big Four victory. Dean Smith, always looking for a psychological edge, actually planted a story with a local reporter, getting him to write a column claiming that Duke would win the game by at least 15 points. Smith then used the column as bulletin board material.

For Foster, this was a big day. A country music freak, he had become friends with the Oak Ridge Boys and they were coming to the game. But they didn't help. Carolina came out hot and built a quick lead. The Blue Devils rallied in the second half and got even. Then the Tar Heels ran off 15 straight points and Duke never came back. The final was 82–67.

More grist for the "Dean's God" mill. Questions suddenly were being raised about Duke's ability to play in the big games. And the Foster-to-South Carolina rumors continued to grow. Foster did nothing to quell the rumors, refusing to talk about them. He had become more and more reclusive, talking to fewer and fewer reporters and fewer and fewer people in general.

Things quickly went from bad to worse. Two days after the Carolina loss, Banks and Dennard collided in practice. Both went down hard. Banks got right up, Dennard didn't. He had seriously bruised his thigh. All season, Dennard had been a model of consistency. He had kept his word of the previous spring to come back with a new attitude. He had worked hard and partied much less. He was averaging 10 points and 6 rebounds a game and was diving for balls as in his freshman days. It was exactly that kind of dive that brought on the collision with Banks. Now, he would be out indefinitely.

In five days, the Blue Devils had gone from an undefeated, top-ranked team to a team with a 1–2 record in its own conference, a team without its number three scorer, and a team besieged by rumors that the coach was leaving.

They managed to win their next three, scraping past Wake Forest 67–66 and then beating State at home and pathetic Georgia Tech in Atlanta. That brought Virginia and freshman phenom Ralph Sampson to town. For Gminski, jockeying for position in the first round of the NBA draft, this was an important game. Even as a freshman, Sampson was a major test of a good big man. Gminski played well, numbers-wise, scoring 20 points and getting 10 rebounds. But Sampson was better. Down the stretch, he made all the big shots and the Cavaliers won, 90–84.

This was a major letdown for Gminski. Coming off his junior year, he had hoped to have a huge senior year, partly to win games, partly to make himself rich. "Something happened to me senior year," he said. "I seemed to get tentative at times, usually the worst possible times. Maybe I was worrying too much about the pros instead of focusing on what was going on right then. Whatever it was, I didn't play that well. I still had good numbers, but I wasn't playing well. I can always tell the difference. There are times when I have good numbers but I know I'm not playing the way I can. I felt that way a lot that year."

By now, there was some tension between Gminski and Banks. The year before, Gminski had been the ACC player of the year and a first-team All-American. Banks had been second team All-ACC. Banks thought Gminski shot the ball too often and too much of the team's offense was designed for him.

This was a little unfair. Gminski was 6-11 and almost unstoppable when his shot was on. Banks, at 6-6, could do more things athletically, but wasn't the scorer Gminski was. Banks didn't think he got the credit he deserved.

"That year, a lot of things started to bother me," Banks said. "It seemed as if when we lost, I got the blame. When we won, Mike got the credit. Then, when things started to go bad, everyone started to write us off."

The Blue Devils won at Pittsburgh and Wake Forest with Dennard still out and Gminski and Banks both playing well. The Wake win upped their record to 17–3 and they moved back up to No. 4 in the polls. Next came Maryland, at Maryland.

The Terrapins were the surprise team in the ACC, perhaps in the country. They had been picked sixth in the ACC before the season but they had blossomed. Albert King had finally become the star everyone had expected him to be, and 6–8 sophomore Buck Williams, considered too small to play center, had emerged as the most fearsome rebounder in the league. They weren't a big team, but they were a great shooting team that loved to run if you gave them the chance.

On a cold Saturday afternoon, Duke gave them the chance. Except for Gminski (17) no one rebounded and absolutely no one got back on defense. The Terrapins put on a clinic in the second half, humiliating the Blue Devils, 101–82. "That may be the best I've ever had a team play," Lefty Driesell said. Foster saw it another way. To him, it was as poor an effort as he had seen from one of his teams in a long time.

They went to Virginia three nights later. Gminski was excited to learn before the game that Red Auerbach of the Boston Celtics was attending. Because of some shrewd trading, the Celtics had the first pick in the NBA draft that year. But Auerbach wasn't there to see Gminski. He was there to see Sampson, hoping to talk him into leaving college at the end of the season. Gminski's pride was hurt when he heard that. The Blue Devils' pride was hurt, too, when they lost 73–69.

Dennard, who had missed eight games, was ready to come back. He did, in a nationally televised game against Marquette. The Blue Devils trailed by 18, switched to a man-to-man defense and rallied to get even. Then, Foster switched back to zone. Marquette made the shots in the last couple of minutes and won, 80–77. On NBC, Billy Packer questioned Foster's decision to switch back to the zone. Foster was furious. Now, it seemed, *everyone* was second-guessing him.

That defeat drained everyone. The long trip to Wisconsin, the comeback, then the disappointment of losing. They went to State three days later and played their worst game since the State debacle of '78, losing 76–59. Gminski played one of the worst games of his career, getting a grand total of two rebounds. There was no fight in them at all, no spirit, no sense that anyone gave a damn.

They had now lost four in a row, the longest losing streak since the end of the '77 season. The record was 17–7 overall but in the ACC they were 5–6. Even with the NCAA Tournament expanded to forty-eight teams—and with no limit on the number of schools that could be chosen from each conference—they were in a deep hole.

The Duke campus that week was like an open-air morgue. Everyone was virtually certain that Foster was leaving and it seemed as if the team had left town ahead of the coach. Maryland was coming in on Saturday for a game that amounted almost to a last stand.

Cameron was full of signs that Saturday: "Bill, please don't go,";

"Coach, you're still our Coach,"; "South Carolina, leave our coach alone." The students still felt the same way as always about Foster and they wanted him to know it. Foster noticed. "I wish they wouldn't do that," he said. "I just want to focus on trying to get this team straightened out."

That wasn't realistic, though. Foster's silence had made it apparent to everyone that he was seriously considering leaving. That wasn't something you could just pretend wasn't happening. The only person connected with the team Foster had talked to about leaving was Wenzel.

"He called me over to the house one night in February and asked me what I thought," Wenzel said. "To me, Duke was exactly the kind of place where he wanted to be and where he should be. But he talked about being an independent, about the fact that they really wanted him and the chance to start fresh. By the time I left, I realized that it would have been out of character for him to *stay.*"

They beat Maryland that afternoon, 66–61. Gminski, embarrassed by his play against State, made the big shots. Banks had 20 points while Bender had 11 points and 9 assists. Then came the home finale against Clemson. This would also be the last home game for Gminski and Bender.

Moments before the seniors were supposed to be introduced, Tom Butters took the P.A. and announced to the crowd that Gminski's number 43 would be retired. It was the first uniform retired at Duke since the immortal Dick Groat had graduated in 1954. A lot of outstanding players had come through Duke since that time: Art Heyman, Bob Verga, Jeff Mullins, Jim Spanarkel. None had rated this honor. Gminski was stunned.

"It caught me completely off-guard," he said. "I had hoped something like that might happen, but I had no inkling. For the first few minutes of the game, I was so emotional I couldn't play a lick."

Gminski recovered just in time. He came on late to finish with 29 points and 19 rebounds. He got ample help from Banks—who had 24 points—and needed every bit of it. For the second time that season, the two teams went into overtime. Once again, the home team won by the score of 87–82.

When it was over, Gminski and Bender took the P.A. to thank everyone for all their support. As Gminski finished, Banks grabbed the microphone and said, "Well, this might be my last home game too. I might pass up my last year and turn pro."

The two seniors, knowing Banks was kidding, grabbed the microphone from him and literally carried him away before he could make things worse. But the crowd didn't react well. It seemed to them that Banks was trying to steal the spotlight from Gminski and Bender. Betrayal was in the air. First Foster, now Banks.

On the final Saturday of the regular season, they went into Carolina expecting to lose and did just that. Dean Smith didn't need to plant any columns before this game. The Tar Heels were flying and they humiliated the Blue Devils, 96–71. Several of the players' girlfriends had planned a party for that night to celebrate the end of the regular season.

"We were in no mood for a party," Gminski said. "We just got drunk and angry. We looked at ourselves and said, 'What the fuck is going on?' We sucked at Carolina, simple as that. We rolled over and died. There was no excuse for that."

They had finished the regular season 19–8, 7–7 in the league. That tied them for fifth place with Virginia but made them the sixth seed in the ACC tournament since Virginia had beaten them twice. The only way they were going to make the NCAA's was to win the tournament. That didn't seem very likely.

Foster had concluded his negotiations with South Carolina. He hadn't signed anything but he had a verbal agreement with USC Athletic Director Jim Carlen. That week, prior to the ACC Tournament, he met individually with Banks, Dennard and Suddath to explain to them why he was leaving before their senior year. All three understood.

"He had to make a move," Dennard said. "The man was making himself sick. Right or wrong, he felt like he had to get away from Duke. As long as he felt that way, he had to do it."

Banks agreed. "If he had stayed at Duke," he said, "I think he would probably be dead now. The man had been like a father to me. I just wanted him to do whatever would make him happy."

The pre-ACC Tournament stories blamed Duke's collapse on the turmoil surrounding Foster. The Blue Devils, in the opinion of most, were done. Ironically, their first-round opponent, N.C. State, also had a lame-duck coach.

But Norman Sloan had announced early in the season his intention to move to the University of Florida. There were no ifs, ands, or buts and the Wolfpack had improved steadily all season. They came into the tournament 20–6, having finished third in the league behind Maryland and North Carolina. They had embarrassed Duke the last time the teams had played in Raleigh. Most people expected the Blue Devils to make a quick exit.

"Everyone thought we were finished, especially after what happened at Carolina," Gminski said. "My dad told me that he was looking for someone to buy his tickets for the last two nights of the tournament because he knew he wasn't going to need them. That's how bad it was."

Everywhere the players turned they heard that all of them had quit, led by Foster. "It finally got to us," Banks said. "Everybody said we stunk, that we couldn't beat anyone. No one wanted to even see us when we got to Greensboro. After all the questions and all of us trying to come up with answers we just said fuck it, we're sick of all this crap. Let's just kick some ass."

In short, they finally got mad. Perhaps for the first time since '78 they felt they had something to prove. And, for the first time since '78, they put aside distractions and jealousies and concerns about who was getting the headlines. They went to Greensboro wanting to show people that rumors of their death had been greatly exaggerated.

—

On opening night, they came out flying, blew to a huge lead on State and never looked back. Banks completely shut down State star Hawkeye Whitney and scored 24 points himself. Their easy victory raised eyebrows but, after all, they had been up and down all season. This had clearly been an up night. Carolina in the semifinals would be a test.

Of course, Carolina had just embarrassed them six days earlier in Chapel Hill. Gminski had a vivid memory of Tar Heel center Rich Yonaker pointing into the stands at his parents after hitting a shot over him. Dean Smith was a big believer in pointing at the teammate who feeds you a good pass, and Yonaker had taken the concept a step further. "When I saw that," Gminski said, "I wanted to get ill."

Now they had a chance for redemption. Maryland, the top seed, had already beaten Clemson in the first semifinal when Duke and Carolina took the court. Foster had put the team through a tough workout during the afternoon shoot-around, wanting his players to sleep for a while after practice so they would be wide awake for the 9:30 tip-off.

They were awake. Gminski, often so unemotional, was on fire. The rest of the team took its cue from him, all of them remembering the roaring Chapel Hill crowd. The game was over by halftime. The final was 75–61. Gminski had 24 points and a career-high 19 rebounds. The team that had been written off forty-eight hours earlier was in the final. Still, to get into the NCAA's, they would have to beat Maryland.

That wouldn't be easy. Maryland had become a wonderfully balanced team with Greg Manning, Ernest Graham, and Albert King all able to score from outside and King and Williams difficult to stop inside. King was the star, the player of the year in the ACC, and a legitimate first-team All-American. Banks, who had already stopped Whitney and Mike O'Koren, would have to try and control King.

For both teams, this game was a crusade. Duke needed to win to get into the NCAA's and to be redeemed. Maryland had not won the ACC Tournament since 1958. In twelve years at Maryland, Lefty Driesell had coached his team into the tournament final four times but had not yet won the title. The Maryland players, knowing that their regular season championship meant little, wanted desperately to win.

The Duke players woke up on Saturday morning, looked out their windows, and couldn't believe their eyes. It was snowing. A real blizzard that would eventually dump sixteen inches on Greensboro, bringing the city—the entire East Coast, in fact—to a halt. To the Blue Devils the snow meant one thing: Duke weather was back, just like '78.

Due to the weather, the Greensboro Coliseum was half empty that night, the first time in memory there had been empty seats for an ACC championship game. Those who couldn't make it because of the snow missed one of college basketball's great games.

Albert King was never better. Banks matched him. Every rebound was contested viciously. Maryland took a 6–0 lead. As it turned out, that was the biggest lead either team had all night. The difference for Duke was Vince Taylor, the sophomore guard. He had the best game of his career with 19 points. Most important, with Maryland up by three and trying to kill the clock, he made back-to-back steals. The first led to a breakaway lay-up, the second to two Gminski free throws. From there, they seesawed to the finish, each team having an answer for every basket.

The pressure kept building, but neither team was willing to fold. With thirty-one seconds left, King hit his 27th point of the night to put Maryland ahead, 72–71.

Now the pressure was on Duke. Maryland concentrated on keeping the ball away from Gminski and Banks. Taylor had to shoot with ten seconds left. The ball rimmed out. Ten bodies crashed the boards. Dennard got his hand on the ball but couldn't control it. Rather than try to grab it, he tapped it back on the board. When it came down again, it ended up in the hands of the surprised Gminski. Never one to look a gift basketball in the mouth, he laid the ball in with eight seconds left. Duke was up, 73–72. Maryland got the ball to halfcourt and called time with five ticks to go.

Everyone in the building knew King would take the last shot. The play Maryland wanted to run was simple: Screen for King at the top of the key to allow him to come out and get the inbounds pass. Then run everyone else down to the baseline to clear room for him. Banks would have to somehow deny King penetration—if he got within eighteen feet he would almost surely bury the winning shot.

As the teams walked back on the court, King and Banks passed one another. Instinctively, each reached out to tap the other, a sign of their mutual respect. Maryland ran the play as planned. King caught the pass thirty feet from the basket and faced Banks one-on-one as the clock ticked down. Banks knew King would get his shot. The question was, from where?

"I wanted to push him out as much as I could," he said. "If I got too close, he would go by me. I tried to force him left [toward the sideline] so he couldn't get as close as he wanted." Banks's slight overplay forced King just a tad wider than he wanted to go. With two seconds left, he pulled up from twenty feet and shot.

The ball hit the top of the front rim and bounded high into the air. Buck Williams went up to try to tip it. He had position. But in a split second, two things happened. First, the ball hit the rim a second time as it came down, throwing Williams's timing off. Then, to make sure Williams couldn't somehow get a hand on the ball, Dennard undercut him, taking his legs out from under him. The two of them collapsed in a heap on the floor. On the second bounce, it was Banks who ended up with the basketball. The clock was at zero. There had been no whistle. Maryland was screaming for a foul on Dennard, but to no avail.

It was over. As soon as he heard the buzzer, Banks began leaping in the air for joy, screaming and pointing at press row. Then, all of a sudden, he collapsed in a heap at center court. At first, amidst the celebration, no one noticed. But when everyone saw Banks not getting up, it was apparent something was wrong. He was hyperventilating.

"I was just so geeked up, I lost it," he said. "I was screaming at the writers because they had said we were finished and I wanted them to know what I thought about that. I was so exhausted and excited that I just got dizzy."

In the Maryland locker room, every single player cried unabashedly.

It had been a brutal, draining game and they had literally come up an inch short. King was chosen as the MVP. Later, that would annoy Banks. For now, he was just trying to breathe.

Foster was dazed. He could not believe the effort his team had put out for three days to win the championship. As he came off the floor he turned to Tom Mickle and said, "How can I leave now? I've got to think about this again."

But he wouldn't have that chance. Tom Butters had had enough with all the speculation and the rumors. Before Foster left the building that night, Butters told him he wanted a decision by the next day. "I didn't think it was fair to the players to go to the NCAA Tournament and be asked over and over again about their coach's status," Butters said. "I wanted Bill to make up his mind."

Foster's mind was made up. He had been emotionally carried away in the aftermath of the victory, but that faded quickly. The next day he submitted his resignation to Butters, effective at the end of Duke's season. Twenty-four hours later he was in Columbia, South Carolina. There, he was introduced as South Carolina's new coach.

The players were still in a fog after the Maryland victory. They were back in the NCAA Tournament with a second-round date against the winner of the Washington State–Pennsylvania game. And they now officially had a lame-duck coach.

"The best thing for us during that period was that everything happened so fast," Bender said. "We had to play three times in three nights. Then we got our bid, then they announced Bill was gone. It was boom, boom, boom. We never had time to think about what was happening."

What they *could* think about was that there was still the NCAA Tournament to play—and there was one more chance to relive 1978.

"We got some of it back during that ACC Tournament," Dennard said. "We were the old, get-after-it Blue Devils. We just wanted to win, do whatever we had to. Gene was never better than he was that weekend. But we were all in it together for the first time in a while. Bill announcing he was leaving put us in that kind of situation again. We felt like this was the last go-round for the old gang and we wanted to make it special."

They started with an easy 52–42 second-round victory over Penn. The Quakers tried to slow the pace, as they had done to North Carolina the year before, but Gminski hit every big shot, the Blue Devils played great defense, and the game was never really in doubt. That put them into the round of sixteen, the Mideast Regional semifinals. The place: Lexington, Kentucky—Rupp Arena. The opponent: Kentucky.

"It was like Notre Dame all over again," Bender said. "No one gave us a chance to win. We had beaten Kentucky in the first game of the season when they were breaking in their new players. Now, they had a whole season of experience and we were playing on their home court."

In those days, the NCAA still allowed tournament teams to play on their home floor, which was unfair. A school should not have home court advantage just because it is wealthy enough to have a large arena. For Duke—or anyone—to play an NCAA round of sixteen game before more than twenty-three thousand fans—twenty-two thousand of them Kentucky fans—was wrong. But that was the hand they had been dealt.

"In a way, it almost became our advantage," Banks said. "We were wired before that game. It was the old 'Let's show these guys' attitude. Instead of thinking we couldn't do it, we were determined to show people that we could."

Foster's status added to the drama of the story. Every game he coached could now be his last at Duke. The players were asked time and again if they were trying to win this one for him. Their answer was honest. "We're trying to win this one," Dennard said, "for us. He's one of us."

The first half of the Kentucky game was a repeat of the Notre Dame game in St. Louis. To the astonishment of the Kentucky fans, the Blue Devils, not the least bit intimidated, came out and proceeded to put a clinic on the Wildcats.

Early in the game, Gminski stepped in front of Sam Bowie on the fast break and took a charge. He jumped in the air and shook his fist. This was totally out of character and it sent an electric jolt through the team. "When Mike did that, I knew we were going to win the game," Bender said. "That kind of emotion wasn't Mike. But it was there that night and we all fed off it."

The first half was almost perfect. Every Bender pass worked. Taylor was superb and Gminski and Banks were all over the boards. At half-time, it was 43–29—the exact same score of the Notre Dame game two years earlier.

It couldn't last. For one thing, Kentucky was too good to get blown out. Players like Kyle Macy, Sam Bowie, and Derrick Hord were not going to just roll over and die, especially with the crowd ready to boo them out of the state if they did. Kentucky began to hit. The crowd grew louder. The Blue Devils got tight and started missing. The lead dwindled and dwindled. Kentucky finally got even at 54–54 with a little more than a minute to go.

Duke wanted to play for one shot, but Kentucky wouldn't allow it. Banks got inside and was fouled with twenty-one seconds left. He went to the line with the crowd screeching. His first free throw rolled out. One left. This one crept over the rim and in. Duke led again, 55–54, but Kentucky had the ball with a chance to win.

The Wildcats looked inside but Gminski had Bowie blanketed. The ball finally swung to Macy, the All-American. He put the ball on the floor and head-faked Vince Taylor. Taylor didn't go for the fake. Macy went up with Taylor all over him. It was a forced shot that hit the back rim and bounded away. The buzzer sounded and Rupp Arena went into shock. Duke–55, Kentucky–54. Final. It was as unlikely a victory as could be imagined. Duke had scored 12 points in the second half—and won. Amazingly, they were one step from going back to the Final Four.

Emotionally drained and physically exhausted, they had to play Purdue on Saturday in the regional final. The Kentucky crowd turned out in force to root against the team that had eliminated their beloved Wildcats. It was like another road game.

Six years earlier, Foster's Utah team had faced Purdue in the NIT final in what turned out to be Foster's last game at Utah.

History repeated itself. Purdue center Joe Barry Carroll outplayed Gminski inside and Taylor, the hero of the Kentucky game with his 15 points, couldn't buy a basket, finishing the game with only 2 points. Banks had 14, but shot poorly also. They managed to lead 30–28 at halftime but Purdue took over midway through the second half. Gminski and Banks were in foul trouble. There was no rally. The final was 68–60.

This was the most heartbreaking loss of all. Kentucky in '78 hadn't really felt like a loss. St. John's in '79, while devastating, was hardly unexpected given the physical condition of the team. But this, two days after the joy of the Kentucky victory, was more than they could bear. Dennard, who had fouled out, chased one of the referees down at game's end and, still enraged, snapped a towel in his face.

"When I fouled out, sitting on the bench the last couple of minutes, it just all kicked in on me," he said. "I mean, this was the end. Bill was gone, Mike was gone, the future was gone. I was in a rage and I directed it towards the ref. The guy had called nine fouls on me in two games. Sometimes you know a guy is picking on you and this guy was. I turned to Mike Tissaw and said, 'When this is over, I'm gonna slug the guy, I don't care what happens to me.'

"When the game was over, I chased after him and started to hit him. Then I stopped myself and started to just walk away. But he was smirking at me, I swear he was. So I just took my towel and went, '*Zap*!' Got him right on the side of his face. As soon as I did that, two state troopers showed up and got between us. But all the way down the tunnel I was screaming at him. It was just pure, pissed-off emotion. I was so mad. We could have won that year. But we didn't and I knew it was never going to be the same. End of an era, all that. Something just snapped inside me."

A few minutes later, a Lexington writer who had witnessed the scene asked Dennard what happened, commenting, "You didn't show a lot of class there, did you, Kenny?"

"Whoever said," Dennard snapped back, "that I had class?"

Everyone else was as upset as Dennard even if they didn't react as overtly. Walking off the floor, it hit Foster that he wasn't Duke's coach anymore, that when he walked out of the locker room, he would do so as an employee of the University of South Carolina.

"He walked in and started to tell us how proud he was of us," Gminski said, "and then just lost it. Then we all lost it."

They all cried. This was a different ending from St. Louis, a more painful and more final one. "There was no way to rationalize losing that game," Dennard said. "To this day, I wish Bill hadn't let things get to him the way he did. He had a bad recruiting year, so what? So what if he lost thirteen games one year? He was the right coach for Duke and Duke was the right place for him. But he just didn't understand. He couldn't deal with things."

Bill Foster certainly couldn't deal with any long farewells. When the team bus pulled up to the hotel, the lobby was packed with Duke people. They were all waiting there to congratulate the team and the coaches on their effort. Foster couldn't handle it. He raced to the steps and went straight up to his second-floor suite. A few minutes later, he and Shirley walked briskly through the lobby, saying good-bye as quickly as possible.

At the door, Foster turned to Wenzel. "Take care of the team," he said. Wenzel nodded. Foster jumped in the car that was there to take him to the private plane—sent by South Carolina A.D. Jim Carlen— and was gone. It took no more than ten minutes.

"I'll never forget that scene," Bender said. "It was such an empty feeling. My career was over and that was sad. But after all Coach Foster had done for Duke, taking us from nowhere to being one of the top programs in the country, it was just sad that he would walk into that lobby, see all those people, and could only think about getting out as fast as possible. It made me want to cry all over again."

Steinwedel was going with Foster to South Carolina. Chili had decided to get out of coaching to pursue a career in business. Wenzel would be interviewed for the job as Foster's successor but never seriously considered. He too would follow his boss to South Carolina. Gminski and Bender were graduating. Of the sixteen men who had walked out of the St. Louis locker room with their arms around one another only three—Banks, Dennard, and Suddath—were left. And Max. That was it.

"It was a feeling," Suddath said, "of being all alone. It was as if Duke basketball had just vanished from the face of the earth."

Ten days later, Mike Krzyzewski, a thirty-three-year-old Bob Knight protégé who had been the coach at West Point for five years, was named to succeed Foster. Banks and Dennard skipped the meeting Butters called to introduce the new coach to the team. That left Suddath as the only representative of the '78 team in the room. The chants of "we'll be back" seemed a lot more than two years past. The era, as Dennard had put it, was over.

III

FOREVER'S TEAM

17

The Coach (I)

Bill Foster's smile had come back. It was the kind of day any Chamber of Commerce would like to bottle, not a cloud in sight and the temperature—in mid-February—climbing up to the 70s.

Slightly less than three years after his departure from Duke, Foster looked much different from the man who had fled Lexington in the aftermath of the loss to Purdue. He was considerably thinner; in fact, he looked too thin. His straight brown hair had some flecks of gray in it but it was neater than it had been in his last days at Duke.

The haggard look was gone. There was a game that night and Foster, as always, was all nervous energy. But the sense of humor had returned. He felt and sounded good. Healthy. "It's a great day to be alive," he said, glancing at the sky, perfectly aware of the irony in his words. "I feel terrific. But I'm going to keep wearing this anyway."

He held up his wrist. Around it was a hospital identification bracelet. "I'm going to keep it on," he said, "so I remember what almost happened."

What had almost happened, exactly nine weeks earlier, was simple: Foster had almost died.

It was December 11, 1982. Foster's third South Carolina team was off to a solid 4–1 start and Foster had high hopes that this would be a 20-victory team. The Gamecocks had gone 17–10 and 14–15 in Foster's first two seasons. He had steadily rebuilt the program, taking the same approach he had taken at Duke: Recruit prospects, not suspects. Get good players and wait for your shot at the great one, the Gene Banks. The program had improved slowly but steadily and Foster was comfortable. He was doing what he did best: building. He was working hard at promotion to bring fans back to the gleaming Carolina Coliseum. He had built up his TV and radio shows and his summer camp. He had gone out and sold himself to the student body the same way he had done at Duke.

"When we first got down there it was a great time for Bill," Wenzel remembered. "It was a new life for him. No Dean. No second-guessers. No Joe Gminski. They were thrilled to have him there because they knew what he could do. He was as happy as I can remember him ever being."

Wenzel was not as happy. He found South Carolina much more southern than Duke. He missed the Duke players and the Duke atmosphere. After one season he was offered the head coaching job at Jacksonville. It was time to move on. Foster, eager to recapture as much of the feeling of the '78 staff at Duke as possible, brought Ray Jones back. Even though the second season was a struggle, they were recruiting good players and their own young players were improving. By the time Purdue came to Columbia on a cold December night, South Carolina was ready to make a move nationally. The Boilermakers were unbeaten and ranked 15th in the polls. This would be an excellent test for Foster's growing team.

South Carolina played superbly. The game went back and forth to the finish. Early in the second half, Foster began to feel queasy on the bench. "I felt kind of dizzy," he said. "And sick to my stomach. I told Stiny I didn't feel great and to keep an eye on me."

Foster made it to the end of the game. The Gamecocks pulled the upset he had been looking for, 59–53. It was, without question, Foster's most important victory to date at South Carolina. He went into his office off the locker room to do his postgame radio show. As soon as the show started, Foster began to feel dizzy and sick again. He made it through the show, then asked for the team trainer. "I have to lie down," he said, and stretched out on the floor of the locker room.

The trainer sent for the team doctor immediately. Foster was quite sick. "Bill," the doctor said, "I think you're having a heart attack. Just lie still. The ambulance is on its way."

Tom Price, the sports information director, went to get Shirley Foster, who was in the basketball office with friends waiting for her husband. Price walked in, took Shirley Foster by the hand and said, "Come with me. Bill's sick."

"I walked into the locker room and Bill was lying on the floor," she said. "He was green. They told me they thought he was having a heart attack. There was no sense telling me later, I might as well deal with it then. Then the medics came in with the stretcher."

The quickest way to the ambulance was directly across the arena floor. Some of the players and their girlfriends were still there, lingering to enjoy the victory, when they saw Foster being carried out. "I could hear people saying, 'Hey, it's the coach, what's the matter with him?'" Foster said. "I wondered if I was going to die. Then I had a thought that almost made me laugh, which probably wouldn't have been a good idea. I remembered that in my last game at Utah, I lost to Purdue. In my last game at Duke, I lost to Purdue. So, I thought, 'I never thought it would kill me to beat Purdue, but maybe it will.'"

When Purdue coach Gene Keady heard that Foster had been taken to the hospital, he went straight there and stayed with Shirley Foster until after 3 A.M. At that point the doctors came out and told her that Bill was out of danger.

"Naturally, I was relieved," she said. "But the funny thing is, I never thought he was going to die. I don't know why. I had never thought about Bill having a heart attack. An ulcer, yes, I always thought that would happen. But I never thought heart attack. When it did happen, for some reason I just felt he was going to be all right. The only scary thing about it was that usually my premonitions about things are wrong.

"I remember a lot of things about that night, but one I'll never forget was Gene and Pat Keady sitting there and refusing to leave until they told us Bill was okay."

By the next morning, a Sunday, the word went out around the country that Foster had had a heart attack. Lou Goetz, who had gotten out of coaching the previous season and moved back to Durham, jumped in his car and headed for Columbia. When he arrived, Foster was conscious but the doctors told him firmly that only family members could see him. "He *is* family," Shirley Foster said, and the doctor backed down immediately.

Bob Wenzel couldn't believe the news when he heard it on Sunday afternoon. He called the house and Shirley Foster, who had just come home for the first time, confirmed it. Wenzel immediately made a plane reservation.

Although the doctors said Foster was out of danger, the blockage that had caused the heart attack had not cleared up. Two days after the attack Foster underwent quadruple bypass surgery. It was a success.

Flowers and cards came from everywhere. Dean Smith attached a note saying, "Winning is important but it isn't worth dying over." Lefty Driesell phoned two days after sending flowers. His team had just won a double-overtime game from UCLA. "During the overtime Aah felt turble," he said. "Aah told my assistants, 'Aah think Aahm havin' one of them heart attacks just like Foster.'"

"I almost broke my stitches laughing," Foster said.

Steinwedel was the acting coach in Foster's absence. Needless to say, the team and the entire South Carolina campus were stunned. The day after Foster had his surgery, Shirley Foster went to see the team. She marched into the locker room just before practice, escorted by Steinwedel and Jones.

She told them that Bill was doing just fine and that her only problem was going to be convincing him to stay in bed when he thought it was time to go to practice. She talked about how proud he was of the Purdue victory and the progress they had made. And she told them in no uncertain terms that he would be back coaching them. "No one, not the doctors, not me, not anyone else will keep him from coming back and coaching you guys," she said. "But for now, he would want you to treat the coaches who are here with you the same way you would treat him if he were here.

"Okay?" she said. "Can we count on you?"

They could.

"Her voice never broke, never wavered for a second," Steinwedel said. "When she walked out, every person in the room was crying."

Shirley Foster knew that trying to convince her husband to give up coaching was fruitless. Once the doctors told him he could coach after the surgery, she knew it was only a matter of time before he returned.

"It wasn't even an issue," she said. "He's a coach, period. This is what he does. I can't say that it makes him completely happy but it gives him joy. He loves doing it. I knew he could do other things and if he wanted that, I would have been delighted. But I knew he wanted to come back and that, in the long run, that was what was going to be best for his health."

Lou Goetz didn't feel that way. He had watched his father suffer with heart disease, never truly regaining his health after his heart attack, and he didn't want Foster to suffer the same way. "He tried, he really did," Foster said. "He told me I would be amazed how little I would miss it if I got out, how many other things I could do. I knew what he was saying but I also knew I hadn't finished what I had started at South Carolina. I had to go back."

Wenzel knew that. "When I saw him lying in bed, I felt sick," he said. "I kept thinking, 'Why didn't you push him more to exercise or go easy on himself?' I knew it wasn't our fault that it happened, but I felt lousy about it and scared. But there was never any doubt that he was going to coach. I mentioned to him one day, 'You know you could get out.' He just put me off, said, 'We'll see.' I knew there was no point pursuing it."

Foster did everything his doctors told him to and was out of the hospital before the end of the year. In late January he got the go-ahead to return. The doctors wanted him to go slowly. The team was playing well under Steinwedel. Let Steinwedel run the team the first night you sit on the bench and see how you feel, his doctor suggested. Foster agreed. On February 12, Holy Cross came to Columbia. The Gamecocks were 16–6. At pregame meal that afternoon, Foster came back to coaching, walking the team through Holy Cross's tendencies. Then he went to take a nap.

"Doctor's orders," he said.

That night, in the locker room, doctor's orders or no, he was his old self. He smacked on his chewing gum and interrupted Steinwedel several times to add suggestions. Finally, it was time to walk back on the court. "I don't think they'll boo me," he said to an old friend, walking out the door. "The last time I was here, we won."

They gave him a long, warm standing ovation. But it was worth noting that the Carolina Coliseum was only a little more than half filled, even on the night of Foster's dramatic return. This was the Catch-22 of the independent status that had been so attractive to Foster when he left Duke. While it was true that, with no league obligations, South Carolina could control much of its schedule, it was also true that it was difficult to bring in opponents who would get the fans and students excited. Without a league schedule, South Carolina had only one real rivalry—with Clemson—and low attendance was a problem. When it came to atmosphere, the Carolina Coliseum, although state of the art in every way, was no Cameron Indoor Stadium. Often, Carolina Mausoleum might have described the place better.

"We play a lot of good, solid teams," Foster said. "Holy Cross is a team that has excellent tradition, has been to the NCAA's quite a bit in the last few years and has good players. But down here, no one knows who Holy Cross is or where it is. They probably don't even know that Bob Cousy played there."

Independence also had put South Carolina in a television bind. Just as Foster arrived, conferences began negotiating block TV deals with the networks, spurred by the arrival of CBS on the scene as NBC's rival for college basketball. Those deals virtually left the independents, with the exception of the name schools like Notre Dame and DePaul, out in the television cold. That hurt financially and it hurt recruiting because of lack of exposure.

As a result, South Carolina had applied for membership in the Metro Conference, a league that included national powers like Louisville and Memphis State. Three years after fleeing the ACC, Bill Foster needed a league.

None of this was on Foster's mind, though, as he walked onto the floor before the Holy Cross game. The ovation was long and warm, then his team went out and played excellent basketball, winning easily. It took Foster, sitting in the middle of the bench away from the rest of the coaches, exactly forty-seven seconds to get on one of the referees. He was back.

Late that night, after taping his TV show, he talked about how well he thought things had worked out for him at South Carolina.

"The family really likes it down here," he said. "Shirley loves our house and everyone, especially [Athletic Director Jim] Carlen, has been terrific. The last few weeks, since I got sick, everyone's been supportive. The president of the school extended my contract while I was still in the hospital. You can't ask for much more than that.

"I think this thing with getting into the Metro will help us in the long run. In the short run, it toughens the schedule. But it also gets us on television and gives us some games to point to on the schedule each year."

Of course, the ACC did all that on a higher level.

"I know that," he said, smiling. "But it was different. I feel very good here."

Dean Smith wasn't eight miles away and his parking lot was paved. But what Foster didn't know that night—couldn't know—was that South Carolina would change, soon. The team would win 22 games that season, but not get an NCAA bid—the NCAA Tournament Committee decided their schedule was not tough enough.

The following year, Carlen would be fired. Foster, after talking to people who had worked with him, opposed the new athletic director, Bob Marcum. Marcum got the job anyway and made it clear to Foster that he knew he had opposed him.

Entry into the Metro Conference made victories tougher to find for South Carolina. Recruiting became tougher because other schools told recruits that Foster wasn't going to stay in coaching much longer because of his health. The program began to flounder. The boosters became impatient. In 1985, the NCAA announced it was investigating the basketball program. Recruiting improprieties were whispered about. In 1986, the Gamecocks finished with a 12–16 record. Two days after the season ended, Marcum called Foster into his office and told him he was fired.

Foster had never been fired in his life. Later, he would joke about it, remembering what his old friend Abe Lemons had said about his firing at Texas. "The guy said, 'You're fired.' I looked around the room and there was no one else there. I figured he meant me."

But that day, it was no joking matter. The NCAA investigation had tarnished him and, forty months after his heart attack—and contract extension—he was out of a job at the age of fifty-five.

Three weeks later, Duke returned to the Final Four for the first time since 1978. Bill Foster was at the Final Four too, attending the coaches' convention. Rumor had it that he was being considered for the job at Northwestern, perhaps the most difficult job there was in all of college basketball. Northwestern had only one tradition in basketball: constant losing.

Sitting in the lobby of the coaches' convention hotel in Dallas, Foster, as always, couldn't resist a joke. "The good news is that I can get the job," he said. "The bad news is I may take it."

There were other jobs Foster could have. Several schools were interested in him. He could also get out of coaching and into administration. That thought barely crossed Foster's mind, though.

Northwestern was a great academic school that had always been overmatched in the Big Ten, which was full of football and basketball powerhouses. So if he was going to stay in coaching, why Northwestern?

Foster smiled, knowing the irony in what he was about to say. "I like the place," he said. "It reminds me of Duke."

One week later, he took the job.

18

Juice

The home of Bruce and Jennifer Bell looks about the way the home of a successful young lawyer should look. The living room is large and comfortable, dotted by the signs of young children at play. The bedrooms are large and comfortable, one of them a nursery for child number three, then due in another month. Off the dining room is a small room that Bruce uses as a study. Jennifer calls it "Bruce's shrine."

The picture in the middle of the shrine's wall catches one's eye immediately. It is the picture that ran in *The Chronicle* the day after Bell's last game in Cameron Indoor Stadium. There is Bell, standing at center court bathed in the spotlight, biting his lip to keep from crying.

Eleven years later, he doesn't look much different. He still has the baby-faced, boy-next-door look that girl-of-his-dreams Kathy Butler couldn't resist, although he is thirty-two now. Standing in The Shrine, looking at The Picture, Bell gets a little bit misty-eyed.

"That season is still one of the greatest things that ever happened to me," he said. "I can still remember after we lost to Kentucky, we all went around the locker room saying, 'I love you' to one another. I have trouble saying those words to my wife, who I love more than anyone, but that night, it was just the right thing because that was the way we felt.

"I never dreamed that they wouldn't make it back. I wish I knew what happened. Rob [Hardy] and I still talk about it sometimes. But when I graduated that year my regret was leaving those guys behind. They were like the brothers I never had."

Bell went back to Lexington after graduating from Duke and worked at his father's law firm for a year. That confirmed Bell's suspicions that he wanted to go to law school, so he applied to the University of Kentucky.

"I enjoyed having that year off," he said. "But I had some problems withdrawing from basketball. In November, when the season was getting ready to start, I got real itchy to play so I went over and played some games with the Marathon Oil team. But I was already out of shape and I hurt my ankle again. That was that.

"Then in December, I started getting real bad headaches. The doctors couldn't figure out what it was, but I think it was just being out of shape and being away from basketball. I had them for a couple of months and then they went away."

Bell kept in touch with the team that year, mostly through Hardy. He could sense Hardy's frustration with what was happening and felt it too. Sympathy pains. "The guys were still my friends and it hurt me to hear what was going on. Some of it I couldn't believe. Or at least didn't want to believe."

The next fall, Bell started law school. He also started dating Jennifer, then a Kentucky senior. Each thought the other was kind of a jerk on their first blind date but they kept seeing each other anyway. "There were some things I needed to have a date for," Jennifer said. "And at least he was cute."

After a while, they started to like each other and by second semester they were dating seriously. That was why Bruce was shocked at the end of the school year when Jennifer announced she was taking a job in Atlanta. "For a while, I figured that was it," he said. "If she was moving, I would date other people. But that next fall, I kept missing her."

They commuted during the fall and on New Year's Night 1981, Bruce proposed. Jennifer said yes.

Jennifer knows the Kathy Butler story. "I figured I better tell her myself," Bruce said, "because if I didn't, one of my god-dang teammates was bound to."

After he graduated from law school, Bell went to work in his dad's firm as an associate. It is a small law firm, but highly respected in Lexington. There was never any doubt in Bruce Bell's mind that he was going to live as an adult in Lexington.

"If it hadn't been for my dad, I probably never would have left Lexington," he said. "Growing up, I thought Lexington was the whole wide world. He was the one who pushed me to go to Duke, and thank God he did. It was the best thing that ever happened to me. I found out there was a world out there and had the best experience of my life playing at Duke.

"But I always knew I wanted to come back here and live. I could have gone to work at another law firm somewhere I guess, but the thought of getting to work with my dad was something I couldn't resist. And I'm glad I made that decision because those three years working together changed our relationship. All my life, he was my hero. But during that time, he became my friend."

Bruce Bell's voice turns soft when he talks about his father. Tommy Bell died in 1986 at the age of sixty-three. Cancer. Bruce admits he still hasn't gotten over losing his father.

"After I graduated from law school and started working at the firm, I was in an office right down the hall from his," he said. "We spent more time together then than we ever had. When I was a kid, he travelled a lot. We saw each other but not all that much. Now, we spent time every day. We had lunch almost daily. We talked about the law and about life and about ball games. He became my best friend. When he got sick, it was very very hard for me to deal with."

Bruce Bell watched his father grow thinner and weaker and he cried often after he died. "The only thing I keep with me is that I was able to tell him how much he meant to me before he died," he said. "And I can still remember the look on his face the night my son was born. I walked into the waiting room carrying him, handed him to my dad and said, 'Dad, this is Thomas Bell. He's named after you.' Then we both cried."

His voice chokes at the memory and at the loss he suffered. The office he works in now is the one his father occupied for years. "At first I had mixed emotions about moving in there," he said. "The firm gave me the choice. When I thought about it I realized that it would be impossible for me to walk into that office and see someone else working in there. And I think he would have wanted me in there, too."

Tommy Bell was renowned as an after-dinner speaker. Bruce knows all his stories by heart. His favorite is the one his dad told often about Fred Arbanas, the Kansas City Chiefs tight end who played for years in spite of having a glass eye.

"Dad always swore the story was true," Bruce said. "He was refereeing an exhibition game between the Chiefs and Dallas Cowboys. Arbanas caught a pass and got slammed. He went down and the trainer came running out. The next thing Dad knew, the trainer had picked up the glass eye, which had popped out on the play and was swishing it around in the water bucket. Then he just popped it back in like nothing.

"Dad was amazed. He went over to Arbanas and said, 'Fred, what would you do if you ever lost your other eye?'

"And Arbanas looked at him without missing a beat and said, 'Why Mr. Bell, I'd become a referee just like you.'"

The most famous Tommy Bell story occurred during Super Bowl III, the famous New York Jets victory over the Baltimore Colts that changed football forever. Prior to the game, Joe Namath had not only predicted a Jets victory but had noted that his team would win even though the referee (Bell) was from the National Football League—the Colts' league.

Late in the game, with the Jets on their way to a 16–7 victory, Namath walked over to Bell and said, "Mr. Bell, I just want you to know I think you're doing a fine job."

"Why would you say that, Joe?" Bell answered. "*My* team is losing."

Bruce loves retelling these stories. It is one way of keeping his dad alive. His mother lives near the house he and Jennifer bought shortly before Thomas was born, and often comes over to baby-sit for the grandchildren. She still thinks her only son is the world's most perfect boy, just as she did when he was growing up.

"I've been very lucky," he said. "I've always had good people around me, starting with my parents, then going through college and now with Jenny. I've been able to do all the things I wanted to and some things I never dreamed of."

His memories of that miracle senior season are still vivid, especially the funny moments: the pregame meals, the Banks farts, his teammates making fun of his accent.

"You know, I don't see those guys very much anymore," he said. "Rob and I live thirty miles apart and we see each other, but not as much as we should. I still talk to Bobby [Bender] on the phone because he's my link to Duke. I think Mike [Krzyzewski] has done a great job and I'm amazed that he manages to remember my name every time I go back there. But my link to the program is Bobby. When he leaves, something will go out of it for a lot of us.

"The other guys, though, I hardly ever see. I think about them a lot. There's a feeling I have for them that will never change. We went through something that can't be explained to people who weren't part of it. A lot of times, when you remember people and experiences you tend to blot out the bad and remember only the good. But that year, it really was all good. It just happened. We didn't expect it or plan for it, we just did it. And no one can take it away from us."

He held up his arm. "I still wear the watch. People down here bring up the championship game all the time. They say all the right things because they won the game but when they do I just kind of smile to myself. Kentucky won the game, sure, and they were probably the better team. But we were the really special team that year. That's why everyone fell in love with us. They could tell we were different. The feeling we had for one another and still have is something I'll bet very few teams that win it all ever have.

"We were young, we were characters, we were all different. We didn't compute. But it worked. Every time I walk in that room, The Shrine as Jenny calls it, I think about those guys and I smile."

And when they think about him, they still smile too. His card says "T. Bruce Bell" but to them he will always be "Juice."

"I still remember a couple years ago I called Gminski on the phone when I was back visiting Duke just to give him a hard time. I was trying to make it tough for him to figure out who it was. I got about as far as saying, 'Mike, how you doing?' when he said, 'Juice, what the hell are you doing?' I couldn't believe he knew it was me that fast. He said, 'Are you kidding, I'd recognize that god-dang country twang of yours anywhere.' "

It is late now on a cold January night. Bell's family has gone to bed and he has to be in the office early. But Bell talks on, enjoying the memories. His visitor is enjoying them just as much.

"I still follow Duke closely," he said. "I get back there a couple of times a year and I drive Jenny crazy because I always have to take a walk around campus. It's like coming home for me."

Like his teammates, Bell worries about his old coach sometimes. "It hurt me when he left Duke. To me, he just belonged there. I couldn't imagine him being happy somewhere else. But then I heard about how unhappy he was at Duke at the end. Now, I see the Northwestern scores in the paper and I remember how he was when we were losing and I say to myself, 'Why is he still doing it?'

"When he had the heart attack, I thought maybe he'd get out. He could do so many other things if he wanted to, but the problem is, he doesn't want to. Maybe he'll turn it around and prove us all wrong. I sure hope so. I still think about him a lot."

But when he goes into The Shrine and looks back, Bell remembers the warmth, the jokes, and St. Louis.

"I have only one regret about my basketball career," he said, laughing. "And that's the three-point shot. If they'd had that dang line when I was playing, well, heck, if there was one thing I could do it was shoot from outside. Who knows what I might have done? Maybe I'll make a comeback. Try out for the NBA."

He still plays basketball, rec league ball once or twice a week. Recently, he got nailed with a technical foul during a game. "I was tired and I wanted to come out," he said. "I'm not in bad shape, but I'm not in great shape either. I went over to the bench and told the guy coaching the team to take me out for a bit.

"But he didn't hear me or the guy he wanted to go in didn't hear him. The next thing I know they're getting ready to start playing again and we only have four guys on the court. So I jumped back on the court. The referee came running downcourt screaming, 'That's a technical foul, illegal substitution, you can't just come in like that.'

"I told him that I'd been in the game and that I never actually came out because no one had subbed for me. 'You can't do that,' he said. 'You can't leave the court. You were off the court.'

"I told him that was ridiculous, that whenever you throw the ball inbounds you're off the court and there was no way I had done anything wrong. Well, he just looked at me and said, 'You don't know the rules. I know the rules. Where did you learn to play basketball?' "

Bell stopped and got the sheepish little-boy-lost grin on his face. "I got mad when he said that," he said. "I looked at him and said, 'Buddy, you're picking on the wrong guy. I played for Duke!'

"He still gave me the technical."

19

The Captain

Something is wrong with this picture. Jim Spanarkel is walking through the suburban New Jersey offices of Merrill-Lynch wearing a blue suit and suspenders. On a basketball court, surrounded by basketball players, he never looked very tall. Walking through an office, surrounded by stock brokers and secretaries, he looks 6-5. Of course, he *is* 6-5.

There are some people who just seem to belong in a basketball uniform. Jim Spanarkel was one of those people. He was so comfortable on the court, so at home, that it was easy to think he would *always* be out there playing the game.

That is fantasy. Reality is the suit and suspenders. Jim Spanarkel is thirty-one now, married to his high school sweetheart, and the father of two children. He lives ten minutes from where he grew up in Jersey City and every morning he comes to this office and makes his living.

He does it quite well too. But he also knows that this will never be home the way a basketball court was. "I'm like anyone else who enjoyed playing the game," he said. "I miss it sometimes. That's why I like doing this broadcasting thing [he does New Jersey Nets games part-time on TV and radio]. It keeps me involved. But I've never wanted to chase the game. I've always understood that it doesn't go on forever."

It did go on for five years after Spanarkel graduated from Duke. As disappointing as the St. John's loss that ended his Duke career was, Spanarkel knew his basketball career wasn't over. At the basketball banquet that spring, he quoted from a Dan Fogelberg song on the ups and downs of life to try to explain what had happened in '79 after the joy of '78.

In many ways, this was classic Spanarkel—always searching for balance and sanity and, most of the time, finding it.

The day of the NBA draft, Spanarkel was home in Jersey City, expecting to get a call sometime in the first round. As always, he was organized. "I knew all my buddies were going to come over for the afternoon," he said. "I went down to our neighborhood liquor store and told them I needed a keg of draft beer. You know, draft for the draft."

The call came midway in the first round—from Philadelphia. Spanarkel and buddies, well into the draft draft by now, were delighted. "It was one hundred miles away," Spanarkel said. "They had been driving five hundred all through college to see me. Now, it would only be one hundred. By the end of the day they had gone out and gotten T-shirts made that said 'Let's Get Silly in Philly.' By the end of the night we had gotten pretty silly in Jersey City."

To understand Spanarkel, one must understand the importance of his Jersey City support group. It starts with his family. He is the fourth of six children. The Spanarkel family was always close. Raymond Spanarkel has worked his entire adult life for Kellogg's cereals, always making a solid living without ever getting rich. Growing up, Jim lived in three different houses—all on the same block, Fairview Avenue. His close friends then are his close friends now.

All through his years at Duke, his buddies from the local hangout, The Peacock Pub, would road-trip to Duke several times a year, led by Jim's older brother Kevin. Their ability to party became legendary at Duke and they provided Jim with a constant support system. They also amazed some of his teammates. "When I first saw those guys, it was like culture shock for me," said Scott Goetsch. "Remember, I was from California. When I met Jim's buddies I realized for the first time in my life that New Jersey was a real place and there were people that talked like that."

Johnny Dawkins, the All-American guard from Washington, D.C., who was the star of Duke's 1986 Final Four team, accidentally summed up the typical Duke team once while trying to describe what Duke was like to reporters. "It's an amazing place," Dawkins said. "You meet people from all kinds of cultures there—Europe, Africa, California. Everywhere."

No doubt, Goetsch and Gray, Spanarkel's California classmates, seemed as foreign to him as his Jersey City pals seemed to them. But they all enjoyed each other nonetheless. "Jimmy's pals were almost part of the team," Bob Bender said. "If we had a big game and they didn't show up we asked him where the hell they were."

His pals didn't have much of a chance to see him play in Philadelphia. Spanarkel was a rookie on a veteran team that included players like Julius Erving and Darryl Dawkins. "I was kind of in awe of the whole thing," he said. "I don't think I gave myself a chance to do well there because I didn't have the confidence I had always had. Confidence has always been a very important part of my game. That year, I didn't have it."

Billy Cunningham was the coach of the 76ers at the time and he thought Spanarkel was a step slow to play in the NBA. Of course, a lot of people had thought he was a step slow to play in college. That spring, the Dallas Mavericks selected Spanarkel in the expansion draft. Now he would be on a bad team but one where he would have a legitimate chance to play.

"As it turned out it was a great break for me to go to Dallas," he said. "I wasn't so sure about going there at first because it was sixteen hundred miles from home. But I knew it was another shot for me, probably my last one. I had signed a five-year contract but only the first two years were guaranteed. So this was it for me.

"I never enjoyed losing and we lost a lot there at first. At least with the Sixers I was with a great team, one that made the NBA final the year I was there. So that was an adjustment. But Dick Motta [the Mavericks coach] liked the way I played and gave me the chance I was looking for."

He was the Mavs' leading scorer his first year and the second-leading scorer his second year. He knew then that he was never going to be a great NBA player—but he *had* proven he could play in the league. It is no coincidence that it was that summer he and Janet McPherson finally got married.

They had met in high school. As a sophomore, Spanarkel briefly dated Janet's older sister, who was a classmate. Janet was just a freshman then, a mere kid. By the time Spanarkel was a senior, Janet was a junior and not a kid anymore. "Our first date was March 1st, 1975," Spanarkel said. "Not that I've kept track or anything."

Janet went to St. Peter's while Jim was at Duke and even with time and distance the relationship continued. By the time Jim graduated he knew he wanted to marry Janet, but he wasn't ready.

"You can call it immaturity or whatever else you want," Spanarkel said, "but I was so into playing basketball and proving myself as a basketball player that I wasn't ready to deal with being married. It certainly isn't a knock on her, but this was just something I had to do first. Who knows, if she had been with me I might have done as well or better but it just didn't seem that way at the time."

After his second season in Dallas, Jim knew he was ready. Fortunately for him, Janet is a patient woman and, a little more than seven years after that first date, they were married. "I guess you could say after all that time we were both sure," Jim said, laughing.

It is interesting to listen to him talk about his wife. He uses words like steady and solid and strong. "You may frazzle her but you'll never know it," he will say. "Put her on an island and she'll find a way to survive." Ask his teammates to describe Jim Spanarkel and they might use exactly the same words and phrases.

In February of 1989, Janet Spanarkel had a miscarriage eleven weeks into her fourth pregnancy. Before James (now three) and Bridget (now two) were born, the Spanarkels lost another child seven weeks into the pregnancy. "Times like those are when I appreciate her most," Jim said. "It's a crushing thing to have happen, but she somehow bounces right back. I've always enjoyed being with Janet because she's smart and she's funny but I also admire her. I think that's a great thing to have in a relationship."

Janet Spanarkel moved to Dallas with her new husband in the fall of 1982. Jim played two more years in Dallas but by that third season Dallas had used high draft picks to stockpile talent and his playing time began to dwindle. The next season, just prior to New Year's, Spanarkel thought the Mavericks might be getting ready to cut him. If they did so before New Year's they wouldn't have to pay him for the balance of the season.

"Twelve days before the deadline I went down in a game against Golden State and hurt my wrist," he said. "I thought it was sprained. But afterwards, the team doctor looked at it and said he thought it was broken. I couldn't believe it because it didn't hurt all that much. He decided to do a bone scan. If the wrist was broken, I would have to go on the injured list and I couldn't be cut while I was on the list. Sure enough, the scan came back and the wrist was broken. That night, Janet and I went out and toasted my broken wrist."

After that season, the Mavericks did not renew his contract. He was a free agent. "The phone did not ring off the hook," Spanarkel said wryly. But he did get invited to the Milwaukee Bucks training camp

and was offered a contract—for less money than he had made as a
rookie. Spanarkel had played five years. "It was time," he said. "I
probably could have hung on another two or three years, sat on the
bench and collected a check. But after a while, playing a professional
sport changes you. You know going in that it's a business, that there
are double standards for stars and all that, but when you see it close
up for a while it begins to get to you. I'd had enough. I wanted to start
doing something where I would be working my way up a ladder rather
than slipping down and just trying to hold on."

Spanarkel had been accepted at Duke Law School at the end of his
senior year and the option to go to law school was still there. He had
made enough money as a basketball player that he could afford to
become a student again for three years. But he had also gotten both
his real estate and securities licenses during the off-seasons and he
thought he could make a good living that way. What's more, when
Merrill-Lynch offered him a job in their New Jersey office it meant
going home. Janet, also one of six children (number three) from a
close family, was thrilled to be back home after two years in Texas.
And so, at the age of twenty-seven, the ultimate gym rat walked away
from the gym.

"It really wasn't that hard," he said. "I didn't miss it as much as I
thought I might. I got involved in my new job right away and I think
I can honestly say I never cheated myself. I was always in shape, always
played as hard as I could, and I always knew how to play the game.

"Sometimes I think I might want to play in some of these organized
rec leagues but the couple of times I *have* played it always seems like
there are a couple of guys who want to prove they can play rough with
the guy who played in the NBA. I don't need that. If I were to get hurt
playing in one of those games, I'd feel silly. It isn't worth it."

And so, like anyone else who puts on a suit to go to work every
morning, Spanarkel works out in a nearby gym and runs whenever he
can. His black hair is shorter now than it was eleven years ago and he
is a little heavier, but he still looks like he could run the wing on the
Duke fast break.

During his time in the NBA, Spanarkel drifted away from Duke. He
was traveling a lot and when Foster left after his rookie year, there was
no natural tie to the school. Given a choice between a weekend off in
Jersey City or a weekend off at Duke, Spanarkel always opted for Jersey
City.

But since his retirement from basketball, that has changed. Interestingly, one of the people who pushed Spanarkel to become more involved with Duke was Foster. "I always thought Jimmy represented all the things that were right about Duke," Foster said. "The school needs people like him to stay involved. And I think Jimmy needs to be involved. It was an important place to him."

Spanarkel agrees. He goes back to Duke a couple of times a year now and is on the national alumni board. He admits there is still a small hurt inside him when he walks into Cameron Indoor Stadium and looks up at the rafters and sees Dick Groat's number 10, Mike Gminski's number 43, and Johnny Dawkins's number 24 hanging there. Even now, he is reluctant to talk about the subject of retired uniform numbers.

"I like Tom Butters, he has always been good to me, and he was good to me from the first time I visited Duke," Spanarkel said. "I still remember him telling me at the time that if Duke wasn't the right place for me he would do everything he could to help me find the right place. You can say that was a smart recruiting thing to say but no one else ever said it to me.

"But to be completely honest, I always thought I deserved to be up there too. Those three guys and Danny Ferry [whose number 35 was retired in the spring of '89] all deserve the honor. But based on what I've been told, that they select people based on performance, on academics, and on how they represented the school, I really think I belong."

It is not an issue Spanarkel harps on, though. He enjoys his renewed association with Duke and he has an excellent relationship with both Butters and Krzyzewski. What he regrets far more than not having his number retired is that he does not see his old teammates more often.

"You know growing up and going your separate ways is part of life," he said. "But as I've gotten older, I feel as if I'm letting something slip away.

"Not many days go by that I don't think about those guys at some point. People still bring up '78 to me all the time and I'm glad they do. It's funny sometimes, people will say to me, 'So what have you been doing since you guys played in St. Louis?' They don't have any idea I played at Duke another year or that I played in the NBA for five years. But they remember *that* team. I hope fifteen or twenty years from now people still remember that team. I know I will.

"The funny thing is I don't remember what you would call the big things. I can't tell you how many points I scored in any one game although I can tell you that Givens scored forty-one to beat us in St. Louis and Ford scored thirty-four to beat us in Chapel Hill.

"I remember different things, like Rob Hardy always coming over to me just before I was introduced and giving me a high-five with both hands. I remember how much Bruce meant to all of us and I remember Gene stinking up the locker room after he drank all that milk. I remember how Harold could always make us laugh and I remember how much I enjoyed working out on my own in Cameron.

"Whenever I do see any of the guys it isn't a big emotional thing. It just seems entirely natural that we start busting on each other and telling the most embarrassing stories we can remember from the old days. We really should all get together more often than we do and I should do something about it. I was the captain."

Indeed he was. It was never something he made a big deal about but there was never any doubt who the leader of that '78 team was. Everything Foster eventually built started with Spanarkel: the program turning in the right direction; the toughness on the floor; the work ethic; the busting on each other in the locker room that made them so close.

"Have you ever thought," Bob Bender, then a Duke assistant coach, once asked, "that you might like to coach?"

Spanarkel paused before answering. "I've thought about it," he said. "I think I would enjoy being part of a team again and the challenge. If I tried it, maybe I'd get to be the coach at Duke someday."

Bender promptly offered to make Spanarkel an assistant when he became a head coach. Spanarkel shook his head vigorously. "No way Bennie," he said, laughing. "You can be *my* assistant. I run the show.

"Every year when the NCAA Tournament starts, I think about our year," Spanarkel said. "I think about how it all happened so fast and I look at how big the tournament is now and sometimes I'm still amazed by what we did.

"You see, every year someone wins the national championship. But I consider what we did special and I think of myself as special because of the *way* it happened. Bill Foster brought me into a program that was down and out and had gone nowhere for a while. We went through some horrendous times, some times when you wanted to just bag it because it got so frustrating.

"And then, we had this magic run. Not really from out of nowhere because we worked for it but in the grand scheme of things, given where we had been a year before, it was out of nowhere. I wouldn't trade that experience for another five years in the NBA or guaranteed success the rest of my life. I'm just damn proud of what we did, no matter what happened the next year. It doesn't diminish '78 at all."

Five months earlier a high school star named Bobby Hurley had announced he was going to Duke. Bobby Hurley played at St. Anthony's High School in Jersey City. He picked Duke, no doubt, because of Krzyzewski, the success the team has had, the academics, and The Chapel. And maybe, just maybe, because of Jim Spanarkel.

"I'd like to think that, in a little, tiny way, I had something to do with it," Spanarkel said softly. "I went down there from Jersey City and did okay and maybe Bobby knows a little bit about our team. Maybe I had nothing to do with it at all. But if my name helped just in a small way, that makes me very happy."

Bobby Hurley is a point guard. The Duke coaches love him because, they say, he is a natural leader. If he becomes half the leader the last Duke kid out of Jersey City proved to be, they are going to have one hell of a player for the next four years.

One who deserves to have his number retired. Just like Jim Spanarkel.

20

Charlie Manson

Steve Gray still wears the ring. But he isn't exactly sure why. "I don't know if I wear it out of pride or if I wear it to remind myself how things can get if you let them," he said, looking at his 1978 Final Four ring. "I know it means a lot to me because I worked a lot of hours and went through a lot to earn it. But the memories it brings back, to be honest, aren't all good ones."

Of all the players who wore Duke uniforms in St. Louis in 1978, Steve Gray had the most frustrating college experience. Like everyone else who was there he vividly remembers the two plays in '77 that became the symbols of his college career: the dribble off the foot against N.C. State and the pass off the rim against Maryland.

"I've tried to figure out a way to describe to people what my college basketball career was like," Gray said. "The best thing I've come up with is that it was like having a nightmare and being in a coma. I couldn't wake up from the nightmare for four years."

He is sitting in a San Francisco restaurant, a decade and a lifetime away from the nightmare. He is here on a business trip, a frequent occurrence in his life. Gray works for a German computer company, managing their business in the western half of the United States. He lives in Hillcrest Estates, a ritzy Los Angeles suburb not that far from where he grew up in Woodland Hills.

All is well with Gray these days. He is making a lot of money and he is married to the girl he dated in high school. He is in excellent shape. Dressed in a gray suit with his dark brown hair cut short and neat, he looks like the affluent young businessman that he is.

"I guess for a guy who everyone called 'Charlie Manson,' I'm doing all right," he said with a smile.

There is no malice or braggadocio in the statement. Once, there might have been. But Gray has grown out of that. "I left Duke with a lot of bitterness about what happened. It took me a while to get over it," he said. "A couple of years after I graduated I was back in the area for a little while and I had just hit big on an investment I had made and I needed somebody local to cosign the check.

"There were a lot of guys I could have gotten to do it but I went and found Bob Bender. He was always ahead of me in the pecking order on the team and I guess I wanted to stick it to him in a way. The check was for $106,000. I remember that. I wanted him to see that number. Now, when I think about that, I feel bad. Bob Bender never did anything to me except for getting to play when I wanted to. In fact, Bob Bender is a hell of a good guy. Someday, if I see him again, I'll apologize even though I don't know if he'll even remember it."

Bender remembers. "You don't forget a guy asking you to sign a check that size," he said. "But I didn't think much of it. Steve was always doing something that was different than anyone else. You didn't question him, you just accepted it. He always marched to a different drummer."

Gray's nonconformism, his outlandishness, is hereditary. His grandfather on his mother's side entered the United States by way of Boston Harbor. Hardly unusual. Only he swam through the harbor having jumped off the Italian Navy ship on which he was serving as a seaman. While Gray's grandfather ran away from the military—he settled in Boston and went to work in a textile mill—his father, Philip Gray, ran away *to* the military at the age of sixteen. He ran away from home and enlisted in the Army until his parents found him and revealed his real age. Two years later, he enlisted again and ended up in Korea, where he received two Purple Hearts and the Silver Star.

Steve is the third of Philip and Virginia Gray's six children. He was always an excellent all-around athlete (another trait inherited from his father) and probably would have stayed on the West Coast to attend college if not for Lou Goetz accidentally stumbling over him.

"Lou had come out to California to watch Paul Mokeski [now with the Milwaukee Bucks] work out," Gray said. "It was the first year that he and Foster were at Duke and they really needed players. I was still in football season but a couple of guys told me to come over after practice and work out because this college coach was coming out to watch Mokeski. When the workout was over, Lou came over and started talking to me about Duke."

Gray visited Duke more for the free trip east than anything else. But like so many others, he fell in love with the campus and ended up joining Scott Goetsch, whom he had played against in high school, in migrating to North Carolina.

"My most vivid memory of arriving at Duke is stepping off the plane into the August heat," Gray said. "It just stunned me. I wasn't used to that kind of humidity."

Gray never quite fit in with his teammates. He and Goetsch, both Californians, roomed together as freshmen but eventually drifted apart; Goetsch joined a fraternity while Gray went to live off-campus. He did become close friends with Harold Morrison and the two of them still keep in touch, especially now that they both live in California. But that was about it.

"I think it's fair to say that I was the outsider on that team, more than anyone," Gray said. "Harold went through a lot of the same frustrations that I did but he always had a role. He was the court jester, the guy who came up with something funny when we needed it most.

"In '78, when we made the run, I was part of it, but I wasn't part of it. I was the guy with the best seat in the house. I felt joy for the other guys. Even though I wasn't close to them, I liked them all. I don't think I ever felt the euphoria they felt, but I did feel happiness for them."

Gray's teammates nicknamed him Charlie Manson because of his appearance and intensity. Back then, Gray's hair was long and wild, brown curls spewing out in all directions. He always had a look in his eye that said, "Don't mess with me." And his personality fit the look.

Goetsch remembers Gray slamming a dorm-mate up against the wall in the hallway late one night because the guy was blasting his stereo so loud that no one could sleep. In practice, Gray was just as likely to square off with someone. "My senior year, things had gotten so bad for me that one day I just threw the ball right in Jimmy Spanarkel's face. For no reason at all. It wasn't him I was mad at, it was the situation. Jim came right at me and if the coaches hadn't gotten between us it would have been a hell of a fight. Neither one of us was the type to back down."

For Gray, basketball was his blessing and his curse. From his first day to his last day at Duke, no one worked harder on his game. He was always in great shape and spent countless hours working out on his own to try to improve his game. But unlike Tate Armstrong and Spanarkel, who benefited greatly from their extra work, Gray never did.

"It seemed like the more I worked," he said, "the worse it got."

Then came Armstrong's wrist injury. Suddenly, Gray had his chance. In the movies, he steps in for the star and becomes a star himself. In Gray's life, he dribbled the ball off his foot and threw the pass off the rim.

"I don't like to make excuses, especially now," he said. "I screwed up, without question. I think my problem was I wasn't really a point guard. I didn't feel comfortable there and when all of a sudden they basically *gave* me the basketball and said, 'Do it, kid,' I just wasn't ready.

"You have to put that time in perspective. I was nineteen years old and I'd come out of California with an ego as big as the Empire State Building. I was like anyone else who had been a star in high school. I expected it to be the same in college. Then it wasn't and it really hurt me, especially at the end of my sophomore year when I got benched for Bruce [Bell, the non-scholarship walk-on]."

Gray's chance had come and gone. He looks back now at his last two seasons with decidedly mixed emotions.

"Sometimes I think about Cameron Hall and the way he walked away from it halfway through that '78 season because he just knew he wasn't going to play anymore. He could have sat on the bench with Harold and me if he wanted to but he said the heck with it, I've got to get on with my life. I admire him for doing that, it took a lot of guts.

"And yet, I don't think I could have lived with myself if I had done that. For me, that would have been giving up because I'd run into problems. I'm glad I was on that team because it was a great group and the success they had was something I enjoyed. When we beat Notre Dame, I felt great. That's why I yelled that thing about, 'What do you think of the ACC now, Digger?' in the locker room. I still remember when Scott hit that shot over Laimbeer and pointed in his face, that was a great moment for me. God, was he happy. So was I; happy for him.

"After we lost to Kentucky, I felt really sad and I'm not sure why. Part of it was lost opportunity. I think we played tentatively against them. If we had played against them like we did against everyone else, I think we would have won.

"But it was more than that. I'll never forget Gene pulling us all together as we went out of the locker room and saying, 'We're together, remember that.' And we all went back out there together. You don't forget things like that. Every year that passes I think I appreciate it more.

"Back then, I couldn't appreciate it. The next year I was even worse. I was a hell of a disruption on that team because I was so bitter about things. When it was over, I was glad. I felt like I had finally gotten out of the coma."

Gray had planned throughout college to go to medical school. Class came to him as easily as rebounding came to Banks and he had very good grades. He took the medical school boards but then decided he didn't want to go to medical school. "I didn't know what I wanted at that point in my life," he said. "I decided to do some traveling, see the world."

He did that, but still clung to basketball. He played semipro ball in Costa Rica for a while and toured Europe with a team. The basketball and the traveling lasted almost two years. Then, in March of 1981, Gray was visiting home and driving down the street in his Corvette.

"This was during one of the gas crises when they had red and green flags to indicate if a station was open," he said. "This lady was in the left lane and she saw a green flag and tried to cut across to get to the station. She gave me about ten feet of room to stop. I can remember literally standing on the brakes to try to stop the car. We collided and my head hit the roof of the car. I got out and all I could think was that my car was ruined. I didn't feel anything—except anger.

"After we exchanged licenses and insurance information and all that stuff, I drove to a friend's house. I walked up to his door and just fell over. The adrenaline had gone out of me and I collapsed."

Gray had ruptured a disc in his back and injured his neck. He had to have two verterbrae fused and spent most of the next six months in rehabilitation. He also sued the woman who had hit him. As part of the suit, Gray claimed that the injury had prevented him from making a living playing professional basketball (he *had* been paid for playing in both Costa Rica and Europe). Among those who gave depositions attesting to Gray's ability to play basketball were Lou Goetz and Bob Wenzel. Gray won the case and a settlement which his teammates heard was worth $500,000.

When that figure is tossed out at Gray, he smiles. "Let's just say," he said, "that I did all right."

The accident proved to be a turning point in Gray's life. Once he was well, he realized it was time to get on with his life. He got a job working for IBM in sales in 1982 and moved up the ladder there quickly. Shortly after he began working at IBM, Gray ran into Kathleen Solomon, his girlfriend from the eighth grade all the way through high school. She had recently been divorced and was living alone with her two young children, a boy and a girl.

"We had had one of those very intense but stormy relationships in high school," Gray said. "She never thought I would go away to college and when I did, that was it. I can remember her calling me at school to tell me she was getting married. When I met her again in California, she was divorced. We started spending time together again. We were both a little more mature and, it just worked."

They have been married six years now and, in addition to Kathleen's two children, they have a four-year-old son. Ironically, Morrison—H— the one member of the team Gray is still in touch with, also adopted two children who were the product of his wife's first marriage.

"It is kind of amazing, especially since the kids are just about the same age," Gray said. "Harold and I went through the same kind of experience in college in a lot of ways and now we're going through similar experiences as adoptive fathers. We compare notes whenever we talk."

It has been several years since Gray last saw any of his other teammates. "There's part of me that doesn't really care about that," he said. "What's past is past. But there's another part of me that would enjoy seeing them, swapping some of the old stories and seeing how they've all done. My memories of all of them are good ones."

The one person Gray still harbors resentment toward is Foster, who he believes gave up on him too quickly, then wasn't there to offer a shoulder to cry on or a listening ear when things went wrong for him. "I just feel that when someone screws up you don't ignore them," he said. "I manage a lot of people now. When one of them messes up I go over and talk to them about it, try to get them to learn from the mistake and then give them a pat on the butt, at least figuratively, and tell them to keep on going."

The question, of course, is how many mistakes is too many? A player's perspective on that will almost always differ from a coach's.

But that is all past for Gray. He has only been back to Duke once in the last seven years but it is indicative of his feelings for the experience he had there that he went out of his way to visit.

"It was back in '86 and I was on the East Coast on some business," he said. "I had to be in Washington and then Atlanta before flying home. I was able to work my schedule out so I would have a few hours to stop over in Durham on my way to Atlanta. I flew in, rented a car, and drove to Duke.

"I hadn't been there since '82, the time I had gotten Bender to cosign the check for me. I had stopped by the basketball office that time to introduce myself to Mike Krzyzewski and he'd been kind of cold to me. Maybe he had heard stories about what a bad guy I had been towards the end. Or maybe he just had a lot of problems of his own. Back then, the team wasn't doing so well.

"Anyway, I didn't stop to see anybody or talk to anybody. I just drove to Cameron, parked and walked in. It was late spring or early summer and the place was empty. I went upstairs, looked down on the empty court and remembered all the hours I had spent in the place trying to make myself a better player. I still think of Cameron as the best place there is to play a basketball game but when I tried to conjure up the ghosts while I was standing there, they just wouldn't come. There wasn't one special memory or moment that came to my mind. Instead, I could almost hear the nervous murmur that seemed to run through the crowd whenever I came into a game my last two years.

"I walked out and was starting back to my car and there was Card Gym, just standing there like always. My best memories of Duke are actually in Card because when we played pickup games in there, that was when I always seemed to shine. Harold and I used to call Card "our gym" because of that.

"So, I walked over there. It was empty too. But there was a basketball sitting there. It was like something out of a Lifesavers commercial or something. I had my workout stuff in the car, so I went and got it, put it on and started shooting around with the ball, all by myself. It felt good. I felt the happiness that I had felt in the place coming back again.

"After a while, I figured I'd had enough and I was getting ready to leave. But just then, a group of guys came in. I recognized several of them: Johnny Dawkins, Tommy Amaker, Quin Snyder. They had all played on the Duke team that had just lost a few weeks earlier in the national championship game to Louisville.

"I don't watch a lot of basketball on television but when they made it to the Final Four, I was really proud. And I watched. All the old feelings came back and the memories of our Final Four. Now I think of it as *our* Final Four. Back in '78 I don't think I did.

"They were coming in to play pickup, just like we did in the old days. So, I hung around and got into a couple of games. My back still gets stiff pretty quick if I play fullcourt for a while, but I am in good shape. On one play, I decided to get right up on Dawkins the whole length of the court, just for the heck of it. He looked at me like I was crazy. Of course if I'd tried to do it a second time, he would have gone right by me. But it was still there, at least for one time.

"At the end, I thought about introducing myself but it didn't seem quite right. I just thanked them for the game, changed, and left for the airport. But when I walked out, I was smiling. It was just a good feeling to be back in Card and still be able to play a little.

"Seven years later, I drove away from Duke with a smile on my face. It took me a long time to be able to do that."

Maybe someday Gray will go back to Duke again, introduce himself to people and say, "Hi, I'm Steve Gray. I was part of the '78 team."

After all, he still wears the ring.

21

The Fonz

For a huge man, Scott Goetsch has a very soft voice. When he becomes emotional, his words seem almost to disappear, flying out the window of his eighteenth-floor law office and plunging into the Baltimore harbor which sits across the street.

Goetsch is remembering the Final Four, Notre Dame, Bill Laimbeer. Every athlete has a moment in his life he can remember so vividly that when he retells it you would swear he is looking at a slow-motion replay.

"I had just come into the game to give Mike [Gminski] his first-half rest," Goetsch says ever so softly. "We had the ball and I started to make a cut across the key. I can still see it in my mind's eye right now because Bobby [Bender] had the ball and I could see out of the corner of my eye that I was open and the thought went through my head, 'Oh God, I should get the ball here.' Asshole [Laimbeer] was a half-step behind me. Sure enough, Bobby throws me the ball and, honestly, I don't think I've ever released a shot any quicker or any smoother in my life. It hit the bottom of the net."

Goetsch's listener is familiar with this story, having heard it from his teammates. Goetsch has forgotten the punch line. "And then you pointed at him," he says, reminding Goetsch.

"*No!*" Goetsch's voice suddenly explodes across the room, filled with disbelieving laughter. "I didn't point, did I?" The memory comes back to him. "I guess I did. Boy I'd love to see the tape of that again. I just remember being so pumped up." The sound of his laughter is bouncing off the walls. "That was so much fun, that game, that whole weekend. Everything."

For Goetsch, hitting that fifteen-foot jump shot over Laimbeer was an extraordinary moment. He had played against Laimbeer growing up in California and didn't like him a bit. "I remember before he went in the game, he was sitting there saying, 'Laimbeer sucks, I'm gonna get him,' " Steve Gray said. "When he hit that shot, I jumped up and said, 'Fonzie wants to kill Laimbeer.' We all loved it."

Perhaps no one on that '78 team understood his role better than Scott Goetsch. He was The Fonz, a nickname put on him as a freshman by classmate Harold Morrison because of the way his straight, thick brown hair would stay slicked back after a postshower combing. "It was one of those things that stuck like glue from the first day I got called it," Goetsch said. "Whenever anyone on the team would introduce me to someone they would say, 'This is Fonzarelli Goetsch.' I can't remember anyone calling me Scott after that. When we got our scouting reports before a game from the coaches, up in the top corner where the coaches would write your name mine always said 'Fonz.' "

But he wasn't The Fonz just because of the hair. Nor was it because he was a ladykiller, à la the *Happy Days* character. It was attitude. Aggressiveness. The Fonz, remember, was a one-time gang member, the guy no one wanted to mess with. He was intensely loyal, always ready to take up for his pals. He was someone you were always glad to have on your side. *That* was Fonzarelli Goetsch.

He came to Duke as part of the Spanarkel class, choosing to come east more because of Duke's academic reputation than because of basketball. Like many of the players Duke was recruiting during that period, he knew nothing about the school when Lou Goetz first showed up to see him play.

"I knew about the ACC because N.C. State had beaten UCLA and won the national championship," he said. "I had gone to John Wooden's summer camp for years although I wasn't that big a UCLA fan. Still, they *were* college basketball at the time and I loved Wooden's camp. Now *there* was a guy who started with the basics. The first day of camp he would have everybody sit on the floor and he would teach you how to put your socks on right."

Goetsch was 6-9 coming out of high school. His size and soft shooting touch attracted recruiters, although not as much as it might have in other years. Size was in that year in the Los Angeles area. "There was a story in the paper about the twenty big men in Los

Angeles, based strictly on height," Goetsch said. "I didn't make the top twenty."

In addition to the height and the shot, Goetz liked him because Goetsch was an excellent student. He was the son of a Wisconsin veterinarian who had migrated to California to find warm weather. Scott was a twin whose brother Steve is only 6-5. "Imagine how big we would have been," Goetsch said, "if there had only been one of us."

Goetsch was bright enough to know he was not destined to be a great player. "Good enough to get a scholarship," he said. "Beyond that, I knew I wasn't a superstar."

That sense of reality made the Ivy League tempting to Goetsch. Cornell and Harvard both recruited him. But when he investigated Duke—and found the combination of excellent academic reputation *and* big-time basketball—he knew he had found the right school.

Duke was never easy for Goetsch. He felt overwhelmed as a freshman, first by homesickness, then by the notion that he was in over his head playing basketball in the ACC. But the midwestern work ethic planted in him by his parents (his mother is from Minnesota) carried him through. He improved his basketball, made friends, joined a fraternity, and did well in school.

"There were times my freshman year when I thought I should transfer," he said. "Gray talked about it all the time. For a while, he was all set to go to Brigham Young. But when I thought about it I realized that even with all the problems, Duke was the right school for me and to move because I was finding the basketball tough going would be a mistake."

Goetsch improved his basketball every year he was there. He was always awkward-looking on the court but by his sophomore year he was a solid backup player—behind Gminski—who even started a couple of games. He also played an important big brother role for Gminski.

"My first day at Duke, I played one-on-one with Scott," Gminski said. "I was kind of cocky, you know, high school star who averaged forty points a game and all. He just kicked my ass. I mean all over the place. He pushed me and kicked me and elbowed me. It was like, 'Welcome to college, hotshot.' I knew right then that this was going to be a different kind of challenge."

Gminski and Goetsch were road roommates, talking about the game and the center position sometimes, acting like a couple of giant children at others. "The day we played Rhode Island in the first round of the NCAA Tournament in '78 we both woke up a little early from our pregame nap," Goetsch said. "We had nothing to do, so to kill time, we found all these pennies and just starting throwing them at each other. Don't ask me why. It just seemed like the thing to do at the time."

Goetsch understood from the first day Gminski arrived on campus that the center spot was his. A year later, when Gene Banks showed up, any hope he had of being a starting power forward was clearly gone. That meant he would be a backup.

Goetsch—like Gray and Morrison—would have liked the chance to start. But he was also a realist. He knew that one could be a contributor coming off the bench and he made the most of every minute he played. "It's very easy to underestimate Scott's value to our team in 1978," Lou Goetz said. "He was the guy who gave the blue team guys their drive. He pushed Mike in practice every day and when he came in to give him a breather, we felt very comfortable because we knew he would play smart and he would play aggressive."

Goetsch was big and strong and wasn't afraid of contact. His strong sense of team was also a plus in the locker room. "Fonz was the guy who you could always count on," Dennard said. "He was quiet, but when it was time to go to war, he was the one who wanted to lead the charge."

Goetsch's memories of '78 are emotional ones. As much as anyone, he feels close to the people on that team. "Twenty years could go by without seeing any of them and it really wouldn't matter," he said. "There's a bond there that can never be broken.

"A basketball team is bound to be close. There are only twelve of you, so you know everybody well. You spend so much time together over the years that you see everything. You see guys getting ripped and getting applauded. You see them laugh and cry and you see them angry as hell. Hell, you see them naked. You know everything there is to know about them. No one in the world will ever know me any better than my teammates did.

"Then, to have an experience like we did in '78, having all the work come together like that, it leaves you with memories of the people that can't be dulled by time. I still remember in '86 I went to Dallas for the Final Four and there was a Duke party I went to. I saw Dennard across the room but couldn't get to him. About fifteen minutes later, someone poured beer on me from behind. I didn't even look. I knew it was Kenny."

Those warm feelings cannot completely wipe out the memory of '79.

"Everybody has a theory on what happened," Goetsch said. "They're all right and they're all wrong too because there were so many things that contributed. But I remember all summer, seeing those T-shirts that said, 'We'll Be Back.' It was almost as if everyone, including us, thought this was a done deal. Bender kept saying, 'It ain't done yet,' but in our minds, it was."

For Goetsch, senior season was especially tough. By then, he had become a pretty good basketball player. But with Gminski now an All-American, his playing time diminished. Even his blue team minutes were gone because Foster had opted not to use the blue team as a unit that year. Goetsch found himself feeling the frustration that Gray, Morrison, and Harrell were feeling, and the four of them became a team almost unto themselves.

"To me, that was a big difference in '79," Goetsch said. "The year before, in some way, everyone felt part of it, with the possible exception of Gray. Now, there were four of us, even five at times with Sudds, who felt like we were getting screwed. The fight that Mike and I got into the day after the Western Kentucky game, brief as it was, was a perfect example of what was going on."

The sudden ending in the St. John's game left Goetsch feeling empty and disappointed. When he didn't get into Duke Law School shortly after that, he felt even worse. But he recovered. He married his longtime girlfriend that summer, enrolled at Emory University Law School and, after one year of stellar grades there, transferred back to Duke Law School.

"Duke was—is—my school," he said. "It was where I wanted to be."

He graduated in 1982 and was hired by a major firm in Baltimore as a litigator. His wife Leslie teaches at a girls' school in Baltimore and they now have two children. Goetsch comes up for partnership soon. "I don't know what will happen," he said, smiling. "Ask my bosses."

Like any lawyer, Goetsch hates the drudgery of research and pretrial preparation. But he loves the theater of the courtroom. "To me, it's a way of still competing," he said. "I get very intense preparing for a trial the way I used to get preparing for a game. When you get a verdict to go your way, it's a lot like winning a big game. It also means that you have a lot of ups and downs in your life because you lose cases too. But I like getting out there and competing with people. Still."

One can almost imagine Goetsch pointing at the opposing counsel after getting a verdict—especially if the guy happened to remind him of Bill Laimbeer. He is not exactly Harry Hamlin in a courtroom. A latter-day Perry Mason perhaps, although, at 6-9 and his current weight of 300 pounds, he would dwarf even the huge Raymond Burr.

"I know my size can be intimidating to a jury," he said. "I try to be aware of it. I think my height can give me a presence if I don't come on too strong. I'm soft-spoken by nature so I don't think I overwhelm the jury. But my size is definitely a factor. To tell the truth though, it's tougher in social situations, company cocktail parties. It can be hard to carry on a conversation with someone when they're looking at your belt."

Goetsch has managed. He jokes often about his size and was quick to warn Dennard about creeping up on him for the team's weight leadership when the two of them ran into each other at a game in Cameron last season.

"If I ever get to Fonz's size," said Dennard, "I'll pack it in."

Goetsch goes back to Duke several times a year, often jumping into the car with friends for a weekend. He likes and admires Krzyzewski but, like everyone else, wishes Foster had not left the school so hastily.

"I'm like all the other guys—I worry about him," Goetsch said. "Bill was never really a motivator, not in the sense of fiery pep talks or anything like that. But he motivated us because we all knew how much he hurt when we lost. It just tore him up. Now, I see him struggling at Northwestern and I know that has to be killing him.

"Funny thing about Bill. I love the man. I really do. I felt a lot of frustration my senior year and I blamed him for it. But I always knew that he cared. He didn't show it by hugging you or anything like that but when I was applying to law school he wrote me a letter of recommendation that was unbelievable. I know now that if I ever picked up a phone and said, 'I need help,' he'd give it to me without even thinking twice about it.

"Steve, Harold, and Johnny [Harrell] are probably the guys who haven't forgiven him for what their college careers became. I understand how they feel because I went through some of what they went through. But you know what, if any one of them called Bill for something, he would help them in a second. I *know* that for a fact and that's why I still care about him and always will. To me, he's like the father you love but can never really talk to. You don't have to be perfect to be a good person. Bill is a good person."

When Goetsch heard about Foster's heart attack, he immediately sat down and wrote him a long letter, telling him how much he respected him and begging him to take care of himself, to ease up on his self-inflicted pressure.

"He wrote me back, thanking me for the note and everything I said," Goetsch said. "And inside the envelope he put a South Carolina media guide. Typical Bill. I couldn't have cared less about South Carolina. I cared about *him.*"

Goetsch also still cares deeply for his alma mater. He isn't one to hang around in the basketball office or in the locker room after games. But he follows the basketball program closely and is keenly aware of the ups and downs.

"I remember sitting there in '86 at the Final Four in Dallas, feeling like I was a Duke student watching the games years ago," he said. "I sat there during the final against Louisville just dying. We had the better team. We should have won the game. We didn't. I looked down at the players' faces when it was over and I felt like I understood some of their pain.

"It wasn't exactly the same as with our team because Kentucky was probably better than us. Maybe not more talented, but because of their experience, better. They handled the pressure of being expected to win. The next year, we didn't. Of course, they were like a machine. They had all those big guys and their mission at Kentucky from the day they got there was clear: Win. We had a different personality. In terms of winning and losing, theirs was better. In terms of life, I think I'd take ours.

"In '78 I wanted to reach out and grab every guy and tell them that I loved them. Funny thing is, I still feel that way. The next time I see Mike Gminski, I would really like to say to him, 'I love you.' Of course if I did, he'd say, 'What are you, a fag?' He would be uncomfortable with my saying that. But the feeling is there."

That was never more apparent than several years ago when Ronald and Nancy Reagan came to services at Goetsch's family's church outside Los Angeles. "I was visiting home on Christmas vacation," he said. "There were going to be two services, the regular one and then a second one for the Reagans and other hotshots. It was a big deal for me. I'd never met a president and everyone in my family, including me, is Republican.

"At the start of the first service our pastor announced that, while we were all excited that the President was coming, we were also very honored to have the basketball team from the University of North Carolina here for services. I turned around and, sure enough, there they were. They were in L.A. playing UCLA.

"When the service ended everyone went outside to kind of line up to meet the Reagans. I went over to say hello to a couple of the guys

I had played against and just as I did, here come the Reagans. I think Nancy Reagan was stunned to see all these giant-sized people. Somebody told her that this was the North Carolina basketball team and she kind of nodded.

"I was standing a few feet away from them when we were introduced but she looked up at me and nodded over towards the Carolina guys and said, 'Oh, are you with them?'

"I said, 'No ma'am, not at all. They're from North Carolina. I'm from Duke.' "

Exactly. He's Fonzarelli Goetsch. From Duke. You can ask Nancy Reagan. Or Bill Laimbeer.

22

H

Harold Morrison is attempting to put his college basketball career in perspective. "My sophomore year, when I was a starter, everybody called me Doctor H," he said. "My junior year, I was coming off the bench, but still playing, so I was Intern H. By my senior year, when I was just watching, I was down to just being H.

"If I had stuck around one more year I would have disappeared completely."

Self-deprecating humor is one of Morrison's specialties. Perhaps more than anything else, his Duke teammates remember Morrison for his humor. "I was a wiseass from way back," he said. "I got it from my mother. By the time I got to Duke, I almost had it perfected."

Underneath the clown's mask one often finds tears. Harold Morrison never planned it that way, but during his years at Duke that was often the case. "I had always heard that college was supposed to be the best four years of your life," he said. "My last two years I often said to people, 'If this is the best there is, shoot me now.' I felt that way for a long time after I got out of school. But now, the hurt has started to fade and I find myself remembering the good things more than the bad."

It has not been an easy process, though. It has been almost ten years since Morrison was last at Duke; only recently has he felt a desire to go back. When he first graduated and was living in New Jersey, going back would have been easy. Now, living in San Francisco with a wife and four children, a trip east is a major undertaking.

"I'd like to go back sometime soon," he said, sitting in his office at Chubb Insurance Company. It is a comfortable office with a view of the Bay Bridge. Morrison is the operations manager for Chubb's San Francisco office, managing about fifty people. He has not disappeared by any means. Like Steve Gray, he still wears his 1978 ring. Spinning it in his hands, he stops at two words carved into the side: Team Unity. He smiles at those words.

"In a way, those last two years at Duke were the most frustrating period in my life. I went from being a starter to not playing at all. I felt as if I was treated unfairly by the coaches and I saw the dreams I had to become a good college basketball player die.

"But I don't think I ever got as down or as bitter as Steve did because of the friendships I felt in that locker room. No matter what happened between the coaches and me, when the team went out to play it was my best friends going out to play. It was *The Guys* and there was nothing I wouldn't do for any of them. I felt a lot of pain, but I felt a lot of joy too."

For Morrison, the turning point in his Duke career came on October 15, 1977. That was the first day of practice his junior year. Morrison had worked hard to help the coaches recruit Gene Banks the previous season because, to him, Banks was his escape from playing power forward, a position he wasn't comfortable or happy with. He had started there for most of his sophomore year and his hope was that Banks's presence would allow him to become the starting small forward.

"I went home the summer after my sophomore year and started losing weight," he said. "I had bulked myself up from 190 as a freshman to almost 230 as a sophomore so I could play inside. Now, I began working my way back to about 210 or 215. I had felt so slow with all that weight the previous season. That was how the 'Doctor H' thing got started. It was obviously a takeoff on 'Doctor J,' because I was about as clumsy as he was smooth."

The path toward a smoother H hit its first pebble during the summer when John Harrell called Morrison. Harrell, who lived in Durham, had been working out with some of the other players who were spending the summer at school, including Banks and the other freshman forward Duke had recruited, Kenny Dennard. "Hey H," Harrell said on the phone, "this Dennard guy is a pretty good player. I think he's better than anyone thought."

Morrison hadn't given any thought to Dennard. He had assumed that as a returning starter the small forward spot would be his to lose. When Harrell mentioned that Dennard looked like a player, his first thoughts were not anxious ones. "I actually thought, 'Great, the more the merrier,' " he said. "We needed good players. But I still came back assuming the job was mine to lose."

When he came back in the fall and began playing pickup ball in Card Gym with the rest of the team, Morrison could see what Harrell was talking about. Dennard *was* good. He was strong and he was fast and he played hard. What's more, there was already a chemistry between him and Banks on the floor that Morrison and everyone else could sense. So could the coaches. They didn't think of Morrison as a returning starter because he had been the starting power forward. That job now belonged to Banks. On the first day of practice, when Foster put his white team on the floor, the starting forwards were Banks and Dennard.

"Pick a word," Morrison says, "Stunned, shocked, devastated, hurt. I didn't mind competing with Dennard for the job, that was fine with me. But I was a junior and I had been a starter. I just thought it would be my job and he would have to take it away from me if he could. But it didn't turn out that way. It was his job and I never really did have a chance to take it away from him. It was an awful, sick feeling that day in practice when I had to put a blue shirt on."

Morrison had never felt close enough to Foster to go to him and complain about the situation. But he did feel close to Lou Goetz. Yet he never said anything to him either. "It just wasn't my way," he said. "Probably, I made a mistake. I should have said something right away rather than just sit around and be angry about it. But really, even with the anger I felt, my focus was on being part of a good team. I was still going to get to play a lot and Dennard was a good player. My attitude was, as long as we paid back some of the teams that had been kicking our ass the last two years, I could live with this."

Living with it early in the season wasn't that hard because Morrison was playing an important role coming off the bench. Then, at Southern California, he took a late shot that Foster didn't want him to take. The Blue Devils lost in overtime.

"He went off on me after the game," Morrison said, the memory still clear and upsetting. "He told me I had taken a stupid shot and that it was my fault that we lost. It's funny how you remember things like that forever. A few days ago I was watching the Duke–Arizona game on television and at the very end that freshman [Christian Laettner] missed the free throw. If he had made two the game would have gone into overtime.

"The first thing that happens is Coach [Mike] Krzyzewski runs out there and puts his arm around him and tells him that it's all right. When I saw that, I thought back to USC right away. I know all coaches have strengths and weaknesses but I just have the feeling, watching Duke from a distance now, that he has a lot better communication with his players than Coach Foster did."

USC was a setback for Morrison but what really hurt him was an Achilles injury he suffered in the last pre-ACC game against Virginia Tech. Until then, he was part of Foster's eight-man rotation, spelling both Banks and Dennard at the forward spots and enjoying the fact that he was part of a good team.

"All of us who had been on the team for a couple of years had almost gotten used to losing," he said. "But the thing about the freshmen was, they had never lost. They just figured we were going to be good and win and that attitude permeated the whole team. It was a great feeling going out there every night knowing that, dammit, we were good."

Then came the Virginia Tech injury, a stretched Achilles tendon. Morrison missed seven games. By the time he was ready to come back, Jim Suddath had taken his spot in the rotation and was playing well. The team was jelling. It had just beaten North Carolina and had cracked the Top Twenty for the first time. Foster was loath to change a combination that was working. That meant Morrison was the odd man out. Suddenly, he found himself at the end of the bench next to his friend Gray.

That was no fun, but the team's success kept Morrison from becoming too unhappy. Like everyone else he got caught up in the joyride that was unfolding. "When we started to get on national television in March, first with the ACC Tournament final and then in the NCAA Tournament, it was a little tough to deal with the idea that all my friends were watching back home in New Jersey and seeing that I wasn't playing," he said. "I almost wanted to stand up and shout from the bench, 'Hey, I can play too!'

"But during that time, we were so tight as a team that no disappointment was going to overcome that feeling. Every day when I walked in the locker room I told myself there was always the chance that someone might get hurt and I would be needed. If that happened and I wasn't prepared, I would never forgive myself. So I stayed ready."

Like Gray, Morrison opted not to take his cut of net after the ACC and East Regional victories but it wasn't out of bitterness or a feeling that he hadn't contributed. "I was caught up in the celebration both times," he said. "I really was. But I told myself, 'You'll take your cut of the net when you really get to show your stuff.' Of course, I had no way of knowing that time would never come."

If Morrison felt any bitterness it came during the national championship game. With Jack Givens beginning to shoot holes in the Duke zone, Goetz walked down to Morrison at the end of the bench. "H, you can guard this guy," Goetz said. "You've got the size and the quickness to get after him. Watch him closely and get ready to go in. I'm going to suggest sending you in to Coach Foster."

Morrison was seized with excitement. Not only was he going to get in the game, he thought, but he was going to be asked to play a critical role. Goetz often made suggestions to Foster about personnel during games. He was considered the coolest head on the bench and the most likely to pick up on something unusual—like the notion that Morrison might be the guy to slow Givens down. Foster didn't always follow Goetz's suggestions, but often as not, he did.

Now, Goetz suggested putting Morrison in. Morrison had played very few minutes in postseason. He had scored two points in NCAA play, in the first half of the Pennsylvania game. Slowly, Foster shook his head. "No, I don't want to do that," he said to Goetz.

Whether Morrison would have made a difference—he certainly couldn't have done any worse than the others were doing—no one will ever know. But when he heard Foster turn Goetz down, he was crushed. "I almost started crying right there on the bench I was so hurt," he said. "But the other blue team guys kind of got behind me and kept me from losing it completely. And then I got back into the game in terms of wanting the guys to win. By the end, I was okay; sad that we lost and the run was over, but okay."

And determined to come back for his senior year in such good shape that he would force Foster to play him. He worked all summer. In the fall, during pickup games, his teammates felt he often outplayed both Dennard and Banks, who by then were into their lackadaisical we're-big-stars-now mode. But Foster, once again, wasn't going to mess with a combination that had brought him to within three baskets of a national championship. Instead of playing more, Morrison—like Goetsch and Gray—found himself playing even less. The blue team concept had been dropped, and Goetz wasn't around to plead their case.

"It was an awful, horrible year," he said. "I wasn't going to get to play. That upset me. Then they benched Johnny Harrell for Bob Bender. Bob's a good player and a nice guy but I always thought Harrell could do more things than he could. Gray, Harrell, and I became a threesome and we really stopped caring very much about basketball. I could feel all the desire draining away from me.

"The only thing I had left was wanting the team to do well. That fell apart too. We became a cocky group, kind of complacent. Then we lost a couple in New York and everyone said we had to get the '78 feeling back. That was impossible. You can't *create* something like that. You can't get innocence back any more than you can get your virginity back. When it's gone, it's gone. But we didn't know that.

"When we lost to St. John's, I felt empty. I was sad we had lost but relieved it was over. That's what I kept thinking, 'It's over, it's finally over.' But my next thought was, 'Okay, now what do I do?' I'd let my grades slip because I was sulking about basketball. When it came time to apply to law schools, the only place I could get in was North Carolina Central. So I decided to go there for a year, try to get my grades up and transfer."

Morrison lasted one semester in law school. Then he packed his bags and went home. "Actually, my grades were good," he said. "But I had no idea why I was there. I kept thinking, 'Why do you want to be a lawyer?' The answer, unfortunately, was because that was what my parents had always wanted me to be. That wasn't good enough. I was really lost, genuinely lost. Even with all the problems, I was used to being part of a team. That gave me direction. I knew each day I had certain things I had to do. I was special and I was pampered. I didn't know it at the time, but it was true. Now, that was all gone. I had no idea what I wanted to do with my life.

"I never had any delusions about playing in the NBA, not after I saw Gene play. I knew I wasn't on that level. But I had put so much energy into basketball for so many years that when it was gone I didn't know what to do with myself. I swear to God, for five years after I graduated from college when October 15th rolled around I would say, 'Hey, I have to start getting ready, lift weights, run, get prepared.' And then I would say, 'Prepared for what, stupid? Getting up to change the television or to open another beer?' But it took me that long to break away."

Morrison went home and moved in with his parents. They understood his confusion and didn't pressure him about leaving law school. He began job hunting, hoping to find something that would appeal to him. In May, one year after graduation, he still hadn't found anything appealing. Tired of looking, he took a job working in the records division at University Hospital in Newark. The job paid $10,000 a year.

"I absolutely blundered into the perfect place for me," he said. "The director of the records division got fired a couple of months after I got there and it took them six months to replace him. I ended up essentially running the division. As it turned out, one thing I can really do is organize, and this was a place that desperately needed some organization. I moved up quickly and in less than two years, I was the hospital's medical records director and was doing work in the management end of the hospital too. I still wasn't making much money, but I had a lot of responsibility. I loved it."

As a management hotshot, Morrison was responsible for a major overhaul of hospital personnel. "There were a lot of people who had been there for years who weren't doing a damn thing," he said. "With as tight a budget as we had, being a state-funded hospital, it was my job to get rid of deadwood."

This meant firing a lot of long-term employees, many of them union members. Morrison became known around the hospital as "The Hatchet Man." Being the son of Harold Morrison, Sr., the secretary-treasurer of the national electrical workers union, Harold Jr. caused some discomfort in his family.

"My dad kept telling me I was a traitor because I was getting all these union people fired," Morrison said. "It wasn't always easy but he understood that I was doing what I had to do to get the place working properly."

A little more than a year after Morrison began working at the hospital, someone came into his office and said, "Didn't you play basketball with Mike Gminski?" Morrison nodded. "Well, he's in the hospital."

Gminski had been brought to the hospital suffering with a staph infection that had made him very sick. Morrison was shocked to see how Gminski looked. "Just the sight of that humongous body stretched out looking so helpless flipped me out," he said. "But more than that, I realized how strong my feelings were for the guys I had played with. I was really concerned about him and kept a close eye on how he was doing.

"When he started getting better and was out of danger, I spent some time with him, clowning around like in the old days. But once I knew he was okay, talking about the old days was just too painful for me. I was still too close to it. I was relieved Mike was going to be all right, but I couldn't deal with spending all that much time with him because then, I still thought of Duke as a painful experience."

Morrison stayed at the hospital for four years. He enjoyed the work but in spite of his rapid rise was still only making $19,000 annually. A friend of his told him that with his management skills he might be able to make a lot of money in the insurance business. Morrison began looking. Eventually, he signed on with Chubb, a $3 billion company that looks almost exclusively for affluent clients.

"What we do is charge people more and give them more," Morrison said. "We insure homes that are worth three hundred thousand dollars or more. And we get involved with businesses that have big accounts. We charge you more and in return, if you have a claim, we don't mess around, we just give you a check. We know about your business, try to understand it and give you high quality service. But you pay for it."

Morrison moved to the West Coast, to San Jose, in 1986. By that time, he had a rapidly growing family. He first met his future wife in a Manhattan club the summer after he graduated. She was going through a divorce at the time. They became friendly and began seeing each other after Morrison dropped out of law school and came home. But for almost two years, both continued to date other people. "By then I realized how important she was to me," Morrison said. "I didn't want to see anyone else."

They were married in 1984, shortly after Morrison moved to Chubb. Donna had two children by her first marriage, Cerrone, now ten, and Shanel, now nine.

Cerrone calls his stepfather "H." The Morrisons have added two more children since their marriage, Philip-Michael, who is four, and Briana, who is almost two. "I tell people I got my first two kids as free agents and the other two the more standard way, by the draft," Morrison said.

He looks very different now from the way he did in his Duke days. He is a natty dresser whose hairline is in retreat. These days, if he made a comeback, it would have to be as a power forward. Look at Morrison now and the first word that comes to mind is prosperous.

But the wise guy is still there. Max Crowder, the trainer who was closer to Morrison than anyone at Duke, remembers the first time Morrison introduced him to his parents.

"It was Harold's freshman year," he said. "I always kid the black players about being the grand dragon of the Cherryville branch of the

KKK. It's one of my routines. Well, after one of Harold's first games here I walked out of the locker room and he was talking to his parents, who had come down to visit. He waved me over and introduced me. He said, 'Mom, dad, I'd like you to meet Max Crowder. He's our trainer. He's also the grand dragon of his hometown branch of the Ku Klux Klan.' He said it with an absolutely straight face. His father got it right away. But his mom looked for a minute like she was going to faint.

"A couple of years ago, out of the blue, I get this cartoon in the mail out of a magazine. It was a spoof on the KKK and how they were trying to reorganize or something like that. The note with it just said, 'Your time is now. H.' "

Morrison remembers the introduction to his parents and the cartoon. "Max is one part of my Duke memory that will always be warm," he said. "In the last few years, my feelings about my times there have changed a lot. More and more, I remember the relationships and the good times and less and less the hard times. I would really love to sit down now with the guys and talk and joke and remember. A few years ago, I couldn't say that.

"I follow the basketball program now and I'm really proud of what they've done. I've never met Krzyzewski but it's pretty obvious he's a hell of a coach. And I'm glad.

"Every year now I turn on the Final Four and if Duke is in there, I root like hell for them. And then I find myself remembering that we were there too. Sometimes that seems like it was in a different life."

He smiled. "But it wasn't. It was part of my life and I'm happy that it was. The hurt has gone away. The pride is still there."

23

Klinger

The office of the general counsel of the Investor's Heritage Life Insurance Company in Frankfort, Kentucky, is handsome and spacious. In addition to a large desk there is a conference table that can easily seat twelve—or more. On one wall is a picture of the man who built the company, Harry Lee Waterfield. Seated on his lap is his newborn grandson. On another wall is a second picture of Waterfield. On his lap, looking remarkably similar to the grandson, is his great-grandson.

It is the grandson who occupies the office now. Ten years after graduating from Duke, Rob Hardy is home, helping run the family business. His grandfather died of cancer in August, 1988, shortly after the second picture on the wall was taken. "That's Harry Lee Waterfield," Hardy says, pointing at his grandfather in the picture, "and on his lap is Houston Waterfield Hardy."

Houston Hardy is now sixteen months old and can imitate animal sounds better than most adults. In a couple of years when it is time for him to go to kindergarten, he will attend the Capitol Day School. His father is a member of the board of trustees. Twenty-five years ago, he was a student there.

Rob Hardy has come a long way: from his grandfather's lap to the Capitol Day School to Duke. Now, he has come back to where he began.

"I never thought when I was in college I would end up coming back here," he said, leaning back in the comfortable armchair behind the big desk. "But I understand that this is really what I always wanted.

266

This is my home and I'm truly happy here. The last few years have been tough at times but I know this is where I want to be and what I want to be doing.

"This company will be my life's work. Every day I come in here and think about the kind of man my grandfather was and know I want to be part of keeping this company strong."

It is a cliché, but Rob Hardy has always been a team player. Maybe it is his family's political background. Before he took over Investor's Heritage Life Insurance in 1960, Hardy's grandfather owned several small newspapers around the state of Kentucky, having gotten his degree from the University of Kentucky in journalism. He was elected to the Kentucky state legislature in the 1940s and eventually became the speaker of the House. In 1955, he was elected lieutenant governor. Four years later, he ran for governor and lost. He was elected lieutenant governor again in 1963 and took one more run at the statehouse four years later. He lost again. "The line about my grandfather back then," Hardy said, "was that he couldn't get elected governor because he was too damn honest."

Hardy's father was also involved in politics. An All-Southeast Conference quarterback at Kentucky, he was good enough to start the Blue-Gray all-star game as a senior ahead of no less a name than Bart Starr. He met Hardy's mother, Sarah Ferguson Waterfield, while at Kentucky. They were the All-American couple: He was the star quarterback, she was homecoming princess. They were married in 1955. Rob, their first child, was born in July of 1957.

Robert Hardy, Sr., went to law school for a year and then went into business for himself, running a small brokerage house. When Harry Lee Waterfield became lieutenant governor for the second time, the Hardy family moved to Frankfort so that Rob's father could help run Investor's Heritage. In 1968, Robert Sr. helped run Hubert Humphrey's presidential campaign in Kentucky and a year later he ran for the state senate—and narrowly lost. Shortly after that the Hardys moved to Columbus, Ohio.

As a boy, Rob was a lot more interested in sports than in politics. He played everything there was to play and was always successful. If he had not fallen in love with Duke while attending Vic Bubas's camp there each summer he might have been a well-recruited player in the Midwest. But his heart was set on Duke, whether he could play basketball there or not.

He got to play, moving from the junior varsity as a freshman to the varsity as a sophomore. More than any member of the '78 team, Hardy is able to remember details from the '78 and '79 seasons. Part of that is his memory; part of it is that he was both a participant and an observer.

"I started keeping a journal [in 1979] because I honestly believed we were going to win the national championship," he said. "I guess we all did. I stopped keeping it in February of that season because I knew we weren't going to do it. The thing just had fallen apart. The feeling we had had in '78 was gone and we all knew it was gone. I kept hoping I was wrong and that it would all come back together in March, but I was pretty certain it wouldn't."

In '78, Hardy and Bruce Bell had been the team's cheerleaders on the bench. Although they never met until college, their backgrounds were remarkably similar: Both were from Kentucky and were the sons of Kentucky football All-Americans. Both had been excellent swimmers as youngsters before falling in love with basketball. Neither was a great basketball player, but both were addicted to the game and loved the idea of being part of the Duke program. Both made the team after walking onto the JV team and moving up.

After college, their paths continued to parallel one another: Bell went to Kentucky law school, Hardy to Louisville. Even though Bell was a year ahead of Hardy at Duke, they graduated from law school the same year because Bell took a year off after college. Both married girls from Owensboro, Kentucky (in fact they married girls whose fathers worked together). Now, Bell and Hardy live thirty miles apart and keep in touch with each other and Duke basketball.

There are, of course, differences. Where Bell was blond and wide-eyed and still has the country accent he grew up with, Hardy is dark-haired and a little more worldly, with just a trace of the South in his voice. Although their teammates love to imitate Bell saying, "god-dang," and "I can't believe it, I just kissed the girl of my dreams," they take almost as much pleasure in remembering Hardy screeching from the bench, *"Box-out!"* or saying over and over again, "Un-believable, that's just un-believable."

Hardy laughs when he is reminded of that. This is right after he has described the 1978 season as "the most un-believable experience of my life. Really, it was just un-believable."

He has just finished reliving the March run: the ACC Tournament victory; the escape from Rhode Island; the snow in Providence; the win over Notre Dame; the loss to Kentucky; and the feeling in the locker room after the Kentucky game. His eyes become misty talking about the post-Kentucky locker room scene.

"I've done a lot of things since then and been a lot of places," he said. "But that's one of those moments that I'll cherish as long as I live. I remember that even the guys who had problems with the coaches like Harold and Steve were hugging people and crying. We all were. We had come out of nowhere to do this and we all understood how remarkable that was. And the thing about it was, people like Bruce and myself, who played very little, felt as much a part of it as Spanarkel or Banks. I think that feeling is what made it so special."

It was the loss of that feeling that made '79 so tough for Hardy—and for everyone else. He graduated not so much saddened by what had happened his senior season as angry. "Everybody lost track of what had made us great the year before," he said. "All of a sudden, everyone wanted to get his picture in *The New York Times.* There were some games sitting on the bench where I could almost feel guys thinking, 'If we're going to win this game, I'm going to be the one who does it.' Well, hell, it doesn't take a genius to know you aren't going to succeed with that kind of attitude.

"When I hear guys on television talking about chemistry I wonder if they really know what they're talking about. It's become such an overused word. But that's what happened to us. The chemistry changed and the new chemistry didn't work. The coaching staff wasn't the same. Gene and Kenny changed. The whole Joe Gminski thing changed everyone to some degree, including Mike. Maybe especially Mike. I felt helpless watching it unravel but there was nothing I could do."

When he arrived at Duke, Hardy had thought he might go to medical school after graduation. One semester of organic chemistry changed that plan. "That class just beat me to death," he said, laughing now at the memory. "I worked like crazy and all through the semester I was getting C's, D's, and F's. I spent a solid week studying for the final. When I walked out of the room, I knew it was a disaster. I had flunked. I went home and prepared my family for the F, which I knew was coming.

"I got my report card and there it was: Organic Chemistry–A. Well, I knew it was a mistake. I had already decided to drop my sciences the next semester to take some economics courses instead. When I got back to school, there was a message to call the professor. He was very embarrassed. He had made a mistake. I had gotten a D-plus. He kept apologizing for the error. I was thrilled. It was better than I deserved."

Hardy ended up majoring in economics and decided to go to law school. No chemistry there. He didn't get into Duke Law School—a major disappointment—but he did get into Louisville.

In law school, Hardy played a lot of pickup and intramural basketball. During his first year, he became friendly with a lot of the players on the Louisville team. In fact, when the Cardinals had some injuries that season, Coach Denny Crum contacted Foster about the wisdom of using Hardy, who still had a year of college eligibility left. Of course, even if Crum had wanted to use Hardy it would have been impossible because of NCAA transfer rules.

Louisville made the Final Four that year and played UCLA in the final. Sitting at home the day before the game, Hardy thought back to '78. "I seriously thought about sending them a telegram saying something like, 'Don't think there's next year, win it *now*,' " he said. "I still think about the fact that we went into the Kentucky game thinking that if we lost it wasn't that big a deal. We were going to be back. I wish to God there had been someone around to tell us that most of the time you don't get a second crack at this thing. I was glad when the Louisville guys won. Their best player [Darrell Griffith] was a senior. I think that helps a team not only in terms of leadership but in terms of understanding there probably won't be another chance."

It was during Hardy's first year in law school that Foster left Duke. When Hardy first heard the rumors, he found them impossible to believe. When they turned out to be true, he was hurt. "To me Bill was The Creator. I don't mean that in any godlike way but in the sense that he was the one who put Duke basketball back on the map. He made mistakes—hell, who doesn't—but he did a great job. It just made me sad to think of him not being at Duke. It's no reflection on Mike Krzyzewski to say it still makes me sad. Clearly his leaving hurt him more than it ended up hurting Duke. It was just a sad thing to see happen."

Hardy moved to Washington, D.C., to practice law after graduating from Louisville. He stayed there for two years, moved back to Kentucky in 1984, and that same year married Lisbon Davis, whose full name is Elizabeth. They had met while Rob was in law school. Everyone at Duke had figured Hardy's wife would be named Elizabeth, but they had a different Elizabeth in mind—the one he dated all through college.

If there is a difference between Elizabeth and Lisbon it is that

Elizabeth always knew Rob would eventually move back to Frankfort. Lisbon, who is tall and striking, is delighted that Elizabeth was right.

Eating dinner at the Frankfort Country Club, the Hardys are stopped constantly by older club members who look at Houston and gape. "Rob," they say repeatedly, "he looks just like you did when you were a little boy." Rob nods, knowing full well from the pictures in his office just how true that is.

As happy as the Hardys are, their life the last couple of years has not been without its share of heartache. In May of 1984, shortly after Rob had returned to Frankfort (he was still practicing law at the time), he and Lisbon were married. They returned from their honeymoon to learn that Rob's parents had split up after twenty-nine years of marriage. Rob's father moved to Boynton Beach, Florida, and has since remarried. His mother recently moved back to Frankfort. Their divorce became final in October of 1986. "That was very rough on me," Rob said. "I think in some ways having your parents split when you're an adult may be harder than if it happens when you're a kid because you *can* understand what's going on. It's been very tough on everyone and, to tell the truth, it makes me very sad when I think about it."

In 1987, Rob went to work for his grandfather as the company's general counsel. He loved the work and the company and enjoyed being with his grandfather, whom he had literally and figuratively looked up to since that day, when Rob was an infant, the picture had been taken. Then, on July 20, 1988, Harry Lee Waterfield was diagnosed as having cancer. It had already spread through most of his body by the time it was diagnosed. Two weeks after the diagnosis, he died at the age of seventy-seven.

"It was a very traumatic thing not only for me and for the family but for the entire company," Rob said. "My grandfather *was* this company. It happened so fast none of us was prepared for it. I still haven't gotten over it. I'm not exactly sure when I will. The last couple of years I feel like I've lost a lot of the family that was important to me when I was growing up. It's made me think a lot about the inevitability of certain things in life. At times, those thoughts aren't just sobering, they're depressing."

The Rob Hardy sitting on the couch with a late-night cup of coffee talking quietly about his family is quite a bit different from the Rob Hardy his teammates remember. He was Corporal Klinger to them, nailed with the nickname by Mike Gminski because of his nose. He was also the cheerleader, the guy who never seemed to get down even when there was every reason to. "Anytime you looked at the bench during a game," Gminski said, "the one guy who was guaranteed to be up and shouting something was Rob. He just never stopped. If he ever did, we would have thought he was sick or something."

"That became my role," Hardy said. "I had one real chance to play and that was my sophomore year after Tate got hurt. After that trip to West Virginia and Duquesne where we almost froze to death and I almost killed B. B. Flennory, we played Wake Forest at home. Bruce's ankle was hurt from the West Virginia game and Steve was struggling. I got into the game while it was still close. On one of our first possessions with the ball, I had an open jump shot and I took it. Heck, I wasn't a bad shooter. I missed and Mike put in the rebound. Bill went nuts. He was screaming at me from the bench not to shoot. I remember Lou and Wenz standing behind him with their palms down just going, 'Don't worry, stay calm.'

"I stayed calm and didn't shoot again. But then late in the game, they went to four-corners and we were in a combination defense. I got lost and Skip Brown got an easy lay-up. That was it for me. I never got another chance.

"But I understood the way it was. Sure, I wanted to play more. Everyone wants to play. But by the next year we had great players in the program. Was I a better player than those guys? No way. But I felt I could make a contribution by getting everyone else to work hard and by helping make other guys better players. I think I did help out that way."

In fact, one of Jim Spanarkel's more vivid memories of Duke is spending lunch hour after lunch hour running up and down the court playing one-on-one with Hardy. There have been other walk-ons at Duke—and at other schools—who have played important roles on successful teams. But Bell and Hardy symbolize how important that kind of player—and person—can be to a team. Their contributions never showed up in any box score, but to the other players on the team—then and now—they were as tangible as points, rebounds, and assists.

That is why Hardy's pride in being a part of that '78 team is justifiable. Like Bell, he often hears about the championship game from the Kentucky fans he is surrounded by. He sets his jaw, reminds people about Bain's technical and how it affected the game, and keeps his cool.

"What I don't say is that as good as that team was, what we did at Duke that year was more worthy of celebration than what Kentucky

did," he said, his eyes shining. "Kentucky was—is—a basketball factory. They have the best team money can buy and I'm not talking about
cheating or anything, I'm talking about all the money that program has.
We were a team from nowhere that loved every second of what we were
doing and never saw basketball as the be-all and end-all of everything.

"The only thing I would change about the whole season was our
attitude going into the final. We just didn't have the sense of *needing*
to win that we had in the other games. If we had, I honestly believe
we *would* have won."

Of course, if they had won, Hardy's life in Frankfort might be a little
more difficult, given the statewide mania over Kentucky basketball.
That would be okay with him. A couple of years ago when he was still
practicing law, Hardy found himself in Floyd County, Kentucky, opposed in the courtroom by an old law school friend named David
Barber. In his opening argument, Barber said to the jury, "I certainly
hope that none of you will be prejudiced against my opposing counsel
just because he played on the Duke basketball team in 1978."

Hardy never blinked. When it was his turn, he walked to the jury
box and said, "I wouldn't think you would be prejudiced against me
for playing at Duke since we lost to Kentucky that year."

Hardy laughed. "Of course what I wanted to go on and say was, 'we
lost, but if we had played the way we were capable, we would have
kicked your tail.'

"I wish," he added, "we could have had a rematch."

That's on the court, not in the court. Hardy won the case in Floyd
County. Given a choice, he would no doubt have traded it for the
basketball game in St. Louis.

24

Johnny Gun

The game had come down to the final seconds. With more than twenty-one thousand people on their feet in the Dean E. Smith Center, North Carolina guard King Rice stepped to the foul line. Three seconds were left and the Tar Heels trailed Duke, 87–85.

A lot was at stake. This was the regular season finale. If Carolina won, it would tie for the ACC regular season title and Duke would be relegated to a tie for fourth place. But if Duke won, the Blue Devils and Tar Heels would be tied for second place. What's more, a Duke victory would ruin the Carolina seniors' last home game and would give them two straight victories in the Deandome.

In a Rockville, Maryland, bar, two Duke graduates watched on a giant television screen. "He'll make both shots," said one, pointing at Rice, "and Carolina will win in overtime. It's the old Carolina piss factor. You think you're going to beat Carolina, then you lose and you're pissed."

The other alum nodded and didn't say anything. Rice made the first free throw. "See, I told you," said the first one. "Overtime."

Rice missed the second. Robert Brickey rebounded for Duke and was fouled. He went to the foul line, made one free throw, and the clock ran out after he missed the second. Duke had won, 88–86.

The second alum turned to the first. "Guess you were wrong," he said matter-of-factly. "They won."

He didn't say "We," he said "They." Even though he once wore the uniform, John Harrell no longer thinks of Duke as We. He had sat and

274

watched the last few minutes of the game without flinching once. His only comment, when Duke's Quin Snyder had missed a free throw in the final minute, had been, "What do you know. He choked." That was it. Nothing more.

"I really don't feel anything when I watch Duke play now," Harrell said. "They won the game today, that's fine. If they had lost, that would have been fine with me too. It really doesn't matter to me. I respect their program but I don't have any emotional attachment to it or to the school.

"I have a lot of good memories of Duke but I also have a lot of bad ones. I'm glad I have a Duke degree and I've got warm memories of a lot of people there, but that can't wipe out what happened."

In many ways, John Harrell personified the 1978 Duke miracle team. He had gone from being an unknown transfer from North Carolina Central to the starting point guard on a Final Four team and the hero of the semifinal victory over Notre Dame. All of that in twenty months.

"When I made the two free throws to beat Notre Dame, it was as incredible as anything that has ever happened to me in my life," Harrell said. "My mother still has a scrapbook full of all the stories about that game and me making the free throws. It was as wonderful a moment as I've ever had in sports."

But it went downhill after that. Duke lost the final to Kentucky. Like everyone else on the team, Harrell was caught up in the emotion of the postgame scene in the locker room and on the court. He was touched—and amazed—by the greeting the team received when it returned home to campus the next day. "I don't think I've ever seen that many people crammed into a space [the main quad] that small all at once in my life," he said. "Seeing how much it meant to all of them was a great thing." Harrell spent the summer at Duke, working out with several other players preparing for the '79 season. Academically, he would be a senior, but he had two years of basketball eligibility left. "My goal was simple," Harrell said, remembering that summer. "I wanted to be the best point guard in the country. I had established myself the year before. I knew the players now, I knew the system, and we were going to have a great team. There was no reason why I couldn't be as good as anyone."

But Harrell wasn't the only Duke point guard working on his game that summer. Bob Bender, who had split time with Harrell during the last twenty-two games of the season, was also improving himself. Harrell and Bender were very different as players. Both were good but not great shooters. Harrell was certainly quicker and less likely to turn the ball over. Bender was more spectacular, more daring. He was also more verbal than Harrell, more of the prototype floor leader.

"Johnny had more talent than Bob, there was never any question about that in my mind," said Harold Morrison, Harrell's closest friend on the team. "But I think the coaches were more comfortable with Bob out there. He was more of a talker than John. He was what they call a coach's player."

Bender was also white. While Morrison wonders if that might have had something to do with what eventually happened, Harrell does not. "I really don't think race had anything to do with it," he said. "I've certainly given that some thought, but I don't think that was it. I just think they wanted Bender to be the point guard when he first transferred from Indiana and I got in the way for a while. When they had the chance to move me out, they did."

There is bitterness in Harrell's voice when he talks about this. Bill Foster decided to switch the roles that season, making Bender the starter with Harrell coming off the bench. Harrell thinks that was unfair, that the job was his and the change should not have been made until—and unless—he had the chance to be outplayed by Bender when the season started.

Everyone on the team, aided by 20–20 hindsight vision, now agrees that the team would have been better off if Foster had left the Harrell/Bender combination intact. Bender thinks that too. But almost everyone agrees that Foster's only motivation in making the change was his belief that it would make the team better.

"Bill was about one thing," said Gene Banks, "and that was winning. He would never do anything to the team if he thought it might hurt the team. He thought we would be better with Bobby starting. He might have been wrong, but there's no way he made the change for any reason except wanting to win."

Harrell could not accept that. He called his mother in tears when Foster told him Bender would be starting, and he never accepted the switch. "I'll say this," he said. "I did not deal with it very well at all. I sulked and I pouted. I thought I had been treated unfairly and I didn't bounce back from it. I became another malcontent very quickly."

Lou Goetz, the one member of the coaching staff Harrell felt close to, had left to become the head coach at Richmond. Harrell is certain that Goetz would have talked Foster out of making the switch if he had still been there. Goetz isn't sure about that. He does concede that Bender was more capable than Harrell of dealing with not starting.

"Johnny always had a tendency to get down on himself very quickly," Goetz said. "I remember when he first transferred over from North Carolina Central, he had some trouble adjusting to the work. He got very upset about it and wondered if he could make it at Duke. Of course he could and he did, he just had to adjust.

"He needed to be told he was doing a good job and to be reminded that we all had faith in him. Bob was much more self-motivated. Coming off the bench didn't bother him. Johnny needed the reinforcement of being a starter. It was important to him. He played great in '78. I mean he only turned the ball over once a game [39 times in 34 games], which is remarkable for a point guard. My instinct, looking at it now, would have been to keep things the same. But I wasn't there to watch them practice every day so I can't say for sure."

If Harrell had dealt with the benching the way Bender had dealt with not starting the year before, the two guards might have continued to split time. But he didn't do that and, as the season wore on, freshman Vince Taylor became more and more of a factor. He was young and innocent, glad to play coming off the bench and not aligned with, to use Harrell's word, the malcontents. Eventually, Taylor moved past Harrell in the pecking order. Harrell really slid after that.

"I called my parents and told them to stop coming to the games," he said. "There was no point in them coming to watch me watch. I hated practice, I hated being on the blue team. I got out of shape, mentally and physically. That's why when Bob got sick [with appendicitis] I wasn't ready."

Harrell became the starting point guard again after Bender got sick. But in his first game back, North Carolina beat Duke in the ACC Tournament final. Harrell, given just a few hours' notice that he would be starting, played poorly. But a week later, against St. John's in the NCAA Tournament, he was playing very well when Wayne McKoy caught him in the eye with an elbow and knocked him silly. He didn't come back until the last fourteen seconds—the last fourteen seconds, as it turned out, of his college career.

"I wanted the coaches to talk me into coming back when the season was over," Harrell said. "I don't mean with any promises but just by telling me that I would have a role with the team the next year, that they felt they had lost something by not playing me. But they didn't do that. They made excuses. I just couldn't see any reason to come back."

And so Harrell passed up his last year of eligibility and graduated that spring with his degree in math. Foster, disappointed that Harrell had not dealt with the point guard switch better, never really knew how bitter Harrell was. But he did understand how disappointed Harrell had been to lose the starting spot. He arranged an invitation to the New Jersey Nets rookie camp for Harrell that summer.

"I felt like I could play with just about all the guys in the camp," Harrell said. "But they weren't looking for a six-foot point guard who didn't turn the ball over. They were looking for someone who could dunk backwards standing still. Something spectacular. I'm not spectacular."

Cut by the Nets, Harrell returned to Durham to become an actuarial trainee for a local bank. He thought he wanted to become an actuary. During that basketball season, Foster provided him with tickets to all the games and asked him if he would talk to visiting recruits about Duke.

"I talked to one kid, Danny Young," said Harrell. "I told him that I thought Duke was a great school and if he was interested in going to law school, which he said he was, Duke would be a great place. But as for basketball, I said I thought there were communication problems between the coaches and the players.

"I felt badly about saying that. It really wasn't fair. After that, I told the coaches I didn't want to take their tickets anymore, that I didn't want to be critical to outsiders but I wouldn't be dishonest either. I just decided to disassociate myself with the basketball program."

A year later, Harrell moved to Washington, D.C. to go to work for a computer company as a programmer. He had worked with computers during that first year out of school and found he enjoyed it. During that time, he put basketball behind him. He didn't play or watch or keep track of any teams. "It hurt too much," he said. "I thought the bitterness would fade but, for a while, it actually grew. I just thought I could have been a much better player than I ever had the chance to become."

Shortly after moving to Washington, Harrell was introduced to Darleen Corbett, who had gone to Hillside High School at the same time Harrell was there, though he hadn't known her then, only her brother. The two were introduced by their mothers, started dating, and were married in December of 1981. But the romance had been too much of a whirlwind and the marriage didn't work. Two and a half years later, they divorced.

"It just didn't work out," said Harrell, who is the only member of the '78 team to have gone through a divorce. "We like each other, but we couldn't live together as it turned out. The good thing for both of us is that there weren't any children so we were able to separate without any problems."

After his divorce, Harrell changed jobs, moving to a consulting firm. From there, he moved to a company called Dialcom, which is one of the largest electronic mail services in the world. He now runs the data base and the directory service.

"It's a great job for me because I still get to work with the computers, which I've always enjoyed," he said. "But it also allows me to get some management experience. I remember what it was like playing for Bill Foster. I think he was an excellent teacher but not a very good manager. I try to be more of a communicator with the people who work for me than he was."

Unlike Morrison and Gray, Harrell has not yet put the anger he felt at the end of his Duke career behind him. His background, growing up in Durham, may be part of this. "I guess I never felt completely comfortable at Duke," he said. "I grew up a Carolina fan and then I went to North Carolina Central for a year. Duke was entirely different. It was never a place I felt I could relate to on any level. Even the black kids there were never very friendly to me until they found out I was a basketball player.

"That's not to say it isn't a great school. I had some great moments there and I have some great memories of people and of what happened to us in '78. I really enjoy it when people recognize my name and remember that I played in the Final Four or that I made the free throws against Notre Dame. But I don't feel an attachment to the school in any way. I haven't been back to a game there since 1980 and I really don't have any desire to go back to a game now. It's behind me.

"I have gotten interested in basketball again the last few years. I watch on television and follow what's going on in the game. But I watch basketball clinically, not emotionally." As befitting a man who works with numbers, Harrell is not an emotional person by nature. At least not outwardly. The hurt of '79 is still clearly there, though. "I get emotional about some things," he said. "I just saw *The Natural* for the first time a couple of weeks ago and I got really emotional watching that. I think it's because the guy got his chance and I felt good about that."

Harrell still talks to Morrison on a semiregular basis and has talked at different times to Banks and Gminski in recent years. And, having gotten engaged recently, he took his fiancée on a tour of the Duke campus when they were in Durham to visit his family.

"When I talk to Harold, it's never for fifteen minutes," he said. "It's always an hour. Or two. There are strong feelings there. I feel the same way about the other guys on the team. I still wear the ring because it brings back memories of the good times there, of what we achieved together in '78. I told my fiancée that when we get married I'll wear my wedding band on my right hand. The Duke ring fits my left hand and I'm not going to take it off."

And yet, when the reunion of the '78 team was being organized last spring, the one member of the team who seemed genuinely uninterested in attending was Harrell. "I would like to see the guys," he said. "I would enjoy that, seeing how they're all doing and telling old stories and remembering how we used to give each other such a hard time back when things were good.

"But I still don't feel like I could look the coaches in the eye—except for Lou. If it were just the players, it would be one thing. But if the coaches were there I would walk in, sit down, and find myself thinking, 'When will this be over?' I know that's how it would be. I can't stop myself from feeling that way, even though I wish I didn't."

His teammates, who would like to see him again, understand. "Johnny Gun was the quietest guy on the team right from the start," Bell said. "It was easy to think he was aloof, but he really wasn't. He was just very quiet."

Perhaps Harrell was quiet because he was an introvert in a room full of extroverts. Perhaps he always felt just a little bit like an outsider since he hadn't been recruited.

Now, though, established in business and in life, Harrell isn't shy or quiet. He is heavier than he was in his Johnny Gun days but he still moves gracefully, like the ex-athlete he is. Maybe someday his feelings about Duke will change. But Harrell doesn't think so.

"I was talking to a guy in a bar a couple weeks ago and he remembered that I played for Duke," Harrell said. "He said to me, 'I went to Ohio State. I remember when we came from way behind to beat you in Madison Square Garden. Do you remember that?'

"Well, of course I remembered it. I think if the guy had brought that up to some other guys on the team, they would have gotten upset, not necessarily with him, but just with the memory of that weekend. It didn't bother me at all. It was just something that happened.

"To me, that's what my Duke experience was, something that happened. If I have a regret, it's that I didn't come back my last year because if I had I would have gotten a free year of graduate school even if they hadn't played me. I should have been more pragmatic about the whole thing but I was twenty-one years old.

"The two things I remember most vividly about Duke are the Notre Dame game and calling my mother, crying, to tell her I was being benched and didn't know why. The high and low, that's what I remember. The rest is mostly a blur. To tell you the truth, I like it that way."

There is some justice in this. After all, to his teammates, Johnny Gun was always something of a blur, on and off the court. Ten years later, nothing has changed. They remember him, fondly. He remembers them, fondly. But that's where it ends. The blur remains a blur.

25

Mikey

It was the first week of February, another day in the life of the Philadelphia 76ers. Practice at St. Joseph's University was over and it was time for lunch. First, though, came the postpractice ritual of dealing with the media. Coach Jimmy Lynam, who, ironically enough, coached at St. Joseph's for six years, stood in one corner talking about the next night's game against the Seattle Supersonics. Charles Barkley, the resident superstar, went from one TV crew to another.

Standing under one of the baskets, Mike Gminski had several writers around him as he answered questions on topics ranging from the team's pursuit of the New York Knicks, to rookie Shelton Jones's chances in the All-Star slam dunk competition that weekend, to how much influence Barkley's grandmother has had on his career.

For Gminski, this was routine. He is what is known among writers as a good talker. That means they come to him every day for quotes on almost any topic. On this day, though, it is a little different. The TV guys want him too. Word is out that the 76ers have offered him a new contract worth more than $8 million over the next five years and everyone wants a comment. Gminski is glad to oblige.

Finishing the last interview, Gminski walks over to an old friend who has been waiting for him. "Eight million," the visitor says, smiling. "Not bad for you Mikey."

An alarmed look crosses Gminski's face and his voice drops to a whisper. "Do me a favor," he says, "don't call me Mikey around here. It might catch on."

Mike Gminski is now thirty years old, the last member of the 1978 Duke team to reach that crossroads. Even before his new contract he was, by far, the wealthiest of the old Blue Devils. He has nine years in the NBA behind him. In Philadelphia, he is "G-Man" (just G to his teammates), the starting center who averages 17 points and 10 rebounds a game. He is one of the most popular members of the 76ers.

But to those who have known him since he first arrived at Duke as a shy but precocious seventeen-year-old, he still is—and always will be—Mikey. "I finally convinced Bender to not call me that in public," he says, laughing, during lunch. "But every time he gets a few drinks in him he goes right back to Mikey. I don't mind it coming from the guys I've known for years, I just don't want anybody new picking it up."

Mikey has come a long way since that first day of his college basketball career, when he looked around the 16,500-seat Greensboro Coliseum and asked, "Do they ever fill this place?"

At this stage of his life, he has played in front of more filled places than he can count. He left Duke as the school's all-time leading scorer (surpassing Spanarkel's record) and rebounder, had his number retired, and was the seventh player chosen in the NBA draft that spring. He was labeled too slow to be an NBA center when he first arrived in the league but has proven his critics wrong. That proof, however, has come only after a lot of hard work.

"That's really been the story of my career," he said. "People have always questioned whether I could move up to the next level and do well.

"At the end of my first contract with the [New Jersey] Nets I had become a starter because Darryl Dawkins was hurt. I had played well. But the Nets kept saying I couldn't do consistently well as a starter in the NBA." He shrugged and said, "Here I am." On the surface, Gminski has led a charmed life. He was a superstar in high school who never had to work hard to get good grades. He was a starter from his first day in college; the ACC rookie of the year as a freshman; a member of a Final Four team as a sophomore; an All-American and ACC player of the year as a junior; and a top draft pick who signed a five-year contract for big money at the end of his senior season.

Those who know Gminski know it hasn't been as easy as it has looked. "One thing people forget about Mike is how hard he worked," said Lou Goetz, Gminski's mentor and prodder his first two years in college. "Except for shooting the ball, which he always did well, things don't come naturally to him on a basketball court. Everything he's become is because he's consistently worked his tail off to get better."

And, through it all, there has been the relationship with his father. In terms of time spent together, no father and son could have been closer than Joe and Mike Gminski. But his father's constant presence has caused problems with Mike's coaches from junior high school on forward. When Mike finally did make it to the NBA, his wife, Stacy Anderson, replaced his coaches as the object of Joe Gminski's frustrations. "It's like there has always been a constant triangle in my life," Mike said. "First it was me, my dad, and whomever happened to be coaching me. Since I became an adult it's been me, my dad, and Stacy. I guess it would help if we could talk about it but we aren't that way. We've never been great communicators. I tend to suppress things anyway, especially my emotions. I don't think my dad and I have ever said to each other, 'I love you.' I know he loves me and I love him but it's never been verbalized. It's been a tough thing for a long time. The last couple of years of college, though, was when it was at its worst."

That was when Joe Gminski was writing letters to the *Durham Sun* accusing Foster of mismanaging the team and demanding that he stop using John Harrell. There is little doubt that it would have been healthier for all concerned if Gminski's parents had stayed in Connecticut rather than move to Durham when Mike went to Duke. But Joe Gminski wanted to be with his son. "He wanted the best for me, I know that," Mike said. "I think that's why the guys were so understanding. They certainly didn't agree with what my dad was doing but they understood his motives were good ones. The problem is that parents don't see a team, they see one person. The coach has to see the whole team."

Gminski's old teammates express frustration, even anger about the way Joe Gminski behaved those last two years. But they do understand his motives and they also understand that Mike had no control over his father's actions. Even John Harrell, who was often the target of Joe Gminski's criticism, knows that.

"What happened with Mike's dad never changed the way I felt about Mike," he said. "Mike was always as nice a guy as you could ever meet. I knew that he was just as upset about what was going on, maybe more upset, as the rest of us were. It never affected my relationship with him."

Nor did it affect Gminski's relationship with Foster. But it did affect Foster. Somehow, Joe Gminski became a symbol of all the doubters, all the complaints, all those who didn't appreciate the coaching or the coach.

"In a lot of ways Bill saw my dad as being typical of all the people in the area who just didn't understand what we had achieved," Mike Gminski said. "He wasn't wrong either. A lot of people, including my dad, *didn't* understand. A lot of *us* didn't understand until after we graduated and got some distance from the place."

In many ways Gminski's senior year was his most disappointing. He was expecting a great season because he had played so well as a junior. The team got off to a superb—12–0—start. Then, things fell apart. "I didn't play very well that season," he said. "To this day, I can't tell you why. I just wasn't very good. Maybe I was trying too hard to impress pro scouts. Maybe I was tentative. My numbers were still good, but I knew I wasn't playing well. Lou [Goetz] used to tell me to forget numbers, that I was the only one who knew when I had played well. He was right. Most of the time that year, I wasn't nearly as good as I could be."

As Gminski struggled, so did the team. The rumors about Foster leaving were everywhere. Then came the resurrection at the ACC Tournament; Foster's resignation; the ecstasy of the victory at Kentucky; and with a return trip to the Final Four at stake, the agonizing loss to Purdue.

"It was like a whirlwind," Gminski said. "It was very hard for me to believe my college career was actually over standing in that locker room after the Purdue game. I definitely felt some relief because it had been such a tough season but I also felt great sadness because we'd never gotten the chance to go back to the Final Four and win.

"No one is prouder of what the '78 team accomplished than I am. I've played basketball in high school, college, and the pros for sixteen years and that team achieved more than any I've played on. By far. In fact, now that I've played for so long I realize how hard it is to do what we did, how few chances you get at something like that. Knowing that makes me a little sad because we didn't quite get it. The championship was right there and we let it get away. That still bothers me a little.

"If we had gone back and won, then '78 would have been a stepping-stone on the way to the top. As it turned out, it *was* the top. That left me feeling a little deflated at the end of my college career."

The best thing about Gminski's senior year had nothing to do with basketball. During Thanksgiving break he started dating Stacy Anderson and the relationship quickly blossomed into something quite serious.

"We had known each other all through school," Gminski said. "And we had always been friends. So we knew each other well. At the start of the year, she was dating a fraternity brother of mine. They broke up, though. Over Thanksgiving break, the only ones on campus were the basketball players and the swimmers and we just started going out."

Stacy had been an excellent swimmer growing up in Pittsburgh and was a backstroker on the Duke swimming team. She was, in many ways, exactly what Gminski was looking for: tall (very important) and attractive, bright and an athlete. "Because she was an athlete and because she had been around the fraternity a lot, she was like one of the guys," Gminski said. "We always found talking to each other very easy."

Most important, though, Stacy got Mike's humor. Like Foster, Gminski has an ironic, deadpan sense of humor. Most of his jokes are delivered without change of expression or tone of voice. A lot of people miss them completely. "Stacy," he said, "always got them the first time."

By the end of the year, they had decided to stay together no matter where Mike was drafted. When it turned out to be in the New York area, Stacy was delighted. She quickly got a job at Dean-Witter and eventually rose to a vice-presidency at Smith-Barney.

The New Jersey Nets had two first-round picks that year. They used the first, the sixth pick overall, to take North Carolina's Mike O'Koren, Spanarkel's old Jersey City teammate, a player Gminski had played against no fewer than thirteen times in college. With their next pick, which was No. 7, they took Gminski. Gminski and O'Koren were both in New York for the draft and before they knew it, they were being whisked by limousine to the Meadowlands to be introduced to the media.

"There was only one problem," Gminski remembered, laughing. "Mike's mom was in the limo and she recognized Stacy as one of those Duke students who had been getting on Mike so viciously for four years. She wouldn't speak to her the whole time we were in the car going over there."

Gminski signed a five-year contract with the Nets and he and Stacy were formally engaged that summer. The wedding was scheduled for the following June—after Mike completed his rookie season in the NBA.

Early in that first season, Gminski bruised the ulnar nerve in his right elbow in a collision under the basket. Part of his right hand went numb after the injury but the doctors told him it would heal on its own. He kept playing. Three months later, the hand was still numb. The Nets were going nowhere that season so the team decided to have Gminski operated on in February. That way he could rehab the elbow and then play in the Los Angeles summer league.

The surgery went well. Gminski regained the feeling in his hand and began his rehab program before the season was over. He and Stacy were married in June and went on their honeymoon to the Bahamas and St. Martin. "We came home for one day, did the laundry, and then Mike left for Los Angeles," Stacy said. "It was a great way to start a marriage. But that's life in the NBA."

Gminski had only been in Los Angeles for a couple of days when, scrambling for a rebound, he caught an elbow in the lower part of his back. The pain was excruciating, bad enough that the Nets told him to come home to New Jersey to get it looked at.

"I had this big bruise and they were treating me for spasms," he said. "For a little while after I came home it started to feel better. But then it began to get worse. I couldn't run. Then I had trouble walking. Then I was dragging my leg behind me. I couldn't figure out what the hell was going on."

By the afternoon of August 1, Gminski was in so much pain that he stretched out in bed—he had moved the mattress onto the floor for extra support—hoping to relieve the pain. A couple of hours later when he tried to get up, he couldn't.

"I couldn't move," he said. "I felt like I was paralyzed."

When Stacy leaned down to put her arms around him she was shocked at how hot he was. "He was burning up," she said. "I told him I was going to call an ambulance. When he didn't argue, I knew we were a day too late."

Just getting the 6-11, 265-pound Gminski off the bed onto a stretcher, down the hallway of the apartment building, and into the ambulance was an ordeal. Mike was in agony. He was taken to Pascack Hospital in Westwood, New Jersey. There the doctors determined that he had a staph infection they believed had entered his body during his elbow surgery, floated around for a while, and then settled in his back when he was injured. Now it was in his bloodstream.

"The problem they had was kind of a scary one," Gminski said. "They knew what was wrong with me but nothing they gave me was making me better."

Gminski arrived at the hospital with a temperature of 103. By the next day, it was up to 106. The doctors were frightened. Dr. Alan Levy, who was treating Gminski, had seen two other patients with this kind of infection lodged in an injured part of the body. Both of them had died.

"He told me later that one had a bruise on the base of his skull and the other in his chest," Gminski said. "I was lucky mine wasn't somewhere where it could spread quickly into a major organ."

The doctors, seeing the panic in Stacy's face when Mike arrived, decided not to tell her just how dangerous Mike's condition was. Two days after Mike arrived in the hospital, he celebrated his twenty-second birthday. He has no memory of it at all. The next morning, Stacy picked up the *New York Post* and found a story saying that Mike Gminski was listed in critical condition at Pascack Hospital.

"They had never told me it was critical," she said. "I went over there and demanded to know what the hell was going on. That's when they told me. I was furious, hysterical, you name it."

The doctors were on the verge of performing surgery on Gminski at this point. If they couldn't find an antibiotic that would fight the infection, they would have to open Gminski up and scrape the infection out. They would then have to leave him open for a while to make sure they had gotten everything out. This was radical, dangerous surgery.

"For a few days there, I would leave the hospital when visiting hours were over and drive home," Stacy said. "Every night I got through the Garden State Parkway tolls, pulled the car over and cried. It just seemed so unbelievable to me. We had been married less than two months and now Mike could be dying. My God what a helpless feeling that was."

After five days of sheer frustration, the doctors tried a drug called napcillin. Bingo. Gminski's temperature began to come down. They began filling him with napcillin, feeding it to him intravenously twenty-four hours a day. The infection started to clear up. He was out of danger.

"It was still a good two weeks before he was anywhere near normal," Stacy said. "He was in another orbit. I would sit by his bed and touch his hand and he would shoo me away like I was a fly or something."

Gminski doesn't remember any of that. "It's like I lost two weeks of my life," he said. "I don't remember any of it."

When he was healthy enough to be moved, Gminski was transferred to University Hospital in Newark. It was here that he ran into Harold Morrison, whose presence cheered him up considerably. "I was getting all these blood transfusions and he was kidding me that I might get some black blood," Gminski said. "One day I told him I thought they had given me black blood because I had a real craving for some fried chicken."

Only after he was on the road back did Gminski's doctors explain to him how sick he had been. "Because I was so out of it, I never went through the fear or worried that I might be dying," he said. "But when I started getting better, I would walk down to the chapel every night at the hospital, just sit there for a while and be thankful. My family has never been religious, we've never gone to church but I've always believed in God. When I started getting better, I just felt very thankful. I don't think the experience made me any more religious but it made me more aware of my feelings than I had been before."

Gminski was in the hospital for thirty days. He arrived weighing 265 pounds and left weighing 215. The weight came back quickly, though, and amazingly, Gminski was in uniform and in the lineup for the Nets' opening game in October against the New York Knicks. He even scored the first basket of the season.

"If you think about it, his playing that first night was unbelievable," Stacy said. "We went from wondering if he would live to wondering if he would ever play to watching him play on opening night. Because of that, I don't think people ever completely understood just how sick he had been."

Which was fine with Gminski. He had no desire to play the role of martyr. When the season began, he was under doctor's orders to play no more than fifteen minutes a game. He was still weak, still taking napcillin several times a day. But the opener was Larry Brown's debut as the Nets coach and he wanted to start off with a win. Gminski played thirty-six minutes. The Nets won. The doctors didn't much care about the victory.

"They went crazy," he said. "They told me I had been lucky once and I was being stupid to try my luck again. I knew they were right. So did Larry."

Knowing Gminski would be limited, Brown and the Nets traded for two veteran centers, Len Elmore and Sam Lacey. Gminski immediately went from starting on opening night to third-string center. He wasn't thrilled. A year later, the Nets dumped Elmore and Lacey but acquired Darryl Dawkins, the one-time prodigy of the 76ers. Gminski became known around the league as a capable backup. It almost became part of his name: "Capable Backup Mike Gminski." Gminski would rather be called Mikey than that.

His opportunity finally came in his fifth season with the Nets when Dawkins got hurt. Gminski became the starter and has been a starter ever since, his numbers improving almost annually. "It's nice that people now accept me as a good player in this league," he said. "Getting to that point wasn't easy."

After his first five-year contract with the Nets, Gminski signed a very comfortable four-year contract. By that point, he had saved enough money that he was making substantial contributions to Duke, even going so far as to endow a scholarship. With the exception of Bender, who has worked for Mike Krzyzewski the last six years, Gminski is closer to the current Duke coach than any of the other Foster players.

"When Bill left, I felt bad about it but to tell the truth, it wasn't going to affect me. I was graduating," he said. "But when Mike was hired, he wanted Bobby and me to help out as much as we could. Mike and I just hit it off. Part of it was because we're both Polish. I think between the two of us we probably know every Polish joke ever told. But I also had a very good feeling for him. I knew he was going to have to learn the hard way as a coach in the ACC but I also knew he would get it done because of the kind of person he is."

Gminski helped Krzyzewski recruit, making visits with him and writing to players until new NCAA rules banned alumni participation in recruiting. He still returns to Duke a couple of times a year, always coming back for a home game during the All-Star break. He and Stacy sit upstairs in Cameron with Krzyzewski's family. When he is introduced to the crowd, they stand and cheer him and Gminski knows he is back home. Scott Goetsch jokingly calls Mike and Stacy "Mr. and Mrs. Duke."

That may be a slight exaggeration, but Gminski would like to settle in the Durham area when he is through playing. He has already looked at property. "That's home to me more than anyplace else," he says, "I haven't lived in Connecticut since I was sixteen and even though I've liked living in New Jersey and Philadelphia, I think eventually I'd like to go back there."

Mike and Stacy were very comfortable in New Jersey. They bought a house on the Hudson River, a ferry ride from work for Stacy, a ten-minute drive to practice for Mike. From 1985 on, Mike was a starter. The only problem was he was starting on a perennially horrid team. The Nets reached the second round of the play-offs in 1984 but began to slide shortly after that. Today they are still wallowing at the bottom of the NBA.

In early 1988, Gminski began hearing rumors that he was going to be traded to the 76ers. He had decidedly mixed emotions about that possibility. He wasn't happy losing, but the lifestyle in New Jersey was very comfortable. The rumors grew. In mid-January, the Nets played the Celtics in the Meadowlands. Philadelphia General Manager John

Nash drove up to the game and sat with the Nets brass. At the end of the third quarter, the deal was done. A Nets office assistant grabbed Gminski by the arm as he walked off the floor after the game. "They want to see you upstairs, Mike," he said.

Gminski knew right away what it was about. "I walked into the locker room, grabbed my warm-ups and turned to Buck Williams. I waved at him and said, 'So long.' I walked into the offices upstairs and John Nash was standing there. He put out his hand and said, 'Mike, welcome to the 76ers.' "

Leaving any team after eight years, even a losing team, is a shock to the system. Mike and Stacy said their good-byes that night and Mike was looking for apartments in Philadelphia that Monday. Once the initial shock wore off, he realized it was the best thing that could have happened to him.

"The tough thing is that Stacy and I have to commute two hours during the season to see each other," he said. "We still have the house up there. She comes down on weekends and whenever she can. It isn't easy on either one of us.

"But professionally, it's been great. Jim Lynam is great to play for, the team is improving, and they've made me feel very welcome here."

To put it mildly. With his contract up at the end of the 1989 season, Gminski would have been an unrestricted free agent because of his nine years in the league. Word on the league grapevine had it that the Los Angeles Lakers were very interested in acquiring him to replace the retiring Kareem Abdul-Jabbar. The Sixers, having traded for Gminski only a year earlier, couldn't afford to lose him. That brought about the huge, long-term contract.

His old teammates express amazement that Mikey is making this kind of money. Not because they don't think he has talent, but because, well, because he's Mikey. "I just can't see him except as the big old kid he was when he first got to Duke," Bruce Bell said. "Every once in a while he'll call me at two o'clock in the morning just to let me know he's still nuts."

Having played so long in the NBA, Gminski has a special appreciation for the closeness he felt on the '78 team. "I've played with a lot of guys, playing one hundred games a year," he said. "But it just isn't the same. It can't be, because you're older and less innocent and you're doing it for a living.

"It's comforting to me knowing that no matter how old I get, no matter how long we're apart, that closeness will always be there. Those guys will always be my friends. In a way, they're like family because I know that in one form or another, they'll always be in my life. When I was sick, seeing Harold in the hospital was better than any medicine I could have taken—almost. There's a feeling there that time and distance won't ever change."

Gminski is lucky. He looks back on his life and smiles. He looks ahead on his life and smiles too. "When this contract is up, I will have played fourteen years in the league," he said. "Very few guys last that long. I'm proud of that and damn happy about it. But nobody can say that it was just handed to me. I worked for it and I'm glad it has worked out so well for me."

As he spoke, Gminski had a bag of ice on a bruised foot and another one on his knee. Ice is a postpractice ritual for him, just like talking to the writers. He is aware that even Mikeys get older. But he looks back to where he was on his twenty-second birthday and is very happy to be rich, thirty, and alive.

"There's a book called *When Bad Things Happen to Good People* that I think everyone should read," he said. "I have a good friend whose mother, one of the absolute best people I've ever met, is dying of cancer. There's no sense thinking, 'Why me?' because there is no answer. Being good doesn't mean you get taken care of.

"I grew up a lot after I got sick. I don't want to sound corny and say I appreciate life more now but I do appreciate *my* life more and how good it has been. I'm very happy to be Mike Gminski."

Or even Mikey Gminski.

26

Coach Benny

In the emptiness of Cameron Indoor Stadium on a cold January afternoon, every word being exchanged by the players on the basketball court could be heard clearly in every corner of the arena.

Bob Bender dribbled down the right side, pulled up and yelled, "Christian!" to get the attention of Duke freshman center Christian Laettner. Too late—Laettner didn't see the pass coming at him and it was intercepted. Point guard Quin Snyder grabbed it and raced the other way with Bender cutting over to stop his advance.

"Okay Quin, good," Duke Coach Mike Krzyzewski said. "Let's do it again." The ball swung back to Bender and he began the sequence one more time. For the better part of the next hour, he ran the wing, took jump shots to start rebounding drills, and threw sharp, crisp passes in to the big men. It was all part of a day on the job as one of Krzyzewski's assistants. Through it all, Bender looked ready to step in to play the point guard spot at a moment's notice.

"Not on your life," he said when that suggestion was made. "The old bones couldn't handle it."

Maybe not, but at thirty-two, Bender's old bones are in excellent shape and, if you were to ask any passing female, holding up quite well. Bob Bender is one of those guys that women look at and sigh, while other men look at him and say, "He's not so good-looking."

Bender *is* good-looking. There's no getting around it. He has wavy brown hair, penetrating blue eyes, and an easy, open smile that most women find irresistible. He is also a fashion plate, always impeccably dressed, even when he is casual, never one to be even a half step behind a trend. Kenny Dennard, talking about the illnesses that have haunted some of the players and coaches on the '78 team, once said, "And then there's Bender. He's terminally good-looking."

Bender is the last of the bachelors from the '78 team, although in May of '89, shortly after he was named the head coach at Illinois State University, Bender asked Alice Hunter, who had just graduated from Duke Business School, to marry him. Against her better judgment, Alice Hunter said yes.

And so, within a matter of days, Bob Bender did two things he never dreamed of doing when he graduated from Duke: He became a major college head coach and he got engaged. "Coaching and getting married were about the last two things on my mind when I graduated," Bender said, laughing. "Anybody who says I'm not different now than I was then didn't know me then."

Bender graduated with a degree in history, a lingering desire to play basketball, and a notion that he might want to go to law school. He felt a little empty about the way his Duke career had ended. Even if his initial move to the starting lineup had been controversial, he had clearly proven himself worthy of the job during his two years as the point guard.

"Our senior year, with Sparny gone, we could have had a real leadership problem, because he had been the guy for almost three years," Mike Gminski said, talking about Spanarkel. "But Benny really stepped up and became the leader we had to have. He held us together through a lot of tough times that year."

The toughest time was the season-ending loss to Purdue in the Mideast Regional final in Lexington. Bender was saddened by the loss, by the down note that ended his and Gminski's career, and by Foster's *need* to leave Duke.

"That's what I think about a lot with Bill," he said, sipping a late-night beer. "How could he think for a second that South Carolina would be a better place for him than Duke? This should have been his place to coach for a long time. And yet, I'll never forget him sprinting through that lobby in Lexington, so uncomfortable that he didn't want to talk to anybody. I guess, what we all know now, is that he doesn't coach anywhere for a long time."

Bender's time at Duke was also up, a fact that saddened him. After his transfer from Indiana, he had quickly become one of the most popular people on the campus and had come to think of Duke as home. But it was time to move on.

Briefly, Bender continued playing. He was chosen in the sixth round of the NBA draft by the San Diego Clippers and went to their training camp. "They were a bad enough team that I was able to stick around for a while," he said. "But it was hardly a shock when I got cut."

He didn't want to play in Europe and he didn't want to go to law school—at least not yet—"because I wanted a break from going to school." After being cut by the Clippers, he signed on with Marathon Oil, an AAU (semipro) team that barnstormed the country playing college and other AAU teams. It was a little bit like the NBA in that there was a lot of travel, but the similarities ended there.

"To begin with, there were no home games," Bender said. "We were based out of Louisville but played all our games on the road somewhere. We traveled around in Winnebagos and had to eat on twelve dollars a day. I still remember when I decided it was time for me to give up basketball. We were in the Winnebago, traveling between Tallahassee and Tampa on one of those endless Florida interstates.

"I looked around me and saw seven guys squeezed into this thing very uncomfortably. It was our fourth night out and the trip was just starting. I said to myself, 'Enough. It's time to get a real job.' I stayed with the team until we got to North Carolina, then I told them that I was done."

The question was what to do next. "I knew I didn't want to coach. Even though my dad had been a coach, I just didn't think that was the direction my life was going in. I was afraid I was going to use basketball as a crutch, just hanging around the game. I thought I could do more, given my Duke background, than hang around basketball."

Bender went to work briefly for a financial consulting firm. He had been there five months when Duke Athletic Director Tom Butters offered him a job as assistant director of the Iron Dukes, the Duke athletic fund-raising organization. Bender liked the idea. The job would give him a chance to renew his ties with Duke; it would give him business experience; it would keep him near athletics without actually being *in* athletics; and, given Butters's contacts around the country, it could be an excellent stepping-stone.

Butters felt that Bender could be a major asset. He was a popular, recently graduated Duke basketball player. He was bright and charming, two important traits in any fund-raiser. And, given the controversy over Butters's hiring of Mike Krzyzewski to replace Foster, someone with ties to that regime would be quite valuable.

When Foster decided to leave, Butters, who had been a major league baseball player and then a baseball coach, felt he needed to consult with basketball people about whom to hire. He knew the new coach would be in a difficult situation, following a coach who had won 73 games, two ACC titles, and gone to the Final Four in three years. The team *also* had no center, a good senior class, one junior, four sophomores who were role players, and no incoming freshman class.

One of the first people Butters contacted was Bob Knight. "Hire Mike Krzyzewski," Knight said, throwing out a name Butters was completely unfamiliar with. But he put Krzyzewski on his list, interviewed him, and decided this was his coach. Butters is a great believer in his own instincts, and those instincts told him that this remarkably sincere, intense thirty-three-year-old coach was the man to replace Foster.

Others, including the players, were not so sure. Banks and Dennard, in particular, wanted little to do with Krzyzewski. Vince Taylor's first response when he heard who the new coach was going to be was, "What the hell is a Krzyzewski?"

One person who didn't ask that question was Bender. He had first met Krzyzewski in 1975 when, in the midst of Indiana's recruitment, he had come to his home with Knight. When, during the final days of Bender's senior year, Krzyzewski's first days as coach, they renewed their acquaintance, Bender remembered why he had liked Krzyzewski so much.

"But I also knew he was in for some rough times," Bender said. "The team wasn't going to be the same the next year no matter who was coaching. Mike was young and he was learning. The ACC is a tough place to learn. But I thought he would do it."

Krzyzewski was just finishing his first season when Bender accepted the job with the Iron Dukes. It had been a moderately successful (17–13, NIT bid) but difficult season. Krzyzewski was an advocate of discipline and man-to-man defense. Banks and Dennard, his two captains and best players, didn't believe in either. There were clashes.

Recruiting had not gone well either for Krzyzewski. His first spring— like Foster's—had been a virtual wipeout. He desperately needed a good recruiting class in 1981, but he didn't get it. He barely missed several key players and settled, instead, for a class similar to Foster's last class: four complementary players, backups. That left the 1982 team with only one top-of-the-line ACC player, Vince Taylor. The record reflected that: 10–17. The season ended with an embarrassing 88–53 loss to Wake Forest in the ACC Tournament.

By now, there were anti-Krzyzewski rumblings throughout the Duke community and Bender, as one of the chief fund-raisers, heard a lot of them. "I had never really been exposed to that kind of second-guessing before," he said. "When you're part of a team, as a player or a coach, you're insulated from most of that. But I heard it all and it bothered me. It was very hard for me to bite my tongue and not tell people that Mike Krzyzewski knew a lot more about how to get the program back on top than they did."

This time, Krzyzewski had a great recruiting year, signing a stellar five-player class, headed by high school All-Americans Johnny Dawkins and Mark Alarie. But with Taylor gone and the freshmen forced prematurely into starting roles, '83 wasn't a lot different from '82. The record was 11–17 and the ACC Tournament game was even more humiliating, a 109–66 loss to Virginia, a defeat Krzyzewski has never forgotten.

Now the anti-Krzyzewski chorus was in full voice. Assistant Coach Bobby Dwyer left to become a head coach at the University of the South, a Division 3 school. There was an opening on the coaching staff of the *Titanic*. Bender decided to sign on.

"I did it for a couple of reasons," he said. "First, I was tired of all the complaining and bitching. I hated watching Mike struggling the way he was and I figured if the ship's going down, I might as well go down feeling as if I was involved in trying to save it. That was one thing. The other thing was, I knew the players were there for us to get better in a hurry. If you watched the freshmen play that year you knew we were going in the right direction.

"And, I realized after two years with the Iron Dukes that one of the things missing in my life was being a part of a team. Some people outgrow that need. I didn't. I really missed that feeling of sharing. No one who works in business knows what a *team* really is. You can't explain it to them. I had been part of something unique in '78 and even though I knew I couldn't ever recapture it, I wanted to see if I could have a role in a team turning things around again."

Bender's *interest* in the job did not mean he *had* the job. Krzyzewski was reluctant. Bender not only had no coaching experience, he wasn't *all* that sure he *wanted* to coach.

"I think if I had not been part of the Foster regime and the success that we had, Mike would have told me to go somewhere else and get some experience," he said. "But that experience, the being part of a winner *at Duke,* gave me something none of the other guys he interviewed had."

Krzyzewski confirms Bender's theory. "Looking just at coaching credentials, Bobby wasn't even in the hunt for the job—because he didn't have any. But he *did* have Duke experience, he did know what it took to be a successful athlete at Duke, and he had always been a winner. That and the fact that I liked him are the reasons I hired him."

The 1978 team underwent minor changes that threw the chemistry *out* of whack in '79. Duke's 1984 team underwent changes that created new and *better* chemistry than the '83 team had ever had.

From the rubble of 21–34 over two seasons, Duke rose to 24–10. After a tough start in ACC play, the Blue Devils fought back to finish in a tie for third place. Then they upset North Carolina, which had gone 14–0 in the regular season, in the ACC tournament semifinals. Even a loss to Maryland in the final and an NCAA Tournament loss to Washington couldn't change the fact that Krzyzewski had turned the corner.

Bender, who has never been part of a losing season as a player or as a coach, helped.

A year later, the Blue Devils went 23–8, though they disappointed many who thought they were ready to make a noise in NCAA play. But in '86, it all came together. The Blue Devils won the ACC regular season, the ACC tournament, and the East Regional. They beat Kansas in a brutal game to reach the national championship game. Eight years had passed since St. Louis. The only two men who had been on the bench that night who were still there were Bender and trainer Max Crowder.

The opponent was Louisville, another basketball factory from the state of Kentucky. But this was a veteran Duke team, one dominated by seniors, not freshmen and sophomores. They had already won an NCAA-record 37 games. This was their game to win. Only it got away. A bunch of missed lay-ups in the first half and a couple of missed jumpers down the stretch cost them the game. The final was 72–69, Louisville.

"In a lot of ways, that loss was more frustrating for me than the Kentucky game," Bender said. "That was our championship. We were a veteran team that started the season thinking about the Final Four. In '78, that thought never crossed our minds. Looking back at that Louisville game, I see shots we had taken and made all season and they just wouldn't go down. Maybe we were tired, I don't know. But it hurt.

"There was a good feeling when it was over, though. Completely different than in '78. There's no question '78 was more fun. It was a joyride all the way, just a lot of laughs from start to finish. A lot of that has to do with age. When you're a coach there are a lot less laughs than when you're a player. But being a coach on a Final Four team, at least for me, was more rewarding than being a player. I understood the work that had gone into it. I had watched the kids get better and overcome things and had put in the hours that all coaching staffs put in to try and make it happen. Both were feelings of gratification, but completely different kinds of gratification."

It is strange to hear Bender refer to the players as "kids." But he is Coach Bender now in every way. No more Benny or Bends or B-squared.

"I know I want to coach," he said on that cold January night. "It will be intriguing to find out how I react to being someplace that isn't Duke. I've always been on the highest level of college basketball. I wonder if I wouldn't enjoy going to a lower level, Division 3 or high school or something like that and just teaching and coaching. I don't know the answer to that. But right now, I want to find out how I'll do running my own Division 1 program. I've worked for Mike for six years, I think I know what coaching is about now and I want to find out if I can compete at the highest level. If it doesn't work, going to a lower level won't bother me. I may even find that I'm happier there. Who knows? Time will tell."

For the members of the '78 team, Bender's departure from Duke will be at least as traumatic as it will be for him. Bender was the link between the new and the old, the conduit of all gossip and news—good or bad. He was the one who always knew where everyone was and how they were doing *and* he could always come up with an extra ticket for a game. Calling the basketball office was never an unnatural thing to do as long as Benny was there.

"When he goes, Duke becomes a different place for all of us," Dennard said. "It isn't that the other guys aren't nice or friendly, they are. They aren't an old teammate, though."

Dennard isn't alone in feeling that way and Bender is certainly aware of that. "I know how the guys feel," he said. "I think a lot of them are comfortable with Mike and the other coaches here now and I know Mike has worked hard to make them feel welcome. But it isn't the same as talking to someone you grew up with, went through the wars with. Duke won't be home the same way it has been for those guys once I leave."

But when the Illinois State job came open in March, Bender knew this was the spot for him. Illinois State is in Normal, just across the river from Bloomington, Bender's high school hometown. "It will be like going home for me," he said. "I know people in the state, I'll be comfortable there, and it's a good place to start as a head coach."

And so, nine years after he thought his days at Duke were over, Bender finally packed his bags for good. Maybe. After all, now that he is a head coach, Bender is on a path that could lead him back to Duke someday to succeed Krzyzewski.

"I haven't even thought about that," he said. "Mike's going to be here for a very long time." He smiled. "But if it did happen somewhere down the road, that would be fine with me."

No doubt, it would *also* be fine with his old teammates. Just don't ask them to call him Coach Bender.

27

The Preacher

Jim Suddath has his eyes closed. There is a wide smile on his face. He is remembering.

"I can feel myself in that locker room," he says. "I can feel the hands of the other guys when we walked out of there to go back on the court. I can feel the bonding we all felt with Bruce because we all knew what our future was and he didn't.

"I can still feel the love we had for each other that night. When I think about any one of those guys, without exception, it brings a smile to my face. I worry about some of them, but the love I feel for them is very real."

If Jim Suddath sounds a little bit like a preacher it is with good reason. In the spring of 1989, after three years of study, he graduated from the Columbia (South Carolina) Bible College as an ordained minister. To his Duke teammates this came as no surprise. In a locker room full of characters, Suddath stood out. "It was very apparent from the first day he showed up that Jimmy was different than the rest of us," Bob Bender said. "It just took us a while to realize *how* different."

The difference stemmed from Suddath's being a born-again Christian. It is that faith that brought Suddath to the seminary. For the better part of three and a half years, he and his wife Jenny have lived with their growing family in a trailer park on the outskirts of Columbia. Now, sitting in the living room of the trailer he and Jenny share with Joshua (four) and twins Alison and Rebecca (one) on a sunny February afternoon, Suddath is talking intently about his life, his Christianity, and his old teammates.

Perhaps if they had known more about Suddath's background, his teammates would not have been so surprised by his devout Christianity. He was born and raised on the south side of Atlanta, the second son of George Newton and Sandra Kay Suddath.

George Suddath had grown up in Atlanta, the son of Foy Suddath, the founder and owner of Suddath Trucking who eventually passed the business on to his son. But Foy Suddath was also an alcoholic. He started drinking at fourteen and didn't stop for fifty years. "I never even knew about it until I was twenty," Jim said. "Then he sat down and told me. It helped me understand why I never saw my father take a drink."

Suddath's mother also grew up in Atlanta. She was the daughter of Hilliard Beddingfield, one of the founding deacons of the Baptist church in his community. But before he found Christianity at the age of twenty-seven, Hilliard Beddingfield had been a member of the Ku Klux Klan.

"He eventually came to understand the stupidity of it," Jim Suddath said. "And when I was a boy, he told me the story of how he started to see how stupid and ignorant it was, to help keep me away from anything like that."

According to the story, Hilliard Beddingfield and a buddy, then teenagers, were cutting across a black sharecropper's land on their way to a friend's house and walked right through his cornfield. Needless to say the man wasn't happy and he came out of his house and yelled at the boys. When they reached town, they told some of the older men about the dressing down they had been given. That night, the robes came out and the KKK paid a visit to the sharecropper. They stoned his house and threatened him. Terrorized, he and his family left town the next day.

"My granddaddy knew what had happened was wrong," Suddath said. "After that, he began pulling away from the KKK. He told me the story to illustrate how sick people can be."

George Suddath and Kay Beddingfield met when they were in high school. He was seventeen and she was fourteen. They began dating and kept dating right up until the day before George Suddath graduated from Georgia Tech. That day, they got married. The next day George graduated and went into the Navy. He came back from the Navy, joined his father's business and, in April of 1957, Jim was born. His older brother Ron had been born two years earlier.

Ron and Jim were about as different as two brothers could be. Jim grew to 6-6, Ron stopped at 5-10. Jim was always an athlete, Ron quit Little League baseball because he couldn't compete. "Ronnie won writing awards, I won trophies," Jim said. "He played chess, I played ball. He read science fiction, I read comics. He could sit for hours and study, I had to be out playing."

He was always a good ball player, always tall, and always on good teams. As a ten-year-old, Suddath played on a team that won the Georgia state ten-and-under championship. He was hooked on basketball from that moment on, although he was also a good baseball player and played right through high school. Being left-handed helped him in both sports: It helped him get his shot off in basketball and made him a more effective hitter in baseball.

"I lived an almost perfect life through most of my childhood," Suddath said. "I had wonderful, loving parents. I remember my father saying to me, 'You will sometimes get what you want, Jim, but you will always have what you need. That I promise you.' My mom went back to work so that my brother and I could go to private school. We were a very typical, southern middle class family. My parents were never into politics one way or another, although I remember laughing at my mother when she voted for Hubert Humphrey in 1968 because I thought Hubert Humphrey was a funny name."

Naturally, in a southern home, the family went to church each Sunday. But religion was never really stressed in the family. Although Kay Suddath had grown up going to Baptist church, she went with her husband to the local Methodist church because that was the way he had been raised. "The only reason I didn't mind going to church when I was young," Jim Suddath said, "was because we always went out to eat afterwards."

Jim noticed his parents moving away from the church. First they stopped going to Sunday School classes. Then, on some Sundays they skipped church altogether. By the time he was fourteen and starting to become a basketball star, Jim Suddath decided he had had enough religion and told his parents he wasn't going to church anymore. They didn't object. "It would have been kind of hypocritical of them if they had," he said. "They had made it clear to me that it wasn't very important in their lives."

By this time, Suddath was at Woodward Academy, the same high school his father had attended. Back then, it had been Georgia Military Academy; by the time Jim got there it was co-ed. As a freshman, he was good enough to make the varsity basketball team and by his sophomore year he was a starter. At the start of his junior year, when Ron went to college, he inherited his '65 Ford Galaxy and had his first serious girlfriend.

"I had it made," he said. "I was a star athlete, I made good grades without any trouble, I had a car and I had a beautiful girlfriend named Sue. Then, it all fell apart for me before I even knew what was happening."

Suddath's troubles were not unusual for a teenager. He began to have arguments with Sue and saw the relationship deteriorating. He was beginning to feel pressure from college recruiters and he was worried about it. Then, on a spring afternoon, he and Sue had a huge argument in one of Woodward's hallways. "I thought for a minute I was going to hit her," Suddath said. "It frightened me."

One of the requirements at Woodward was that every student take two quarters of Bible study. The class was taught as literature, not theology. Suddath's teacher in that class was Jim Donovan, an assistant basketball coach as well as the school's chaplain. "Even though he taught the class the way it was supposed to be taught, as literature, I could hear his belief in Jesus Christ every day in class," Suddath said. "After a while, I really began to listen. This was someone I respected. If he thought there was meaning to this, I thought it was worth listening to.

"One afternoon in class, I was sitting and listening to him talk. I was really confused and hurting. So I bowed my head and I prayed, really for the first time in my life. I said, 'Jesus, you claim to be the savior of the world; you claim to give people new life; you claim to heal the hearts of people who are hurting. Well, I'm hurting. I'm a rotten person. I've been selfish and I've messed up. If you're there, I'd like you to come into my life and make me a new person.' "

Suddath paused, the memory clearly still vivid. "I didn't see any lights or hear any ding-dong bells but right then I felt the peace and the reality of Jesus entering my life. At that moment, I became a Christian. At that point, I didn't tell anybody, except my best friend, Ed Richardson. He took me to his church and I told his minister. He encouraged me to tell the Methodist minister in my church, which I did. He suggested that I be baptized and I was that summer."

Suddath didn't begin to study religion or think about the ministry until later, but from that point on, Christianity became the driving force in his life. A year later, when he began to narrow his list of colleges, he seriously considered the University of Florida because John

Lotz, the coach there, was a born-again Christian and he felt very comfortable with him. "In the end, it came down to this when I chose a college," Suddath said. "I wanted to play for John Lotz but I wanted to play for Duke just a little bit more."

Suddath was heavily recruited. Six ACC schools and seven Southeast Conference schools pursued him. He was bright enough, however, to understand that even with all the attention, he was not a superstar. "I was six–six and I could shoot," he said. "I had good grades and I was a good kid. But I was also very skinny [180 pounds] and not very fast. The reason they all wanted me was that I was a pretty good player *and* I was white. If I had been the same player and black, I would have been recruited, but not as heavily."

The University of Georgia wanted Suddath badly enough that it prevailed upon Governor George Busby to place a recruiting call on its behalf. Georgia also arranged for Suddath and a couple of his friends to buy tickets for the Final Four, which was in Atlanta that year. "We sat in the second row," Suddath said. "I remember thinking I would never get a chance to be any closer to a Final Four than this. Little did I know."

Duke got involved with Suddath after Ray Jones saw him score 31 points and get 30 rebounds in a game early in his senior year. Jones knew that Duke had already signed Dennard and was in hot pursuit of Banks, but he felt Suddath's long-range shooting ability could add an element that Duke lacked. "The kid can really stroke it," he kept telling the other coaches. They listened.

Suddath's visit to campus was almost a disaster. Not knowing about his devoutness, Foster turned him over to Spanarkel. This was the night of one of the big SAE fraternity parties of the year and, needless to say, Suddath was aghast at what he saw. "I had never had a drink," Suddath said. "I had never danced. Let's face it, I was sheltered and I was naive. The whole thing shocked me. I remember going back to bed that night and saying to myself, 'No way am I coming here.'

"But the next day was Sunday. I had breakfast with the coaches. It was the first time I really talked to Coach Foster and I liked him a lot. We went to church in The Chapel and then we walked around campus. It was a beautiful spring day and the place looked gorgeous. I began to think maybe this wasn't such a bad idea."

In the end, Suddath chose Duke over Florida and Georgia largely because its academic reputation appealed to his parents. He also liked the coaches. And loved the campus.

He made his decision the night Marquette beat North Carolina for the national championship, giving away his Georgia-provided tickets and spending the evening with Jim Donovan. "We drew up a list of Duke's pluses and Florida's pluses," he said. "Duke won. I signed the letter of intent the next day. I didn't pay any attention, really, to North Carolina–Marquette. That was another orbit to me."

Suddath didn't really know what other orbits were until he arrived at Duke and was told by Foster that he was going to room with Dennard. "To say that I had never met anyone like Kenny doesn't begin to describe what went on," Suddath said. "That was a very tough time for me. I was very young in my Christian faith and, especially rooming with Kenny, I was being exposed to a lot of temptation."

The most famous Suddath–Dennard story is, of course, the "bottle it and sell it" story. But even though he speaks warmly of Dennard and laughs at that story, Suddath admits he was baffled by him. "Even putting aside my Christianity, I was very committed to basketball," he said. "I couldn't believe the hours Kenny kept. I couldn't believe that an athlete would drink the way he did. I couldn't figure out how in the world he came to practice every day and played so hard and so well because it seemed to me that he never slept.

"Actually," he added with a smile, "it's a good thing he didn't sleep much because I swear to God he didn't change his sheets once the whole semester."

Dennard and Suddath were the Odd Couple in real life. Their partnership is best put into perspective by Harold Morrison. "In one bed, you had a born-again Christian whose path to heaven has been paved for him," he said. "In the other bed you had a guy who needed to be exposed to the other guy just to have a shot to get into hell."

Suddath fit in with the team because he was easygoing, likeable, and never tried to preach to his teammates. Bruce Bell took him under his wing, which also helped. On the road, his roommate was Banks, which was almost as much of an adventure as Dennard. His playing time increased after Morrison's injury and, after wondering if he could compete during preseason, he found himself part of Foster's eight-man rotation during the last two months of the season.

"There were times, especially during the NCAA Tournament, when it was my time to go in and I would get very nervous," he said. "I think when you're a starter you can get the jitters out because you go out and play. You don't have a chance to look around. You sit on the bench, you look around and you realize what a big deal this is."

Suddath scored four points off the bench in the national championship game and, like his teammates, wonders what might have happened if Jim Bain hadn't called the technical on Bill Foster. But it is the postgame scene that makes him pause, slow down, and savor the memories.

"The feeling that we had then is exactly why we were so successful that year," he said. "No one thought about himself. Everyone just thought about winning. As different as we all were, there was real caring. I think it started with Coach Foster. Whenever I think about him, the first thing I think about is that he really cared about all of us. He's a good person. I think our approach that season was the right way to approach sports and it paid off for all of us."

But the next year it all changed. Everyone was looking for a piece of glory. Suddath looks at the goings-on that season as sin because of the selfishness he felt in the locker room. "I can still remember a team meeting where Coach Wenzel had this flow chart showing us each step we were going to take during that season. He kept talking about where *we* were going to be but I know everyone in that room was thinking where am *I* going to be. I did it too. We were all guilty."

Because he came in with Banks and Dennard, Suddath was never a starter at Duke, except late in his senior year when Mike Krzyzewski went to a three-forward lineup. He had some excellent games, including an 11-point, 5-steal, 5-rebound performance against Kentucky in the overtime victory that opened his junior season.

"After that game I sat in the locker room and cried my eyes out," he said. "Playing them again really affected me. But looking back, the national championship game in '78 was a pinnacle for us, in terms of success and disappointment. Winning that game two years later didn't make it even, but it meant a lot to me."

Suddath's junior year was an important one for him for several reasons. Early in that season, when he was getting substantial minutes off the bench and playing as well as he ever had, it occurred to him that while he was a decent college player he certainly was not an NBA player. This was not a great moment of revelation but it forced him to focus on his future—a future without basketball.

"During my sophomore year I had gotten very involved with the FCA [Fellowship of Christian Athletes] and I felt myself growing as a Christian. By the time my junior year came around I was seriously thinking that my life's work might very well be in doing mission work. I had gone overseas to play in Sri Lanka and India during the summer with an FCA team and I knew I wanted to go back and do more."

It was also during that season that he met Jenny, who walked up and introduced herself when Jim was manning an FCA booth in front of The Chapel on Religious Activities Day at Duke. She was a field hockey player who wanted to join the FCA. Suddath not only signed her up, he started dating her. The summer after he graduated (Jenny was one year behind him), in the middle of the Duke quad at two in the morning, he asked her to marry him. She hesitated briefly before saying yes.

Dating Jenny and working often with the FCA, Suddath had several excellent games his junior year, but because of the rumors that Foster was leaving, it was a roller coaster ride. Foster felt most guilty about leaving the three juniors—Banks, Dennard, and Suddath—because he knew it would be hardest on them. He talked to each of them individually the week before the ACC Tournament to try to make them understand why he was leaving.

"I didn't want him to leave but I understood that he felt he had to," Suddath said. "He was unhappy. There's no point being someplace where you're unhappy. Naturally, it was tough for Gene, Kenny, and me because we didn't have any options. The younger guys could transfer if they felt really strongly but for us it was too late."

Suddath did not get off to a great start with the new regime—through no fault of his or Krzyzewski's. Late in Foster's last season he hurt his knee. At the time the injury didn't seem serious and Suddath continued playing. In March, another examination showed damaged cartilage. The first week Krzyzewski was on campus, Suddath was in the hospital being operated on.

But the problem wasn't solved. During the summer Suddath's knee swelled again. He came back to campus in late August, had the knee examined, and on the first day of classes was back in the hospital for a second operation. Once again he began rehabbing the knee. On the first day of practice he was ready to go—he thought.

"By the end of practice, the knee had locked on me fifteen times," Suddath said. "I knew it wasn't right. I just broke down and cried."

The next day he was in the hospital again. The third operation got all the cartilage and chips but it wasn't until the week the season began that Suddath was able to start practicing again. "Imagine yourself being Coach K," Suddath said. "The first week you're on campus, the first day of classes and the first day of practice, I'm in the hospital or on my way. He never saw me go through preseason. If I were him, I wouldn't have counted on me for much that year."

Suddath did work his way back into his super-sub role by January.

Duke came into the final home game in Cameron with a 14–11 record, everyone knowing that one more victory would at least salvage an NIT bid. But it would not be easy. North Carolina had already beaten them twice and, as always, Dean Smith was dying to win in Cameron. For Suddath, Banks, and Dennard this was their final home game.

It was an emotional afternoon. The students all showed up wearing T-shirts that said, "Dennard and Banks, So Long and Thanks," a tribute to the 87 victories they had contributed to over four years, the two ACC titles, and the Final Four trip. Suddath was, in a way, an afterthought.

"To me, that game symbolized my Duke career," he said. "I can remember when we were all introduced before the game, how emotional it was for me because I had changed so much during my four years at Duke. Then, the game was unbelievable."

With two seconds left, North Carolina's Sam Perkins hit two free throws to put the Tar Heels up 56–54. Duke had to go ninety-four feet in two seconds to somehow tie the game. The Blue Devils inbounded to halfcourt and called time with one second left. Then, Dennard threw the ball in to Banks, who turned from twenty-three feet and threw a rainbow over Perkins's outstretched arm. The ball swished at the buzzer, sending the game into overtime. In the overtime, Banks won it with a rebound basket with nine seconds left. They tore down the nets and carried him off the court.

But it couldn't have happened without Suddath. On the winning play, Vince Taylor missed a jump shot and the rebound went right to Carolina's Matt Doherty. But just as Doherty was about to grab the ball, Suddath came up behind him and knocked the ball right to Banks, who hit the winning shot.

"That game was me at Duke," Suddath said. "I was never a star or the hero but I was part of it. Gene got all the accolades and he deserved them. But I had to get my hand on that ball for him to make the shot. It wasn't a big deal or anything, but it mattered. And that has always made me feel good about what I did there for four years."

Suddath ended up starting his last four games and starred in an NIT upset of Alabama, a game Duke won without Banks, who had broken his wrist. Suddath's career ended drearily, though, on a snowy night at Purdue. Duke lost that night and Suddath could barely finish the game. He had dislocated his thumb in warm-ups.

"Gene was out there rebounding for us in his street clothes and he whipped the ball back to me with his good hand," Suddath said.

"Just as he did, somebody called my name and I turned my head. The ball bent my thumb back. I was in major pain the whole game. The doctor said it would heal on its own and it did. But it was a sad way to end up."

Suddath graduated that spring, asked Jenny to marry him during the summer, and went to work as the basketball coach at his old high school, Woodward Academy. "My old coach retired after a year in which the whole starting team graduated," he said, laughing. "I went in there and won four games my first year. It was a long season."

The following September he and Jenny were married. They remained at Woodward for three more years but the entire time, Jim was preparing himself to go to the seminary. "I wanted to try and save some money because I knew it would be difficult financially to not work for three years," he said. "We got involved in being dorm parents at Woodward and that helped us with living expenses quite a bit. I knew I wanted to go to the seminary, it was just a matter of being able to afford it."

One of the Suddaths' dorm "children" was Amy Carter, daughter of ex-President Jimmy Carter. "Amy came to Woodward as a junior," Suddath said. "Early in the year, there was a Parents Day and the Carters came down to see Amy. I was away for part of the day at a reunion with a friend of mine but I got back in time for the dinner that night.

"By the time I got back, Jenny had met the Carters and spent time with them and was getting along real well with them. I came back and just before we walked in to dinner, Jenny wanted to introduce me. So, I'm walking over and Jenny says, 'Mr. President, I'd like you to meet my husband, Jim Suddath.'

"Well, I'm just about to shake hands with the President when this little eighth grader, hearing my name, turns around and yells, 'Jim Suddath! My God, it's Jim Suddath! I saw you play at Duke! Wow, I can't believe you're here! What are you doing here?'

"By now, I'm standing right next to Jimmy Carter. The kid has no idea while he's screaming my name that I'm standing next to a former President. But when he said, 'What are you doing here?' I couldn't resist. I just pointed at the President and said, 'Oh, I'm just here with what's-his-name.' Fortunately, both Carters cracked up. They thought the whole thing was hilarious."

The Suddaths stayed at Woodward for four years. During their last year there, Joshua was born. The next fall, the three of them moved into the small trailer that would be their home for most of the next four years. Three years later, Jenny's second baby turned out to be twins and now the family was five. But they managed. When Jim graduated they were debt-free.

"It's been tough at times," he said. "We spent four months in the Philippines as part of my required mission work and, with two babies, that wasn't easy. But it's been worth it. I know this is my life's work. This is my calling. I want to do mission work overseas until God tells me he doesn't want me there anymore."

Before he goes overseas, though, Suddath will be an assistant pastor at a church in Chattanooga, Tennessee. He turned thirty in April '89 and he thinks this is the perfect time to begin his work as a missionary.

That doesn't mean he has left his teammates behind. "I think about them a lot," he said. "It would be great to see everybody again. If I walked into a room and they were all there, I'd have two instincts. One would be to preach to them, but the other would be to hug them all. I think the second one would be stronger though. I also think if I preached, a lot of them would look at me and say, 'Come on, Sudds.' But that's the way they are—and the way I am."

Every once in a while, Suddath has a recurring dream. "It happens every month or two," he said. "All of a sudden, I'm back in college and I've got one more year to play. Coach Foster is still there and I've got another chance to play." He smiled, understanding the irony in the dream. "It's as if I'm born again as a basketball player."

Born again with the same wicked, looping lefty jump shot. And why not? After all, preachers can dream too.

28

Tinkerbell

Gene Banks is in serious trouble. Most of the time, he can talk his way out of any situation. He can charm or cajole or just BS his way through. He is as famous for his ability to convince people that the sun will rise tomorrow morning in the west as he is for his ability to play basketball.

But now he has met his match. Standing in the living room of her grandparents' home, India Banks is not buying any of the famous Banks excuses. "Honey, I don't want to leave, believe me," he says, almost pleading. "I'll be back tomorrow, I really will. If there was any way I could take you I would."

India has heard the speech before. She doesn't like it now any more than in the past because she knows the bottom line is the same: Her daddy is leaving her behind.

"Daddy," she says mournfully, "will you be home for my birthday?"

Gene Banks drops the excuses. "Honey, I would never miss your birthday," he says. "That I can promise you."

India's face lights up. Her birthday is Saturday—in two days and she knows when Daddy is telling the truth. She may be one of the few people in the world who knows when Gene Banks is handing out a line and when he is handing out the truth. India will be four on Saturday.

"Children always know," Banks says, climbing into the car. "I can BS adults any time I have to. But not my children. They can always tell when I mean something and when I don't."

The trip from Greensboro to Durham will not be an easy one. A major snowstorm has blown into North Carolina and the interstate is down to one lane. But Banks needs to get there, not because his alma mater is playing at home against North Carolina State tonight but because his agent, Herb Rudoy, is in town. So are a number of NBA scouts and coaches.

Gene Banks is looking for work. He talks about this fact almost casually. He isn't in need of money; in fact the Italian team that he left at the beginning of February paid him off quite handsomely. But he is three months shy of thirty and he knows his basketball life is slipping away. He isn't ready to quit yet. So he sits by the phone and waits for it to ring. It hasn't rung yet.

The man every college in America chased through the streets of Philadelphia in 1977 is living with his wife and their two children in his father-in-law's house, waiting to find out if he will get the one last shot to play basketball that he craves so much.

"If I didn't think I could still play, I'd do something else," he says, sounding like many players near the end of their careers. "I've worked hard, I'm in shape, and I know there are teams I could help. I'm just waiting for someone to give me a chance."

Looking at him, there is little doubt that Banks is in shape. Eleven years after he awed his teammates with his teenage physique, he is still impressive to look at, even in an overcoat. His face is a little fuller than it was back then, but he is still handsome and his body looks rock hard.

"After I got hurt I got almost up to 240," he says. "But right now, I weigh 215. I'm in as good condition as I ever have been. No one but me knows how hard I worked to come back. It was the hardest thing I've ever done in my life."

There is no BSing going on here. The last eighteen months have been as challenging as any Banks has ever lived through. In July of 1987, having completed his sixth and best year in the NBA, Banks was playing in the Baker League, a staple of summer life in Philadelphia. Although he had never become the megastar he had been cast as when he first arrived at Duke, Banks had become a solid NBA player and had started for much of the previous season with the Chicago Bulls. He had one more year left on his contract, which called for him to make $345,000 in salary and possibly another $100,000 in incentive clauses.

After that, he would be a free agent, able to sell his services to the highest bidder. Then, on a warm July afternoon in a Philadelphia schoolyard, it all changed for Banks. "I got a rebound and spun around to throw an outlet pass upcourt," he says. "I reached back to throw the pass and pushed off on my back [right] foot. I felt this sudden pain and

I knew I had done something, but I wasn't sure what. I hobbled off, figuring I had pulled something and shouldn't take any chances."

It was too late. The pain Banks had felt was his Achilles tendon snapping. He went back to Chicago where the Bulls doctors confirmed that he needed surgery. It was after the operation that the Bulls told him they had no intention of paying him for the upcoming season. With all its tradition, the Baker League is not formally sanctioned by the NBA the way some other summer leagues are. That meant, according to the Bulls, that they did not have to pay Banks for the lost season. NBA teams routinely encourage their players to take part in summer leagues to stay in shape. Now, though, the Bulls were claiming that Banks was at fault for injuring himself in an "unauthorized" league.

"I was really hurt by that," Banks said. "I thought I had really contributed the previous season and been an important part of the team. Now, it was like they wanted to discard me and try to save themselves some money because I wasn't any use to them. I was shocked."

All athletes find out sooner or later that the teams they play for are more than willing to discard them if they are no longer useful. For Banks this was a particularly painful discovery. He had always been sought. Now he was being dumped.

This was not the first time the NBA had disappointed him, but that didn't make it easier to take. Banks had come into the league in 1981 as a second-round draft pick of the San Antonio Spurs—the twenty-eighth player chosen overall. That was about twenty to twenty-seven players later than most people had thought Gene Banks would go when his time came to be drafted.

But his senior year at Duke had ended painfully—literally and figuratively. Bill Foster's departure the year before had been harder on Banks and his alter ego Kenny Dennard than on anyone else. Both said they understood why Foster had to leave. But both, especially Banks, knew they had lost something when Foster left.

"Let's face it, he was like a father to me," Banks said. "After all was said and done, the main reason I chose Duke was because I really liked Bill. I felt I could relate to him and get along with him.

"He put up with a lot from me. When I got into trouble, he got mad at me, but he was always there to help. He kept that can of BS repellant in his desk to use when I came in with a story, but he always said yes when he knew I needed something. It would be very hard for any other coach to understand me the way Bill did."

Banks had arrived at Duke as the father of a son who had been born

in Philadelphia his senior year in high school. Foster helped him deal
with that. Two years later, Banks fathered another boy. Foster was
there to help him with that too. He constantly counseled Banks to
change his partying ways, and Banks listened—sometimes.

"I've always tried hard to be good," he said. "My parents met in a
Pentecostal church. I believe very much in God and I pray all the time.
I believe he has a plan for me and I want to do what is right."

He smiled. "But the problem is, there's always been fifty percent of
me that wants to be good and fifty percent of me that wants to have
fun. I'm like Dr. Jekyll and Mr. Hyde. When I was at Duke, Mr. Hyde
took over a lot."

Dr. Jekyll and Coach Foster usually bailed Banks out when Mr. Hyde
got into trouble. Banks could BS his way through most things, usually
with a story so wild it *had* to be believed—because how could it have
possibly been made up? Foster and the other coaches and players would
shrug their shoulders, say, "That's Tink," and life would go on.

But Mike Krzyzewski wasn't Bill Foster. He told Banks and Dennard
in no uncertain terms that the partying, the constant use of the basketball office telephones, the trips home or to Florida, and the general
anarchy would *stop*. Foster had figured that if he could get Banks and
Dennard to go to class and keep them out of jail and showing up at
practice every day, he was doing well. Krzyzewski wanted more.

"It was toe-the-line time," Banks said. "With Bill, we always knew
there was a line we better not cross. But Mike moved the line and when
he did, we were way over it. We were seniors. We didn't really want
some new coach coming in and telling us what we had been doing for
three years didn't work anymore. It was tough for me; just about
impossible for Kenny."

Even though the two team captains and the former Army captain-
turned-coach clashed often, Krzyzewski soon learned there had been a
reason why Foster had put up with Banks and Dennard. For all their
wildness, both came to practice ready and came to games to play.
"There was always a respect between us because we were all competi-
tors," Krzyzewski said. "Gene and Kenny had faults, no doubt about
it. But they never once backed away in a game."

Banks had a superb senior year. Playing on a team with no center
and inexperienced guards, he was the key to victories over Top Ten
teams like North Carolina and Maryland. He kept the team competitive in the ACC. And he finished his home career with exactly the kind
of flourish one would expect from Tinkerbell.

When the seniors were introduced, Banks went last. Dennard and

Jim Suddath were already on the floor when Banks was introduced. When they called his name, Cameron shaking with cheers, he came out carrying roses. He ran to each corner of the court and laid a rose in each corner. It was his way of saying thank you—and making sure no one would ever forget it.

There is a picture of that pregame scene, with Dennard and Banks exchanging their traditional hug. Dennard has his hand over his eyes, apparently overcome by the emotion of the moment. "I wasn't crying," Dennard says of that picture. "I was covering my eyes because I knew what Gene was about to do."

The roses may have been hokey, but the game itself was truly unforgettable. Banks scored 25 points and had 16 rebounds. That didn't tell the story, though. The Philadelphia legend played a legendary game. First, he hit the rainbow twenty-three-footer over Sam Perkins at the buzzer to send the game into overtime. It was easily the longest—and most remarkable—shot of his Duke career. Then, in the overtime, with Suddath's assist, he scored the winning basket. Duke had won, 66–65, and Banks was as heroic as a hero can possibly be. "When the game was over, I couldn't believe what happened," he said. "Before I knew it, I was up on everyone's shoulders and they were carrying me around. It was so loud, I thought I was dreaming.

"I saw this movie last week, *Everybody's All-American,* and there's this scene where the hero scores the winning touchdown in the Sugar Bowl and they pick him up and carry him around, and, as he's sitting there he knows his life can never get better than it is right at that moment. That's the way I felt. I can remember thinking, 'It will never be like this again. Never.' The love I felt that day . . ." He stops and shakes his head. "Wow. Just talking about it chokes me up."

Much like Gavin Grey, the hero of *Everybody's All-American,* Banks has never achieved a moment quite like that one again. He and Grey both understood that pure joy such as that would probably never come again—but that didn't prevent them from seeking it.

Duke was invited to the NIT that season, thanks to the victory over Carolina. They opened play at home against North Carolina A&T. Six minutes into the game, Banks went up for a rebound, got shoved, and came down hard, landing on his right wrist. Slightly more than four years later, he had suffered the identical injury Tate Armstrong had suffered at Virginia: a broken navicular bone in his right wrist.

He underwent surgery that night. The break was a serious one, serious enough that the doctor told him he might not play again. "I knew I would play basketball again," Banks said. "But when the word went out on the grapevine that the wrist injury was serious, it hurt my draft position a lot."

Banks showed up for Duke's second-round NIT game against Alabama dressed in a tuxedo—"Gene never did anything quietly," Suddath remembers—and received a huge ovation when he was introduced. But it wasn't the same, of course, as Carolina. He did have one more gratifying moment at Duke, though, when he was selected as a student speaker at graduation. Four years after people had whispered about Duke admitting him in spite of his low SAT scores, he spoke to and for his classmates.

"I still have the speech," he said. "I talked about the fact that all the people in the world are like an orchestra and we all play different instruments. But if we're going to survive, we all have to play together and in harmony or the orchestra will fall apart.

"That was important to me. After all the talk that I could never get through Duke and I would never graduate, it meant something to me to show people that not only did I graduate but I was able to stand before my classmates and deliver a speech. It was the most nervous I've ever been. Playing in the Final Four was nothing compared to that."

The NBA draft was a disappointment to Banks, but he went to San Antonio and became a solid role player. At 6–6, he wasn't big enough to dominate NBA games inside the way he had done in college. He was not a good enough shooter to step outside. "Gene is a power forward in a small forward's body," Dennard said. "It's a tribute to him that in spite of that he became a good NBA player."

After four seasons in San Antonio, Banks was traded to Chicago, where he became a starter. Michael Jordan was on the scene and there was no question about who the team's superstar was, but Banks had a very definite role before the Achilles injury. He was a consistent rebounder, a good defensive player, and he could score inside well enough to take some pressure off Jordan. Still, being a solid role player is a lot different from being Gene "Tinkerbell" Banks.

"It sure is," he said, shaking his head. "In college, I usually had more ability than the guys I played against. I was bigger or stronger or faster. In the pros, I had to work my ass off to be a good player. There was satisfaction in it, though. I enjoyed finding out that I could be put in a tough position and not only handle it, but prosper and get better."

The NBA lifestyle did not make things easy on his marriage. Banks had met Belle Johnson as a sophomore at Duke. He, Harold Morrison, and John Harrell had been wandering around a Greensboro mall before a preseason scrimmage down there when they had spotted a good-looking woman working in one of the stores.

"We went in to talk to her and I was kind of clowning around with her," Morrison said. "She seemed to like me. Well, Gene couldn't take that. So he started talking about the fact that yes, he was planning to go on to the NBA after college. You could see her eyes go wide. I said, 'That's it, I'm out of here.' "

Her name was Debbie and she and Banks exchanged phone numbers. A couple of weeks later she called Gene to say that she and a friend were coming down to Durham for a party. Did Gene want to go? Of course. "I was standing on the porch of this house where the party was," Gene said. "And they pulled up. Debbie gets out of the car and then comes her friend. It was Belle. I mean, she was beautiful. Absolutely beautiful. I said to myself, 'I have got to get to know her.' "

Banks had a problem though. Debbie was his date. He raced into the house and called Morrison. Would he come over and bail him out by taking Debbie off his hands? Morrison was sick in bed. He also remembered that initially, Banks had taken Debbie off of *his* hands. "You're on your own, Gene," he told his friend.

Banks handled it. He told Debbie that he really liked her but his friend Harold *really* liked her and he would feel guilty if they kept seeing each other. Debbie wasn't too sure about all this. After all, where was Harold? Sick in bed and sick with disappointment that he couldn't be there to see her. Debbie still wasn't buying all this. It didn't matter. At the end of the night, Banks got Belle's phone number. Debbie was history.

"But it wasn't easy," Banks said, laughing at the memory. "First of all, Belle was four years older than I was. She had already graduated from North Carolina A&T. She couldn't have cared less about me being a basketball star. She kept telling me I was just a baby and I should leave her alone.

"But I courted her. I mean, really courted her: flowers, telegrams, playing a guitar under her window . . ."

Whoa. Playing a guitar under her window?

"Well, not exactly, but you know what I mean."

Belle finally broke down. Maybe it was to avoid having Tink play a guitar under her window. They were engaged when Gene graduated and were married a year later. But the NBA lifestyle, with all the time that is spent on the road, does not always lend itself to monogamy.

Gene and Belle were separated for eighteen months beginning in 1983, got back together, and separated again briefly after India was born. Now they have two children. Banks's two sons, Benjamin, twelve, and Eugene, ten, both live in Philadelphia with their mothers, although he sees them often. Benjamin went to his first basketball camp in the summer of 1989—at Duke.

Having learned to deal with not being a superstar, having learned how to be a consistent NBA role player, having learned how to be a husband, Banks was riding high on that summer afternoon in Philadelphia when his Achilles snapped. That is why the injury was painful in so many ways. He went through rehab and by the summer of '88 felt he was ready to come back and play in the NBA.

But no one wanted to give him a tryout. The fact that he had sued the Bulls for his salary—and won a settlement that paid him the $345,000—may very well have influenced NBA owners to stay away from him. They are, after all, a fraternity just like the owners are in all sports. Banks had taken on one of their own—and won.

Banks thought he was going to get a tryout with the expansion Charlotte Hornets. This would have been a perfect setup for him. His wife's family lived ninety miles away in Greensboro and he certainly could help an expansion team.

"I had worked my tail off for a full year and I was ready to go there and perform," Banks said. "But I never got the chance."

At the last moment, the Hornets told Banks they were not going to offer him a contract. He was a man without a team. Herb Rudoy made some phone calls and found an Italian team in Bologna that was willing to pay Banks $200,000 to come and play for them. Artis Gilmore would be the other American on the team. Banks accepted. He, Belle, India, and their newborn baby girl moved to Bologna in the fall.

The next five months were difficult. The American players are generally looked to in Italy to carry a team, and Gilmore, who is forty, struggled. That left a lot of the burden on Banks. At times he played very well, at other times not so well. He and the family were not happy in Bologna and when the team began looking for someone to take his place, Banks and Rudoy negotiated a buyout of Banks's contract. He came back to the U.S. the first week in February and set up headquarters in Greensboro hoping the phone would ring shortly.

"There are a lot of possibilities out there," he said on that snowy February day. "Several teams have said they're interested. We just have to wait and see."

The end of the season came and Banks was still waiting. He played in the Los Angeles Summer league for the Hornets hoping they would invite him to training camp. Banks knows he could go back to Europe and play and extend his career that way. But that isn't what he wants to do.

"For one thing, I don't want to move my family again," he said. "I'd like for us to pick a place to settle down. I've thought about building a place in Charlotte and I still own a place back in San Antonio. I don't need to go back to Europe for the money. I want to play at the highest level, that's the way I want to go out."

Looking at him, it is difficult to believe that Banks can't help someone in the NBA. Anyone who saw him at Duke back in that glorious freshman year—or even on that remarkable day when he beat Carolina single-handed—has trouble coming to terms with the notion that a day will come when Gene Banks can't play basketball anymore.

Bob Bender explained it better than anyone. "From the very first day we practiced with him, Gene was Superman to all of us. He could do anything. The night we beat Villanova to go to the Final Four Gene won a *dance* contest, for crying out loud. To us, there's never been anything that could stop Gene when he wanted something."

All he wants now is a final chance. Before it's too late, Tinkerbell wants to fly one last time.

29

The Dirty Dog

As the car pulled into the parking lot, Kenny Dennard whipped a snowball right at the windshield. *Whap!* It splattered right before the driver's eyes while Dennard shook his fist in the air to celebrate his direct hit.

This was a relief to the driver, who had heard reports that Dennard had grown up. If Dennard had passed up the opportunity to zing a car with a snowball it would have been a sobering indication that those reports were true. But the snowball was thrown with great zest. The dirty dog lived.

Up close, however, it was apparent that this was not the same dog who had romped through four years at Duke. Shortly after turning thirty, Dennard started wearing glasses. That, combined with the weight he had put on, made him look entirely different from the nineteen-year-old who had sprawled across the press table in St. Louis screaming, "Ain't this fun?"

"I've come a long way in a short time," he said. "And where has the journey brought me? Right back to where I started."

Twelve years after he left Stokes County to go to college and see the world, Dennard was back home. He and his wife Nadine were living in the house that Kenny and his family lived in while they waited for the big house up the hill to be constructed. His parents live in that house now. In the doorway leading from the kitchen to the garage of Kenny and Nadine's house, the chart kept by the Dennards tracking Kenny's height is still on the wall. It stops a couple of inches below the ceiling at 6-8. When Kenny walks by the chart now, his frame fills the entire doorway.

"When I left here to go to Duke, I never thought I would come back except to visit," he said. "I knew there was something better out there for me. But a lot of things happened, some good and some bad. They say that life is a circle. I guess I'm proof of that."

More than anything, Dennard is proof that you can't judge a book by its cover. He was always the self-designated crazy man of the Duke teams he played on, the guy with the most enthusiasm and the penchant for getting into the most trouble.

He had two nicknames, Dog and Dirt, but it was the second one that mattered most. Whatever else you wanted to say about Dennard, he would do anything to win a basketball game: dive, sprawl, fight, you name it. To his teammates, he was Dirt because he would roll in the mud to win if that's what was necessary.

But beneath the Dog and Dirt image, Dennard was perhaps the brightest member of the team. Jim Suddath can still remember sitting up late at night with Dennard—on the rare occasions that he was home—arguing about Suddath's born-again Christianity. "Kenny pointed out a lot of the hypocrisy in my life," Suddath said. "He was fun to argue with because he made so much sense. After a while, I decided that Kenny was an instrument sent by the Lord to make me think about my life and my Christianity."

Dennard might not see it quite that way, but there is no doubt that he has a questioning, analytical mind. More than anyone on the team he has thought about the experience the '78 team went through and how it changed them—and him.

"If I had been Gene, I might have handled our success as freshmen differently," he said. "He had been a star when he was a sophomore in high school. I didn't even have pubic hair until that year. I was still playing junior varsity basketball and not doing it all that well. I was a pudgy kid. Gene was a man playing against boys.

"When he came to Duke he expected to make the program into a winner. What happened was no surprise to him. I had no idea what to expect. I didn't know if I would play or start or what would happen. Then, in one season, it all fell into place. I became a star too. Everyone wanted to be my friend. If I had been thirty, I might have dealt with it differently. But I was nineteen and you couldn't possibly tell me I didn't have everything in the world completely under control."

Dennard was rarely in control the next three years. He did just enough school work to stay eligible, often taking off during spring semester for long trips to Florida. He decided at the end of his sophomore year that he wanted to play in the NBA; he worked very hard to fulfill that goal. His junior year he played well but was set back by the collision with Banks and the subsequent thigh injury that put him on the bench for eight games.

Then came the comeback in the ACC Tournament, the sad ending in Lexington, and Foster's departure. Like Banks, Dennard was nowhere to be found at Mike Krzyzewski's first meeting with his new team. When he came back from Florida, Krzyzewski was in Foster's office. "I couldn't even pronounce his name," Dennard said. "You know there are times when you don't really think straight in life. The last couple of weeks of the season I knew Bill was leaving. But it never really occurred to me that they would replace him."

This is not a facetious comment. Dennard simply hadn't thought in tangible terms. That was one reason why he had agreed to pose for a local magazine in a mock *Playgirl* centerfold: Dennard stretched out, his body covered by nothing but a basketball placed strategically just below the waist. "I knew Bill was leaving when they shot it so I figured it was no problem," he said, laughing at the memory. "Of course I'm sure Mike was thrilled when he saw it."

The magazine came out the week after Krzyzewski arrived. He never said a word to Dennard about it but the tension between the two of them was there from the very first day. "He always told us he wanted us to act like men," Dennard said. "Then he gave us an eleven-thirty curfew and did everything but tuck us in. Is that treating us like men? Bill never gave us a curfew but we were always in bed the night before a game. Then he [Mike] started making us stay in a hotel the night before home games to make sure we were in by curfew. He said it was because some guys couldn't sleep with the noise on the quad. Hell, I had an apartment. Let them sleep in a hotel. I wanted to sleep in my own bed."

The conflicts between Dennard and Krzyzewski were inevitable. Both were (and are) stubborn and strong-minded and each had different ideas about discipline. Krzyzewski believed in it; Dennard didn't. What they shared, though, was the desire to win. That and that alone got them through their one season together. But it wasn't easy.

"Actually, a lot of it was Gene," Dennard said. "To be honest, I was pissed off when he didn't turn pro after his junior year. I thought he should have. It would have been good for him and it certainly would have been good for me. Senior year, to be honest, I was thinking selfishly. I wanted a chance to show the pro scouts what I could do. That didn't mean I didn't want to win, but I also wanted my chance. With Gene around I never really got it." After 14 games, with the Blue Devils 7–7, Krzyzewski slowed his offense to a crawl and built everything the team did around trying to get the ball to Banks. This did not sit well with Dennard. Still, he kept playing hard and was a key player in the two best victories of the season over Maryland and North Carolina.

After the Maryland game, the first player Krzyzewski hugged was Dennard. After the Carolina game, while giving full credit to Banks for his superhuman effort, Krzyzewski pointed out that on the last play of regulation, Dennard's pass fake toward Chip Engelland in the corner had given Banks an extra split second to get off the shot that tied the game.

"That game was the one really great moment of my senior year," Dennard said. "I was happy for Gene to go out that way and I was happy that we had played well, that *I* had played well. It was a nice way to finish. But the rest of the year wasn't a lot of fun for me."

As soon as the season was over, Dennard took off for Florida. He had stopped going to classes altogether once the second semester had started, knowing that he wasn't going to graduate on time. "My plan all along was to come back and finish after I was through playing ball," he said. "My mind wasn't on college at that point. It was on playing pro basketball."

He was drafted in the fourth round by the Kansas City Kings, meaning he came to camp with only an outside chance of making the team. He was the last player cut, but Coach Cotton Fitzsimmons told him that the team wanted to bring him back if it could make a trade or if someone got hurt.

Encouraged, Dennard signed on with the Continental Basketball Association team in Great Falls, Montana. He was a long way from the pampered life he had led at Duke. "I was being paid two hundred and fifty dollars a week," he remembers. "I rented a small apartment, bought a bed for twenty dollars from the Salvation Army, and brought my stereo with me. That was all I had in the apartment.

"When we played games at Billings or Lethbridge, we were expected to get there on our own. When we played up in Anchorage we would fly all night to get there, play three straight nights and then fly all night to get home. It was a bitch. We played in front of three hundred people most nights in freezing cold gyms. It was a long way from Cameron Indoor Stadium.

"But I felt happy. I was reborn. I didn't have all the expectations to deal with that we had at Duke. I knew exactly what my goal was and I went out every night working towards it. There was no BS with classes or saying the right things to people. I just played basketball."

He played it well. He led the league in rebounding and was a starter in the CBA All-Star game. Two days after that game, the call came from Kansas City. The Kings had traded backup forward John Lambert for a draft choice, opening up a spot for Dennard. "I went out, bought myself a bottle of champagne and drank it so fast I got sick," Dennard said. "I looked around at that tiny little apartment, thought about all the road trips and said to myself, 'If you can survive this, you can survive anything. Little did I know.' "

He went to Kansas City and played off the bench for the remaining thirty games of the season with a very poor team, one that finished the year 30–52. But when the season was over, Fitzsimmons told him to work hard all summer—the club had big plans for him the next season. "I really thought I might end up a starter," Dennard said. "I worked harder that summer than I've ever worked in my life. I was in better shape than I'd ever thought about being in while I was in college. My heart rate when I was standing still was forty-seven. I was lifting weights and running five miles a day. I was twenty-four years old and stronger and more ready to play basketball than I ever had been in my life."

Training camp was supposed to begin the last week in September. About two weeks prior to the September 28 team meeting that would open camp, Dennard noticed a small lump on one of his testicles. At first, he thought nothing of it because it didn't hurt. "I just thought it would go away by itself," he said. "But a week later it was still there. I still didn't think it was a big deal because there wasn't any pain. But I thought I should have a doctor look at it. If there was any problem I wanted to get it over with before training camp started."

On Friday, September 22, Dennard went to the doctor's office. "It was a gorgeous day, warm and sunny but not too hot," Dennard said. "I went for my run and then went to see the doctor. I felt like Superman that morning. I'd never been stronger."

The examination was brief. When it was over, the doctor looked at Dennard and said, "Kenny, I want to check you into the hospital on Sunday night."

"What the hell for?" Dennard asked.

"We have to take a look inside your testicle," the doctor said. "Usually these tumors are malignant, nine times out of ten in fact. If it isn't, we can put the testicle back. But if it is, we have to take it out, examine the tumor, and see how serious it is and whether or not it's spread."

"You're talking about cancer," Dennard said, stunned.

"That's right, Kenny."

"I want to talk to my father."

Jack Dennard was back home in North Carolina when his son called. Kenny laid the facts out as the doctor had explained them to him. He listened calmly and said softly, "It sounds to me like the doctor knows what he's talking about. You might as well find out what you're dealing with right away."

Dennard remembers the conversation vividly because he was looking out a large picture window at the beautiful day as he talked to his father. He knew he was right. "I was in shock," he said. "You have to understand, I had never *heard* of testicular cancer." The surgery was scheduled for Monday morning.

Dennard says that he and Nadine—who was then his girlfriend—spent most of the next two days in bed. "We sent that nut off good," he says proudly.

On September 26, Dennard's left testicle was removed in a forty-five-minute operation. The tumor was malignant but, fortunately, it was what is called a pure seminova, meaning it had not yet spread to other parts of the body. Still, the doctors had to remove the entire left side of Dennard's reproductive system.

"The postsurgical pain was unbelievable," Dennard said. "It was like nothing I had ever felt before. I kept drifting in and out of hallucinations because they had me so drugged up."

Dennard's parents flew to Kansas City. Remarkably, this was the first time they had ever met Nadine, who had been Kenny's girlfriend since his junior year in high school. They had never before dealt with the relationship in the past because Nadine is black.

"When I was in high school, I never got into trouble, never got involved with drugs or got arrested or anything," Dennard says. "But I did have a black girlfriend. In Stokes County, North Carolina, that made things tough for my parents."

This was not a time to be petty. The Dennards and Nadine had a common cause now: Kenny's health. What's more, it turned out they liked each other. "I was operated on on Monday," Kenny said. "By Friday, my mom and Nadine were shopping together."

The doctors told Dennard they wanted him to undergo radiation treatments for four weeks and that it would be a couple of months before he could think about working out again. Dennard got out of the hospital in time to go to the opening day team meeting. Fitzsimmons told him there would be a place on the team waiting for him when he was ready to come back.

But the Kings refused to pay him. Since he had not been injured while playing for them, they were not liable, they said. Dennard had signed a contract for $55,000 for that season. He was eligible to collect disability insurance but if he did that, he could not return to playing basketball. And playing basketball again was what he wanted to do most.

"From the very beginning the whole thing was goal-oriented for me," Dennard said. "I didn't think about death. Nadine and my parents went through all that. I was basically unconscious during the scariest times. By the time I was really conscious again, I was getting ready to get out of the hospital and try to get back to playing.

"Then, when the Kings wouldn't pay me, it really upset me. *They* didn't need the money, I did. A guy who tests positive for drugs the first time in the league is suspended *with* pay. I had cancer and I was on the suspended-without-pay list. How is that fair?"

Still upset with the team and general manager Joe Axelson—"a scumbag if there's ever been one," according to Dennard—Dennard made it back for the last thirty-two games of the season. But it wasn't the same. The desire that he had felt the previous summer was gone.

"All of a sudden it just didn't matter that much anymore," he said. "First, I couldn't believe the Kings wouldn't pay me. Then, when I came back, I realized that my time had passed. I was never going to be in the shape I had been in before I went into the hospital. My shot to be a ten-year player in the NBA had been right at that moment when I got sick. I was never going to be that ready again. Now, it was just a question of how long I could hang on in the league. I wasn't as strong, as fast, or as motivated. The first day I went out to run in January I hurt so much I thought I'd never play again. Just making it back to play was a miracle."

At the end of the season, Dennard asked Fitzsimmons to trade him. He was suing the Kings for the $30,000 he said they owed him and he didn't feel he would be given a fair shot to make the team the next fall. Fitzsimmons, who always liked Dennard, complied with his wishes and traded him to Denver. Doug Moe, who had played for Dean Smith at North Carolina, was the coach.

"I know Dean would deny this but I think he talked Doug into trading for me," Dennard said. "He always liked me and was always good to me, even when I was playing against his teams. I've always felt thankful towards him because I think he was the reason I got to play in Denver."

Dennard played in sixty-two games for the Nuggets during the '83–'84 season and made $85,000. His operation had attracted national attention and that winter he was interviewed in *Penthouse's Forum Magazine.* The headline was, "The basketball player with one testicle."

In the story, Dennard described the operation and, quite graphically, how it had changed his sex life. It was classic Dennard. "When I was first operated on the Kings put out a release saying that the problem was in the lower abdomen," he said. "How stupid is that? I lost a testicle. It's part of my body. Why can't people say that? I started working with the American Cancer Society in Kansas City because I thought it was important that people not be afraid to deal with the disease. Now, most high schools teach boys about testicular self-examination. Back then, they didn't do it."

Dennard was released by Denver at the end of the season. He wasn't surprised. He had never been the same player after his illness. He was known as a renegade and, because of his suit against the Kings, a troublemaker.

An arbitrator eventually ruled that although Dennard was entitled to his salary, he had not filed his complaint within the time required to receive the money. He did order the Kings to pay Dennard five thousand dollars in bonus money because it was separate from his salary.

"I felt good that they had to pay me something," Dennard said. "It was a matter of principle with me. Hell, they were trying to screw me. I suppose you could say I lost because of the technicality but it was important to me that, on the merits, the arbitrator said they should have paid me."

Two days after his arbitration hearing, Dennard flew to Rome and signed a contract with Valentina, a team in the Italian A-league. He only stayed two months. "Italian teams can be very slow in paying Americans," he said, echoing one of Banks's complaints about his time in Italy. "Every time I went in to get paid, they said, 'Domani (tomorrow).' I finally told them in February that if they didn't pay me by the following Monday, I was leaving. I went in the following Monday and they said, 'Domani.' I said, 'Domani, my ass.' The next day I got on a plane and flew home.

"I was done. I really didn't even want to play anymore. The summer after I lost the testicle I had several seizures that felt like epileptic fits. Twice, it happened while I was in the car. I didn't know what the hell was wrong with me. One time I thought it was a heart attack.

"The doctor gave me a complete examination. Nothing was wrong. He thought it was delayed stress. I had suppressed all my fears when I had the operation and now it was coming out this way. It was a physical reaction to an emotional thing. All the time when I was trying to focus on basketball, I still hadn't completely dealt with the cancer. Pro basketball just wasn't meant to be for me. So, rather than hang on, I just decided it was time to quit."

That summer, after living together for four years and dating for ten, he and Nadine got married. Both had been with other partners but they kept coming back to one another. When it was time to start his life without basketball—an unknown to Dennard—he knew he wanted the person he knew best—Nadine—with him.

At the same time, he decided to go back to school and get his degree. While he was in Italy, he had read a story in *USA Today* about graduation rates among basketball players. In the story, Duke had been cited as a shining example of academia because only one player who had stayed four years had failed to graduate in the last twenty years. That player, according to Tom Butters, was Kenny Dennard.

"I clipped that story," Dennard said. "I took it with me when I went to see Butters about coming back to school. I asked him why he couldn't have just said there was one player without a degree and left it at that.

"People like to say I went back because I was embarrassed I was the only one without a degree. That's not true. I went back for myself. I had always planned to go back and this was the right time."

But it wasn't that easy. Dennard wanted his athletic scholarship back. He had one full year of school to finish and that would cost $8,300. Under NCAA rules, he was no longer eligible for an athletic scholarship. But he was eligible to apply for a President's Scholarship. This was a scholarship fund made available to the university president. He could use it any way he chose. Dennard applied for a President's Scholarship and Terry Sanford, then the school president, recommended that he be given one. When the board that approves such scholarships met, there was only one vote against Dennard: Tom Butters.

"We gave Kenny Dennard the opportunity to get his degree," Butters said. "All of us, Bill Foster, Mike Krzyzewski, myself, and others pleaded with him to go to class. He chose not to. I didn't think he deserved the privilege of that kind of scholarship and I said so."

Butters told Dennard exactly how he felt. Dennard still resents it. "I made contributions to Duke that go well beyond an athletic scholarship," he said. "I was part of a team that did as much for Duke and its image as anything that has ever happened to the school. I don't think they could be having the success they're having right now if not for our team in '78.

"Did I make mistakes while I was there? Sure. Am I not allowed to make a mistake or be immature? I really don't think I was asking for that much. I just wanted the chance to get my degree."

He got that chance, Butters's opinion notwithstanding. He wrote a fifty-page paper on how being a member of the '78 team had affected him, breezed through his classes, and graduated in August of 1986. Then he went into business with his brother David.

David Dennard had two inventions: a tote bag that turned into a hat and a vest that became a sleeping bag. He and Kenny formed a company, built largely on the money Kenny had made playing in the NBA. "Most small business start up with a couple of million dollars or more in capital," Dennard said. "We started with $150,000. We tried. We came close to making a couple of deals that would have really gotten us going but they fell through. Finally, the banks started calling in our loans. We didn't have the money to pay off."

Broke and unable to pay the banks, Kenny Dennard filed for bankruptcy in May of 1988. He had to file for personal bankruptcy because he had put his own name on most of the loans. "I went from a great credit rating to no credit rating," he said. "I'm back to square one."

Square one brought him home to work for his father. Jack Dennard and his partner, Jack Keiger, had started Carolina Medical Electronics in 1955. The company's main asset then had been an invention he and Keiger had come up with that measured blood flow. It became a key instrument in the development of open heart surgery.

But thirty-two years later, Jack Dennard had resigned as CEO of Carolina Medical Electronics in a dispute with the board. The buyout of his stock was generous but it was still a difficult time for the family. Kenny and Nadine were without assets and Jack was without work, so it made sense to form a family business. Thus was born Dennard Associated International, a small computer marketing and sales company. But a few months after the company was formed, Jack Dennard needed spinal surgery.

"He just doesn't want to get heavily involved in building a company right now," Kenny said last winter. "We'll keep it going on a small scale for now [DAI operates out of the Dennard house] but Dad's looking to sell the land here [35 acres], move south and take it easy. That means I'm looking for work again." The Dog would find work quickly. He is thirty, has a Duke degree, and is extremely bright. The problem is, he is no closer now to knowing what he wants to make his life's work than he was when he was an innocent Duke freshman.

But in June he found a starting point when a laser graphics firm in Mobile, Alabama, called RLQ, hired him to do public relations work. "Right now Nadine and I feel like we're kids again," he said. "We're starting fresh but we also have some experience behind us. I've been through a lot, I've learned a lot, most of it the hard way.

"I'm alive, I'm healthy, and I've got my whole life ahead of me. The way I look at it right now, cancer saved my life. If I had become a star in the NBA, I'm not sure I could have handled it. I certainly didn't handle it at Duke. Maybe I would have gotten into drugs or who knows what. As it was, I had to pause, take a deep breath, and fight my way back. It hasn't been easy and I'm not back yet. But I'll get there. Mark my words, I'll get there."

No jokes, no wisecracks. Just serious talk about growing up and learning tough lessons. All this from Kenny Dennard.

Maybe, just maybe, you can teach an old dog new tricks.

30

The Jewish Mother

Lou Goetz pours himself another cup of decaf and sits down at the table shaking his head. It is just after 8 A.M. but already Goetz has been out for his morning run and is eating a health-food breakfast topped off by the fake coffee.

"Watching them all season, you can tell something's not right," he says. "Their offense is totally out of synch. They don't look confident out there. Great teams have a certain look when they play. This team doesn't look that way. Even when they were undefeated you could tell they were heading for a fall."

Almost eight years removed from his last night on a bench, Goetz still analyzes basketball the way a coach would. But now he is a Duke season ticketholder and, by his own admission, a fan. This morning, in the wake of a 20-point loss to North Carolina, he's a frustrated fan.

"I don't sit up there and scream and yell," he said, smiling. "I would hope that I'll never be that kind of fan. But I do get emotionally involved. There was a period of a couple of years when I didn't even watch the game on television. But now, especially with my son starting to play, I'm really into it again. And, being back here near Duke, it's very easy for me to have feelings for the team."

He is sitting at this moment on the Duke campus, no more than 250 yards from Cameron Indoor Stadium and the office that was his home for four years. He is a little heavier now than he was then, but the curly hair is still brown and his face breaks into an easy smile as he talks about both the past and the present. Then, he was a quiet presence, the calm one. Now, he is still calm, but there is emotion in his voice as he remembers the past.

He comes here, to the Duke cardiac center, every morning for his workout, having been diagnosed recently for high blood pressure and a high cholesterol count. Goetz's father had a heart attack when Lou was a high school senior. He lived another ten years but was never really healthy again. At forty-two, with a history of heart disease in the family, Goetz is being careful.

"I have a wife and two little kids who I love very much," he said. "I have no intention of doing anything that will jeopardize my chances of being with them."

His family was one of the reasons Goetz got out of coaching after three years as the head coach at Richmond. It was an extremely difficult decision for him because coaching was the only thing he had ever done.

"I always wanted to be a coach," he said. "My role model as a kid growing up was my high school coach, Dick Tarrant. There was a bond between us when I played for him, just as there's a bond between us now. Even when I decided to go to Rutgers, I knew that someday I wanted to coach."

Goetz grew up in Passaic, New Jersey. His father was the son of Polish and Romanian immigrants who worked in a factory to feed his family. His mother was, in Lou's words, the family tyrant.

"All of my type-A characteristics come from my mother," he said, smiling. "She was the classic Jewish mother. Loving, but tough. I always believed there was something wrong with me growing up because my mom was always telling me there were things wrong with me. I always had a tendency to do that to people when I was coaching—demand more than they could give."

His family was not highly religious, but very traditional. Both his parents spoke Yiddish—"My brother and I only learned the curse words," he said. At one point, Goetz thought he wanted to become a cantor. His friends, growing up, were Jewish. It was not until he got to Rutgers that he began to have friends who were not Jewish. When he started dating non-Jews, his mother was furious.

While at Rutgers, Goetz did some coaching at the Jewish Community Center. At the end of one season, he brought Jim Valvano in to speak at the awards banquet. Jim Valvano, then Foster's graduate assistant, had just married his high school sweetheart, who was Jewish. He told a number of jokes about Catholics (like him) who marry Jews. At the end of the dinner the head of the center and the rabbi told

Goetz that they were shocked that Goetz would bring in a speaker who would imply that interreligious marriage was acceptable.

"Their reaction made me sick," Goetz remembered. "I was so fed up with the whole concept of religion that I walked away from it completely for a long time."

Only recently has Goetz started to deal again with his religion. His wife, Tracy, is Episcopalian. "If I am anything, I am Jewish," he said. "I have a lot of questions about my religion but one thing I do know is that I'm not Christian. We have to deal with this with our kids now and one thing I know is it will bother me greatly if my children grow up Christian."

Goetz was a younger brother—by two-and-a-half years—and was always driven to prove himself to his brother and his friends.

He was driven first by his mother, then by competition with his brother, and then by a driven coach, Tarrant. He was good enough to be recruited by many schools in the East but chose Rutgers because he liked Bill Foster, liked the school, and because he decided at the last minute that he didn't want to go to West Point.

His decision not to go to a military academy proved to be significant. "I graduated from high school in 1964 when going into the military didn't seem like such a bad thing," Goetz said. "By the time I graduated from Rutgers, we were deeply involved in Vietnam. Rutgers was the scene of a lot of antiwar marches and sit-ins. I was very involved in all that."

Goetz's coaching career actually began while he was a student at Rutgers. During the summers, he coached in the Kutscher's Summer League, learning his craft from Joe Lapchick, the legendary St. John's coach. When he graduated, after a solid playing career, Foster had an opening on his coaching staff, created when Valvano left to become the head coach at Johns Hopkins. When Foster offered Goetz Valvano's spot, he took it immediately.

His two years as a Rutgers assistant were not comfortable ones for Goetz. He was learning on the job. That was okay. But he was also a young liberal in an athletic department populated by older conservatives. When students took over the ROTC building, the members of the athletic department were asked to unanimously support a statement condemning the students.

"You can't say it's unanimous," Goetz said softly in the middle of the meeting called after the sit-in. "I just can't support a statement like that."

Goetz shakes his head now at the memory. "There were like sixty people in the room and most of them came from the 'love it or leave it' school of patriotism, especially the football coaches. I really felt for Bill, because I knew it was killing him. But he never said a word to me, even though he was getting a lot of pressure from people because of my politics."

Goetz was a child of the '60s in an environment that came straight out of the '50s. It was a relief for him when Foster accepted the job at Utah. Even though Utah was an even more conservative place than Rutgers, it was not the same place where Goetz had been a student and he didn't feel caught in the middle.

It was at Utah that Goetz became Foster's major confidant. He was the person Foster leaned on. That meant a lot of late nights for Goetz, sitting up with Foster and Bob Wenzel—who had come to Utah as a graduate assistant—trying to figure out how to get the Utes turned around.

"I didn't have much of a social life during those years," Goetz said, laughing. "The experience at Utah was a tough one, but it was also a good one. Sitting up all those nights with Bill was really how I got to know him. I had never been that close to him when I played for him because he isn't the kind of coach you get that close to. You look up to him but you don't get close to him.

"But at Utah, we spent a lot of time together. Bill is a very driven man, driven, I think, by a fear of failure more than anything. While we were at Utah, I began to understand that."

Goetz was delighted when Foster got the Duke job. He had never been entirely comfortable in Salt Lake City and he felt guilty about recruiting black kids from the East into the lily-white atmosphere. At Duke, he was back in the East at a school he felt very comfortable selling to anyone.

Just as he had done at Utah, Goetz spent a lot of time keeping Foster sane, especially during the trying first three seasons. Goetz loved it. He loved the school, the atmosphere at the games, and the kind of people on the basketball team. The only problem was the losing. Then, in February of 1977, things turned around.

First came Gene Banks's announcement that he was coming to Duke. Later that same month, during an otherwise disastrous trip to West Virginia and Pittsburgh, Goetz was invited to the home of Dick Groat. If there is a legendary figure in Duke sports history, it is Groat. Until Gminski's number was retired in 1980, Groat's number 10 was the only number that had ever been retired at the school. He played baseball and basketball there and is one of a handful of men to have ever played in both the NBA and the major leagues. After three years in the NBA, he decided to only play baseball and became an All-Star shortstop. He retired after playing with the Pittsburgh Pirates and still lives in Pittsburgh.

Goetz was visiting Groat, paying a visit to a distinguished Duke alumnus, when Groat's daughter, Tracy, came home from a night on the town with several girlfriends. "She and her friends were bombed," Goetz remembered. "But she was a knockout."

Six weeks later, during the Final Four in Atlanta, Goetz ran into Groat, who mentioned that Tracy was on the trip with him. Goetz called her, they spent most of the next four days together and, to make a long story short, they were married nine months later in the Duke Gardens. "At first I was embarrassed by the way I felt," Goetz said. "She was twenty, I was thirty. But by the end of the weekend in Atlanta, I knew I was going to marry her."

Their honeymoon was the 1978 season. "Tracy thought we went to the Final Four all the time," Goetz said. "She hadn't been there for all the bleeding."

The team's success that season brought Goetz a lot of attention. As often happens when a team does well, the top assistant becomes a candidate for head coaching jobs. "The more we won," Goetz said, "the better coach I became. I understood how the game was played. I knew this was the time when I had to make my move."

He accepted the Richmond job the day after the Kentucky game. "It was one of the hardest things I've ever done in my life. I knew it had to be and I had to go out on my own. But I had been with Bill for fourteen years. I loved Duke and felt like I was leaving with one more thing left to do. That's why I cried in the locker room after we lost to Kentucky. I hated the thought that I wasn't going to be part of this team anymore."

He took over a program at Richmond that was in horrendous shape, having just gone 4–22. His first move was to talk his old coach, Tarrant, into coming to Richmond as his top assistant. Then he went about rebuilding. "I did," he said, "all the Bill Foster things."

And, like Bill Foster, he steadily rebuilt the program. The team went from 4 wins to 10 wins to 14 wins to 15 wins. The third year, Richmond came up one victory short of getting into the NCAA Tournament. The Spiders hadn't signed Gene Banks, but they weren't playing in the

ACC. Goetz had brought in good players who knew how to compete.

But after three years of building, Goetz wasn't happy. He had verbally agreed to a four-year contract, with a clause that would automatically extend the contract at the end of each season. But when Goetz was handed his contract, the rollover clause wasn't in it. "We'll take care of it later," he was told.

"I was naive," Goetz said. "I just wanted to sign and get to work. I signed."

He never got the rollover clause. At the end of his third season, Goetz went to the school president for a contract extension. Wait till next year, he was told. Goetz walked out of the meeting furious.

"I had a lot of different thoughts right then," he said. "My son had been born in April and each time I went on the road it was tougher and tougher. I had watched Bill from up close all those years spending so much time on the road while his daughters were growing up. I didn't want to be an absentee father. I felt the school had let me down. For the first time in my adult life, I started to think about life without coaching."

While at Duke, Goetz had become close to a man named Barry Bergman, who ran a string of record stores, The Record Bar, in the Durham area. When he told Bergman how frustrated he was at Richmond, Bergman suggested he come to work for him. Goetz thought about it for a week. "I finally decided to tell Richmond to go to hell," he said. "That part was easy. The tough part was telling the players. I can still remember four of the guys coming into my office and asking me if it was true I was leaving. I told them yes, then we all sat down and cried.

"*That's* what made coaching special for me. The relationships with the players. I always wanted to feel like I could be a positive influence on someone's life. Walking away from that was very, very hard to do. It was hard at Duke, hard at Richmond. But in both cases, it was something I had to do."

After more than twenty years of building his life around basketball, Goetz shut himself off from the sport completely. He didn't go to games, watch games, or talk about the game. He knew who was winning and who was losing from reading the newspaper, but that was it. He didn't keep up with coaching fraternity gossip. And, he found out that he was still breathing in spite of it. Then, eighteen months after Goetz quit coaching, Foster had his heart attack.

"I had never in my life tried to tell him what to do," he said. "But now was the time. I wanted very badly to convince him there was something else in life besides coaching. I thought this was the time for him to gracefully get out of it and go on to something else. But I don't think he heard me."

Goetz stayed at The Record Bar as the personnel director for three years. In the meantime, Tracy went to work for a local real estate company. She did so well that eventually she bought the company. Two years later she sold it, for a substantial profit, to Merrill-Lynch Realty and signed a five-year contract to manage the company for Merrill. Watching his wife do so well in real estate intrigued Goetz. He decided to try his hand at it and formed his own small development company.

"I'm just now getting to the point where I might have some real success with it," he said. "It's a challenge for me and I like that. I need that. I need to feel like I'm competing for something and I get that from what I'm doing now."

As successful as he is, as happy as he is with two young children, a beautiful wife, and a lifestyle that gets him home from work at a reasonable hour every night, Goetz admits he sometimes misses coaching.

"If there's one thing in life I know I'm trained to do and do well, it's coach," he said. "Sometimes I think about coaching again, but I know I tend to focus on the good things, on the things I enjoyed.

"I'd like my son to be a player. I was a pretty good player and his grandfather was a great player. So he has the genes. But will he have the toughness? Will he have the desire to go out and play six hours a day? I don't know. If I coached, he would. But every time I think that, I know I don't have the drive to do it again. The carrot just isn't out there for me. I coached in the national final. For a lot of guys, that's not enough. For me, it was. I feel very good about what we accomplished."

Goetz knows that the team is virtually unanimous in pointing to his leaving as one of the keys to the failures of '79. He feels flattered by that but doesn't want to be made into a hero. "There were things that were going to happen to that team no matter what," he said. "The expectations were going to be there, no matter what. The pressures that come with success too.

"What happened to us in '78 was unique because there was no master plan. It wasn't *necessary*. We had this strange mix of personalities that just clicked. If you tried to plan a group like that, it would never happen. There was luck involved. John Harrell walked in off the street. Terry Chili discovered Gminski. But one thing about that team: It never backed down to anyone.

"And you know what else? Losing to Kentucky, in the grand scheme of things, didn't matter that much. Really, it didn't. Bill still would have been unhappy and he still would have left. Beyond that, the sense of pride we all feel now wouldn't be a lot different. We got more out of the experience than Kentucky did because we were playing for *ourselves*. Kentucky, players and coaches, played to satisfy everyone else. Our joy will never go away. Never."

Goetz is speaking almost in a whisper, the memories clear in his mind. He enjoys going to games in Cameron now, sitting up in the stands and watching. When one of the guys comes back for a game, he inevitably finds Goetz and the story-trading begins.

"When people are important in your life," Goetz said, "they never fade. If anything, your feeling for them grows stronger because as you get older, you understand the experience you lived together was unique."

Last season, when he was back at Duke for his annual visit, Gminski spent some time with Goetz. At the end of their talk, after all the kidding, joking, and insulting, Gminski turned serious for a moment. "There's something I'd like you to do for me," he said, turning for a second into the shy teenager he was when he first came to Duke. "I'd like you to come see me play an NBA game. You've never seen me play as a pro."

Goetz, touched that Gminski felt that way, nodded. "I'll get there, Mike," he said. "I promise."

Goetz didn't understand completely, but Gminski's request made perfect sense. Like his teammates, he wanted his Jewish mother to see that he had listened and he had learned.

What Gminski couldn't know was that when his Jewish mother thinks about him and his teammates, he smiles. All of them have accomplished the impossible. They have given their Jewish mother enough.

31

The Little Buckaroo

He worked his way through the lobby like a politician working the polls on election day. Everyone was an old friend. Names rolled off his tongue easily. If he spied someone he couldn't get over to say hello to, he waved enthusiastically. In the lobby of the coaches' convention hotel at the Final Four, Ray Jones was in his element.

"Actually, it makes sense that I would know everybody," he said, laughing. "After all, I've worked just about everywhere in the country."

Almost. He has gone from Jacksonville to Houston to Cincinnati to Duke to Furman to South Carolina to Minnesota to Wyoming. At the very least, he has covered all the regions. He is forty-two now, eleven years and four jobs removed from his two years at Duke. He is the epitome of the transient college basketball coach. Yet, no one associated with the 1978 team becomes more emotional when talking about those days than Jones.

"When I try to explain to people what that experience was and what it meant to me, they look at me like I'm crazy," he said. "It's impossible to explain it. To me, those two years were like the three years John Kennedy was president. It was Camelot. Nothing in my life, before or since, has been like it."

It has been a life full of adventure almost since the day he was born in Clifton, New Jersey, with two holes in his heart. He had congenital heart disease and the doctors told his parents that his chances for survival were not good.

He was always sick as a little boy; he had to make four trips a year to a cardiologist. When he was five, he asked his parents why he couldn't go out and play like the other little boys. They explained to him that he had a problem with his heart and had to be careful.

"Am I going to die?" he asked them, not quite sure what that involved. They told him no, but he always had to be careful.

His father, Raymond Robert Jones, Sr., was a superb athlete, a bicyclist skilled enough to qualify for the U.S. team that went to the 1936 Olympics in Berlin. After that, he served under Patton during World War Two and came home to marry his high school sweetheart, Norma Liptak. He started his own trucking company, "Ray's Parcel Service," and quickly made it a success. Raymond Jr. was a baby boomer, arriving in 1946.

By the time he was twelve, the doctors told Ray and Norma Jones that without open heart surgery Ray Jr. would probably live for less than another year. His heart was enlarged and was not properly pumping blood into the rest of his body. The Joneses first took their son to the best hospital in the area to meet the doctors there. The chief surgeon explained to Ray Sr. that while he had never done this operation on a human being before, he had performed it successfully on chimpanzees.

"Chimpanzees!" Ray Jones roared. "You must be kidding. This is my son we're talking about. You can kiss my ass before you can operate on him!"

Little Ray was shocked. He had never heard his father talk that way before.

Two months later, just before Ray was to fly to the Mayo Clinic in Minnesota for the heart surgery, Ray Jones Sr. had a heart attack at the age of forty-three. "It was a wonderful Christmas at our house," his son remembered. Several weeks later, Ray and his mother flew to the Mayo Clinic, and two weeks after that, the surgery was performed. But within a week of returning home, Ray was having terrible trouble breathing. The doctors told his mother to bring him back. One of the holes in the ventricle had reopened. There was no choice but to operate again.

The day before the surgery was scheduled, Dr. John Kirkland came to see Ray. He wanted him to understand why the surgery was necessary. In a scene straight out of a movie, Ray Jones looked up at the doctor and said, "What are my chances, doc?"

John Kirkland didn't believe in lying to patients, no matter what their age. He thought they should know what they were dealing with.

"With the surgery, you've got about a twenty percent chance to live," he said. "Without it, you've got no chance. The only thing I can promise you is that if you do die, it won't hurt. You'll never feel a thing."

To Ray Jones, this was almost a relief. "At that age, you're more scared of pain than of dying," he said. "My mother was furious that the doctor told me what was going on. But actually, he didn't tell me everything. He didn't tell me I was only the third patient to come back for a second operation and that the first two had died."

Ray Jones survived the surgery. This time, the sewing held and he was able to compete, on a limited basis, in sports. He never grew beyond 5-3 because of his heart problems (his dad is 6-1) and his mother went crazy whenever he went out to play ball. But he played anyway. "I once told my mother that I would rather die than just sit in a chair my whole life and do nothing," he said. "She couldn't understand. I needed to feel like I was as normal as was possible."

His father passed on his love of sports. He took Ray and his brother Ron to Yankee Stadium to see both the Yankees and the football Giants and to Madison Square Garden to see the Knicks. When Ray went to LaSalle, he became a manager on the basketball team.

By then, he knew he wanted to coach. People told him that wasn't possible. He had never played the game and he was too short. Jones went home after graduation, and worked as a part-time coach and substitute teacher at his old high school. During that year, he met and fell in love with Rita Santobono. They were married on August 7, 1971. Six days later, his mother died of cancer at the age of fifty.

"That was a very tough time for me," he said. "Watching the disease kill my mother killed me. She insisted that we go through with the wedding. She was in a wheelchair, but she was there. We had been so close when I was a kid because of all the time I spent going to doctors and now here I was just starting my adult life and she was gone. It really hurt."

He worked at meeting people in the coaching profession, hitchhiking to summer basketball camps, working the circuit. Shortly after marrying Rita, Tom Wadsden, the coach at Jacksonville, offered him a job—with no pay. Jones found a paying job at a local high school— getting himself hired by a man who had picked him up when he was hitchhiking—so he and Rita headed for Jacksonville. A year later, he moved to Houston as a graduate assistant, two years later to Cincinnati as a full-time assistant. He made his reputation by being hard-nosed and hardworking. No one would outwork Ray Jones recruiting a player. The three schools all recruited the inner city and Jones became comfortable dealing with inner-city blacks and their families. They also recruited right on the edge of—or over—the line between illegal and legal. Both Jacksonville and Cincinnati ended up on probation during the 1970s. Ray Jones learned the tricks of his trade in the school of hard knocks.

"Let's put it this way," he said. "I'm not proud of everything I've done in coaching. I'm no virgin."

But that kind of experience made him the kind of coach Foster thought could help Duke. He, Goetz, and Wenzel had all been at the same places at the same time. Jones's recruiting experience was more varied—and more streetwise.

"I think they had been kind of pollyanna in their approach," Jones said. "They felt that kids should want to go to Duke because it was a great school. With some kids, that worked. But with others, you had to dig, dig, and dig. Be with them constantly, make them think they were the most important thing in the world to you. Until Banks, I don't think they had ever approached recruiting a kid that way."

Jones was immediately popular with the Duke players. They heaped nicknames on him. "Electric" came first and then Max Crowder started calling him "Short Fuse," after he went off during a JV game. But the one that fit was "Little Buckaroo." When Foster's daughter Mary, then three years old, started calling Jones "The Little Buckaroo," it was evident that was the one that was going to stick.

Jones was especially close to Gminski, the classic giant-mouse friendship, and to Bob Bender, whom he had recruited long and hard while at Cincinnati. His job at Duke was to recruit, recruit, and recruit some more. He had almost no responsibilities on the floor. John Harrell, in his first year, wasn't even sure Jones was a coach because he almost never saw him on the practice floor.

But he was very much part of the team. He and Wenzel shared an office where players spent a lot of time clowning around. Jones was responsible for the signing of Jim Suddath that first year; the next year he played a key role in the successful recruitment of Vince Taylor. He was part of Camelot.

"When we added Banks and Dennard, it changed the team completely," Jones said. "It had been a long time since Duke had had two inside guys who were as tough as they were. Spanarkel was tough, but he was a guard. These guys just got after you every single night. When we went up to Maryland in January and kicked their butt, I knew we were good. When we blew Maryland out of Cameron the first week in February, I thought we were the best team in the ACC. It just went from there except for Ford having that unbelievable game against us in Chapel Hill."

Jones was an icebreaker when things got tight. On the morning of the ACC final against Wake Forest, he sensed that everyone was down because the opponent wasn't North Carolina. The pregame meal, usually so lighthearted and up, was almost silent. Finally, Jones stood up and threw down his napkin. "That fucking Dean!" he yelled. "The one time we wanted him to win, he loses. All he ever does is screw us!"

The whole room cracked up and was immediately filled with Dean jokes.

Being associated with Duke was important to Jones. He loved the campus and the players and the whole idea of being at a school where you could win with players who would graduate. At his three previous schools, they had won—period.

"That was my feeling when we made it to the Final Four," he said. "By then, I knew we had a good team and even though it had seemed farfetched at the start of the season, by that time we were clearly good enough to be there. But when I looked around the locker room and saw guys like Spanarkel and Harold Morrison and Bruce Bell and Gminski, I thought, 'Christ, no one has ever gotten to the Final Four with a group of guys like this.' We had a group of guys who just didn't think they could lose. You know what that team had? That team had *chutzpah.*"

Jones was as pumped to play Notre Dame as anyone. He had recruited against them both at Cincinnati and at Duke and was no fan of Digger Phelps. There was also the mystique of Notre Dame for someone who had been raised as a Catholic.

"When we won that game, it was a feeling like I've never had in my life," he said. "I went into the locker room with the guys for a few minutes and then I had to get off by myself. I couldn't stop crying. I thought about being twelve years old and the doctor telling me I had a twenty-percent chance to live through surgery. I thought about being told I was too short to be a coach. I thought about my mom. Then I called my dad and my brother and we all cried."

As he tells the story, Ray Jones is crying again. "I'm sorry," he said. "This isn't something I'm good at putting into words."

They all cried again after the Kentucky game and Jones can still recite Bell's prayer almost word for word. "Two things I remember about that game. I remember that SOB Jim Bain calling that ridiculous technical on Bill like this was some CYO game and I remember going back on the court and all the fans chanting, 'We'll be back.' "

But Jones never had the chance to come back. When Goetz left, he felt he deserved to move into the slot vacated by Wenzel, who moved up to Goetz's spot. Foster felt he needed someone taller to work with the big men. He hired Steve Steinwedel and asked Jones to continue in the same job. Jones couldn't deal with that. When Ed Holbrook called and offered him a full-time job at Furman, he accepted.

"God, I hated leaving," he said. "I was devastated when he didn't move me up. Just devastated. I couldn't believe he didn't have faith in me. I'll always wonder what would have happened if I had been around the next two years. Maybe nothing would have been different. Or maybe I could have gotten a couple of really good players who would have inspired him to stay. Who knows? All I know is, it was Camelot. But it didn't last."

Two years later when Foster moved to South Carolina, he brought Jones back. The reunion was a happy one at first. Then Foster had his heart attack. Wenzel left after one year and the two full-time assistants, ironically enough, were Jones and Steinwedel. Word went out on the recruiting grapevine that Foster was too ill to coach. South Carolina started losing players and losing games. By the summer of 1985 it was apparent to the coaching staff that if the Gamecocks didn't turn things around that winter, they would be gone—Foster's post-heart attack contract extension notwithstanding.

With all that on his mind, Jones went to see his doctor on a hot July afternoon, wanting to know why he was feeling pain when he urinated. The doctor wasn't certain what the problem was but suggested he soak in a hot tub every day for a week, then come see him again if the pain persisted. It did. The doctor ran some tests. They were virtually identical to the tests the doctor in Kansas City ran on Kenny Dennard almost three years earlier. And the results were the same. "We have to do a biopsy, Ray," the doctor told him.

Alarm bells went off in Jones's head. His mother had died of cancer at fifty. He was thirty-eight. "I was really frightened," he said.

The biopsy showed a malignant tumor, although, as with Dennard, it didn't appear to have spread. That meant radiation treatments. Initially, Jones went every day at midmorning, but sitting in a waiting room full of children waiting for their treatment was more than he could bear. He found a nurse willing to come in at 7 A.M. to give him his treatment. "I just couldn't look at the kids," he said. "It was bad enough for me, but the kids . . . *Jesus.*"

Jones's own children were five and four at the time. Once, as a five-year-old, he had asked his parents if he was going to die. Now, his son, Raymond Robert Jones III, asked him if he was going to die. Just as his parents had done thirty-three years earlier, he shook his head and said no.

"I was never really afraid of dying," he said. "I didn't want to die and I really didn't think after all I had been through that this was going to be what got me. I just didn't believe it. But there were times when I thought about not getting to see my kids grow up, missing out on all that, and I got hysterical. Rita and I waited nine years to have children; it was a big decision, one that we didn't take lightly. Now, I faced the possibility of not being around my kids. That was the part I couldn't deal with."

But the tumor didn't spread and, even though he was weak and ill for a while, Jones never missed any work. South Carolina offered a paid leave of absence, which he refused. Unfortunately, eight months later, after a 12–16 season, he, Foster, and the entire coaching staff were asked to take a permanent leave of absence. That wasn't the worst of it. Not only were they fired, but they were being investigated by the NCAA for rules violations.

It took a year for Jones to clear his name of the major charges made against him—most notably, he was accused of running a ticket-selling operation, a charge he proved, to the satisfaction of the NCAA infractions committee, untrue.

That year was a nightmare for Jones. He was hired by Minnesota, then taken off the road during the NCAA investigation. The controversy damaged his reputation and ended his friendship with Foster. He and Rita separated briefly. He was fighting his health the whole time. "It was not a great time in the life of the little buckaroo," he said. "If the cancer had killed me, that would definitely have been worse than what was happening. But that was about the only thing that would have been worse."

Slowly though, things turned back around for Jones. He was hired at Wyoming as a full-time assistant to new coach Benny Dees in the spring of 1987. He and Rita got back together. His health improved.

He loves living in Wyoming. What little buckaroo wouldn't? After two years, he is comfortable there, as is his family. He has recruited well for Dees. He was a candidate for the head coaching job at Northern Illinois last spring but withdrew his name because he thought it would be almost impossible to build a winning program there.

"I would like to be a head coach someday," he said. "I don't know if I'll ever get the chance though. But I won't go someplace where I feel like I have to cheat to win. I know that sounds like BS because I have made mistakes in the past. But emotionally, I couldn't go through it again. I just couldn't be happy doing it the wrong way.

"I'm not trying to claim I'm perfect, but I have learned a lot of lessons, most of them the hard way. I'm forty-two now and if I make another coaching move, I'd like it to be my last. I love coaching, even though I've had my ups and downs. I had one experience that was truly special in my life and that was at Duke.

"There are still times when I catch myself daydreaming about those days. I can see the students all running into Cameron before a game to get the best seats. I tried to convince Wyoming to go to festival seating for the students downstairs but they wouldn't do it. Then I realized that was silly. You can't manufacture that kind of thing any more than you can manufacture innocence or any emotion.

"What we had at Duke was something that happens once in a lifetime—if you're lucky. When the word first got out that I had cancer, the first phone call I got was from Kenny Dennard. He wanted me to know what I was dealing with and wanted to make sure I knew all the statistics about how good the survival rate was. He came down just to spend a couple of days with me. Gminski called. And Bender. And Wenz. It didn't matter if I had heard from them for a while or not. It would be the same with anyone connected with that team. If someone needs help, the guys would be there. I don't think I can say that about any other team I've been associated with. It was just different. I can't tell you exactly why."

One story that Jones remembers might explain why. On the night of Duke's victory over Notre Dame, he and Rita were having dinner in an Italian restaurant with their friend Frank Dascenzo, the sports editor of the *Durham Sun.* Guy Lewis, who had been Jones's boss at Houston, walked in. He walked over to the table, shook Jones's hand and said, "Little guy, you've come a long way. No one thought you'd ever be where you are tonight."

Jones starts to cry again as he finishes the story. "It's been thirty years since my heart surgery," he said. "I guess I'm a survivor. For me, the future is tomorrow, that's the way I look at it. But there's no question, I've never felt more alive than I did that year at Duke. If the Good Lord came down from the sky and said to me, 'One wish little buckaroo,' it would be to go back there."

He smiled. "And to have all those guys back there with me."

Camelot is long gone. But in Ray Jones's memory it remains very much alive.

32

Wenz

The tension in Louis Brown Arena had been building for most of two hours. Now it was almost unbearable. The team that was supposed to win, Penn State, had led most of the evening, once by 11 points. But the underdog home team, Rutgers, kept scrapping back. This was a team that, a year ago, had won just seven games. Their home games were played in a virtually empty arena.

Now, the place was almost full, alive with noise. It was February 3 and already Rutgers had won as many games as it had a year ago—seven.

But Penn State was a bigger fish. Nittany Lions Coach Bruce Parkhill had steadily put together a solid program and they were rated just a notch below the two powers of the Atlantic 10 Conference, West Virginia and Temple. Considering that Rutgers had finished tenth a year ago, this was Penn State's game to win.

Only Rutgers, with its aggressive rookie coach, didn't know that. The game was in overtime and the Knights led 79–78 with ninety seconds left. They had the ball. Bob Wenzel, the rookie coach, Rutgers Class of '71, stood in front of his bench directing his team's offense. He sensed a kill and he wanted his best player, Tom Savage, to take the shot. Point guard Rick Dadika drove to the right, stopped and reversed the ball to Savage, who had popped from behind a screen on the other side of the floor. Savage was a step behind the three-point line when he caught the ball. He never hesitated. Swish. The building exploded. Rutgers led 82–78. Penn State was dead.

"Boy, did that one feel good!" Wenzel said when it was over. "That's the kind of game you have to win to regenerate interest in the program. We've got a long way to go, but we'll get there."

As always, Bob Wenzel brims with confidence and self-assurance. He has come back to his alma mater to rebuild a fallen, once-proud program in much the same way that he came to Duke as an assistant to Bill Foster in 1974. Back then, Foster wondered *if;* Lou Goetz wondered *how;* Bob Wenzel only wondered *when.*

"That was always my role," he says with a laugh. "Bill was the worrier, Lou was the thinker, and I was the ass-kicker. We would sit around and talk about a team for a while and shake our heads and analyze and reanalyze. In the end I was always the guy who stood up and said, 'Hell, we're gonna kick their ass.' "

They didn't always do so, but Wenzel's instincts and self-belief were almost always right when it mattered most. Wenzel was the first one to believe that Gene Banks could be successfully recruited. He was the first to think the ACC title could be won in '78 and he, more than anyone, was absolutely convinced Duke would beat Notre Dame. He also thought the Blue Devils would beat Kentucky.

"Any game you play you can go back to a play here, a play there, and what-if it," he said. "But the technical Jim Bain called on Bill, I swear I can still see the whole thing as if I was looking at a tape right now. Spanarkel makes a great play, jumping in front of the kid [Truman Claytor] and Bain freezes. Bill never says a word. I mean, damn, how ridiculous was that call?

"See, the thing is, that call bothers me more now than it did then. When we lost that game, the feelings of pride and togetherness and look-what-we-just-did still overwhelmed all the other emotions. Now, eleven years have gone by and I've never been back. None of us have. You realize how hard it is to do and that it may not come again. *That's* when Jim Bain really pisses you off."

As he talks, Wenzel is sitting in Patty's, a small restaurant a few blocks from the Rutgers campus. It was in this same restaurant, eighteen years ago, that he met his first wife, Sue Bloch. "I was walking in, she was walking out," he said, smiling. "I was a senior, captain of the basketball team. She was a freshman and I mean, she was beautiful. She walked by me and said, 'I like the way you play.' I took one look at her and did a U-turn."

He smiles, warmed by the memory. It is a dreary, rainy day but Wenzel is still aglow after the victory over Penn State. He is doing exactly what his mentor, Foster, did here twenty-five years ago—building from scratch. For someone who never for a moment considered coaching as a career until the day he started coaching, Bob Wenzel has become quite a coach.

"Even now, I still relate a lot of my experiences back to playing," he said. "When I was growing up, all I did was play, play, play. I never thought about the games as anything but competition. Even now, I almost never give my players scouting reports. I just say, 'Let's go play.'"

He grew up on Long Island, the second of six children. His father, Arthur Wenzel, graduated from college at sixteen, went to work at Chemical Bank and never left, working his way up from the bottom to a vice presidency. His mother, Lillian, was, in Wenzel's words, "a classic mother. There was nothing she wouldn't do for her children."

The Wenzels moved from the Bronx to Long Island when Bob was five and all six Wenzel children went to West Islip High School, a giant, middle class suburban high school. There, Bob Wenzel was a star. He was captain of the football, basketball, and baseball teams and twenty-fifth in a class of three hundred. He even dated the head cheerleader.

He was recruited by most of the eastern schools and chose Rutgers because it was close to home, it had gotten a lot of attention with its run to third place in the 1967 NIT, and because both starting guards, Bob Lloyd and Jim Valvano, were graduating. He thought he would have a good chance to play.

His freshman coach was Valvano. "He was a lousy coach," Wenzel said, laughing. "He didn't play me enough."

Wenzel didn't play much as a sophomore either but as a junior became a starter. He scored 34 points in the first game of the season and went from there to stardom. He was a typical late-'60s college student with long hair and the same antiwar attitude that Goetz—three years older than he—had. He was into Buddhism for a while. "I was more into it on dates than anytime else. I used to quote it a lot. I thought of myself as a young rebel but all I ever really did was talk about being rebellious and wear sloppy clothes. It never got much further than that."

Wenzel was a big man on campus and enjoyed every second of it. "I was into three things at that point in my life," he says. "Basketball, fun, and school. My last two years, I always thought I would play pro ball when I graduated. I knew I wasn't a great player, but I thought

I was good. I always thought I was good no matter what I was doing."

He wasn't quite good enough to make it in the pros, though. He went to camp with the Carolina Cougars of the American Basketball Association and made it to the final cut. But when Coach Jerry Steele made his last cut it was Wenzel he called in to tell he was sorry. It was too late to catch on with anyone else and the phone wasn't ringing off the hook. Wenzel called Foster, who had just moved to Utah. Foster had an opening for a graduate assistant. Wenzel got on a plane, took the job, and enrolled in graduate courses at Utah.

During his two years there, he played a lot of basketball, staying in shape, working out all the time. In the back of his mind was the notion that he would take another shot at playing pro basketball. Even now, he wishes that he had done that. "I guess I'll always believe that if I had gone back and tried again the next year, I would have made it," he said. "It really took me a long time to get over being cut because I thought I was good enough. It wasn't until we got to Duke that I really started to think of myself as a basketball coach, not a player who was doing some coaching."

He and Sue Bloch were married after Wenzel's first year at Utah. They lived in an apartment in the married-student housing section of the university for eighty-two dollars a month. Foster cut a deal with a local furniture store to get them furniture. Wenzel began to enjoy coaching. The all-night sessions with Foster weren't as tough on him as they were on Goetz because he was married and had someone to go home to regardless of the hour. After two years at Utah he got a full-time job at Yale. He was there one year when the call came from Foster to join him at Duke. It was then that the coaching bug really bit him.

"I'll never forget being in Greensboro at the Final Four with Bill a few days before he was going to formally take the job," Wenzel said. "The word was out that he was going to Duke and Lefty Driesell walked up to us in the lobby and said, 'Bill, you got the worst talent in the league at Duke. You guys ain't got a thing.'

"We knew it was going to be rough but not *how* rough. The league was a bitch. Cameron's facilities—locker room, weight room, offices—were terrible. The feeling on campus seemed to be you couldn't win at a school with good academics. The academics were a crutch. They were used to losing. But Bill, Lou, and I were very comfortable together and we knew exactly what had to be done. Bill had been through it before and he was completely organized from day one."

Wenzel was the consummate recruiter. He was young and eager;

players could relate to him. He was handsome and charming, perfect when dealing with the mothers. He was also selling two products he believed in—Duke and Bill Foster. Through those first three years Wenzel was always the guy whose head never seemed to droop, even when Foster was nearly apoplectic about a tough loss. When Banks committed to Duke, Wenzel raced through the basketball offices all day long yelling, "The worm has turned folks, the worm has turned.

"I always tell people that The Force was with us that '78 season," Wenzel said. "I think, in a way I appreciate it as much as anyone on that team because I've had so many basketball experiences since then. For a lot of the players, basketball was over shortly after that season. But for me, there's been a lot of basketball, a lot of it good, some of it not so good. It's made me appreciate how extraordinary what we did that year was.

"There was a lot of luck involved. I know people always wonder what went wrong the next two years and second-guess a lot of things. I've done that myself. But you know what? We couldn't really have changed anything. If you try to make people something they aren't, they fail. Suppose we had made Kenny Dennard into an altar boy? He would have been a lousy player. The same with Banks. You take people as they are and do the best you can. We had one year where that was enough and two others where it almost was, but wasn't."

Wenzel was disappointed when Foster decided to leave Duke but knew there was nothing that would stop him. He also hoped he would be given the chance to succeed him, but Tom Butters wanted someone from outside. When Mike Krzyzewski was hired, Wenzel followed Foster to South Carolina. The move put a strain on his marriage. Sue had been working at the *Durham Sun* as a feature writer; leaving wasn't easy for her. She got a job in Columbia working for the state film office but was not terribly happy.

For Foster, the move worked superbly—at first. "He was as happy as I've ever seen him," Wenzel said. "He was a hero because he was going to rebuild. He was doing all the things he liked doing to put a program back together. He felt appreciated. But for me, it wasn't the same. I missed Duke. Being an independent was great for Bill because there was control over the schedule and none of the constant intensity of league play.

"But I *missed* that. I lived for *the battle* and the full arena, even on the road. We played some games that year in front of nine hundred people. The fun just wasn't there for me."

At the end of that season, Wenzel interviewed for four head coaching jobs: George Washington, Rice, the College of Charleston, and Jacksonville. He thought Rice would be perfect for him because it was much like Duke, an academic school trying to play big-time basketball. But he didn't get the job, much to his surprise. He did, however, get the Jacksonville job.

"It was a real rebuilding situation," he said. "The place was in shambles in every way. But in a sense, that was perfect for me. That was exactly what I had always been involved with under Bill."

It wasn't perfect for his marriage though. Sue couldn't deal with yet another move. When Bob went to Jacksonville she went back to Durham where, ironically, she got a job working for the Duke alumni magazine. As might be expected, Bob buried himself in the rebuilding process at Jacksonville.

After he and Sue were divorced, Wenzel didn't stay single for very long. He had known Neva Lapan since Rutgers and, after he and Sue separated, they began dating. "It was very comfortable because we had been friends for so long," he said. "It wasn't like starting from scratch with a stranger." Two years later, they were married.

It was during Wenzel's second season at Jacksonville that Foster had his heart attack. Like Goetz, he went to Columbia to see his old boss. Wenzel was thirty-two at the time and had never given much thought to mortality. Seeing Foster in the hospital made him realize that there was a lot more to life than winning games. Here was Foster who had built and won, built and won. But where had it gotten him?

"It didn't deter me from what I was doing," he said. "But it made me think about not letting it consume me. I want success. I'm definitely someone who is drawn to the limelight. But the limelight only does so much for you."

Wenzel was quickly in the limelight in Jacksonville. After winning seven games during his first year, the Dolphins improved steadily. In a city of 700,000 with no pro teams, Jacksonville was *it* for local sports fans. Wenzel quickly became a popular figure. He was turning the team around, he was articulate and approachable. His fourth season looked like the one when the school would return to postseason play. The Dolphins were 13–9 when Sun Belt Conference rival South Alabama came to town for a key game on the second Saturday in February. "We were right on the verge of becoming very good," Wenzel said. "We were still a little young, but gaining confidence. I knew if we could win that game, we were going to at least make the NIT, maybe even have a shot at the NCAA's. Every game seems like a big one when you're building, but this one really was. We had a packed house and a team that was ready to take a step up."

Before the game, Wenzel felt a little bit sick. A virus had been going around and he thought he might be coming down with it, a thought he dreaded.

"Once the game started, I forgot about it," he said. "But about midway through the first half, I stood up to yell something at one of the guys and all of a sudden I felt like someone had hit me over the head with a sledgehammer. I fell back onto the bench and for a second I thought I was going to black out. But the pain passed and I went back to coaching. I really felt lousy in the second half but I got through it. We won the game and I did my press conference just like normal.

"But my head really hurt and I felt nauseous. I let Neva drive home because I felt kind of dizzy. By the time we got home, I knew I was really sick."

In the car, Neva Wenzel asked her husband if he wanted to go to the hospital. He said no, just wanting to get home and into bed. But when he couldn't stop vomiting after they got home, she called the team doctor, Duane Bork. He told her to take Bob to the hospital immediately. By that point, Bob felt so sick he didn't think he could walk to the car. "I practically carried him," Neva said.

At the hospital, Bork ran several tests. This was clearly not just a virus. Bork tested Wenzel's reflexes. They didn't respond. Bork sent for a neurologist. He explained to Wenzel that they were going to take some fluid from his spine. Wenzel asked what for.

"We want to see if there's any leakage at all in your brain," Bork said. "We'll be able to tell right away. If the fluid comes out clear, then that isn't the problem. If it comes out pink, then there's probably some kind of aneurysm that we'll have to deal with."

Wenzel understood. He was still lucid and the pain in his head, while steady, wasn't unbearable. He had no idea that he had already been in the hospital for almost three hours. The doctors ran the test. "When they looked at the fluid," Wenzel said, "it was blood red. The next thing I knew everyone was grabbing my head, pushing me back on the bed and saying, '*Do not move your head. Stay absolutely still.*'" This was no small aneurysm. Wenzel was sedated almost immediately because the doctors were afraid that any sharp movement of his head would burst a blood vessel and kill him. The only question now was when to operate. To do so immediately was risky because of potential clotting. The best thing to do was wait for as much as a week, although that too was risky. Either way, the risk factor was high. "Fifty percent of the people who have an aneurysm like this don't make it to the operating table," Wenzel said. "Fifty percent of those who do don't make it *off* the table."

Wenzel had been born with this defect in his brain, a tiny leak that had now opened up. The only way one ever finds out that he or she has this leak is if it pops, as Wenzel's now had. The doctors explained the situation to Neva. They decided to wait. If they could keep Bob alive for a week and then operate, his chances for survival would increase greatly.

Wenzel spent most of the next week drifting in and out of a drug-induced haze. At times, he knew how serious his condition was. At others, he had no clue. "I remembered we had a game with Old Dominion and a lot of the time my only thought was that I had to get the hell out of here and coach the game. I remember telling the doctors that I had to go coach the game and then I would come right back and they could operate."

When he was lucid enough to understand what was going on, Wenzel thought often about his son, Alex, who was six months old at the time. "When Alex was born, it was, without question, the peak experience of my life," he said. "When I was in the hospital I thought about him a lot and when I did, I would start to cry. The thought that I might never see him again tormented me and, more than anything, scared me."

Most of the fear was felt by Neva, who did not have the advantage of being sedated most of the time. She forced herself not to think the worst but instead to prepare for her husband's recovery. Fortunately, she was kept busy, not only with Alex and the time she spent at the hospital but with answering constant questions about Bob's condition. Bob Wenzel had become a big man in Jacksonville and his illness was daily front-page news.

One week after he entered the hospital, Wenzel underwent brain surgery. In theory, the operation was simple: Open up the cranium and place a clip on the broken blood vessel. The operation took seven and one-half hours. Throughout, doctors kept coming out of the operating room to give Neva and Bob's mother, who had flown down, updates. When he came to, Wenzel looked up and saw Neva. The first thing he said for some reason was, "Will I still be able to ski?"

The operation had been a success. Wenzel would ski again, but not for a while. The doctors wouldn't let him watch his team play, even on television, because they were afraid any stress could cause a seizure. Several days after the operation, when Wenzel was able to sit up, Neva brought Alex to the hospital to see his father. When she placed their son in his arms, Bob Wenzel started to cry. Then they all cried together, mother, father, and baby, the latter no doubt wondering why his father had no hair.

Wenzel's surgery attracted national attention. Letters and good wishes poured in. Dean Smith wrote and said, "I know you like to follow in Foster's footsteps but isn't this going a little too far?" Foster came down to visit and, for the first time, understood how Wenzel and Goetz had felt when he had his heart attack. Others who had survived similar surgery wrote or called Wenzel to tell him the worst was over, that there was no reason why he couldn't lead a normal life.

"It's a little bit like being in a fraternity," he said. "They really were helpful. The doctors told me I was just like anyone else after the operation except that I knew it couldn't happen to me because it already had and it had been repaired. Hearing it from them was nice. Hearing it from people who had been through it was even better."

That didn't mean there were no anxious moments. Whenever Wenzel got a headache, it frightened him. "I was afraid to go to sleep because I thought if I did I might die," he said. "It took me a while to get beyond that feeling." The doctors told Wenzel there was no reason for him not to coach. In the wake of his illness, Jacksonville had fallen apart, but there were still high hopes for the next season. The Dolphins opened at Southwest Louisiana, the opening game in a new arena there. In the locker room prior to the game, Wenzel went through his normal pregame talk.

Then, at the end, he turned to his players and said: "I just want to let you guys know how important it is to me that we're here together as a team." There was more he wanted to say, but he never got any further because at that point, he broke down and cried. All the tension and all the fear and all the relief of having survived came out at that moment with his players. They all cried with him, then went out and won the game.

That started a storybook season that reached its climax when the Dolphins stunned Alabama–Birmingham on the Blazers' home floor in the Sun Belt Tournament championship game. The victory put Jacksonville into the NCAA Tournament and it made Wenzel a national hero. One year after almost dying, he had written one of the more miraculous coaching stories of 1986 or any other year for that matter.

That same month, he and Neva had their second child, a daughter. Truly, it was a magic time for Wenzel.

"I had never really prayed before I got sick," he said. "And I'm not one for saying, 'If you let me get better, I'll do this or that.' But I did pray in the hospital and after I got out and got better. I really believe my prayers were answered."

Jacksonville won 20 games again in 1987. Wenzel's name was being mentioned often when prestige jobs came open. But it wasn't yet his turn. When Dave Wohl, then the coach of the New Jersey Nets, offered him a job as an assistant coach, Wenzel took it. "I thought it would broaden me," he said. "There really wasn't much more to do at Jacksonville in terms of building and I wanted to find out what the NBA was like. Neva told me I wouldn't be able to deal with being an assistant again. As it turned out, she was right."

His season with the Nets was difficult. Wohl, who had hired him, was fired fourteen games into the season. Wenzel found himself working for interim coach Bob McKinnon, then for Willis Reed. Three bosses in one season. He found the NBA fascinating but Neva's instinct about being an assistant was right.

Yet the year had its benefits. Until he was traded in February, Mike Gminski was on the team. He and Wenzel enjoyed being reunited. Gminski was struck by how much Wenzel had grown as a coach and a person. "I had known him as a very eager, young, aggressive assistant coach," Gminski said. "Now, he was different. Much more mature, clearly a guy who was a head coach playing an assistant's role for a while. I liked him much more as a person. I had always liked him, but in a different way."

It was more of a peer relationship now, Gminski being an adult, not a teenager. But his experience as a head coach, as a father and as someone who had survived a very real brush with death, had changed Wenzel.

"I'm as intense and competitive as I ever was," he said. "But I think I'm more understanding of people's foibles now. I'm less likely to get upset with people when they make a mistake. I'm certainly more conscious of spending time with my family and with my friends. And, without question, I appreciate things more. It isn't anything miraculous or dramatic. It's a learning experience just like becoming a father was."

The NBA was a learning experience too. If the Nets had decided to make Wenzel the head coach, he no doubt would have stayed in the pros. It is a purer coaching experience. All one does is coach. There is no recruiting, no worrying about who is or who is not going to class, no stroking of the alumni. But the NBA was not about to make someone with less than a year's experience a head coach. When the Rutgers job came open, Wenzel was the logical choice. He interviewed for the Providence job too but ended up deciding to go home.

Ironically, his third game as Rutgers coach was against Northwestern. The coach of the Wildcats: Bill Foster. When he saw the schedule, Wenzel decided to make the game a real homecoming for Foster. Along with another ex-Foster assistant, Dick Lloyd, he arranged for a number of Foster's ex-players to come back for the weekend for a party at Lloyd's house. On the night of the game, he presented Foster with a plaque thanking him for building the Rutgers program to prominence in the 1960s. Foster normally shies away from nostalgia but he was clearly touched by this.

"It was really, really nice," he said. "I doubt if most of the people at Rutgers now remember me at all. But Bob made them remember. It was just a nice thing to do."

To Wenzel, it was the only thing to do. "If the brain surgery changed me in any way, it was in dealing with things like that," he said. "I don't think you should ever let an opportunity to do something for someone go by. It's so easy to put it off and say, 'later,' or 'next time.' But who knows about that? None of us. So, if you can do something good, you should do it now. Don't put off doing things that are the right thing to do."

As always, Wenzel threw himself totally into his new job. "It is not an easy job because we're in a league that doesn't get on television very much," he said. "We're competing with Seton Hall and the Big East right in our backyard and, at least for now, getting the attention of the New York media is tough." He smiled the Wenzel smile of complete confidence. "We'll get it done though."

Wenzel is a man of his word. The Penn State victory started Rutgers on a winning streak that climaxed during the Atlantic 10 Tournament. In the semifinals, Rutgers stunned Temple, the defending champion, in the Philadelphia Palestra. That meant the final would be played at Rutgers against—you guessed it—Penn State.

The game was similar to the one that had been played there four weeks earlier. This time, the building was packed to overflowing and it was Dadika, the little point guard, who hit the key three-pointer down the stretch to clinch the victory for Rutgers. Amazingly, one year after the school had won seven games and finished tenth in the league, it was the league champion and in the NCAA Tournament. The students stormed the floor at the buzzer, putting on a victory celebration worthy of Cameron Indoor Stadium at its best.

Wenzel was up all night savoring the victory with family and friends. The next morning, even without sleep, he was still buoyant. "It's a special moment because it's the first time," he said. "We may win again at Rutgers, I hope like hell we do, but it won't be the same as this one. The first time is something you can never repeat."

Wenzel enjoyed the first time at Duke in '78 and he enjoyed this first time too. But in a different way. "Back then I assumed it was just a beginning, that it would somehow get even better," he said. "Now, I cherish that memory as I look back as much as anything in my life, short of my kids. This one though, I'll cherish right now because I know from experience there's no guarantee it will ever happen again."

Six weeks after the second Penn State victory, Bob and Neva Wenzel's third child, a son, was born. "I think three is enough," he said. "But boy am I glad I've had the chance to see each of them born. It's like a brand new miracle each time."

If anyone can appreciate the miracle of life it is Bob Wenzel.

33
The Coach (II)

When Bob Wenzel called Bill Foster in November of 1988 to tell him that he was planning to honor him before the Northwestern–Rutgers game, Foster was very uncomfortable with the idea. "I'm not a big one for looking back," he said. "If I could have talked him out of it, I would have."

But when Wenzel went through with his plan, no one enjoyed it more than Foster. Seeing his former players brought back happy memories; the notion that he is still remembered fondly at Rutgers gave him great pleasure. At fifty-eight, Bill Foster seems to have learned—at least a little bit—about how to have fun.

"If I had the whole Duke experience to do over again, the one thing I would change would be the time right after our run in '78," he said. "I never did stop to enjoy it or appreciate it. Now, finally, I can look back at it and say it was a hell of an achievement. But it took me a long time to do that. I tended to dwell a lot more on the Kentucky loss than on all the victories that came before it."

His former players and assistant coaches still worry about Foster. He has been at Northwestern three years now and the record is 23–61. He is popular there, just as he was popular at Duke before the winning started. He has made the team much more competitive and pulled some significant upsets, including 1988 victories over Indiana and DePaul. Still, there have been many more losses than victories. Northwestern started in a hole much deeper than Duke's. This school isn't likely to go 27–7 in Foster's fourth year.

Knowing how Foster deals with losing—or doesn't deal with it—is what worries those who care about him. "I still can't accept losing," he said. "I feel like I have to be the one to be the bad loser here because there's a real tendency to accept losing. It's been a fact of life for so long that people don't get that upset by it. It's nice that I've gotten support from people at the school. I appreciate that. But I still feel that I was hired to do a job and that job is to win games. So far, I haven't done it."

No one is quicker to question himself than Foster. Even now, after twenty-nine years and 436 victories as a head coach, Foster still thinks of himself as the kid from tiny Elizabethtown College who must prove himself every single day.

"When he first started moving into the so-called big time, I think he thought he had to work twenty hours a day to be successful because he wasn't as good as other guys," Wenzel said. "When he won, he figured it was because of the work, not because he was any good."

Foster knew what he was getting into when he took the Northwestern job. He knew all about the losing tradition and about how tough the Big Ten was. But he also knew he didn't want his coaching career to end on the sour, tainted note of South Carolina. When he visited Northwestern, it brought back memories—of Duke.

"That was definitely a factor," he said. "The school itself is a lot like Duke. You're coaching and recruiting the same kind of kids. That doesn't make it easy, but it makes it fun. I like the campus and we've really enjoyed living near Chicago. I think that's where I have managed to change. We go to Bulls games on occasion or Blackhawks games. During the summer we go to baseball games. This is a fun place to live. I've actually had some fun even with the losing."

There is a cruel irony in Foster's seeking happiness at a school that is similar to Duke. He understands that although he categorically refuses to dwell on it. "I look at what they've done and I can honestly say I feel good about it. There really are good guys and bad guys in this sport and Duke is always going to be one of the good guys. When they win, what the school stands for wins. And I like seeing that."

Before Foster took the Northwestern job, the school had started a series with Duke. In his fifth game as Northwestern coach, he found himself back in Cameron Indoor Stadium—as the visiting coach. When he walked onto the floor at Cameron for the first time in almost seven years he received a warm standing ovation. That was all well and good. But the 105–56 final score took a lot of the pleasure out of the homecoming.

Going back to Duke will never be easy for Foster. He can walk into Cameron and see the two ACC Championship banners he produced and the 1978 Final Four banner. But there are also three Mike Krzyzewski-produced Final Four banners and, outside the front door, a paved parking lot.

"Looking back is pointless," he said. "I can't go back there, so why think about it? When I think about those years now, I don't think about the wins or the losses or even the frustrations. I think about the guys I coached. My memories of them are still vivid and still warm.

"But I don't like to think of myself as someone sitting around reminiscing about my career and my past. I'm still coaching and I still think we aren't all that far away from making some tangible progress at Northwestern. We've done a lot of the little things: getting attendance up, getting the students out to the games, building up the camp and the TV and radio package. Now, of course, we have to win or the result of improving those other things is that more people are watching us lose."

Although Foster says he has learned to enjoy himself more, he is still a basket case after losses. Often, he will drive around in his car by himself or sit up late in his office working on the next day's practice plan. Shirley Foster still worries about him largely because she knows that trying to change him is impossible.

"I married a coach," she said. "He was this way when he was young and he's always going to be this way. I wish he could relax a little bit more but it just isn't going to happen."

If anything, Foster worries more about how his behavior affects his family than about how it affects his health. "I know it upsets them when I'm up late or stay at the office working," he said. "Shirley's been trying to quit smoking but during the season she starts again. I know it's because of me. I'm not exactly easy to live with. But knowing that and doing something about it are two very different things." Foster's heart attack did make him more aware of his health. He had a bed set up in an office at South Carolina so he could lie down when he felt tired. He is in excellent shape and exercises every day—almost to the point of being obsessive about it. He has done well on his annual stress tests since the heart attack but it took him a long time to put the fear behind him.

"For a couple of years there, every time I felt a little bit sick I was really afraid that I was dying," he said. "I can remember one game in Memphis where I was absolutely convinced just before we went on the floor that I was having another heart attack. I didn't feel good a lot of the time and I'm sure a lot of that was psychological. I just wasn't convinced that I was actually healthy. I spent a lot of time being scared."

All of that made perfect sense given what Foster had been through. What didn't make sense was his insistence on staying in coaching, especially at a school where winning is almost an impossibility. But Foster, who has never found happiness in any one place for very long, honestly believes that he may find happiness here.

"This is the last stop, I know that," he said. "I was lucky that my first two daughters went to Duke and I'd like to see my last one go to Northwestern. Mary [the youngest] is fourteen. That's not a reason to keep coaching though. Thinking I can still get it done is. I know a lot of people don't think I can. But not many people thought we'd get it done at Duke."

He smiled. "Of course," he said, "we *did* get it done there. It just took me a while to figure that out."

Was there a *specific* time Foster came to that conclusion?

"I think, really, it was after the heart attack," he said. "I did stop to do some thinking after that, especially after I saw how many people really were concerned about me. That was nice. I suppose I should have understood all that before I got sick but I didn't. If there was anything good that came out of my being sick it was that I learned to appreciate a lot of the good things in my life. Before that, I had tended to focus on the bad."

The down side of the heart attack, other than the obvious, was that it marked a turning point in Foster's tenure at South Carolina. The Gamecocks slid steadily after the 22–9 season in 1983 and that led to Foster's firing. What hurt more than that, though, was the NCAA investigation. Foster had always had an impeccable reputation. After he left South Carolina, that reputation was tainted forever.

"That crushed me," he said. "I've been in the profession thirty years, I've been president of the coaches' association, and I think people, whatever they thought of my coaching ability, always thought of me as honest. Since South Carolina, no question, there are some doubters."

A lot of that has been put behind him at Northwestern. Now, though, he needs wins—and players. "We've done a decent job in recruiting," he said. "But decent isn't good enough in the Big Ten. Our power rating [based on computer analysis] this year puts us ninetieth in the country. That may not sound great but, based on that, we're in the NIT. In a lot of leagues, we probably contend. But we're in a league where this year the team that finished ninth had a power rating of thirty-fifth. That puts us behind."

The funny thing is, if Foster walked away tomorrow, no one would question him, doubt him, or criticize him. In his office, on his Rolodex are the names, phone numbers, and addresses of most of the players who have played under him during his career. Virtually all of them know that if Foster could help them with something he would do so in a second. Loyalty is something he has always treasured—whether giving or receiving.

He enjoys feeling as if his players, past and present, will come to him if they have a problem. And yet, there is really no one he takes his problems to. "All the years I worked for him, I don't think he ever opened up to me about what was bothering him," Lou Goetz said. "You could usually guess, but he would never really tell you."

Shirley Foster says she thought her husband would end up not with heart problems, but with an ulcer because he has always internalized his frustrations. Foster has always been someone who wants to give to people but he has always held back one thing from everyone: himself. When things aren't going the way he wants them to he buries himself in even more work rather than burden others with his troubles.

During the past season he organized a postseason seminar for coaches on how to use videotape. More and more, coaches are finding dozens of different ways to use tape. Foster set up a weekend at a Chicago hotel to tutor them on exactly what can be done.

"I feel like I've been a little bit brain-dead the last couple of years," he said. "I need to have things going during the off-season or I get bored. Especially now, with all the dead periods in recruiting when you can't go on the road, there's a lot of free time."

Free time is never something Foster has believed in. Goetz and Wenzel both remember him creating work for himself even when there was really no work to do. He says he does that less now, but does still do it. It is as if he is searching for something and feels as if he is running out of time to get it done. But *what* is he searching for?

"I don't know," he said. "All I do know is I still feel as if I have something to contribute as a coach. To the players, to the school, and to myself. As long as I feel that way, I'll want to coach."

In 1988, Foster became a grandfather for the first time when his second daughter, Debbie, had a son. Foster is a doting grandfather. But when the subject of being a grandfather came up last winter, his first reaction was instinctive: "Hey, don't spread that around."

Why not? Certainly Foster loves his grandson. But somewhere deep down he is still rebuilding. Coaches who are rebuilding aren't grandfathers. And, more than anything, Bill Foster is a builder. He was a builder at Bloomsburg at twenty-nine, at Duke at forty-three, and he still is at Northwestern at fifty-nine.

Still building. Still trying to prove himself. Again and again. For Bill Foster, the answer to the question, what is enough? is simple: nothing.

"He's always been searching for something that doesn't exist," Lou Goetz said. "Complete acceptance. No one ever finds that. No matter what you do, no matter how well you do it, especially in a high-visibility job, someone is going to be unhappy with you. Bill has always wanted to please everyone."

Ever so slowly, Foster is learning to understand that. Maybe at some point in the future he will look back on his accomplishments and his friendships and be able to please not everyone but someone: himself.

"I hope that will happen," he said. "Maybe after I retire, I'll be able to look back and realize that a lot of good things have happened to me."

And maybe by then he will also realize that he has made a lot of good things happen to others.

Epilogue:
The Reunion...Day Two

Banks and Dennard were late. Of course. Their teammates were neither fazed nor surprised.

"Maybe Kenny forgot how to find the place," Bruce Bell suggested.

"One of Tink's aunts probably got sick," Jim Spanarkel said, remembering one of the more famous Banks excuses.

It was Saturday afternoon and they were all sitting down to a lunch that Tom Mickle had put together for them. Mickle had been the sports information director in 1978; now he was the director of the Duke Varsity Club, a fund-raising arm of the athletic department that focused on former Duke athletes. Technically, it was Mickle's *job* to put together events like this. But in the case of this team, this was an act of love.

Mickle had planned this weekend even though Tom Butters, the athletic director, saw no reason to bring the '78 team back together. Not enough time had passed, he said. Of course Butters had no way of understanding either the bond these players felt toward one another or how much had happened to them since graduation.

After all, on the surface, this was a team full of achievers. Dennard's graduation meant that all twelve players had Duke degrees. Three of them—Bell, Rob Hardy, and Scott Goetsch—were lawyers. Two more were making a lot of money working in the computer business: John Harrell and Steve Gray. Spanarkel was a successful stockbroker; Morrison a top manager in a major insurance company. Mike Gminski was a millionaire basketball player and Bob Bender was about to become one of the youngest college head coaches in the country. Jim Suddath would be an ordained minister in another two months.

Only Banks and Dennard were in flux and that fit too. Always late, remember? Banks had made plenty of money playing basketball; even if he didn't get to play again, he would do just fine. And Dennard? Well, Kenny was Kenny. He had survived cancer and bankruptcy and his teammates had little doubt he would find his way into something profitable shortly.

That didn't mean they didn't get mad at him sometimes. "Every once in a while I just say, 'Dammit Dog, quit with all these schemes and find something you can do well,' " Bender said. "Heck, he can do just about anything he wants to. It's just a matter of him deciding to do it."

Now though, the tardiness of the Dynamic Duo caused great amusement in the room. If they had showed up on time, their teammates would have been disappointed. They were all taking bets on when—or if—Banks and Dennard would arrive, when the door opened and in walked Banks.

Before he had gotten two steps into the room or had a chance to open his mouth, every player in the room had grabbed a spoon and started clinking it against a glass. "Joke, joke, joke," they shrieked joyfully. Banks broke up. He knew that if he walked into a meal with this group fifty years from now, they would all go for the spoons in a second. Banks went around the room formally saying hello to everyone, making sure to hug the wives and the two female managers, Mary Kay Bass Haynes and Debbie Ridley. He was just about to sit down when the door opened again and Dennard came in, along with his wife Nadine.

Banks and Dennard had run into each other a couple of weeks earlier at an NBA game in Charlotte. Banks had told Dennard to wait for him after the game so they could get a drink. Dennard hadn't waited.

"Hey Kenny, why didn't you wait for me that night in Charlotte?" Banks demanded to know almost immediately.

"Are you kidding?" Dennard said. "Wait for you? I don't have that much time. I'm not that young anymore."

Banks looked around him to see everyone nodding their head in agreement with Dennard. He laughed. In this room, there was no point trying to BS anybody. They all knew the act too well.

When lunch was over, Spanarkel felt as if he had to get up and say something. Foster had flown home that morning. As captain, he was the acting spokesman. He tried to keep it serious, thanking Mickle and his assistants, Johnny Moore and Jill Mixon, for organizing the weekend. He talked about how much fun they had had in the past. But finally, he couldn't resist becoming himself.

He ripped Banks for overdressing and Dennard for arriving even later than Banks. He got on Bell and Hardy for drinking too much the previous evening, even though he had had at least as much to drink as they had. He congratulated Suddath on making it through the seminary. "Seems to me Sudds you had it easy," he said. "After all, anyone who roomed with Dennard *and* Banks should be guaranteed a free pass into heaven."

Kevin Hannon, the ex-head manager, had flown in from Denver for the weekend. He stood up and tried to be serious for a minute. "You should know," he told the '78 team, "that people really think of you guys as special."

One of the things that made them special was that they never thought of themselves that way, and this reunion was evidence of that. No one felt the need to stand up and tick off the accomplishments of the team. No one stood up and compared what they had done to what Duke teams before or after had done. All they wanted to do was enjoy being together, just as they had eleven years earlier.

That night, Duke held its annual Hall of Fame banquet. For the players, the highlight was the formal announcement of the Max Crowder Endowment. Max hadn't escaped Spanarkel's routine either. "For four years everyone in the ACC thought I was knock-kneed and pigeon-toed," he said. "What they didn't know was that it was just Max's lousy tape jobs."

Bringing up tape jobs brought up the "Banks Rule." As a sophomore, Banks had emphatically passed gas one evening while Max had been taping him. Max had simply walked away from the training table with the tape dangling from Banks's ankle saying, "Finish it yourself," while Banks convulsed with laughter.

That incident had brought about the creation of the "Banks Rule." The first time you did that to Max, you taped yourself that day. The second time you taped yourself for a month. It had been passed down through generations of Duke players. The members of the '89 team knew the rule just as the members of the '78 team had.

There was no question how the players felt about Max. All of them remembered his exact words to them the first time they met him as freshmen: "Just remember one thing, kid," Max always said, "I was here before you came and I'll be here after you're gone." The implication was that the players better not mess with Max.

Of course, they all messed with him—constantly. Spanarkel and Morrison had been particularly adept at giving him bad directions on the road when he was driving them somewhere. Once, after they had guided him into a tour of the entire parking lot of the New Orleans Superdome, Max had told Foster he would never, repeat *never*, drive those two SOBs anywhere again.

There were lots of Max driving stories. The most famous one had occurred in Knoxville the night before a game against Tennessee. Max had gone to get the car in the hotel parking lot and, thanks to one wrong turn, gotten completely lost. He was already steaming when he finally got out of the lot. Naturally, the players gave him bad directions to the hamburger joint they were going to.

By the time they arrived, Max was so angry he refused to go inside. He sat in the car with his arms folded on his chest. He quickly disappeared from view as the windows and windshield on the car steamed up. The players didn't know if the steam came from the car's heater or from Max's head. As soon as they returned to the hotel, Max went directly to Foster's room, hurled the car keys on the floor and said, "Get yourself another driver. I'm through!"

Foster tried to get angry, but couldn't pull it off. Max tried to stay angry but he couldn't do it either.

▬

At the dinner that night, they made Mickle seat them all at the same table. As Bell explained, they hadn't come back to sit with a bunch of strangers, they had come back to spend time with each other.

Max was clearly touched when he was introduced to a standing ovation, led by the '78 players. He went out of his way to thank Mickle, the key person in raising the money to endow the scholarship, all of it from ex-Duke athletes. "Anyone who can convince a group of players who I worked with for four years to give money to a scholarship named after me must be a damn genius," Max said. "This is about the nicest thing anyone has ever done for me."

If he hadn't been such a mean old man, Max might have cried.

The only sour note of the entire weekend came when Butters only made passing reference to the '78 team's presence at the dinner. In talking about Max and all the different Duke athletes he had worked with over the years, Butters mentioned almost offhandedly that eight members of the '78 Final Four team and all the team's managers were in attendance.

But nothing more. He didn't ask them to stand and be recognized. He didn't even pause for applause. The players were hurt. "Did we do something wrong somewhere along the line?" they all wondered.

Perhaps Butters didn't want to detract from the honorees of the evening. He did, however, introduce Krzyzewski. Maybe the players were being overly sensitive. Maybe Butters hadn't been sensitive enough.

The slight was quickly forgotten at the postdinner party in Max's honor. It was held in the training room—where else?—with drinks and snacks set out on the various taping tables around the room. Everyone got a button walking in that said either "Max" or "Howie." Spanarkel had stuck Howie on Max years ago for the very logical reason that Max's *real* name was Howard.

Max set up his own personal bar in one corner of the room, mixing killer drinks for anyone who dared. The '78 players stayed long enough to give Max a hard time—Banks demanded a tape job, claiming that Max still owed him one—and to make sure everyone who wanted to talk to them got the chance.

They were in no rush. But as midnight came and went, Spanarkel began organizing. He wanted the group to get away together for a little while before the night was over. They would all be heading home the next morning and they all wanted some time alone—as a team—before they split up.

"After all," Spanarkel said, "They probably won't bring us back again until the year 2000. Every eleven years, right?"

The players began to make their excuses, talking about early plane flights or long drives home. They gave Max hugs and thanked everyone for inviting them back. Then they all went to a local sports bar a few miles away. Nothing formal. They drank some beer, played some pool, and told stories until closing time.

It was after 2 A.M. when they left the bar. It was time to say good-bye. They were all going in different directions, back to their own lives. They stood there for a moment exchanging good wishes and promises to see one another again soon.

They were about to turn and head for their cars when Banks said, "Hey!" He was standing there with his arms spread wide, the way he used to hold them when the team huddled up on the court after being introduced. Without pausing for a second, they all put their arms around each other and went into their huddle.

They stood there holding on to one another in the empty parking lot just as they had stood in that packed arena in St. Louis eleven years earlier with millions of people watching them. They were a team then. They were a team now. Always, they will be a team.

Forever's team.

From left to right, seated: Kenny Dennard, Deborah Ridley, Kevin Hannon, Mary Kay Bass Haynes, Rob Hardy, Jim Spanarkel; standing: Gene Banks, Bob Bender, Jim Suddath, Max Crowder, Scott Goetsch, Bruce Bell.

GARY A. CAMERON

1977–78 DUKE UNIVERSITY VARSITY BASKETBALL TEAM

No.	Name	Pos.	Hgt.	Wgt.	Class	Exp.	Hometown
14	Rob Hardy	G	6–3	170	Jr.	1VL	Columbus, Oh.
15	Bruce Bell	G	6–0	165	Sr.	2VL	Lexington, Ky.
20	Eugene Banks	F	6–7	205	Fr.	HS	Philadelphia, Pa.
21	Bob Bender	G	6–2	175	So.	TR	Crown Point, In.
22	John Harrell	G	6–0	170	So.	TR	Durham, N.C.
23	Steve Gray	G	6–2	180	Jr.	2VL	Woodland Hills, Ca.
24	Harold Morrison	F	6–7	200	Jr.	2VL	West Orange, N.J.
30	Jim Suddath	G–F	6–6	185	Fr.	HS	College Park, Ga.
33	Kenny Dennard	F	6–7	200	Fr.	HS	King, N.C.
34	Jim Spanarkel	G	6–5	190	Jr.	2VL	Jersey City, N.J.
35	Cameron Hall	F	6–9	215	So.	1VL	Dundas, Ontario
43	Mike Gminski	C	6–11	245	So.	1VL	Monroe, Ct.
44	Scott Goetsch	F–C	6–9	215	Jr.	2VL	Chatsworth, Ca.

1977–78 DUKE FINAL BASKETBALL STATISTICS

RECORD: 27-7 (ACC: 8-4) HOME: 12-0 AWAY: 5-5 NEUTRAL: 10-2

PLAYER	G	FGM-FGA	PCT.	FTM-FTA	PCT.	SM	REB-AVG.	PF-D	AST.	PTS.	AVG.
Jim Spanarkel	34	244-460	.530	220-255	.863	251	116-3.4	83-3	126	708	20.8
Mike Gminski	32	246-450	.547	148-176	.841	232	319-10.0	60-0	50	640	20.0
Gene Banks	34	238-451	.528	105-146	.719	254	292-8.6	99-1	120	581	17.1
Kenny Dennard	34	140-254	.551	51-76	.671	139	215-6.3	112-7	72	331	9.7
John Harrell	34	68-140	.486	38-46	.826	80	34-1.0	72-0	54	174	5.1
Bob Bender	22	41-84	.488	31-42	.738	54	32-1.5	49-1	82	113	5.1
Scott Goetsch	32	41-66	.621	12-19	.632	32	69-2.2	45-0	21	94	2.9
Steve Gray	25	32-69	.464	18-21	.857	40	18-0.7	38-3	30	82	3.3
Jim Suddath	31	30-62	.484	18-25	.720	39	49-1.6	35-2	15	78	2.5
Harold Morrison	22	16-40	.400	13-17	.765	28	32-1.5	23-0	9	45	2.0
Bruce Bell	21	10-25	.400	5-10	.500	20	12-0.6	9-0	13	25	1.2
Rob Hardy	13	8-14	.571	0-1	.000	7	8-0.6	11-0	5	16	1.2
Cameron Hall	7	9-16	.563	6-7	.857	8	11-1.6	15-1	4	24	3.4
Team Rebounds	34						88-2.6				
Dead Ball Rebounds*							66-1.9				
Duke Totals	34	1123-2131	.527	665-841	.791	1184	1295-38.1	651-18	601	2911	85.6
Opponent Totals	34	1047-2236	.468	434-634	.685	1389	1129-33.2	733-26	415	2528	74.4

Turnovers   Duke: 610-17.9   Opp. Team Rebounds: 103-3.0
Opp.: 614-18.1   Opp. Dead Ball Rebounds*: 83-2.4

*Dead Ball Rebounds do not count in Team Rebound Average

About the Author

Forever's Team is JOHN FEINSTEIN's third book on college basketball. His first book, *A Season on the Brink*, is the best-selling sports book of all time, having spent twenty-five weeks on the *New York Times* best-seller list, fourteen of those weeks at number one. His second book, *A Season Inside*, was also a national best-seller. Mr. Feinstein spent eleven years at *The Washington Post* and has worked as a special contributor to *Sports Illustrated*. His stories have also appeared in *Sport, Inside Sports, The Sporting News*, and *TV Guide*. He has won twelve U.S. Basketball Writer's Awards and three National Sportswriter's and Sportscaster's Awards as Washington writer of the year. Currently, he is the chief feature writer for *The National—America's Sports Daily*, a contributing editor to *Basketball Times* and *World Tennis*, and a commentator for National Public Radio. He lives in Bethesda, Maryland, and Shelter Island, New York, with his wife, Mary Clare.